A Different Shade of Gray

A Different Shade of Gray

Midlife and Beyond in the Inner City

KATHERINE S. NEWMAN

Published in the United States by The New Press, New York, 2003
Distributed by W. W. Norton & Company, Inc., New York

Grateful acknowledgment is made to the following for permission to
reprint previously published material:

Excerpt from *King Hedley II* © 1999 by August Wilson.
Reprinted by permission of the author.

Library of Congress Cataloging-in-Publication Data

Newman, Katherine S., 1953–
  A different shade of gray : midlife and beyond in the inner city / Katherine S. Newman.
    p. cm.
  Includes bibliographical references and index.
  ISBN 1–56584–615–X (hc.)
    1. Urban poor–United States. 2. Inner cities–United States. 3. Middle aged
  persons–United States. I. Title.
  HV4045.N476 2003
  362.5'1'0973091732–dc21   2002024426

The New Press was established in 1990 as a not-for-profit alternative to the large, commercial
publishing houses currently dominating the book publishing industry.
The New Press operates in the public interest rather than for private gain, and is committed
to publishing, in innovative ways, works of educational, cultural, and community value that
are often deemed insufficiently profitable.

The New Press, 450 West 41st Street, 6th floor, New York, NY 10036
www.thenewpress.com

Printed in the United States of America

2 4 6 8 10 9 7 5 3 1

To the next generation

Steven and David Attewell
Jonathan, Jessica, and Jack Attewell
Bill and Nicole Newman
Jennifer and Lauren Newman
Katie and Daniel Wright

Contents

Acknowledgments

This book has been a long time in the making and along the way has benefited from the support and the resources of a number of different organizations and individuals. It would not exist at all were it not for the MacArthur Foundation Network on Successful Mid-Life Development, directed by Bert Brim. Brim led the national research effort and was instrumental in creating a special research group under the auspices of the Social Science Research Council in New York, which I directed for several years. Dr. Bob Rose, our program officer at the foundation, was an essential intellectual force in the network. Professor Diane Hughes, Department of Psychology at New York University, succeeded me as director of that New York seminar and was a particularly important participant. She designed the special survey we conducted, which provided the basis for my own qualitative study of African Americans, Puerto Ricans, and Dominicans in middle age and beyond.

The other members of that seminar—Larry Aber, Jeanne Brooks-Gunn, David Featherman, Orlando Rodriguez, Rick Shweder, and Mary Waters—were sounding boards, constructive critics, and fellow explorers in the territory of midlife. I appreciate their creative input.

The MacArthur Foundation Network on Socio-Economic Status and Health, led by Professor Nancy Adler, was also a critical component in this project. Adler provided support for the aspects of this project that dealt with health and created a stimulating atmosphere for exploring the impact that inequality has on the well-being of people at the bottom of the income distribution in our society. I wish to thank the other members of the SES/Health Network who listened to my ideas with more patience than they deserved over the years of this book's preparation. David Williams was particularly helpful in educating me on the impact of racial discrimination on health outcomes. Sheldon Cohen, Mark Cullen, Ralph Horwitz, Ichiro Kawachi, Michael Marmot, Karen Matthews, Bruce McEwen, Joe Schwartz, Teresa Seeman, Judith Stewart, and Shelley Taylor are among the best colleagues one could ever hope to have. Dr. Idy Gitelson at the MacArthur Foundation has been a major supporter of the network and we are all in her debt.

I would not have been able to put a single word to the printed page were it not for a very talented group of students who did the original interviews for this project. They combed the neighborhoods of New York and spent hours talking with the men and women who figure here. Linda Benbow, Marissa de la Garza, Nancy Lopez, Laura Ortiz, and Rose Williams deserve special recognition. Students who helped me with the analysis were also critical to its completion and I thank Carrie Conaway and Shelley McDonough for all of their assistance. Shelley was so important to the research in chapter two that I invited her to be my coauthor for this part of the book in recognition of her labor.

The extensive notes that accompany the text represent a huge amount of scholarly work in and of themselves. They are provided mainly for readers who want to learn about the academic debates that surround the issues discussed in this volume and as a place to provide additional data. I had a lot of help in preparing them and wish to thank Audrey Amalforque, Cybelle Fox, Margot Minardi, and Gesemia Nelson for the sociological imagination they contributed to them. Kevin Psonak, my faculty assistant at the Kennedy School, did a great deal of editorial work on the manuscript, for which I am grateful.

My colleague at the Kennedy School, Professor Jeffrey Liebman, contributed in very important ways to the discussion of social security reform in chapter eight. From 1998–99, Liebman served as special assistant to President Bill Clinton for economic policy and coordinated the administration's Social Security reform working group. He subsequently prepared position papers and detailed suggestions for reform to the Gore campaign. I have quoted liberally from his work in my conclusion, but wish to thank him here for educating me on the impact of social security on the urban poor.

My colleagues in the Wiener Center for Social Policy at the Kennedy School—especially Mary Jo Bane, David Ellwood, Christopher Jencks, Julie Wilson and William Julius Wilson—have all done important research on poverty and labor markets that has helped to inform my thinking here. We are all fortunate to inhabit the Center, which Malcolm Wiener has helped to sustain over the years.

Several people read this manuscript in draft form and gave me extensive comments that improved the work. I am especially grateful to Professors Jill Suitor and Scott Feld in the Department of Sociology at Louisiana State University. Suitor is a nationally respected authority on aging who has been waiting for me to finish this book for more years than I care to remember. Suitor and Feld have welcomed me many times into their home and their university department and given me the opportunity to talk about my work with all of their colleagues. My agent, Lisa Adams, has helped me in more ways that I could possibly list. Diane Wachtell, my editor at The New Press, was beyond patient in seeing this manuscript through its many revisions. André Schiffrin, the director of The New Press, has provided many civic-minded academics a forum for expressing themselves, a rare opportunity in commercial publishing. Many people, myself included, owe him our gratitude for keeping public scholarship alive.

Finally, as is true with every book I have written, my husband, Professor Paul Attewell, listened to me worry out loud, helped me think through my ideas, and critiqued the whole manuscript from beginning to end. I have never been able to thank him sufficiently and this book is no exception. Our children, Steven (age nineteen) and David (age thirteen), have long been tolerant of their mother's obsessions and will be very happy to see the book in print.

Cambridge, Massachusetts

2002

A Different Shade of Gray

Introduction

America's favorite aging hippy, Michael Doonesbury, adorns the cover of the April 3, 2000, issue of *Newsweek* magazine.[1] "The New Middle Age: A Boomer's Guide to Health, Wealth and Happiness" is the theme of this edition. Doonesbury is sitting in a field at the side of a river, his laptop humming away, cell phone at his sandled feet, and a thoughtful look on his face. This is the portrait of midlife in America: pensive, comfortable, and just mildly anxious about the problems *Newsweek* highlights: "Handling the Inheritance," "Bourgeois Bohemians," and "How to Get Your Golden Years."

The country is aging, but in very different places. In every rural hamlet and well-heeled suburb, gated community and gentrifying city neighborhood, the United States is growing gray. In the next thirty years, as the baby-boom bulge works its way through America's population structure, we will see the over sixty five age group double in size to 70 million.[2]

The prosperity of the late twentieth and early twenty-first centuries has meant that middle age and elderhood is comfortable and secure in ways that would have been hard to imagine a century ago. Older Americans have the highest rates of home ownership of any age group in the country.[3] Wealth is concentrated in the hands of the World War II generation, now poised to confer on the Doonesburys of this world a massive inheritance windfall. The first in the nation to go to college in large numbers, today's seniors exemplify the promise of a wealthy nation. Their boomer children—now in their forties and fifties—are the best-educated, highest-earning group of Americans ever seen.

While much of this good fortune is concentrated in the hands of whites, it is one of the signal achievements of the post–civil rights period that minorities have shared in the bounty. The minority middle classes—black and brown—

have grown at an astounding rate,[4] following the expansion of equal opportunity in the public sector, the successes of affirmative action in the private sector,[5] and an unparalleled period of economic expansion in the 1990s. Where "black" and "brown" were once synonymous with ghetto poverty, we can now point to communities like Prince George's County in Maryland or St. Albans in Queens, New York, where African-American civil servants, lawyers, doctors, and teachers have staked their own picket fences.[6] Success has come to people of many colors.

If this had been a universal experience, there would be no subject matter for this book. We would not need to ask how growing old in the inner city differs from the experience of passing through middle age and elderhood anywhere else. But millions of Americans did not reap the benefits of economic expansion and occupational mobility. They did not decamp for the suburbs. Instead, they stayed put in the Bronx, on Chicago's South Side, in the barrios of Los Angeles, and the poorest enclaves of Oakland, California, and watched the world outside their doors—and the members of their families behind them—crumble. They aged in place, and in a very troubled place.

For these folks, moving into middle age and beyond represents a dissonant experience of stock taking, a confrontation between their genuine achievements and some profound disappointments. On the positive side of life's equation, they can point to the upward trajectory that leads from the life stories of their truly impoverished parents (now long gone) to their own adult lives. Inner-city Latinos and African Americans now in their fifties and sixties were raised by parents who endured enormous hardship in the sugarcane fields of the Caribbean islands or poultry processing plants outside small southern towns in the grip of Jim Crow. "Now those folks were *poor*," their descendants tell us. Turning around to examine their own accomplishments, today's middle-aged and elderly minorities in the inner-city have much to be proud of even though they may still live in troubled, urban neighborhoods. They eclipsed their own parents just by completing high school. Where their mothers worked as housekeepers and their fathers scrambled to find backbreaking day labor, they point with pride to their own careers as secretaries or car repairmen.

The disappointments are many as well, however, for these inner-city residents have little in common with their middle-class counterparts—whatever their color—in the suburbs. They raised their families in enclaves bedeviled by poverty, the raging damage of a crack epidemic in the 1980s, and increasing racial and class segregation that followed as middle-class flight gathered force. Conditions like these left their treadmarks on the life histories of young people. The teenagers that our older generations raised in the ghetto were surrounded by a "code of the streets"[7] that encouraged them to walk right into the deep end. Drugs, out-of-wedlock pregnancy, and high levels of unemployment interrupted the upward movement of their parents and plunged the family line toward an unwelcome detour into poverty.

We know a great deal about the impact on young people of this sad chapter in America's urban history. Classic works like William Julius Wilson's *The Truly Disadvantaged*, or Alex Kotlowitz's searing account *There Are No Children Here*, describe in painful detail the deterioration of housing projects, the spread of slums, the breakdown of families, and the war-zone atmosphere that surrounded inner-city youth in the 1970s and '80s. We know what became of young men and women who grew up in these nightmare scenarios because their difficult lives have been the subject of so many chronicles of poverty, joblessness, single parenthood, and crime.

What we know less about is how those conditions ultimately affected their elders, the people who crested into midlife and started down the road to old age in the very same neighborhoods. We might imagine that this older generation was a wreck that produced a wreck. Not so. Most of them were examples of upward mobility when compared to their own parents. Civil servants, blue-collar factory workers, secretaries in law firms, security guards, they caught the wave of postwar economic expansion and equal opportunity and were able to make something of themselves along the positive arc that separated them from their own, poorer parents. Even those adults who did not have good jobs in the 1970s and '80s were still working. But they had trouble sustaining an upward path through the next generation, where low-wage jobs and unemployment become a more troubling norm.

This is something of an untold story. We have grown accustomed to thinking of poverty as a condition that is handed down from one generation to the next in an unbroken string of unemployment and welfare. Surely inner-city elders got there because they were poor like their parents before them and their children after them. There *are* families who followed just such a descent. Yet they are rarer than most people realize. More common is a tale of interrupted mobility: one generation's fragile stability dashed on the rocks of conditions faced by the next. Neighborhoods went bad, marriages broke up and children were raised by working mothers who couldn't keep a watchful eye on them. As they reached their teens, the upward momentum unraveled.

Now that these middle-aged and elderly residents of our inner cities are approaching the age when they need to rely on the kindness and support of those adult children, reliable relatives may be in short supply. At the same time, the need is great and often arrives early in the lives of inner-city dwellers, who tend to develop chronic health problems earlier than the norm.

The accidents of biography that determine whether growing old is a graceful experience or a hardship afflict us all. No one is immune to the toll that unemployment or ill health take on the shape of middle age. And many elderly people in the United States, including plenty of whites who have nothing more than social security to rely on, face hardship. Yet for the people described in this book, accumulating troubles cascade into insurmountable burdens. Inner-city dwellers often have no health insurance, small pensions or none at all, and more problems in their extended families for which they are often the last, best refuge. Worries that would bedevil anyone in their fifties and sixties—health problems, money concerns—are harder to regroup from when one lives in the inner city. Managing on a fixed income is more difficult in a high-crime neighborhood. Contending with chronic illness is more complicated when one's nest is not empty but instead filled with young children who are now under the care of a grandparent.

Why do all these pressures descend more on black and brown shoulders than on others? When they read about leisure cruises, retirement villages full of amenities, minority men and women who have never had those luxuries wonder why not. How do they explain to themselves why crime and poverty plague their communities? What do they make of the fact that others, mainly those of other skin colors, are so privileged? Aging is at least in part a process of coming to terms with where one sits in a social hierarchy. When the men and women in this book think about that question, they recognize not only how far they have come relative to their own parents, but how far from the ideal they are as well.

The conclusions they draw from these unsettling thoughts are informed by contradictory explanations for their personal fate and the destination of the racial and ethnic groups to which they belong. There is a fault line between perspectives that emphasize the role of individual responsibility and perspectives that recognize the power of impersonal forces like discrimination to shape a person's life chances. African Americans and Latinos know they are on the receiving end of special burdens that have a bearing on where they have ended up. But in the main they do not conclude from these observations that society is always at fault. For they share with mainstream American culture a powerful commitment to the idea that we make our own pathways in the world. They are convinced, often in the face of evidence to the contrary, that they are masters of their own destinies, able to rise above the bad decks they may have been dealt. This is not a conclusion most social scientists would readily accept, prone as we are to emphasize the impact of structural forces compared to the efforts of individuals. Yet we have to credit the influence of mainstream American culture when we discover how much weight it carries in the inner city, where many observers would least expect to find it.

The conclusions inner-city adults draw about the role of race are not the obvious ones that might be inferred from the pronouncements of racial nationalists. They are more nuanced meditations on how some groups managed to turn disadvantage into self-determination, while others collapsed in heaps and gave up. At one level this has nothing to do with aging. At another, it is the essence of growing older, for it connects the middle aged and the elderly with the family "mobility project"[8] that is an essential aspect of American culture as a whole. To understand one's fate in these terms is to move beyond the self and its sphere of control to the organization of the wider society, the way it deals with race and poverty, immigration and displacement.

Growing old can be thought of as a biological process, a decline of the body. It is also a social transformation that reshapes a person's identity or social role, moving from parent to grandparent, worker to retiree. This much has been said many times over. What is less often noticed is that aging is also an historical phenomenon.[9] The slice of time each of us moves through contains its own possibilities and limitations. The oldest people whose lives are chronicled in this book were born when the country was stuck in the rut of the Great Depression and came of age during World War II. They moved into middle age with this very particular history under their collective belts, a history of early poverty and dramatic recovery. The next generation, the war babies, knew nothing of the Depression's hardships and hit their early adulthood in the 1960s, when Fair Employment opened up opportunities in the public sector that truly built the modern black middle class.

This is more than an abstract economic history. It had political dimensions that shaped the experience of minorities for better and for worse. Men and women who grew up in the police state of the Jim Crow South and migrated north in the interwar years have moved into the sunset of their lives under the leadership of black mayors in some of the nation's largest cities. Puerto Ricans who formed the tidal wave of migration that moved off the island in the 1940s watched their children grow up in an entirely new culture of Nuyoricans, an immigrant society that grew ever more distant from the homeland. Dominicans who remember all too well the terrors of Trujillo and the abject poverty of rural life have defined an old age in immigrant enclaves that are now beset by urban poverty. It is a harsh existence by some standards, but vastly more comfortable than anything they knew as young people in the Dominican Republic.

To understand how these divergent groups moved into their middle age and elderly years in America's premier city, New York, I draw on the research sponsored by the MacArthur Foundation's Network on Successful Mid-Life Development, including a special study of inner-city residents in New York. These sources help us understand trends and numbers as well as personal histories and private perspectives, in the words of middle-aged and elderly men and women who live in Harlem, Brooklyn, and the Bronx.[10]

These rich sources yield a picture of the trajectories that brought the present generations of mature men and women to their places in the inner city. They open up a window on the social history they share, crosscut by race and ethnicity. Each separate box, defined by generation, race, and gender, opens a different pathway for growing old. Collective memory provides a common backdrop for the ups and downs, a set of benchmarks for evaluating whether this mature phase of life should be considered hard or blessed. We will come to grips with what it means to wear a "different shade of gray" only by moving back and forth between the trails these generations have followed and the conditions they face now in the inner city.

1 – In the Shadow of White Flight

W e came from Mobile, Alabama, in 1949, when I was five years old," remembers Darlene Cawley. "Mobile was a [terrible place] as far as my mother was concerned. She couldn't cope with the black-white issue." Born in Trinidad, to Barbadian parents, Darlene and her family were newcomers to the racially charged landscape of the American South.

> Where my mother came from black, white, green, English, Italian, everybody could ride the bus. That's the truth in the West Indies. They have social classes. Certain people have [better] kinds of houses and stuff like that, but everybody gets the same thing down there: the blacks, the Indians, everybody goes to the same kinds of schools.

The Cawley family landed at the epicenter of Jim Crow America. "Whites only" water fountains. Gun-toting sheriffs who would just as soon run a black man off the road as let him pass. Black schools with dirt floors, textbooks in tatters, sixty kids to a class, and a five-mile walk with no school bus coexisted with gleaming schools and shiny yellow buses for the white kids.

The social mores of the Deep South came as a total shock to the Cawley family. Darlene's father, a merchant marine shipping in and out of Mobile, was gone for months at a time and wanted his wife and children nearby in a port city where he could see them during shore leave. Waiting stateside, the family did its best to adjust to Mobile, but the lid blew off their patience the day Darlene's mother was ordered to give up her seat on the bus.

They wanted her to move out of her seat and give it to [a white person].
My sister and I were with her. She told the people she wouldn't get
up. The driver kept the bus there for a long period of time and finally
started up and went on his route. But from that day on, whenever we
were waiting at that bus stop to go downtown, he never stopped. We
would always have to wait forty-five minutes for the next bus. He
wouldn't let my mother get on. He told her, "I know you're one of
those smart-assed foreigners." We used to tease my mother that she
could have been the first Rosa Parks, but she didn't make an issue out
of it.

After that incident, my mother couldn't handle [Mobile]. People calling her by her first name that she didn't even know, business people,
you know, and passing all kind of remarks. When my father came off
the ship, she told him, "Either take me somewhere different or take me
back where I came from."

The North beckoned. Along with thousands of other black families from
the South, the Cawleys found their way to the Bedford-Stuyvesant section
of Brooklyn. Crammed into a tiny apartment, with nosy neighbors below
who complained, incessantly it seemed, about the noise Darlene and her sister
made moving across the wooden floors, the family settled in to city life.
Sitting on the stoop of the apartment building, playing jump rope in the
streets, opening up the fire hydrants on hot summer days, waiting for Daddy
to come home from months at sea, Darlene slowly forgot Barbados and
Mobile, and began to melt into the great metropolis of New York City.

Merchant marines made good money in those years—the boom time following World War II. The austerity of rations and families doubled up on
top of one another gave way to the pent-up demand for toasters, refrigerators,
cars, and, above all, new houses. When Mr. Cawley came home with his
pay packet, his Mrs. was waiting on the stoop. What she wanted more than
anything was to move out of that apartment building and into a house. Joe
Cawley got the message. So a year or two after landing in New York, the
family packed up once again and moved into their first real house on Willoughby Avenue, in a quiet, leafy neighborhood in Bedford-Stuyvesant. They
were among the first black families to join the block. Italians, eastern European Jews, Irish now two or three generations deep in the United States, and
a smattering of island-born blacks surrounded them.

Oh I remember so many people: the Dodsons, the Chamberlains, the
MacDonalds. The people who owned my house and six other houses

nearby were an Irish family, a doctor from King's County [Hospital]. One of the sisters was a nun; another was in business. They had all these houses for rent and we used to go from one backyard to the next.

When Darlene thinks back on the Willoughby Avenue neighborhood, what she remembers most of all was the diversity of the community, and the ease with which her family fit in.

I have very fond memories of Willoughby Avenue. I grew up on that block as a child. I lived on the left-hand side. There was a Jewish temple on the corner which had to have been three hundred or four hundred years old. It's a landmark. I remember wonderful people [in that neighborhood]. I remember Monty, the Jewish guy on the corner who owned the delicatessen. I remember Miss Carter, who came afterwards, from Barbados. The majority of the block when I first got there was Jews and Italians and they were kind of segregated because they lived on certain parts of the block.

The little Jewish ladies and the black people, everybody was friendly. Everybody used to sit outside in their yard at night, till three, four in the morning. The apartment house around the corner, they'd be sitting out on those mesh chairs that they use, those old-time beach chairs. Nikki's Candy Store was on the corner, where you could get an egg cream or a cherry soda and talk. . . . They'd sit out on the concrete, knitting and talking, especially in the summer when it was hot.

Movies were all the rage in those days and Darlene was eager to trot off to the pictures every Saturday. Twenty cents would buy her a ticket; "two bits" and she had a candy supply that would last for the whole double bill. Her mother wasn't about to pay for these treats, though, so Darlene had to earn her own way. Monty, and the other Jews on the block, were only too happy to oblige. "I used to make a little money on Friday afternoons," Darlene remembers, "because the Jews didn't turn on the electricity and stuff; it was against their religion. So I used to do that. I used to get paid weekly for that!"

The Cawley family was religious, traditional, and keen on raising the children to be disciplined and respectful. Joe Cawley was a good provider and a strict disciplinarian. When their father was in port, the children knew they were under watch and had less freedom to hang around with their friends in the neighborhood, a point of some frustration for young Darlene.

I became a different person when he was home. I wasn't outside running up and down the street. I wasn't allowed outside. Everyone always
knew when my father was off the ship because I used to be in the
house. He didn't believe in gallivanting and, as he said, mixing with all
the riffraff off the block in the neighborhood and people that's beneath
you.

The riffraff Joe Cawley was worried about started to turn up in larger
numbers in the 1960s. A second great migration lured whites from the city
to the burgeoning suburbs. Black families from diverse class backgrounds
took up the vacant spaces. Families that weren't so respectable, with kids
running a bit wilder, started to make their way to Brooklyn. This wasn't
quite what Joe Cawley had in mind and he was not keen on letting Darlene
mix with the new element.

Nobody imagined that these stable, middle-class neighborhoods were
about to self-destruct. But the trickle of middle-class families, white and black,
attracted to the distant suburbs grew to flood stage by the middle of the
decade.

In the 1960s, the area started to change. You started to find a lot of
absentee landlords. Everybody running—the whites, they had started to
run to Nassau County, Long Island. Some of the blacks, too, were
running, to St. Albans. But a lot of them still kept their house. An
absentee landlord don't know what's going on in his building. You can
check people's credentials and their job, which is what people do now.
But years ago they didn't really check your job. They asked if you
worked and so long as you had that month's rent, month's security,
or whatever they asked at the time, they would take it.

The community Darlene knew so well started to draw inward, its residents
looking out from behind their curtains with wary eyes, bolting the doors with
double locks. It took a long time for the quality of public life to deteriorate.
Yet as the old folks began to die off or move in with their children elsewhere,
the people who replaced them started to tip the balance toward a less settled,
less safe neighborhood. The newcomers did not seem to value public decorum in the way the old-timers had. Community life began to slip through
the fingers of Willoughby Avenue's longtime residents.

Some blocks were better than others. Willoughby Avenue remained
basically the same way it was because a lot of the people never left.

The old-timers just stayed there . . . and most of them died there. So it's only in the last [fifteen] years that the area around [my family] really started changing. By then, the different people they let come in to a lot of the apartment houses, they tore them up. They had fires, they burned down things, they demolished the building. Then you get debris. Mattresses left on the street. The neighborhood started to look bad.

Poor communities are often portrayed as passive sponges in tales of decline.[1] They stand by and watch as garbage, lost souls, decaying buildings, and crime descend upon their heads, unable to stem the disaster. Willoughby Avenue did not give up so easily. When local transit authorities announced that the closest subway stop would be closed as a cost-cutting measure, protests erupted in the form of a petition drive, visits to Borough Hall, and angry phone calls to the Metropolitan Transportation Authority. Women coming home from work late at night would have to walk through dangerous neighborhoods in the dark. Safety concerns galvanized community action. Yet to no avail; subway authorities prevailed and the stop was shuttered.

Darlene's neighbors had better luck when they blocked an attempt to open up a liquor store across the street from the now-defunct subway station. The next street over from Willoughby Avenue had already seen what kind of damage a liquor store could do to the quality of life. Over on Park Street, families now had to thread their way through derelicts and winos, hanging around the store's front door, harassing people for spare change, weaving down the sidewalks, heaving when they'd had too much to drink. Graffiti was starting to appear on the storefronts nearby. The whole scene reeked of a neighborhood on the downward spiral. Darlene, her family, and the people who lived on either side of her were not about to let that happen to Willoughby Avenue if they could help it.

We picketed that man! He remodeled that whole storefront, put all his liquor in it, and we managed to put him out of business in a week. [We] had a school right up the street and we just felt it was bad. When you have liquor stores, you have people that drink, with their hands out in front, and you got a lot of young girls coming from schools. The people in the community just felt it was bad. They're working, their kids are coming home from school, and they have to pass this liquor store. And we already *had* a liquor store up the block, you know. So that's how we shut him down.

Despite these efforts, the Willoughby Avenue neighborhood, too, began to look more like a slum. Tree-lined blocks that had once been decorated by flower boxes and neat, though tiny, green lawns were now overshadowed by broken bottles in the gutters, fast-food wrappers on the sidewalk, broken paving stones, and dubious characters on the corner. Newcomers to the neighborhood were poor families from Puerto Rico, Haiti, and the Dominican Republic. As Darlene saw it, these folks cared little for public decorum. They didn't own the property they lived in and so they didn't care what it looked like. Neither did the landlords, who divided single-family dwellings into smaller sublets in order to cram as many of the poor migrants into the space as they could.

> They broke up people's houses. One guy subleased to about thirty different people. And one of them caught the place on fire. The woman owner had insurance, but they almost burned that house down to the ground. But she was an absentee landlord. So after that, she got the insurance, but she decided not to fix the house. So right now the house is still an eyesore on the block. It looks terrible. Since then, another fire's been in it and that messes up other people's homes.

The problem, as Darlene saw it, was not race or ethnicity. Home ownership was the issue. Renters of all colors are less concerned about the condition of the property they occupy. People who have a stake in the place where they live will take pride in its appearance and invest a little sweat in making it look nice. They will make it their business to intervene if the young people get out of hand. They will pick up a picket sign and let the liquor-store owner know that he's not welcome to do business on their street. Renters are another cup of tea.

> Renters don't care. And it's all ethnic groups: whites, Spanish, blacks. You're going to find those kind of people. They just don't care about anything, live from one day to the next. They don't take care of garbage—they'll come outside and see the cat knock over the garbage can, walk right over it, and go on to work. I mean they live in the building. What's to stop them from just tilting up the garbage can?

By the early 1970s, Darlene was riding high on good wages, especially for a black woman with only a high school diploma to her name. Starting as a service clerk in New York Telephone and Telegraph, she worked her way up to management. With that solid bank account in hand, Darlene claimed her own little patch of the American dream, a small starter house across the street from her parents. At twenty-five, she had what no one else in her family had been able to put together in all the generations that had preceded her. She had her own place that no landlord could control. No greater asset, from a purely material point of view, was required.

Darlene always felt comfortable on Willoughby Avenue, even when it began to turn down. The security of the old, familiar neighborhood, not to mention the proximity of her parents, was an important source of support as she navigated the waters of single parenthood. Darlene's first husband died young and she was left to raise a son on her own. Her mother, a lifelong housewife, pitched in and made it possible for Darlene to continue working for the phone company, hence Darlene never skipped a beat at work. The arrangements worked smoothly until her mother had to return to the West Indies to take care of her own mother, who had fallen down and broken her hip. Suddenly the support structure wobbled.

Scott was two at the time. My next-door neighbor, she was very good. She would baby-sit, but he used to cry so much. I'd call in the day and he'd be crying. I'd call at lunchtime, he'd be crying. I couldn't do my job properly. I [thought to myself], "Is it better to send him to my mother, where I know he'd be well cared for?" But I knew my mother would be in Barbados for at least a year or so [and it would be hard] for me to make the trip down there. So I made the decision and I sent him to the West Indies. He stayed there for four years. Those four years I went about every summer for two weeks. But he had already known the difference between mother and grandmother. So it wasn't like he didn't know me. But that was the only time I ever had to do that. He came back here at seven.

Darlene was looking to give Scott the best upbringing she could arrange and the kind of solid schooling that would stand him in good stead as he grew into adulthood. She was careful with her resources and managed to put away enough money to put him in a Catholic elementary school where the nuns were strict and the uniforms were starched. When the workweek was done, Darlene would slip back into the mothering role. She made it her business to center Scott's recreational life around her own home.

Because we lived on Willoughby where I knew everyone, Scott's friends were always welcome at my house. They would play baseball, watch TV, play with baseball cards, whatever. Whenever I had any function, he had a [best] friend who joined us. Whenever I took him to a baseball game or the circus, I invited his friend along and explained to his mother that it was an invite, meaning that whether she had the money to send him or not, as long as I had her permission, I would pay the expenses because I took him for company for Scott. I was very involved with his friends.

Yet as the blocks surrounding Willoughby Avenue began their descent into poverty, the decay spilled over into Darlene's life. When Scott hit his late teenage years, in the mid-1980s, the combustible combination of his adolescence, the death of Darlene's father, and her mother's permanent departure for the West Indies started to take its toll. As a full-time, working Mom, Darlene was unable to supervise the boy's whereabouts after school. Scott started running with the wrong crowd, getting involved in minor scrapes with the law. It is possible none of this would have mattered had it not been for the coincidence of Scott's young adulthood and the appearance of crack cocaine in New York City. But his minor lapses with the boys in the 'hood turned into something more serious as he reached his twenties and got further involved in the trade.

The contrast between Darlene's childhood decorum and Scott's out-of-control behavior was razor sharp. Never in a million years, Darlene recalls, would she have acted up, disobeyed, swore, or run around the way Scott did. Joe Cawley would have tanned her hide! Indeed, before he died, Joe did what he could to control his grandson, lending a man's presence to his daughter's household. When Joe passed away, all that discipline went with him.

Scott did finish high school and even attended junior college in Brooklyn for a while. He had a variety of jobs, including one Darlene helped him get at the phone company. But these positives were swamped by the negatives as Scott got more deeply involved in the world of drugs, all the while living in his mother's house. Darlene would leave for her job at the phone company every morning and come back to find her house in a shambles and money missing from her top drawer. Scott exploded whenever Darlene challenged him with evidence of his drug habit. The confrontations made no difference. Bit by bit, the life she helped Scott to build for himself unraveled.

After he got hooked up on drugs, he lost his job with the phone company. They gave him an option to resign or be fired. He resigned. Lost his seventeen-dollar-an-hour job. Now he's working as a temp for seven-fifty. It's a big difference. . . . He didn't pay rent. Very disrespectful and I couldn't get him out. Then he got hooked up on crack and that just like took over his mind. He had no respect. He started hitting on me and stuff like that. He broke out the windows of my house. He threw big rocks and broke them all out.

The conflict escalated until, at her wit's end, Darlene called the police and busted her own son.

He threatened me. . . . He had a terrible temper. I finally said, "I've got to stop letting you do what you want to do to me." And he turned his cap around and said, "Now call the motherfuckin' cops, ma." And that's what I did. I pressed charges. I locked up my own child. He couldn't believe it. He called me up. He said, "You're not going to post bail?" I said "No. Maybe the fifteen days in jail will do you some good."

This sobering confrontation with the lockdown ward put Scott back on a path toward a decent, if not particularly goal-oriented, life. He earns his own way now and has his own place to live. It is a bare-bones existence, one Darlene softens by helping him as much as she can, short of having him live in her house.

I launder his shirts. I feed him. He doesn't give me any money; he doesn't have any money to give. I do [what] I can to help him, but I will not let him live with me again. He's been clean now about a year. He doesn't have a real good job. I usually give him dinner at night because he's not making a whole lot of money. But it reaches a point where I've got to come first. And I've done all I can for him and will continue if he's in need. But I will not give up my space for him.

Now in her late fifties, retired from the phone company, and living on a fixed pension, Darlene has no margin for Scott's foolishness. She has to find ways to help from a distance. Darlene is not heartless, nor is she looking to slam the door in the face of the only blood kin she has nearby. Like many other inner-city parents in the older generation, she has come down on the side of her own sanity in order to be sure she will have the resources she needs to keep body and soul together into her old age.

When Darlene scans her own biography, she sees a woman who stepped eagerly on the up escalator and has a lot to show for her hard work. If it all stops with her, though, if her son ends up a part-time messenger on a low salary, she will not take great satisfaction in the trajectory of her family. And she wonders whether she is to blame for the way in which Scott turned out. Could she have done more to make sure he stuck to the straight and narrow?

> Sometimes I think I failed my son because maybe I should have had a man figure, a father figure for him and stuff. But then when I think about it, I say, "I didn't fail him. He's failed hisself." I gave him all the necessary ingredients he needed to make a life for himself. And he just didn't know what to do with it. He felt that because he was my only child, I was supposed to just keep giving him and giving him and giving him. Every time he fell behind or owed somebody some money, I was supposed to go to the bank and just take it out and give it to him. And I did that for some time. And then I stopped. You know. I don't really have any failures [of my own], except sometimes I reminisce about him, what I could have done better to make him be a little different from how he is.
>
> I told him, "You can't live with me. We can't hardly get along just you coming here [to visit]. Because you start telling me about what you don't have and what you need, and when I tell you I'm on a fixed income, you tell me about all the money I have." But all that money I have is not all that much.[2]

Darlene's story is familiar to inner-city families where the good fortune of one or two members has not been repeated in the lives of their extended kin. To be the one stable earner in a sea of relatives who need help is to be caught in a dilemma without easy solution. Scott does his best to make his mother feel guilty, privileged, withholding in the face of his needs. He argues that by denying him comfort she is refusing to act like a mother. Darlene has discovered the hard way that if she bends to these demands, she will deplete the only reserves she has. She will deliver her security to a son who is completely unreliable, who has shown that he cannot be trusted to care for her. Multiply Scott times the many cousins, nephews, nieces, and grandchildren who could come knocking on the doors of the more fortunate elderly in the inner city, and you have a recipe for intergenerational heartache.

Darlene protects herself from these demands by engaging in a little subterfuge. She is now responsible for husbanding her own mother's nest egg as well as the modest savings she has squirreled away. To guard against her own impulse to help everyone who calls upon her, she has put the money into accounts that cannot be accessed. They bear her mother's name, in trust to Darlene. This seemed the only way to maintain the fiction that she actually couldn't help the relatives who turn to her.

God forbid, anything happens to my mother, [the money] is going to be mine anyway. It will be mine because it's in trust for me. I figure if I get it into my hands, I'm a sucker for a sad story. I have so many people that owe me money. "I was sick, the car broke down." Some of them repay me, some of them pay me when they feel like it. And then when I question them they tell me, "Well it's not like you don't have money." I say, "Yes, but if I keep lending it [this way], I won't have any." So I've gotten to the point where I lend no money.

Family and friends who are refused when they ask for help do not just wander away and lick their wounds. They get angry. Darlene has lost some of these people from her circle because she wouldn't deliver.

Her relative prosperity, coupled with the financial distress of her closer relatives, forces her into a kind of protective shell that leaves her alone much of the time. Loneliness is a problem for many singles in late middle age. It can become even more intense as the aging process takes its toll and limited mobility restricts their range of motion. Even for people in their fifties, as Darlene was when she was downsized out of her phone-company job, "getting a life" entails a bunch of problems that bubble up out of a history of rocky relationships.

After her husband died, Darlene had a series of short-term relations with men who never quite stayed the course. Granted, she was working, raising a child, and trying to help her parents as they got older. There wasn't much energy left over for a man. But more than energy was at stake. A certain wariness set in, a circling of the emotional wagons, that has stayed with Darlene into her fifties. She opened herself up on a number of occasions to men that just were not ready or willing to make a commitment to her or her son. They were content to take what Darlene had to give short term and walk out at the first sign of conflict, boredom, or responsibility.

Some days Darlene stares out the window and thinks it would be nice to have someone close, someone to share the time with. Other times, she remembers how hard it was to ride the roller coaster those relationships put her on·and she swears never again. The ups and downs have left Darlene leery and slightly callused around the edges. She expects people will try to take advantage of her and she turns inward, like a turtle in its shell, to shield herself. Darlene both wants and doesn't want close emotional attachments. She isn't sure it is possible to enjoy those bonds without losing either money or sanity. After a while, the walls she puts up become hard for anyone to breach, and they don't try.

Is Darlene having a miserable middle age? Will her elder years be fraught with isolation and loneliness? She doesn't think so. Like most people, she looks at her life with a mixture of satisfaction and frustration. Darlene is unusually blessed, particularly as compared to the widows that she knows, who have a lot more to worry about. Traditional women who left the work world to their husbands and never learned to fend for themselves often find themselves in trouble when they lose their partners.

> Some people get to this age and they really don't have anything to show for it. They don't have a substantial job—especially the women. Their husband might have been the major breadwinner and [the wife] never took their job seriously or they never worked or wanted any kind of career. The husband up and dies. You know, death doesn't always bring a lot of insurance or a lot of money. They're left to face with young kids and sometimes they feel they missed out on life. At this point they don't have this, they should have did that. But me, I'm content. Anything I get now is a plus.

Ten years ago, Willoughby Avenue got so rough that Darlene really couldn't take it anymore. She was getting older and the young toughs were getting bolder. Even though she had lived there most of her life, she had come to the end of her tether. The house went up for sale and Darlene moved to a more middle-class community, nearer the gentrifying sections of Brooklyn. Here she discovered a whole new collection of neighbors who have accepted her as one of their own. She knows everyone in her new building: the black family from South Africa, the Italian "super" who will come and change a lightbulb for her or fix a leak, the single mother who is a student at the Pratt Institute. Everyone is invited to the cookouts in the park when the children in the building have their birthday parties. Her new neighbors are pleased that Darlene is around to keep an eye on the apartment building during the day, when the working people are gone. She lets the gas or light company in to check the meters, which helps everyone in the building (because they used to get high "estimated bills" without the actual meter check). If the mailman has a package to deliver, he knows Darlene will take it and give it to the right person when they get home.

The value of a supportive community became all too clear to Darlene the day her high blood pressure got the better of her. She blacked out, fell down, and had to go to the hospital for tests.

> I had some trouble and they brought me out of there on a stretcher. My face looked bad, but I didn't know any of this because I was

[passed] out. My neighbors all came, they kept calling, leaving messages on the phone. I didn't get home for a week. But after I got out of the hospital, they brought me fruit, they brought me juice. I mean, I only knew these people a couple of months! So it's friendly. It just reminds me of where I grew up, when the old-timers were on the block.

She knew she'd moved to the right place.

This episode cast a bit of a pall on Darlene's future. She hopes that her own old age will be like her mother's, who in her late eighties spends her days in a rocking chair on the back porch of her home in the West Indies. But she could just as easily have her father's bad luck. Hypertension led to a stroke and left him an invalid for several years before he died. Her mom nursed her dad. Who would do that for Darlene? Her neighbors and friends are good to her, but they couldn't be called on for that kind of caretaking. She has no siblings and her only son does not appear to be a good bet over the long run. The cousins she might have been able to turn to may not be so eager since she has had to push them away in recent years when they have asked her for money.

The pension Darlene has now from her phone-company days takes care of her needs with some to spare. When social security kicks in, nearly ten years after her retirement, she will have a bit more to count on. None of this would stretch to cover round-the-clock care. Yet Darlene is truly one of the more fortunate black women in New York City. She has had the benefits of a good job over the whole of her working life, a job that provided her with a reliable pension, health care for life, and enough of an income to make her a home owner. Indeed, she had enough resources to pull herself out of a neighborhood that, in some sense, dragged her son down.

Darlene's life testifies to some of the key themes I raised in the introduction to this book. She can measure the distance between her parents and herself in the accoutrements of middle-class life that she earned: a home, a steady white-collar job, a pension. Her life has been spent in the company of people of all colors, at least for a time before white flight stripped Willoughby Avenue of so many of its white residents. Only in her later adult years did the community become a segregated enclave defined by increasing poverty, and she finally managed to wave good-bye to it. In all of these respects, Darlene has a great deal to be proud of.

Yet the legacy of her personal life was one of constraints that blunted the impact of her good fortune. The loss of her husband left her to raise a son on her own. Without a second steady income, she had little choice for many years but to stay put on Willoughby Avenue as it spiraled downward. She needed her parents' help to raise her son and on a single salary could not have afforded a more affluent neighborhood anyway. Instead, she stayed put and watched the disappearance of home owners and the increasing presence of unstable renters, the growth of the drug trade, the overcrowding of the schools, and the rising crime in the area. These conditions created the environment that dragged Scott into the drug trade and made him a predator in her own home.

What this has meant for Darlene, now that she is well beyond the child-rearing years, is that she is largely alone. She has many friends who have stayed with her through thick and thin, and they are her real family now.

Rita Tilly, a seventy-one-year-old black woman who lives in a modest apartment not far from Darlene, took a different approach and has paid a price for it. Rita's parents were from the southern cities of Memphis and Charleston. Like millions of other African Americans, they joined the great migration of the interwar years, moving to Manhattan in the early 1920s. Rita grew up lucky, living in high style among the high society of the Harlem Renaissance. Her father was a successful musician who parlayed his talents into a solid career and a big apartment in the middle of a neighborhood that was a melting pot of American society. Chinese launderers, Irish laborers, Italian grocers—these were Rita's neighbors. But all of that changed, as Rita explains: "Just before the war, I guess around 1940 or so, the whites on Amsterdam Avenue started moving out and it all became black."

Rita's family joined the exodus. In the mid-1950s, they began searching for a home in Brooklyn where they could enjoy more space and escape the segregation that was enveloping their Manhattan neighborhood. The Brooklyn realtors were only too happy to help them find a new home.

> Real estate agents wanted to buy those houses from the whites. They got the house for ten or fifteen thousand dollars. They charged the black people twenty-five, thirty, maybe fifty thousand dollars for the same house. After we moved in, we used to get letters asking us to sell because black people are moving in. They'd just stick these letters under the door, because it was still a predominantly white neighborhood. They used to say, you know, you better move because the blacks are moving in.

For the princely sum of $15,000, Rita's family moved into what is now an historic preservation district. Their gorgeous three-story brownstone was graced by a curving mahogany staircase, leaded-glass windows, twelve-foot ceilings, and more rooms than they knew what to do with. The house could easily accommodate several generations. So when Rita married it was only natural that the new couple took up residence in the Tilly family household, where they could live in splendor.

The neighborhood around the beautiful brownstone was another matter. By the time Rita had her second child, the familiar hallmarks of the ghetto had begun to creep a little closer.

We had the brownstone house and our own neighborhood was nice. But two or three blocks away, it's drugs—a lot of drugs around. There's a [drug] rehab center down there and you had to ask your councilman to do something about them hanging out after the [addicts] go in for their treatments. They'd hang out on the corners and you'll be afraid to walk to church because they're out there.

Rita did what she could to shelter her own kids from bad influences. She read to them when they were little. She paid attention to their schoolwork. She was a working woman, too, however. For almost forty years she held down a full-time job as an administrator in a Manhattan publishing company, returning home at night to her latchkey children. Her husband, a West Indian, was a good man who did what he could for the family, but Rita lost him to a gunshot wound. Her second marriage was a disaster. Still, she managed to keep her head afloat and her children on an even keel until they reached their teenage years. By then they were beyond her immediate control and the impact of living in a dicey area created a tug-of-war for Rita's son. She was able to keep Eli on the straight and narrow for quite a while. Indeed, he got a job as a bus mechanic in the city's Transit Department. It paid well and promised job security. Unfortunately, friends in the neighborhood pulled in the other direction, dragging Eli down into addiction. By the time he was in his thirties, Rita's boy was a heroin addict married to another drug addict and HIV positive to boot.

Rita's daughter developed a devastating illness in her thirties, sapping most of her mother's retirement money to pay for a series of operations that did not restore her health.

Before I retired, I had money put aside . . . but my daughter got sick with a brain tumor and she had bills. . . . My money was eaten up in all that, paying her bills. Now it's not like she can get her job back.

She quit her job just about two weeks before she had to go in for this operation.

The tumor destroyed her daughter's eyesight and much of her hearing. It has rendered her completely dependent on her aging mother, and since mother and daughter have had strained relations since high school, it has brought two unwilling women into close proximity and stripped Rita of any prospect of a comfortable retirement. Now she must nurse her daughter as well as take full responsibility for the two grandchildren her son and daughter have left to her care.

I've been taking care of my grandson [my son's child] since he was born, because the baby's mother is a drug addict also. I took care of him since he came home from the hospital [where] his mother gave him up. I've minded him until I got my granddaughter two years ago, and I started taking care of her. We all live in the same house. I feed them and most of the time I clothe them. Since my son went on public assistance, he's doing something [financially] for the one grandson now, but all the other time, I did it all on my retirement money.

Rita is not a saint. She has had her share of struggles with alcoholism and depression, but she also has her God and the help of AA to keep her on the straight and narrow. She is not a well-educated woman and she blames herself for not pushing harder to get an education. Still, she has soldiered through a difficult life and has done what she could for her family. Now, at seventy-one, she would like nothing more than a little peace and quiet. Instead, she is saddled with the care of two grandkids and her sick daughter, plus the worries that come from years of contending with addicts and relatives who are seriously ill. She has not shirked from sharing her money with family members who are in need, but as a consequence there isn't much left over to cushion her own old age.

Rita and Darlene have many things in common. Both of them have been working women their entire adult lives. Neither of them has ever crossed the threshold of a welfare office, and they have precious little respect for those who make a habit of it. They both lost husbands and had rocky relationships with men thereafter, leaving them, for all practical purposes, the sole bread-winners in their households. Because they were the only earners in their homes, they didn't have the cash it took to take leave of neighborhoods that turned downward. Work was a source of pleasure and a steady, though not terribly lucrative, income, but it also took them away from their children, a problem they managed, though not easily, when the kids were small, by relying on a combination of their own mothers' help and baby-sitting by the neighbors. They both heaved a sigh of relief when their kids were old enough to go to school, for this solved the childcare problem.

Latchkey kids have been a working-class norm for many decades. By the time Scott and Eli were adolescents, it was no longer cool to be under close adult supervision anyway. Hence the kids were on their own and free to mix with whomever they pleased. Try as they might to keep track of exactly which kids that might be, neither Darlene nor Rita was able to control her adolescent after he had turned fifteen. The combination of freedom and the increasingly unsavory aspects of the neighborhood undermined the pathway both mothers had laid out for their children. Drugs, particularly crack cocaine, crept into the streets and alleyways of Brooklyn just about the time their kids reached their twenties.

This is where their stories diverge. Darlene "divorced" her son. Rita might have done the same if her son's life were the only one hanging in the balance. She couldn't ignore the needs of her grandchildren, who are now Rita's to raise on the retirement pension she had been saving for herself. Then she was faced with the unexpected burdens of her daughter's very serious illness. She is not content; she is not happy. She is pretty miserable.

What Rita's tale adds to our understanding of aging in the inner city is the dimension of health as a key turning point. Ironically, though, it is not Rita's health but that of her daughter that has had such a forceful impact on her mother's life. Left to her own devices, Rita would probably have managed her middle age and elderly years without much complaint. She would have agonized over her son's drug problems and the children he left her to raise, but in this she would have been like millions of other black grandmothers who have stepped in to fill the holes that their errant children have dug. What has pushed Rita over the edge and made her financially vulnerable is the devastating illness of her daughter. It has drained her savings, pushed her own health to the brink, and added to the stresses she was facing already, which, as she would be the first to point out, were "quite enough, thank you." Unfortunately, as we will see in the following chapter, the incidence of serious health problems is high among poor minorities. They descend early and are more debilitating than we would expect to find among the middle class.

How people cope with these pressures, what they do to deflect or embrace the problems that fill their lives dictates a great deal of what they will face as they age. Social problems larger than any one individual are at fault for depositing the troubles on their doorstep. Whether they open the door or slam it shut is another matter.

Cancion Naciento illustrates a third pattern of contending with inner-city disorder. He elected to close his home to the trouble that was brewing in the life of a nephew, one of two he was left to raise after the first was orphaned and the second abandoned. Cancion wasn't going to go Rita's route and saddle himself with a problem child; nor was he inclined to try Darlene's way of giving and then retreating. Tough love, self-preservation, and strict order: these are Cancion's watchwords.

Born in 1936 in eastern Puerto Rico, Cancion comes from many generations of agricultural workers.

> My father grew up on a ranch where eighty cows a day were milked. From the house, you could see the sea from side to side. . . . We had many neighbors—though they were at least a mile away—a beautiful view, many mango trees, all kinds of tropical fruits. The houses were all wooden except for some made during the Puerto Rico Reconstruction Administration, when houses were made for First World War veterans. Two bedrooms, kitchen, dining room, and living room. My father got a house for a hundred dollars!

By the 1950s, Cancion's teenage years, the trickle of Puerto Ricans bound for New York City's west side became a flood. His parents, three brothers, and sister all migrated before him, while Cancion stayed behind to finish school under the watchful eye of his grandmother. In 1956, at the age of twenty, he found himself on 83rd Street and Columbus Avenue, the center of what was then a poor Puerto Rican slum on the upper west side of Manhattan. A shopkeeper who befriended his mother offered Cancion a job repairing shoes and taught him the trade. For the next seventeen years, until the shop went bankrupt, Cancion had a steady job, a new church (Episcopalian), and the English language to learn.

Over time, his brothers and sister married and started their own families, but Cancion remained a bachelor and, when his father died, assumed responsibility for his mother. He was always an austere man, good at saving money, on the lookout for investment opportunities. Slowly but surely, he accumulated enough money to think about buying a place of his own. When one brother died young and left Cancion a nephew to look after and his sister abandoned her own son to his care, Cancion took the home owner plunge, moving everyone—his "sons" and his mother—to the Bronx, where he has lived ever since.

This part of the Bronx is no paradise. The blocks that surround Cancion's house are littered with overturned trash cans and check-cashing stores that cater to the poor, with brightly lit signs advertising lotto tickets and beer. Small groups of boisterous young men hang about the nearby subway station. The run-down commercial area gives way to a short row of wooden two-story houses painted white, with grass in their small front yards and bunches of bright red and pink peonies in flower boxes against cement foundations. One house has now been converted to a law office—"Spanish spoken within"—while another is for sale. Cancion's home is next door. He paid for his modest home from his salary as a security guard for Chase Manhattan bank, a position he landed thanks to the recommendation of his Episcopalian minister, who was a personal friend of the branch manager.

For twenty-eight years now, Cancion has worked full time for the bank, where he has been blessed with a retirement fund, health insurance, and overtime pay that brought him up to $35,000 a year at the age of sixty. By being prudent, he has achieved his piece of the American dream: his own home, money in the bank, and enough resources to take care of his eighty-two-year-old mother for the rest of her days. A steady parade of uncles (his mother was one of eight) and fictive kin who "go for" cousins streams in and out of his house on weekends, while Cancion presides from his living room perch, a couch covered in protective plastic.

One of the reasons Cancion has been able to enjoy his accomplishments is that, unlike Rita or Darlene, he has never been at the mercy of teenagers caught up in the drug trade. At the first sign of difficulty with one of his nephews, he cut the troublemaker out of his life. Cancion came early to the conclusions Darlene reached belatedly and acted on his convictions without hesitation. One of his nephews prospered under this regime and has now become a sergeant in the army. He is always welcome in the family home. The other nephew couldn't hack it.

> My brother's son was always negative. He never tried to follow positive individuals. In one year he was in six or seven different schools and since he didn't continue in school, I kicked him out. . . . I don't want him here. Period. What he does, that's his problem. He's done here. I got rid of the rotten apple and the barrel was saved.

Cancion applies the same no-nonsense approach to virtually every task he has confronted in life. He gives no quarter to people who do not toe the line of self-discipline and personal responsibility. He has no time for liberal ideas about the damage poverty does to self-esteem or the drive for success. He has seen real poverty in Puerto Rico and believes New York is a picnic of opportunities by comparison.

The inner city is not a particularly forgiving place in which to pass through middle age and on to elderhood. Those who have done so are marked by the experience, by the history they have lived through. Economic upswings that opened up options in the 1960s gave way to downturns in the '70s and '80s. The impact of these macro forces on local neighborhoods is traceable to this day: home owners gave way to renters, grocery stores gave way to liquor outlets, mixed-race communities descended into segregation, and families had to pick up the pieces, even as they themselves were often in disarray.

Today, many of the same neighborhoods have started to see a renaissance sparked by gentrification, as many middle-class Manhattanites find themselves unable to afford downtown rents and turn to these outer boroughs and poor neighborhoods as commutable alternatives. New immigrants have also arrived in droves, turning first to the poorest New York enclaves in which to settle their families. All of this is, at least in most respects, to the good. The quality of life improves, at least for those who are not forced out by rising rents. It is particularly important for the elderly because they were the ones made most vulnerable during the truly dangerous years of the crack wars. But it came too late to shape the trajectories of their families, particularly their adult children. Hence aging takes place against the backdrop that history has bequeathed to them.

What does that history mean now? How does it shape the economic resources they have to support them in retirement? What about the emotional terrain of family life, relations between now adult children and their aging parents? Or the bonds between men and women who bring to their elder years a rocky history of intimate relations? Inner-city adults develop a "different shade of gray" from that of their suburban age mates because the pathway that has shaped their lives in inner-city neighborhoods has been dramatically different.

To understand why those differences matter, I turn now to explore the diversity of the middle-aged and elderly population of the United States at the beginning of the twenty-first century. What kind of educational background, income history, and family structure did they develop in their younger years that so powerfully altered their options later on? How did the limitations imposed by racial discrimination or migration affect their health profiles? These number-driven portraits are the focus of chapter two because they define the structural circumstances within which the history of these generations unfolded in the inner city.

With this framework in place, I move to two critical factors that helped to shape the aging experience: work and neighborhood location. Chapter three explores the kinds of jobs available to these adults, which determined the income they could rely on and set the limits on what kind of neighborhoods they could live in. It also looks at what happened to the communities where people like Darlene or Cancion spent their early adult years.

It would have been much easier for black and Latino families to hold those pressures at bay had they been able to rely on stable marriages. Family structures began to change in relation to the rising poverty of inner-city neighborhoods. We know this history from the vantage point of young families. Indeed, the literature on poverty is largely about young single mothers and absent fathers. But we know very little about how those patterns of family formation mattered later in life. Hence in chapter four, I ask what happened to romantic relationships decades after the kids were born. Where do all those older divorced men and never-married fathers go when they have not been part of family life for many years? How do women cope in their fifties and sixties when men are not part of their lives? And what do they do when those long-lost men come knocking on the door once again?

One of the consequences of growing up with hardship is that the wear and tear on the body advances at a rapid pace. In chapter five, I look at how the stress of economic hardship, economic insecurity, and lower social status combine to produce patterns of illness that make many inner-city dwellers in their fifties look more like middle-class people in their seventies. We know that stress ages people prematurely, but that observation is confined mainly to statistical relationships between poverty and disease. We need to dig deeper into the lives of inner-city dwellers to find out how the early onset of chronic illness affects middle-aged mothers, working sisters and brothers who have to drop everything to assist their elderly parents, and the elderly themselves, who often have to set aside their own aches and pains to care for sick relatives who are decades younger but have nowhere else to turn.

How much of that stress is a function of race relations? Chapter six considers the ambiguous nature of racial hierarchies seen from the viewpoint of African Americans, Puerto Ricans, and Dominicans. Who is on top, who is on the bottom, and why? I explore how those who live in segregated communities see these dimensions of social life in a divided society and how they apportion responsibility for the inequalities they know so well.

The legacy of those divisions poses problems for what we have come to call "social capital," those essential forms of participation and engagement that make American communities what they are. Chapter seven details local understandings of social responsibility, of the ways in which minority families radiate out from their most intimate relations to the broader community of which they are a part. To whom do they feel obligated? Where do they draw the lines of extra-familial commitment? These are pressing issues for those who are crossing the line from middle age to elderhood because they are often retired and therefore at least potentially able to contribute energy to community building.

Finally, I conclude with some thoughts on what we might do as a society to support those who are aging in America's poorest enclaves. How might we address the special needs they have as a consequence of many years of struggle in difficult neighborhoods on meager resources?

Whatever the answers, we should not think of the aging experience as one defined solely by the lifestyles of the rich and famous, or even by the middle class and ordinary. For below them in the pecking order are the working poor in communities like Harlem, Bedford-Stuyvesant, and the Dominican and Puerto Rican neighborhoods of Washington Heights. To understand what it will mean for the country to have a multicultural elderly population, we need to explore their experience as well.

2–The Big Picture*

Darlene, Rita, and Cancion are participants in a great transformation under way in the United States, a transition to a society dominated by older people.[1] We have fewer children under the age of five and more elders than we used to. People are living longer: the average American born in 1950 could expect to live to about age sixty-eight; a child born today can expect to live to seventy-seven.[2] Our "graying" trend will become only more pronounced in the coming years,[3] a shift driven both by the aging of the baby boom generation and by medical advances that have increased the life span.

At the same time that the American population is growing older, it is also becoming more racially and ethnically diverse. In 1990, more than three-quarters of Americans were white.[4] Over the next fifty or so years, however, the number of white Americans is expected to grow by only a modest 10 percent, such that by 2050 whites will represent just over half of the U.S. population.[5] In contrast, during that same time period, the population of African Americans[6] will increase by more than 75 percent[7] and the number of Americans of Hispanic origin will jump by approximately 300 percent.[8] Older minorities, particularly those of Hispanic origin, will see the fastest growth in the coming decades[9]:

*Coauthored by Shelley McDonough

Figure 2-1

Projected U.S. population change by age group and race, 1990–2050

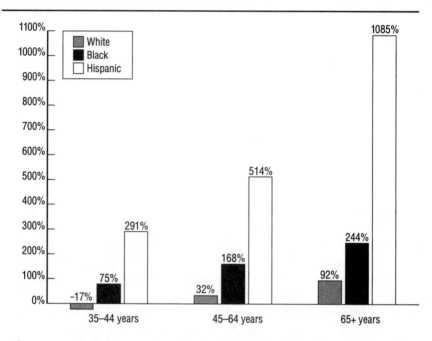

Important challenges to the well-being of the whole country lie at this nexus of aging and diversity. Minorities, particularly poor minorities, arrive at middle age and elderhood with more problems and fewer resources to address them than their white, middle-class counterparts. To understand what that means for domestic social policy, for urban communities, and for families who have to step in and patch up the safety net, we have to come to grips with why the pathways to old age are so different in the first place. What are the forces that lead older men and women in the inner city to age prematurely, to encounter serious health problems sometimes decades before anyone else? Why do they end up facing these difficulties without partners to help?

Anyone with family members approaching retirement on a fixed income will recognize some of these strains. We all have relatives who worry about their finances, physical disabilities, and the inevitable but terribly sad consequences of widowhood. Is there any reason to single out inner-city dwellers for special attention? I believe there is. Confronting these problems—problems that invade the lives of poor minorities sooner and more severely than anyone else—is even harder against the backdrop of concentrated neighborhood poverty, seriously dysfunctional adult children who cannot raise their own kids, and a legacy of single parenthood. There is a tangle of social problems at issue here, whose origins lie much earlier in the life span but whose consequences become most visible and pressing during the middle age and elder years. To understand the backdrop against which these burdens have accumulated, we have to detour into the numbers that reveal just how different the inner-city aging experience is from its more familiar counterpart in the suburbs.

To provide this context, I have adjusted the lens of our investigation to two different settings. First, we look at some statistics that contrast minorities with whites in terms of childhood poverty, education, employment, income, marriage, and health. My purpose here is to show that there really *are* distinctive patterns that make aging a different kettle of fish for minorities. Through this initial lens of race, we consider the broad generations of people who inhabit this book—those who came of age just after World War II (now elderly) and those whose lives were shaped by the opportunities created after the civil rights movement became the law of the land (now middle aged). I then move the lens all the way down to the most local level, to explore the African-American, Puerto Rican, and Dominican communities of New York City whose stories are chronicled in this book. Theirs are the "real lives" that are unfolding within the contours and constraints described by these impersonal statistics.

Childhood Poverty

So many of the problems that emerge in midlife and beyond are clearly a function of poverty. While financial hardship is difficult to bear at any age, when experienced in childhood its consequences—for cognitive, emotional, and physical development—can be particularly damaging.[10] The Great Depression which shaped their childhood crippled the economic security of both white and minority families. But for African-American families, who already existed on the employment margins, the hit was even more severe. "Blacks who were concentrated in the South were hit hard by the crisis in agriculture; those in the North, who worked primarily in domestic service and less skilled industrial positions, were hit by massive and persistent unemployment."[11] The vast majority of African Americans who are now in their seventies spent a good portion of their formative years in deep poverty.[12] Conditions improved dramatically after the Depression and with the onset of the war economy. Even so, the racial divide persisted: while 20 percent of white children[13] lived in poor families in 1959, 66 percent of black children were in the same boat.[14]

It is difficult to paint an accurate portrait of poverty among Hispanics during the first half of the twentieth century,[15] though it seems likely that Puerto Rican and Dominican children were no better off than their African-American peers. Puerto Rico's economy has historically tracked that of the United States. Thus, the fallout from the Great Depression in the 1930s pushed many island dwellers into deep poverty.[16] Given its reliance on exports such as tobacco and sugar, Puerto Rico experienced significant economic problems when the price of these commodities dropped elsewhere in the world. For many, this translated into a loss of jobs and increased difficulty in meeting the basic needs of the family. Dominican families, most of whom were completely dependent on sugar production for survival, faced similar hardships. When the stock market crashed on Black Monday in 1929, sugar prices fell dramatically, as did the jobs and wages that supported most Dominican households.[17]

While migration in the succeeding decades delivered new job opportunities and higher incomes, Hispanics quickly found that their earnings on the mainland simply did not stretch far enough. This was a fact felt all too readily by the children of these immigrants. Some of the earliest data available demonstrate the pervasiveness of childhood poverty among Puerto Ricans in the United States. In 1970, nearly 4 in 10 Puerto Rican children under the age of eighteen were living in poor families,[18] a rate rivaled only by the depths of black child poverty (42.2 percent). Over the next decade, things only got worse for Puerto Rican families, as the percentage of children living in poor homes eclipsed that for African Americans, and exceeded the rate of white child poverty by fourfold.

This may sound like a blizzard of numbers that have no concrete meaning. Yet the conditions under which the individuals whose lives are chronicled in this book grew up had profound importance for their life trajectories. In the most obvious sense, many more blacks and Hispanics than whites spent their formative childhood years lacking the basic life necessities—nutritious food, consistent shelter, reliable health care.

Education

The financial vulnerability evident among most inner-city residents has many sources. One of the most powerful is the problematic educational background many minorities received. This produced serious limitations for blacks and Latinos, though the patterns vary between them.

Black Americans in School

Only 45 percent of this country's elderly[19] African Americans graduated from high school. In contrast, 72 percent of white Americans in the same age group have a high school diploma. Racial inequality in college education is even more dramatic: more than twice as many elderly whites as elderly blacks[20] managed to get a baccalaureate degree.[21]

The postwar period saw a rapid growth in enrollment at the college level, as the GI Bill sent a whole generation of servicemen (and some women) into higher education and, to an unprecedented extent, democratized a university experience that had hitherto been reserved for children of real privilege.[22] Nevertheless, a college education was hardly a universal entitlement, even among those who qualified for the GI Bill. Getting a B.A. became increasingly necessary for managerial and professional employment. Hence the racial gap in college attainment had profound consequences.[23] Younger generations of African Americans have been steadily closing the educational gap over the years, but their elders lacked these credentials. The impact on the older generation's individual and household income was significant, limiting their capacity to pile up assets like real estate, savings, stocks, and other forms of wealth that are particularly important in the elder years.[24]

While graduation rates signal the degree of educational disadvantage, they do not tell the whole story. Educational *quality* is important too, and here the racial divide has long been pronounced. It wasn't until the landmark *Brown v. Board of Education* case (in 1954) that blacks were even allowed to attend the same schools as whites in some parts of the country. Thus, virtually *all* of those members of Rita's generation were educated in segregated schools, and many of Darlene's contemporaries spent their childhood years in black-only school systems.[25]

How much did segregation matter in determining the quality of the education that "our" generations received? Opinion on this subject is mixed. Gary Orfield, professor at Harvard's School of Education and national expert on desegregation, argues that kids who go to racially segregated schools have classmates that are mainly from poor and poorly educated families. Students in these schools are more likely to drop out, have low test scores, and learn from poorly qualified teachers.[26] That has been so for decades. On the other hand, segregated schools were one of the few venues in which African Americans could see middle-class role models of their own race. Black teachers, like the black preachers, undertakers, dentists, and other professionals who served the racially isolated communities on the "wrong side of the tracks," were respected leaders. Though they were sharply constrained by the limited funding afforded by the state authorities under Jim Crow, they could do more to impact the future of the children in their community—to shape what W.E.B. Du Bois called the "talented tenth"—than they were able to do under desegregation.[27]

The loss of this authority is something that older African Americans from the rural South readily remember. They recall key figures from their youth who were important to the black community and they lament the loss of their standing. Indeed, education itself was treated as something precious when it was a route to prestige and mobility that whites in power actively tried to deny to black children. When integration was declared, it not only came about on white terms, and resulted in the demotion of black teachers and principals, it reduced black kids to unwelcome interlopers in white schools whose teachers thought of the newcomers as unruly, uneducable, and socially damaged. Although the oldest African Americans in this book attended segregated schools and suffered many of the negative consequences, in some respects they were better off than their grandchildren and great-grandchildren, who decades later formed the bottom tier of more integrated schools.

Latino Education

The trends in education are perhaps even more troubling among Hispanics.[28] Only 32 percent of this country's elderly Latinos hold high school degrees, and fewer than 6 percent graduated from college, rates below those of their black peers, and dramatically lower than whites.[29] The persistent poverty that Puerto Ricans, Dominicans, and Mexicans experienced in their homelands, and later in America's urban centers, fueled the demand for young people to find work and generate income for their families rather than stay in school.[30]

The legally enforceable right to attend desegregated schools was not granted to Hispanics by the Supreme Court until 1973.[31] Thus, minority-only schools—and the lack of funding, social capital, and basic resources that constrain them—were a fact of life for Latinos who were educated on the mainland. Most Hispanic students in the United States had yet another

Table 2-1

Mean Income By Ability to Speak English for
Hispanics 40–65 Years of Age in New York City (1990)*

English Proficiency	Mean Income
Bilingual/Use English only	$18,271
Speak very well	$17,162
Speak fairly well	$14,001
Do not speak well	$10,287
Do not speak at all	$7,434

*It is possible that this relationship may also be a function of the amount of time spent in the United States (i.e., those who have been in the United States for longer periods may speak English better, and be more economically established, than recent immigrants), or of the level and/or quality of education attained. This table does not allow us to pull these factors apart.

significant strike against them—language. For the majority of the Hispanics in this book, schooling in the United States was almost entirely in English. For monolingual speakers of Spanish (or any other language, for that matter), movement into English-speaking schools can be problematic, especially if it comes about after the second grade. Learning English was harder to do in the midst of segregated barrios, and retaining Spanish was reinforced by the circular migration that took many Puerto Ricans back and forth from the mainland to the island. Intermittent return to Puerto Rico—and the disruption in schooling that came with it—was quite common. (Entry into the Puerto Rican school system did not always bring relief, however, as these students would often find themselves lacking full Spanish literacy as well.[32]) This language barrier, it is important to note, had significant consequences not only in school but also later in life, as Table 2.1 suggests. Those with a limited command of English felt the consequences in their pocketbooks.

What about those Hispanics who received all of their schooling in their native land? The rural schools that people like Cancion attended were rife with problems. Most teachers lacked qualifications and textbooks were rare, yet stringent achievement standards employed in the primary school grades meant that many students were forced to repeat first grade several times. While many parents were eager for their children to receive an education, critical household activities often assumed a higher priority in daily life, making regular school attendance a near impossibility for many students. Furthermore, "for many, school [was seen as] a 'holding operation' until the time some other social or occupational role became available: marriage or motherhood, employment, or migration to the United States."[33] Not surprisingly, then, rates of school attendance in the mid-twentieth century were low. In 1960, less than 40 percent of high school–aged Dominicans were enrolled in school.[34] Even the most "advantaged" of the Dominicans—urban residents who eventually migrated to the United States—spent far less time in school than U.S.-born whites or blacks.[35]

For Puerto Ricans educated on the island, things were not much better. As Geoffrey Fox noted, "Until the 1940s, public schools were required to teach in English, which many of the teachers themselves barely knew. But the dropout rate was so high that most Puerto Ricans neither acquired English fluency nor more than basic literacy in their own language."[36] In addition, given its status as a commonwealth, Puerto Rico has historically received lower levels of federal education aid than the states.[37]

Why is education so important? It confers options in the labor market, more so now than ever before. For many years, minority workers could get decent jobs for good pay even if they weren't well educated. Skilled blue-collar work paid fairly well. Even Cancion, who not only had no education but also could barely speak any English at all, had a steady job in a shoe repair shop. These kinds of jobs disappeared in large numbers throughout the decades when the generations in this book turned toward middle age. It got tougher out there and those who were well educated, like Darlene, were able to pull away from the pack in terms of income and steady employment. She did so because she did finish high school and even went on to complete some college, an accomplishment that paid off handsomely for Darlene. For millions of other blacks and Latinos, low levels of education made for lifelong problems.

Employment

What were the early work experiences like for today's middle-aged and elderly minorities? The oldest of them began looking for work in the 1940s and '50s, a period long both in time and in social history, for it spanned the tail end of the Great Depression, the tight labor markets and rising wages of World War II, and the first eight years of the long postwar boom. For the younger cohort (those between the ages of forty-five and sixty-four today), there were far more highs than lows. They entered the labor market between 1954 and 1973, a golden age of prosperity, high wages, increasing equality, and a boost in our standard of living—trends that began to "go south" after 1973. But these broad snapshots obscure some important underlying differences. Labor market opportunities and outcomes throughout the decades varied markedly by both race/ethnicity and gender.

Perhaps the most striking aspect of employment over these periods was the increase in the number of women in the work world. African-American women led the way. While employment rates[38] for white women have risen steadily throughout the century[39], working for a living was old news for their black sisters.[40] Puerto Rican women followed a different pathway. Those born on the island tended to be traditional, stay-at-home mothers. U.S.-born women of Puerto Rican ancestry were much more likely to be in the workforce.[41]

This huge sweep of history saw some dramatic changes in the kind of employment available to minorities, particularly women. According to economic historian Claudia Goldin, as late as 1940 fully 60 percent of all employed black women were servants in private households.[42] Domestic service was in high demand, but it was hardly the job of choice.[43] Poorly paid and lacking possibilities for advancement, black women were eager to leave behind their lives as housemaids. The advent of World War II made this possible as opportunities opened up for black women in shipyards and munitions plants, with much higher wages and greater dignity on offer. One domestic who left work for a higher-paying factory job put it this way: "Lincoln freed the Negroes from cotton picking and Hitler was the one that got us out of the white folks' kitchen."[44]

For many, the good fortune was short-lived. Black women were often the first to be pushed out of the high-wage factory jobs when the servicemen returned from the war. Their white sisters were not far behind. However, while white women often retired to the home as housewives and full-time mothers of the fast-approaching "baby boom," black women still had to work. Their menfolk were less likely to be employed once they got out of the service, and their pay packets were comparatively small as measured against whites. As a consequence, black women headed back into service work in large numbers. As Figure 2.2 shows, more than half of all working black women were employed in the service industry as late as 1960.[45]

While black women moved in and out of the service industry, Hispanic women established a foothold in the manufacturing plants that were popping up in many urban centers. In particular, island-born Puerto Rican and Latin American women found themselves occupying spots in the apparel and leather industries in New York in massive numbers—more than 70 percent of those working in manufacturing in New York in the 1970s were concentrated in these few jobs.[46] Dominican women followed suit (so to speak)—by 1980 more than half of all female Dominican workers in New York City

Figure 2-2

Occupational distribution of women aged 16–64: 1960

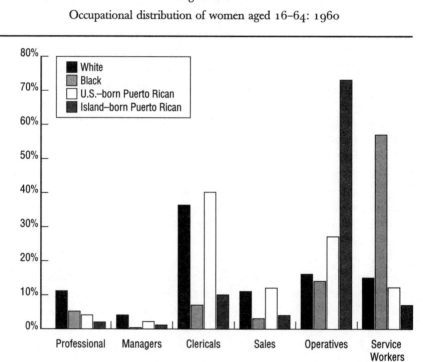

were factory workers, predominantly in the apparel industry.[47] Not surprisingly, these industries were among the lowest paying and most labor intensive in the city.[48]

These patterns reflect the divergent educational opportunities open to women from these ethnic groups. White women, even those from poor immigrant backgrounds, were able to move into white-collar occupations because they were literate, had at least some high school education, and were steered toward shorthand, typing, and related clerical skills in school. Black women made the same move, but did so much later in the twentieth century because it took that much longer for them to access the educational background required. Like black men, they were held back by the force of racial exclusion, which relegated them to domestic service and blue-collar trades. Hispanic women, in particular island-born Puerto Ricans and Dominicans, remained in occupations that did not require spoken or written English—namely, manufacturing and domestic service work. By the 1980s they, too, had moved into the white-collar world, but that was too late for most of the women who figure in this book.[49] Their occupational lives were set by the

Figure 2-3

Occupational distribution of men aged 16–64: 1960

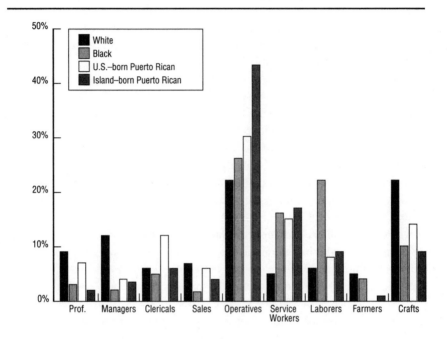

trends that shaped the period from roughly 1940 to 1970, hence few of them became white-collar working women.

How did the pattern for men's employment compare to the experiences of women? Prior to World War II, African-American men could be found mainly in agricultural employment—more than 40 percent were farmers or farm laborers.[50] After the war, however, farm work dropped sharply. Mechanization of agriculture pushed men off the farms and war-related factory labor pulled them northward.[51] By 1960, black men had taken up positions as laborers, service workers, and factory operatives in large numbers, as shown in Figure 2.3.[52] Most of these jobs tended to be better paid than farm work, but not nearly as lucrative as the professional and managerial occupations from which they were barred. The most fortunate black men moved into the blue-collar occupations, cracking the barriers that had excluded them from unionized manufacturing jobs as craftsmen and operatives. Those were good jobs with higher wages, greater security, and more benefits than anything men had seen in the agricultural fields of the South.

What black men have not been able to do is move in large numbers into the professional and managerial occupations that their white counterparts occupy. This is where the money is now, and has been for several decades. While there were clearly more black men wearing white collars in 1980 than was true in 1960 (and certainly in 1940), they still lagged well behind their white counterparts. For the generations of particular interest to us, the predominant employment niche for black men was in the urban factory system, a system that began to crumble in the mid-1970s.

The vast majority of Hispanic men, particularly those born outside the United States, moved into the factories and service jobs, like the security job that Cancion holds. Comparatively few of those born outside the mainland were able to assume the white-collar positions their white peers did.[53] Even by 1980, 56 percent of Dominican men in New York City were still employed in manufacturing jobs or "personal service" employment, such as gardeners or home health aids.[54] Most were unskilled and spoke no English. If they hailed from a rural environment (as many did), they had very little experience with any type of machinery. Thus, most ended up in service occupations or laboring in repetitive factory jobs. For example, in one sample of Dominicans who had immigrated to New York from Aldea, a small village in the Dominican Republic, 30 percent of the workers held positions in a garment factory, 26 percent worked as factory laborers and machine operators, and 20 percent took jobs in restaurants, mostly as dishwashers.[55]

Overall, the trends in the labor force participation of men are almost the exact opposite of women's. Men have been pulling out of the work world rather than increasing their commitment to it, and this is true of all races and ethnic groups.[56]

Economic Status

What impact did these patterns of educational and occupational disadvantage have on the earning power of today's middle-aged and elderly minorities? Here, the story is somewhat mixed. On the positive side were the impressive economic gains made by black women relative to their white peers. In 1960, median wages for a black female worker were roughly 65 percent of those paid to her white counterpart. By 1980 black women had nearly closed the income gap, taking home 92 percent of the earnings of their white peers. Earnings of black males also increased relative to whites, though the gains were not nearly as substantial. In 1980, the median wage for a black male worker, while clearly better than what he earned in 1960, was still only 63 percent of that paid to a white worker. In contrast to the gains experienced

Figure 2-4

Median wages and salary, female workers aged 16+

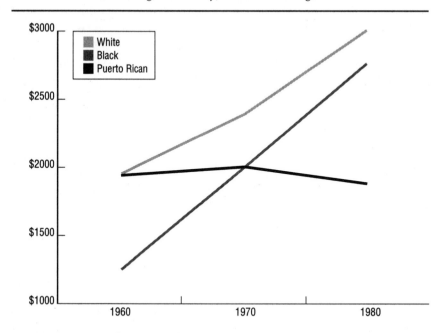

by blacks, wages for Puerto Rican men and women stagnated, and then actually *dropped* between 1960 and 1980.[57]

Income disparities by race have been reflected in substantially lower poverty rates for whites over the past several decades. As Table 2.2 demonstrates, throughout the 1970s, '80s, and '90s, African Americans and Puerto Ricans were two to three times as likely as whites to be poor.[58]

When we look specifically at the recent poverty statistics for Puerto Ricans (rather than for the Hispanic population as a whole), the story appears even more troublesome. The 1990 poverty rate for U.S.-born Puerto Ricans eclipsed that of African Americans, while more than half of island-born Puerto Ricans were poor.[59] Between 1970 and 1980, the proportion of overall income Puerto Rican women derived from public assistance increased dramatically from 2.4 percent to more than 18 percent, significantly higher than that for black women (6.2 percent) or white women (1.3 percent).[60]

Dominicans resemble island-born Puerto Ricans in that both groups are likely to be monolingual Spanish speakers. However, Puerto Ricans are U.S. citizens and thus have automatic rights to work and to receive public benefits (including public housing, Medicaid, food stamps, and the like) while Do-

Figure 2-5

Median wages and salary, male workers aged 16+

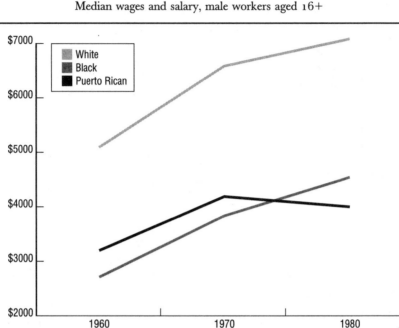

minicans, especially those who are undocumented immigrants, are less likely to access these financial supports.[61] Without employment papers, Dominican workers are confined to the underground economy where pickings are slim. Forty-four percent of the Dominican men who were "undocumented" earned less than $150 per week in 1981. Only 21 percent of the legal male immigrants earned that little.[62] Marriage provides very little respite from the resulting economic pressures. The census tells us that married couples in New York City earned, on average, about $20,000 in 1980. Dominican couples took home only $12,000.[63]

Many Dominicans and Puerto Ricans came to New York at a point in the region's industrial history that was far less favorable than it was when Cancion arrived. By the late 1970s, New York was mired in a deep recession, its manufacturing industries had begun to head south or overseas, and poverty rates started to climb. Without manufacturing to turn to, poorly educated, non-English speakers had relatively few options for earning a living. That stands in marked contrast to the conditions that lured so many Puerto Ricans, in particular, to the mainland in the postwar heyday. They found

Table 2-2
Percent of People Below Poverty Level,
by Race and Hispanic Origin

	White	*Black*	*Hispanic*
1973	8.4%	31.4%	21.9%
1983	12.1%	35.7%	28.0%
1993	12.2%	33.1%	30.6%

booming factories and relatively high wages (certainly when compared to equivalent jobs on the island).

Twenty years later, the story was quite different: factory jobs all but disappeared in the city proper. New Yorkers who worked in factories were now likely to be commuting long distances to the outskirts of New Jersey where land was cheaper. For many, the factory life was no longer possible. Service jobs, generally low paid, replaced the assembly line. The best educated found their way into clerical and technical positions.

How did these economic trajectories play out into the middle-aged and elder years? First, the good news: adult poverty has fallen pretty steadily over the past fifty years. Next, the bad news: racial disparities are still with us. In 1998, three times more elder blacks than whites reported incomes below the poverty threshold.[64] Elderly Hispanics were more than twice as likely as whites to be poor.[65] The statistics for middle-aged minorities are equally grim.[66] Those who live alone are most vulnerable to economic hardship.[67]

The likelihood that an individual is poor is obviously closely related to his current employment situation, though the importance of work decreases with age.[68] The financial benefits of employment do not extend to all Americans equally, however. African Americans who work are twice as likely to be poor as working whites; Latinos have it even worse.[69] This has nothing to do with who is working hard in this country. The vast majority of middle-aged people in all three ethnic groups work year-round and full time.[70]

Education, employment, and earnings are key "social facts" that shape the conditions under which these generations reached their middle-age and elderly years. Race, gender, region, and family history interact to set the stage for the development of each individual's portfolio of resources—financial and personal—which constitute the "bank account" from which to draw in the later years. For some, this means a comfortable cushion of savings, pensions, equity in housing or the stock market, retirement accounts, and life insurance. For others, growing old means growing poorer, because a lifetime of economic marginality means there are no savings. The jobs that poor people hold throughout their working careers typically do not provide pensions or retirement health insurance, and they do not yield the kind of income it takes to be a home owner. Most of the people who appear in this book were not poor throughout their entire lives. They experienced *periods* of poverty, particularly if they grew up in single-parent households. But as they reached adulthood they moved into the labor market and many experienced the upturns in economic fortune that were characteristic of the postwar boom.

Yet there are important differences in the fortunes of these minorities that grow more evident as they age. The most financially secure members of these generations—like Darlene—tended to hold jobs in the phone company or the public sector that did indeed have pensions. The least secure worked in domestic service, child care, construction, or in factories where they earned enough to keep their heads above water but had no margin for error. Growing old in the inner city means being careful about bank accounts. Like most Americans, the individuals we are concerned with here have come to depend on Social Security, the most important component of the American safety net.[71]

Safety Nets

Minorities rely heavily on Social Security as a mainstay of their retirement support precisely because they are less likely to have other sources of income, like pensions. Yet they have not always been welcome participants in the Social Security system. When Franklin D. Roosevelt inaugurated this universal retirement program, it wasn't so universal. In particular, it did not cover two categories of workers who loomed large in the history of poor immigrants and internal migrants like the generations of African Americans who came out of the rural South: both agricultural and domestic labor were specifically *excluded* from Social Security coverage in 1939.[72] At the time, this eliminated virtually 80 percent of black workers from this essential source of support.[73] It wasn't until the early 1950s that farm workers and household employees were added to the Social Security system at all.

Even then, the irregular conditions of seasonal employment conflicted with the provisions of the Social Security Act. Workers were required to put in forty quarters (about ten years) in covered employment to be fully insured, though they could qualify for some retirement benefits with a less steady work record. For many older minority workers who had spent their lives in the fields or cleaning houses, full benefits were thus not available. In such occupations, seasonal work, frequent layoffs, and injuries resulting in disabilities are quite common. The vulnerability of one's Social Security coverage is still a reality for many service or construction workers who are part-time or part-year workers, because they are more likely to experience layoffs. Frequent spells of unemployment translate into fewer completed quarters of work. The bottom line here is that the eventual expansion of Social Security meant that more minorities were included, but they tended to receive only partial benefits as they reached retirement.[74] And yet they are far more likely than whites to depend upon Social Security for all of their income, since private pension levels are dropping among minorities.[75]

Clearly we have a long way to go before retirement will mean the same thing to blacks and Hispanics that it means to whites. And because the differentials have their origins in patterns of employment and asset gathering[76] that stretch back to early adulthood, a great deal more is involved than a focus on aging alone would suggest. This is what inequality means at the tail end of the life span. The accumulated consequences of differential access to good jobs and good pensions, combined with pressures on family structure that create high-resource demands and low income during crucial adult years, add up to this very divided old age.

Marriage and Childbearing

While education and employment are key domains for understanding the life chances of the individuals at issue in this book, we are also interested in how these aspects of "human capital" translate into the more social domain of the family. This is particularly important where families at the bottom of the economic ladder are concerned. The income of poor, single parents does not stretch far enough to take care of basic needs, much less launch the next generation in a fashion that leads to success in school, for example.[77] For this reason, marriage trends and childbearing behavior matter a great deal. They are also important in the context of the aging story. Are men and women growing old together? Or do they face the challenges of growing older alone? The answer to this question depends a lot on the "marital careers" that predate the beginning of middle age. Here, too, we have seen dramatic change across the decades of the twentieth century.[78]

Overall, men and women are marrying later in life,[79] and the proportion of people who will never marry has risen.[80] But hidden in these general trends

Table 2-3
Percentage of All Persons Age 15 and Older
Who Were Divorced, by Sex and Race,
1960–1998, United States

Year	Males Total	Males Blacks	Males Whites	Females Total	Females Blacks	Females Whites
1960	1.8	2.0	1.8	2.6	4.3	2.5
1970	2.2	3.1	2.1	3.5	4.4	3.4
1980	4.8	6.3	4.7	6.6	8.7	6.4
1990	6.8	8.1	6.8	8.9	11.2	8.6
1998	8.2	9.2	8.3	10.3	12.2	10.2

are some important racial differences. Up until World War II, whites typically married much later in life than did African Americans. When the war was over, however, the trends flipped. After the 1940s, blacks began to marry much later than did whites and the rates of nonmarriage in the black community began to climb dramatically.[81] This important change is written into the lives of the people in this book. While most elderly blacks (like elderly whites) married at some point in their lives, fewer than 75 percent of black women born in the 1950s were ever married. This is a much lower rate than that of their white peers, 91 percent of whom took a mate.[82]

Certainly part of the change has come about because more American couples are simply living together without the benefit of marriage, period. "Cohabitation" has become increasingly popular. Indeed, in the past forty years, the number of unmarried couples living together jumped by 1,000 percent![83] Cohabitation is more common among those of lower educational and income levels. Among women in the nineteen to forty-four age range, 60 percent of high school dropouts have cohabitated, compared with 37 percent of college graduates.[84] Recent studies suggest that this may be at least in part a reflection of income inequality.[85]

A decline in the propensity to marry is only part of this story, however. Divorce is another critical ingredient. The percentage of all people who have been divorced rose steadily from 1960 through the 1990s. As Table 2.3 illustrates, this upward trend is evident across gender and racial lines, although blacks have experienced higher rates throughout the decades.[86]

It is difficult to get accurate estimates of the rates of marriage for Latinos much before 1960, but the trends we have studied are unsettling. Latinos have always married at higher rates than populations from comparably poor backgrounds. Catholicism and the traditional orientation of many immigrant communities from Latin America make a difference in this intimate sphere. But the more time these communities spend in the United States, the more they begin to resemble poor blacks. The proportion of Puerto Rican females who had ever married by the age of twenty-five fell from 79.8 percent in 1960 to 67.4 percent in 1980. Similarly, the percentage of Puerto Rican women, aged fifteen to sixty-four, who divorced or were separated increased by more than 50 percent[87] between 1960 and 1980.[88]

So what are the consequences of these marital trends for middle-aged and elderly minorities? For women, in particular, the economic implications are significant.[89] Women who age alone because they never married (as well as many women who have divorced) are women who lack a husband's pension, Social Security, and dependent health care coverage. This is particularly worrisome for those women who find themselves unable to work but too young to qualify for Social Security in their own right. Of course, these never-married women have long had to fend for themselves and provide for their children and grandchildren, often with little or no help from the men who have been part of their lives. But it is one thing to do so when you are young and relatively healthy. It is quite another matter when the chronic diseases of the aged develop, as they do at a comparatively early age for many minorities (in particular, for African Americans).

Most families experience some hardship with the arrival of kids, for resources are stretched and they often have to forgo the earnings of one adult—usually the mom—for some period of time. Indeed, among the older generation in our line of sight, the common pattern for middle-class white women was to leave the labor force altogether after they started their families.[90] Minorities have rarely had that luxury.[91] Yet when a married couple has children, they typically have more resources—in the form of household labor and income—to support the demands of parenthood than the vast majority of single parents.

Having a child outside marriage was considerably less common in the first half of the twentieth century than it is today. In the 1930s, only 8 to 9 percent of the first births to women aged fifteen to twenty-nine were pre-marital. Twenty years later, the numbers were still quite small: 90 percent of the young women giving birth for the first time were married in the 1950s.[92] This figure masks vast racial differences, however. Less than 6 percent of the first-time births to white women occurred outside marriage in the '30s, while roughly one-third of births to black women were out of wedlock. In addition, more than half of the single white women who *got pregnant* pre-maritally had married by the time their child was born. This was true of only a quarter of their black counterparts.[93] By the late '6os and early '7os, well more than half of all the first births to black women, compared to 18 percent of the births to white women, were out of wedlock.[94]

The U.S. Census Bureau did not begin reporting data on marital and childbearing trends for Hispanics until the mid-1960s, which is too late to catch the important trends for the older generation of Dominicans and Puerto Ricans we are concerned with here. Nonetheless, the data from the '6os and '7os reveal that, while Hispanics were about twice as likely as whites to have a first child out of wedlock, their rates of premarital birth were still considerably lower than those for blacks.[95] Indeed, for the generations that inhabit this book, marriage followed by childbirth was the more common experience. For their daughters, though, this is less likely, as suggested by a steady rise in out-of-wedlock births. This is a social fact we will return to when we consider how the behavior of the succeeding generations has influenced their elderly parents.

This trend is evident at worrisome levels among Puerto Ricans in particular, whose longer period of residence on the U.S. mainland may portend the trends that other impoverished immigrant groups will encounter.[96] Throughout the last half of the century, African-American families have been consistently more likely than families of other ethnic backgrounds to be headed by females. Yet the percentage *increase* in female-headed households over the past three decades has been even greater among U.S. Puerto Ricans (140 percent) than among African Americans (99 percent).[97]

This is not just a question of normative behavior, or some cultural change in ideas about what makes for stable homes. The trend has powerful implications for the economic well-being of Puerto Rican households. While white, African-American, and island-born Puerto Rican female-headed families were less likely to be poor in 1990 than they were in 1970, the opposite is true for U.S. Puerto Rican families headed by a woman. As Table 2.4 reveals, a significant majority of them are poor and the trends are all in the wrong direction.[98]

Child Support

One of the reasons that single parenthood pushes families into poverty is that child support is so poorly enforced. Since the advent of welfare reform in 1996, we have done a much better job at making sure that fathers contribute to the support of their families. But in earlier decades, when the now

Table 2-4
Poverty Rates of Female-Headed Families

	1970	1980	1990
European American	25.7%	21.0%	23.7%
African American	53.1%	46.2%	44.5%
Island-born Puerto Rican	73.7%	71.7%	57.3%
U.S.-born Puerto Rican	57.5%	66.8%	69.9%

middle-aged and elderly were bringing up their kids alone, this was not the case. That hurt them in the pocketbook.

As Table 2.5 shows, minority women are considerably less likely to be awarded child support upon gaining custody. Even in those cases where support is awarded, minority mothers fare worse; far fewer actually end up getting the money they are due. Even if they are lucky enough to receive payment, black and Hispanic women see significantly less money flowing into their overburdened households.[99]

The child-support picture looked much the same more than two decades ago, when the adults in this book were busy raising young children. In 1978, the average child-support payments made to black and Hispanic women were only slightly more than two-thirds of the amount paid to white women.[100] Poorly educated women lost out on child support[101]: mothers without a high school diploma received an average of only $2,858 in child support in 1978, compared to the $4,895 that the average woman with a college degree took in.[102]

Parents who lived through divorces, or who never married in the first place, spent their child-rearing years living close to the edge of their resources. Raising kids took all of their earnings, not to mention the kindness of many family members, particularly since child support was rarely forthcoming. Little was left over for a savings account that would come in handy now that they are older.

Grandparents on the Front Lines

We generally think of middle age and the sunset years as a time when one's children have grown up and left home. Yet in poor households, like Rita's, the nest never does empty. Adult children recapitulate their parents' struggles

Table 2-5

Child Support by Race, 1997

	Percent awarded	Percent received	Mean support received
White	68.3	74.9	$3,996
Black	48.4	53.3	$2,600
Hispanic	46.7	62.9	$3,012

with rocky marriages and single parenthood. When it all becomes too much, Grandma has to step in and pick up the pieces. In ever increasing numbers, grandparents have shouldered the burden of raising the little ones after the middle generation collapses in a heap of drug problems, ill health, or financial instability. The number of children living in grandparent-maintained households has climbed over the past thirty years. In 1970, 2.2 million children were living in homes maintained by their grandparents (with or without a parent present). By 1997 this figure had nearly doubled.[103]

What is worse, the generation in the middle has disappeared. Between 1970 and 1992, children living with *both* a parent and their grandparents were the trendsetters. But between 1992 and 1997, the greatest growth occurred among "skipped generation households," in which grandchildren live with grandparents *only*. More than half of the households in which the children live with their grandmother alone are black.[104]

Grandmothers who take care of their grandkids on their own are considerably worse off than are grandmothers who have husbands or adult children living with them, providing those crucial extra hands to take care of the young ones. Nearly two-thirds of "lone grandparents" did not work at all in 1996. More than half[105] of single grandmothers raising grandchildren alone are officially poor, compared to only 10 percent of those whose spouses and (at least one) adult child are still with them.[106] The health statistics on these single grandmothers are not encouraging either. More than half report that they are in fair or poor health, a far higher proportion than married grandmothers or those who have their adult children with them to help raise the third generation.[107]

Table 2-6
Co-resident Households (with Children under 18),
by Composition and Race,
1997

	All Co-resident grand-parents*	Both grand-parents, some parents	Both grand-parents, no parents	Grand-mother only, some parents	Grand-mother only, no parents
White	46.9%	56.7%	62.8%	38.6%	27.9%
Black	27.8%	16.0%	18.8%	45.4%	53.5%
Hispanic	17.7%	20.5%	15.3%	12.5%	15.8%

*For example, 46.9 percent of all co-resident grandparent households are white, 27.8 percent are black, and 17.7 percent are Hispanic.

Health: The Bottom Line

What is the most telling marker of the inequalities between middle-aged and elderly Americans of different racial and ethnic groups? The answer has to be health. If you have your health you can put in the effort to cope with the curveballs that life throws in your direction. If you don't, then all bets are off: you will age prematurely, lose jobs more often, suffer poverty more frequently, and have far less energy to do anything for your children or for yourself. This ultimate bottom line tells us a great deal about why growing older in the inner city really is a different experience.

Death rates are particularly telling.[108] Annual death rates for black women aged thirty-five to forty-nine are more than twice those for white women of the same age. While the racial gap gets smaller with each successive cohort, it persists at every age grouping up to eighty-four years. A similar story can be told about men. The annual death rates for black males between the ages of thirty-five and fifty-nine are more than twice the corresponding rates for whites in the same age groups.[109] Racial gaps disappear among the "oldest old" and may even reverse, but that is largely because so many others have passed away before they reach those milestones.

We can translate these rather abstract numbers into something a bit more concrete if we look at the way specific causes of death hit these communities differently. Heart disease and cancer, the leading causes of death for those aged forty-five and older, strike black Americans particularly hard. Black

women in middle age[110] die from heart disease at rates that are two and a
half times greater than the rates for white women of the same age. Diabetes
death rates are even more disproportionate—three times higher for black females. Black men in their middle years die from cancer 1.6 times more often
than whites. They are in even worse shape when it comes to heart disease
and diabetes.[111] While these racial gaps narrow considerably in the age sixty-
five and older cohort, the death rates for blacks—particularly from diabetes—
remain stubbornly above those for whites.

Despite their poverty, Latinos actually do better in most of these disease
categories than either blacks or whites.[112] Their death rates from heart disease
and cancer are markedly lower. As with blacks, however, Hispanics are hit
harder by liver disease and diabetes than are their white peers.[113]

The killer diseases discussed so far—cancer, heart disease, and diabetes—
are not the only sources of illness plaguing minority elders. Chronic health
problems that can take a turn for the worse and cause permanent disability
or death are common as well. For example, more than one-third of black
men and women between the ages of twenty and seventy-four suffer from
high blood pressure, a major risk factor for strokes. This is significantly
higher than the rate among whites.[114]

Obesity is, no doubt, one of the burdens that lead to these disparities in
disease rates. While racial differences in weight among men are modest,[115]
the differences among women are striking. More than half of the country's
African-American and Mexican women are overweight, while only about
one-third of white women are carrying extra pounds. Weight problems
contribute to high blood pressure, high cholesterol, and a host of other health
troubles.[116]

High stress levels can produce "coping behaviors" that relieve stress for a
time, but they have tremendously negative consequences for health over the
long run. Smoking is a chief culprit. Younger minorities are less likely than
their white counterparts to be current smokers, but their older counterparts
did not get the message: among men aged forty-five to sixty-four, more than
a third of African Americans smoke, while only a quarter of whites do. The
differential is even greater among elderly men: twice as many black males as
white males[117] light up regularly. Black females are also more likely than
white females to smoke, but the gap is considerably smaller.[118]

These patterns reflect the cumulative consequences of stress borne of inadequate income, heavy burdens for the care of dependents, crowded housing,
poor diets, and the burdens of living in neighborhoods with high crime rates,
low education, and a high proportion of single-parent families that have fewer
shoulders to bear the responsibilities for child-rearing. And though these prob-

lems are clearly vexing for the poor, they are also more prevalent among working- and middle-class families than they are among elites: health outcomes reflect a gradient that influences each income group up the ladder.[119]

Does Insurance Matter?

Health insurance, the focus of much political rhetoric, turns out to have a more modest impact on health outcomes than most of us would expect. Gaps in health outcomes turn out to derive more from who gets sick in the first place rather than from access to care among those who become ill. But health insurance is not irrelevant. For those who have the misfortune to contract breast cancer or lung disease, access to a doctor's care is obviously crucial. Fourteen percent of middle-aged Americans[120] lacked health insurance in 1998. Among poor people, however, the uninsured rate was more than three times higher. Because blacks and Latinos are more likely to be poor, they are also much more likely to lack insurance.[121] This probably helps to explain why there are disparities in preventive care.

Compared to people who came into adulthood during the Great Depression, practically everyone in our story is advantaged. But if we shift the benchmark away from such a low point, we see striking evidence of mounting burdens. Education, employment, income, family formation, and health all point in one direction: poor minorities start out with many strikes against them and the strikes build up over time. By the time an individual reaches middle age and then elderhood, the cumulative consequences of these disadvantages can become quite profound. When they unfold in the inner city, where so many friends and neighbors are similarly burdened, the aging process is that much more vexing.

Yet each individual and family confronts these "social facts" differently. Some fold their cards in bitterness and defeat. Others soldier on, working in their churches, taking in their grandkids, reconciling with past lovers, finding comfort in old friendships. We learn a bit more about how they do or don't take those hurdles in stride in the following chapters.

3–Work and Neighborhood

Way back in 1919, Macon, Georgia, was a small southern town not un-like the thousands of others that launched the Great Migration of African Americans toward the northern cities. Lena Sharpley's parents were just starting out when she was born at the tail end of World War I. The family was fortunate in those years because Lena's father was one of the elite, educated blacks in town, holding down a respectable white-collar job. Having trained in theology in a nearby black college, Mr. Sharpley was able to secure a position selling insurance. He was held in high esteem by the black community because he was a college man. That reputation, in turn, cemented his success in business. Relative to the other African-American families in Macon, the Sharpleys lived well, but not well enough for Lena's mother to forgo the fate of most black women in Macon, working as a domestic in the houses of white families on the better side of the tracks.

The black community in Macon was almost as class bound as the whites they worked for.[1] On the top of the heap were the clergy, teachers, nurses, and doctors—elites who served an exclusively African-American clientele. White professionals would have nothing to do with black residents of Macon, which, ironically, left open the possibilities for minorities to rise within their own ranks. Lena remembers that the black bourgeoisie were the object of respect and a little envy. Churchgoing, proper, honorable families living in good (though segregated) neighborhoods surrounded her own home, set off from the houses of lower-class black families. She was, in these respects, a child of privilege.

For a while I went to public school, but then I moved to a private school taught by Caucasians. They were very good about trying to teach us. They wasn't just there [doing nothing]. They taught us a lot. They wanted us to play tennis and all the good things of life. A lot of us didn't take advantage of it, but I thought it was the best and a lot of the parents [agreed]. That's why they wanted [their kids] to go to this private school.

Of course family privilege was not enough to break down the racial barriers that separated white and black in the Deep South. Lena remembers playing with the little white girl who lived nearby while waiting for her mother to come home from work. Whenever they were "caught," her friend's mom would holler out the window, "Eleanor, come here!" and everyone would scatter. "Eleanor would come to her window to show me her doll instead." Lena was disappointed, but the divisions around her were so ubiquitous that she didn't really think much about it. Her life, on the whole, was serene and comfortable.

The cocoon began to unravel in the 1930s, when the Depression began to tighten its grip on the South.[2] By the late '30s, Lena's father had lost his job and the family was in difficult straits. Her mother moved to Miami in 1937 in search of work and her father followed shortly thereafter. Lena stayed behind with relatives for the remainder of that school year, but then she, too, moved to Miami and a new life. That was the last Lena saw of private school and tennis lessons. Both parents took whatever work they could find and lived with her mother's sister as long as they were tolerated. As the war years approached, New York City beckoned and the family moved north.

The story of what happened to Lena once she arrived in New York is centrally about work. It is about the options that opened up in her life because of the dynamics of the labor market, especially in the period of the great consumer boom that emerged following World War II. How Lena negotiated this "switch point" tells us a great deal about the resources that she was able to build up, both before and after she married, which influenced her later years. It is a story shaped by a particular historical moment, when jobs were plentiful and unions strong enough to deliver for their members. Tracing that work story over time, particularly as it intersected family responsibilities in later years, tells us a lot about the pathway toward elderhood that Lena and millions of other African Americans in the World War II generation have followed.

Lena married in the early 1940s. She had been sheltered from the demand to work full time in her teenage years, but once she was a married woman in her twenties Lena had to shoulder her share of the burdens. The war years brought tight labor markets to the big cities,[3] which made the task of finding work fairly simple. In a short time, she landed the job she most wanted.

> A girlfriend and I would go downtown and look for jobs together. . . .
> It was easy to get a job. If you quit one, you could go to the next building and get [another] one. And somehow or another I got into hats because I was always interested in creating, sewing something. I got this job with a guy that made all fabric hats on 37th Street.

So began a thirty-year career in millinery. Well-dressed women always wore hats in those days. Greta Garbo, Ingrid Bergman, all the leading ladies of the stage and screen were cosseted behind black netting, bedecked by sequins, smartly turned out with sleek feathers trailing. Fashion demanded skilled workers, but it was factory labor, part of the larger garment trade that made New York a fashion capital. Even though hers was a manual labor job, Lena enjoyed it, as much for the company on the shop floor as for the creativity of her output. She was working in the heart of New York's bustling fashion district, near enough to Macy's, Lord & Taylor, and Saks Fifth Avenue to do a bit of window shopping at lunchtime. What more could a girl want?

Lena was also reasonably well paid, at least for jobs that didn't demand much education or past experience. Lena was pleased by the pay packet that came to her every Friday, but she knew she could do better if she could find a unionized job. So five years later she made the move to another hat factory and collected a fatter pay packet because the union was behind her.

> When I moved to 39th Street, I joined the union because the fellows and girls working [in those shops] didn't want you to be there unless you were in the union. It was better for you because you got a little more money, though of course you had to pay the union dues. But I loved being down at 39th and Fifth Avenue. I thought I was in heaven there because I was in the heart of town and I could go to any of the stores around and have lunch.

By the mid-1950s, Lena had worked her way up to being the assistant "floor lady" in the factory. Floor ladies were the first line of quality control, responsible for making sure that the hats in production were good copies of the samples customers had used to place their orders. Lena was supposed to get the samples out of the showroom and compare them to the hats ready for shipping. Only if she and her boss approved the end results could the hats go to the shipping clerks.

Up above her in the ranks were the "preparers" who looked up the patterns in large books and figured out what was needed in the way of ribbon, flowers, and base patterns to assemble the hats. If ten flowers were needed for ten hats, it was the preparer's job to be sure all the necessary items were on hand. Lena never claimed this job officially, but on many occasions she filled in for the preparers on the floor. She was piling up skills that made her valuable to management, even if she felt she wasn't fully appreciated.

The factory boss was an Eastern European Jew who had survived the concentration camps and made his way to New York. He wasn't an easy person to work for and Lena thought he played favorites in hiring in ways that did not favor black people. Looking back now, she sees him as the norm rather than the exception.

> The boss made a lot of noise and tried to drive people, but I didn't pay him any mind. He hired a lot of Spanish girls. They came after I did, and he wanted them to tell me how a certain hat was supposed to be and I wouldn't accept it. If he wants to tell me, let him tell me himself, you know? I told the [Spanish] girl she couldn't [boss] me and I didn't let her tell me [what to do]. But the boss never bothered me that much because I would ignore him. He was kind of like a slave driver at times, making so much noise yelling and making the girls that were sewing hats very nervous. I don't know how they stood it, but I'd just ignore him.

The waves of postwar immigration that streamed into New York filtered into the hat factory and gave Lena a chance to mix with fellow workers from all over.

> There were some Haitian girls there and then there was this floor lady who was French. She was trying to teach me to speak French, which was good. I could speak it a little. A lot of the Haitian girls that worked there were nice, but the trimmers, the ones that actually sewed the hats, were way up there in age and I was younger. So I didn't associate with them. But you'd contact with them, give them back work when it wasn't right and stuff like that. So you had a chance to talk to them and all.

Lena's work had an ebb and flow to it, moving with the demands of the fashion seasons. They had slack periods and frantic times when they worked around the clock.

We worked a regular thirty-five hours every week, but then we did make a bit of overtime sometimes, like two or three hours. When it was the buying season, we worked like mad. When the work was slow, then they'd lay you off. Of course, I had one boss that I wanted to lay me off and he wouldn't! He kept me there folding up papers just so that I'd be on hand. But most of the time I worked straight through and then maybe a month or so I'd be on unemployment. Other than that, the work was going on all year.

She earned $75 a week and that was good money. She held on to that job for nearly twenty years, and on the strength of her earnings, and her husband's post office salary, Lena and her family were able to buy their own home in Corona, Queens, not far from Shea Stadium. The co-op apartment, where she lives to this day, was a mixed-race building in an integrated neighborhood when they moved in. Over time, it began to lose its white population, as whites increasingly moved out to the suburban ring in search of single-family homes and proper backyards. But many of the original families stayed put, and today there are Jewish widows, and Italian musicians, as well as black families like Lena's. For her, this was a little bit of heaven: a safe neighborhood, a building with its own guards, and a place she and her husband could call their own. It took her earnings as well as his to afford this security, but it was well worth the effort.

Lena kept her job in the millinery business until her ailing father needed her help during the daytime. Her mother was working and couldn't take care of his needs, so it fell to Lena to leave the world of hats and find something more flexible and close to home.

I ended my job before I retired from it because I had to help my mother and father. I had to give my father insulin injections and I was the only one who knew how to do that. My mother was working and she didn't want to leave her job. I had to go with my father back and forth to the hospital and so I had to end the job. And then when my father passed, I had to keep track of my mother. So I worked part-time in Brooklyn and never went back to the hats.

As was true with so many of the inner-city families in this book, Lena's work history wound around her obligations to kin. Particularly in her later years, this precluded going after jobs that paid better and had decent benefits. While her millinery job was unionized and therefore paid better wages than the jobs that weren't subject to collective bargaining, she had no retirement benefits coming from it and nothing in the way of a health plan either. The movements Lena made in and out of the job market were clearly not for her alone to decide. Family obligations, her own sense of duty, and the collective decisions made by the whole kinship group about who could best afford to leave a job to care for sick members were critical. This is true in most of the families I have interviewed over the years and it is often a sore subject, for what might be most beneficial for a single individual is often subordinated to the needs or opinions of other family members. Poor families are more likely to turn inward and demand sacrifices of their members than richer families who can afford to let children go their own way, knowing they have money in the bank to cover needs that might arise in their absence.

Lena's own job history was shaped by family demands, and in some respects this was to her detriment. Still, she had more resources than many African-American widows. Lena's husband worked for the post office and was then killed in an accident not long after Lena retired. The loss was enormous in every respect. She was alone for the first time in many years. Her mother and father were both gone. She had no children; widowhood was a lonely life. In Lena's case, though, it was not compounded by poverty. She receives her husband's monthly pension (small, because he worked for the government for only eleven years before his death, and his previous jobs did not carry pension benefits). And Lena collects Social Security because her own job was in the formal sector.

One of her close lady friends coaxed her out to a senior center, just to have something to do. Lena remembers that she "wasn't quite old enough" for the place, but it was better than forced isolation and she reckoned her friend was right when she said, "You're staying in the house and not going out and that's bad. You've got to meet people or you'll get sick." The advice rang true, and Lena started going out to the senior center where, almost by accident, she found her next job.

> There was an Italian fellow there. He watched me—I don't know why. But he told his daughter that he was lonely. His wife had died sixteen years before. He wanted somebody to come and have dinner with him a couple of times a week from the center. His daughter came over and talked to me and she got me to do that. I would go to his house from

the center. Then he broke his hip and he was in the hospital, and that's when I really got back to working. I went to the hospital for eight weeks straight and sat by his bed from nine to six. The daughter finally put him in a nursing home and then I was really needed. I had to go see him quite often because his children were younger and they were working. They couldn't go. And the last year of his life, I went to see him every day. I think that's why the family likes me and is very good to me. So work is good. It keeps your mind active.

Lena spent two years in the "caretaker labor force"[4] and in this fashion supplemented her earnings. It is a role that minority women have played for decades in the United States, both as child-care workers and as companions for the elderly. Most often, this is classic "informal sector" labor, unregulated, without benefits, and not particularly well paid. But it is the kind of work that an elderly woman can get when other possibilities disappear and it helps to make ends meet. The motivation was at least as much psychological as it was financial. Taking care of the gentleman helped Lena recover a sense of purpose in life. Once again she had a place to go where she was needed; she had an important role to play. Now that the gentleman has passed on, Lena would not mind finding another placement of this kind.

The census for the year 2000[5] shows that widows and divorced women are returning to (or just remaining in) the labor force for many more years than has been typical in past decades. For middle-class divorcées, the need to work beyond their sixties owes itself to their inability to access their ex-husband's retirement funds, a potential source of income that many divorce lawyers seem to have neglected. For widows like Lena, the need is great because the kinds of jobs they held—and the sort their husbands held as well—did not provide for the kind of nest egg required for a comfortable retirement. Social Security alone is not enough. And, as I noted in chapter two, the oldest minority families, who may have worked in agriculture or domestic service, were not covered by Social Security at all until the mid-1950s.[6] Finally, for men and women whose earnings come to them via the underground economy, there are no legal wages to report and no Social Security accrued. Hence a lifetime of irregular work, or just low-paid work that carries no pension benefits, puts a huge dent in the economic security of inner-city families when their members move into retirement.

Working conditions and wages play a critical role in supporting most American households. Hence it comes as no surprise that in the national study conducted by the MacArthur Foundation, 99 percent of all adult respondents had worked for pay at some point in their lives, as had 94 percent of the minorities in our New York survey. Unemployment patterns were largely the same as well: about two-thirds of the national and local samples had experienced periods of unemployment, with the problem most frequent among those in households with annual earnings below $10,000. However, the consequence of being in that low-income population was more pronounced in New York, with households at the bottom of the income distribution significantly more likely to experience unemployment than those in the national sample with comparable incomes.

Table 3-1
Percent Ever Unemployed by Annual Household Income

Income Group	New York Sample	National Sample
<$10,000	90%*	77.1%
$10–24,999	64.5%*	76.0%
$25,000+	55.8%	64.5%

*Difference from the national sample is significant at the 0.05 level.

The current employment status of the New York respondents also reflects their more tenuous position in the labor market. A lower proportion are employed, a higher proportion are unemployed, and a somewhat larger group are permanently disabled.

Table 3-2
Present Employment Status

Status	New York Sample	National Sample
Employed	46.2%	61.5%
Unemployed/looking for work	9.7	3.3
Retired	15.1	15.0
Homemaker	11.8	8.4
Permanently disabled	3.2	1.5
Self-employed	2.2	2.2
Student	3.3	3.3
Maternity/sick leave	1.1	0.3
Temporarily laid off	0	1.3
Other	5.4	1.0

Figure 3-1

Perceptions of Discrimination and Stereotypes in
the Workplace*

Do you agree or disagree that at the place where you work . . .

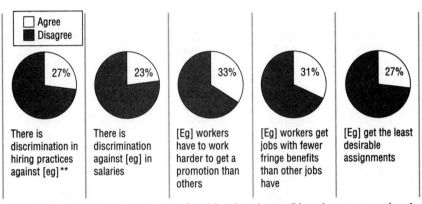

| Agree |
| Disagree |

| There is discrimination in hiring practices against [eg]** | There is discrimination against [eg] in salaries | [Eg] workers have to work harder to get a promotion than others | [Eg] workers get jobs with fewer fringe benefits than other jobs have | [Eg] get the least desirable assignments |

*For ease of interpretation, "strongly agree" and "moderately agree" have been aggregated, and similarly "moderately disagree" and "strongly disagree" are combined.
**Ethnic group of respondent

We need to know more about the work environment than just an individual's status to appreciate how their work impacts on their lives, particularly where minorities are concerned, for the workplace is one of the key venues where conflict may emerge across race lines, creating stresses that affect other domains of life, including the home front. We asked African Americans, Dominicans, and Puerto Ricans in New York a series of questions about their experience with discrimination and stereotyping on the job. Their responses are revealing, both for the progress they suggest and the barriers that remain.

By a substantial majority, the workers in our study do not believe that discrimination is at work in the institutions where they are employed. They do not see their own ethnic group at a disadvantage in hiring or salary, nor do they think that they are on the receiving end of less desirable job assignments. When it comes to promotion or fringe benefits, they are slightly less convinced of racial equality, yet more than two-thirds still believe that, on these dimensions as well, race is not playing a significant role.

However, when we turn to less tangible issues, which nonetheless have a powerful impact on one's sense of well-being, social acceptance, and fairness, the picture is less encouraging. With the exception of the most overt and socially disrespectful conduct (ethnic slurs)—which is not perceived as a sig-

Figure 3-2

Perceptions of Discrimination and Stereotypes in
the Workplace*

Do you agree or disagree that at the place where you work . . .

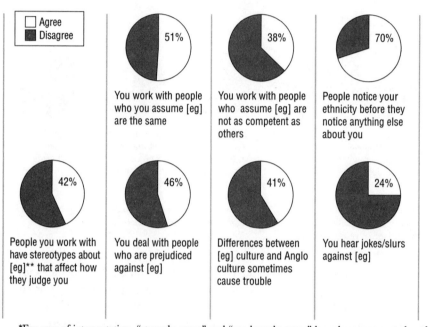

*For ease of interpretation, "strongly agree" and "moderately agree" have been aggregated, and similarly "moderately disagree" and "strongly disagree" are combined.
**Ethnic group of respondent

nificant issue—most of the other questions in this section met with more divided and pessimistic opinion. The minority workers *do* think their fellow workers engage in stereotyping, judging individuals by perceived group qualities.

Perhaps for this reason the New Yorkers are more negative about their contemporary work situations than are those in the national sample. When asked whether their work situations were better now than ten years ago, the national respondents were more likely to say "yes" than those who responded to the New York survey.[7] Midlife and elderly minorities were not so happy with their current situation, but they were surprisingly optimistic about what the future would bring.[8]

A number of explanations may contribute to the negative evaluation of the present. Having a low income doesn't help. The median family income of these minority households is vastly lower than the median income of the national sample.[9] Indeed, the New Yorkers have median household incomes ($19–19,500) that are less than half that of the national respondents ($45,000).[10] More than 50 percent of the New Yorkers say that it is somewhat or very difficult to pay their monthly bills, compared to 37 percent of the national sample, with those at the very low income level (less than $10,000 per year) in the most trouble. In that group, 86 percent cannot meet their monthly bills.

Within the minority groups there are significant variations as well. Dominicans are the poorest and African Americans the best off. Long accustomed to thinking of the nation's black population as its most impoverished group, we must recognize instead that new immigrants from very poor countries often occupy a rung far down the ladder from African Americans. Within all racial categories, elderly people are the most likely to be at the bottom of the income distribution.[11] Yet for the minorities in New York, being at the bottom means being very close to the official poverty line.[12]

Hence, money troubles may be at the root of the New York minority view that at work the present is not so wonderful. If those concerns are wedded to vexation about being on the receiving end of stereotypes, a certain amount of discomfort and stress is bound to surface. It might spread to engulf the private sphere as well. It might, but it turns out not to be the case, for this is one domain in which the New York minorities are in better shape than the rest of the country. They are considerably less likely to claim that stress at work seriously affects their home lives and vice versa.

On virtually every count, Dominicans, Puerto Ricans, and African Americans in New York City look to be better adjusted, more comfortable with the balance they have achieved between work life and the home front than respondents from the national sample. They are far less likely than the national sample to feel stress in either domain or to let problems in one spill over into the other. Whatever problems may crop up, they are more effectively able to compartmentalize the stress and not let work affect family life or vice versa. Here, too, we see evidence of resilience. Table 3.3 tells us that there are indeed troubles in the workplace of the kind that could easily be undermining, but the next set of data suggests that minorities in middle age and beyond have learned to buffer their private lives against the strain. At the same time, they have found ways to prevent the considerable stresses that we know attend low-income families, contributing to lower concentration or effort at work.

Table 3-3
Work/Home Balance

In the past year, how often did the following occur:

	All the time	Most times	Sometimes	Rarely	Never
Stress at work made you irritable at home					
New York	2.2%	0.0%	35.6%	17.8%*	44.0%*
National	1.8%	5.8%	44.8%	35.0%	12.7%
Your job made you too tired to do needed things at home					
New York	4.4	0*	22.2*	33.3	40.0*
National	3.2	13.4	49.4	25.7	8.4
Job worries/ problems distract you when at home					
New York	2.2	0	17.8*	31.1	48.9*
National	1.5	5.6	35.2	39	18.7
Stress at home makes you irritable at work					
New York	0	0	17.8	22.2*	60.0
National	1.1	2.2	21.9	46.9	27.9
Responsibilities at home reduce the effort you give at work					
New York	2.2	0	8.9*	24.4*	64.4*
National	0.9	2.7	20.4	47.1	29.0

*Difference from the national sample is significant at the 0.05 level.

The Magic of Public Employment

No account of the work lives of New York's minorities would be complete without a discussion of "city jobs." They are the holy grail of employment and have been since at least the 1960s, when the initial push toward fair employment began. The first domain to take the commitment to fairness in hiring seriously, federal, state, and municipal employment became a mecca for minority workers. Because pensions, health insurance, and decent wages were all assured in the public sector, civil service jobs were sought with great intensity. Middle-class black communities, like those in St. Albans in New York, or Prince George's County in Maryland, were largely creations of the upward mobility that public employment made possible. Nobody took this good fortune for granted because its beneficiaries—especially the generations that occupy the center of this book—had seen too much hardship and disappointment in the generations that came before them. Their parents had worked as domestics; they worked as post office employees. Two different worlds.

Missy Darden saw exactly this kind of trajectory in her own work life. Born in a small town in North Carolina in 1926, Missy moved to the northwest section of Washington, D.C., as a small child. Her mother remarried there and they lived in a humble, all-black section of the city. The family managed on the modest income of the mother's earnings as a domestic for rich white families and her stepdad's income as an auto mechanic. Missy remembers her family as being poor. That meant she had to find a job as soon as she could navigate the neighborhood on her own. One of her early jobs, at age fifteen, was in a shoe store in the "S Street Northwest" district, made up of exclusive stores and lunch counters where black people were not otherwise welcome.

In 1947, Missy decided to move to New York to seek her fortune and escape both her family and the southern racism that was still very much in evidence in Washington. To her surprise, New York turned out to be more of the same.

> When I came to New York, I thought I would get the same kind of job I had in D.C., but I found it was a very prejudiced town. Most of the jobs for blacks were not on Fifth Avenue. They were not in the offices. They were in factories. I couldn't get a good job when I first came to New York. Jackie Robinson had not been heard of. There were very few blacks in Chock Full 'o Nuts [coffee shops].[13] So I took a job working in a printing and engraving place.

This job was considerably below Missy's station, but she figured that to do any better she would have to get more education. She enrolled in college, hoping to qualify for something better, and there she met her husband. She continued working while she was pregnant with their first child, but once he was born she quit school and never did go back. Still, the business courses she took in what she called "technical and labor colleges" put her way ahead of many of her age mates, particularly women, who had not gone beyond high school. In 1957, now with two young children, she got another civil service job.

> I was interested in civil service because that was one of my early jobs in Washington. So I used to look in the paper in New York. I didn't particularly like working the job I had. I learned a lot working in the printing concern, but that was, to me, only temporary until I found something else. I looked for the civil service papers, went to the offices, and took the exam. I passed it and was appointed. I saw more of a future in that, more security.

Missy has been employed almost continuously in civil service jobs ever since. Thirty years ago she landed a position she still holds today, at age seventy, as a claims examiner in the unemployment office. Of all the civil service jobs Missy has had, over her nearly fifty years on the government payroll, this is the one that she has most enjoyed. It gave her the opportunity to work with people, to make a difference in their lives.

> We didn't only deal with unemployment issues. We referred people to social service, so my educational background came into play at that point, especially when I worked with welfare clients. We had to send them on job interviews and such. For the African-American people who were working in there, especially people like me, sometimes a [client] would come up to you and they needed some kind of spiritual uplifting. They needed some kind of nutritional talk or a referral to other social service agencies. They didn't just need a job. I found a great satisfaction in sending people to jobs and servicing people with whatever they need in order to make them a full person. That gave me great satisfaction because I felt I was using what I was given to share with them.

Finally Missy had a job that was intrinsically rewarding and paid well, too. She spent the next five years, until about 1975, working in the unemployment office, taking time off only to have her other children, who by that time numbered four. Thereafter she had a series of jobs that were less interesting, but still secure. Missy was one of the few people she knew who did not have to worry too much about being laid off as the economy of New York City began to reel from the financial pressures of the 1970s. As a civil servant with seniority, she could expect that paycheck every month and that was a blessing, especially as layoffs began to mount and the recession of the late '70s started to bite.

Job security was something Missy treasured, but there were other, less tangible aspects of her employment that did not make for an entirely happy situation. Civil servants probably experience the closest thing to a military hierarchy apart from workers who are actually in the armed forces. Each job is graded; each job sits inside a supervisory system. Labor/management relations are often fraught with conflict.[14] Missy had her share of trouble with what she regarded as officious bosses with insufficient respect for the people under their supervision.

> When our former supervisor retired, this [new guy] came and he brought some of what we called the "UI [unemployment insurance] syndrome." We're all professionals and he came down with what we considered a slave-owner mentality. That is, he had his thumb on us [as if] we don't know our job. We've been working at this job for some time, we already know it, and right away he came with this negative criticism. He'd only been there a week without learning. We were the better section of all the sections he supervised. We had worked four or five months without a supervisor. The work got done. So this person comes in and the first week he wants to make negative criticisms of us.

Racial divisions between management and the front line did not make things easy. Missy's perceptions of the problem fit squarely with the survey evidence presented earlier in this chapter.[15] She would never have said that she was discriminated against in hiring, nor did she think her salary was less than what anyone else at her grade received. But when it came to promotion, or to the subjective elements of race relations on the job, she saw some significant barriers in the way. White supervisors seemed to her to go out of their way to see faults in their black and Latino employees.[16] They harbored attitudes, she thought, that lumped all minority workers together and could not see the individuals behind the categories. And they were clannish.

> Our supervisor is Irish. We have about seven people in our section and five of them are black and there are two Jewish ones. The alternate

supervisor is Jewish too. We notice there's [more] of a comradeship between the Irish and the Jewish alternate than with us. I mean, it's constantly looking at the watch to see what time, if you're a few minutes late. And being in the location that we are, it's very difficult with the shuttle buses and the traffic to try and get back within a certain time. So we, the black people, we sometimes don't even take our breaks. We work, but the others take their breaks. They don't miss a beat taking their breaks. So this gets on your nerves after a while that you're constantly [being watched]. Now with me, he really harassed me a lot and he made an ethnic insinuation and I really should have written him up.

The whole atmosphere changed when he came. With the former supervisor, we had such a camaraderie. Whenever it was anyone's birthday we had a little celebration. She was that kind of a person. She didn't bother you. As long as you got your work out, fine. This man came in and we tried to have the same . . . parties, but the whole spirit of our unit changed.

The incident that really tipped the boat for Missy had nothing to do with birthday parties. Instead, it epitomized a quiet racism that wouldn't quite be called discrimination but is oppressive all the same. Missy's friend Cecile had a teenage son who was attacked on the streets. The boy was in and out of court pressing charges in a state building not far from Missy's office. Because Cecile had to be at work herself, Missy offered to let the boy come and sit with her so that he could ride home at the end of the day and not have to return alone to the neighborhood where the attack had taken place. With a lot of fellow workers out on a Friday afternoon, there were plenty of vacant desks. Missy sat her young charge at one near hers and went back to her "in box."

He was sitting at one of the empty desks and the supervisor came over to me at the Xerox machine in the next room. He asked, "Who is that?" I said, "Oh, I'll introduce you." He starts to tell me that the manual says we're not supposed to have any visitors. I said, "Wait a minute. First of all, supervisors bring their young people in and stay all day. We don't see the public, so why are you harassing me?" So he says, "Well, I'm the supervisor and anything gets stolen . . ." And I blew my top. I said, "Had that been a white kid sitting there, would you have made the same [comment]?"

I said, "How dare you insinuate that I would lower my integrity to bring someone in here [who would steal]. Just because he's a black male sitting there." Because I was going to tell the young fellow later on to go down to the lounge if he wanted to relax because I knew he had gone to the doctor because he had a big knot on his head where they had attacked him.

Missy couldn't let the young man go to the lounge after a confrontation like that, so she left early that day. Ever since she has had a sullen relationship with her supervisor. She cannot afford to tell him off "for real" because she has to keep the job and he's the boss. She treats him very formally nowadays, however, and limits the conversation to "what is extremely necessary as far as work is concerned." Missy no longer sees her job as enjoyable or fulfilling; it is now a means to an end. It puts bread on the table and moves her down the road toward retirement and the day she can return to what she calls her "creative side." At age seventy, she would like the chance to work with teenagers.

How Neighborhoods Matter

One of the reasons Missy would like to do volunteer work with young people is that her own children did not turn out so well. She would like to find a way to make amends in a sense, to start over again and see if she can help teens in her neighborhood in ways that she was not able to help her own. The story is worth telling for the way it underlines the point that a good job is not enough to sustain a household. If other parts of life run off the rails, a job can offer only modest protection from sorrow. In Missy's case, ironically, the good job she found became a source of tension on the home front.

It was very difficult because my husband had trouble finding jobs, you know, although he had a college background. It was still difficult to find jobs and I found myself earning more money than he did. Consequently, that led to a lot of problems. He was unemployed more than he was employed.

In the 1970s, black women tended to be better educated than black men and this put the women at the front of the line for decent jobs. While men's earnings continued on average to eclipse women's earnings,[17] the occupational prestige of women's jobs outran that of their menfolk. Even now this would be a difficult social situation in many households, since tradition dictates that men are to be of higher status than their wives. Thirty years ago, with the women's movement not yet in full flower (and having relatively little impact in the black community anyhow), the imbalance was very hard to manage. The resentment in Missy's household grew too serious and the marriage broke up.

So Missy, even with a good career and decent income, was left to raise four children without anyone nearby she could turn to for help.

> I had to do everything for the kids. My mother was still employed, so I couldn't count on her. I had to be breadwinner, mother, father, aunt, uncle ... because I had no family to speak of in New York. I didn't have anyone down south like some people did with their grandparents or something [to whom I could send my kids] because all my family was working too. So there was nobody.

There was also less income. Her ex-husband moved to Pennsylvania where he tried to start a business of his own, and while he was always on "good talking terms" with Missy over the phone, he didn't have much to contribute to the family's support. Missy moved the family to a less expensive neighborhood, which worked well until the kids got older and started hanging out with troublemakers.

> I had them in church, Boy Scouts, and the after-school center. But when they started junior high school, they started to associate with people that I consider to be not so savory. I had moved out of the old neighborhood, Clinton Hill, to Crown Heights and I didn't like what I saw them associating with.

Her older boy was managing and did finish high school. But the younger one started getting into trouble, skipping school, acting up, hanging out with the negative element. Missy knew where this was headed and became desperate to get him away from the bad influences in Crown Heights. Even with her civil service job, however, and the steady paycheck it provided, a single income did not stretch far enough to send that child to boarding school or move to a better neighborhood. Because she had to put in full-time hours to collect the check—and took on a second weekend job to help her oldest daughter with college expenses—Missy could not keep a watchful eye on her boys. Yet they were broadcasting "trouble signs," showing in unmistakable ways that they were bound for more serious difficulty.

Reluctantly, she turned to her ex-husband, who agreed to take the boys to the small town in western Pennsylvania where he had settled after their marriage ended. Missy made arrangements for her sons to go into the Job Corps, one of the nation's largest training programs for "at risk" youth, so that they could gain some useful skills. Her husband managed to miss their interview appointments and they forfeited their chance. The second son dropped out of high school, and the first son started a rocky career in college that ended almost before it began. They returned to New York with nothing to show for their Pennsylvania venture.

The armed forces came to the rescue, as they have for countless wayward young young people. Missy's oldest son enlisted in the Navy and he has straightened himself out. Regimentation did not appeal to the second son, so he got a CETA job[18] laying cement for sidewalks. That didn't last long and he began a descent into drugs and drifting. One by one, Missy's children married, had kids of their own, and then lost their sense of direction. Their marriages foundered, then broke up, and the grandchildren began coming home to roost with Missy. As her adult children drifted back home, they brought the next generation with them, so that Missy's civil service salary had to stretch to take care of the lot. One daughter died, leaving four children behind, most of whom came to live with their grandmother.

Missy's story reflects the power of neighborhoods in determining the direction of adolescents in single-parent households. Single parents cannot work and keep close tabs on the whereabouts of their kids. In a middle-class community, this is perhaps a less urgent matter because trouble is not brewing on the streets where they live. But if petty crime is just around the corner, the story may take a different turn. When the neighborhood goes down, it can take those young people with it, even when their mothers are working full time to provide them a decent life.

Albert Fields's example shows that dicey streets can be a problem even with two caring parents in the family, especially when both work. Albert is a retired New York City policeman in his early fifties who never expected to face the issues that have dogged Missy. He is a "law and order" man who believes in discipline, respect, the church, and the obligations of men to their families. Over the years he has worked hard to impart those values to his teenage son. Yet he found it a struggle to inoculate the boy against the pervasive problems that engulfed a nearby neighborhood during the crack epidemic of the 1980s.

Albert was born in a housing project in Harlem, where he grew up, finished high school, and started college. He met his first wife in his senior year, and they were married not long thereafter. The marriage lasted almost ten years but then broke up. Albert met his second wife because they were both on the police force. They have a young daughter together and have jointly assumed responsibility for Albert's teenage son from his first marriage.

The Fields's immediate neighborhood is a comfortable, middle-class enclave in the South Bronx. To step outside Albert's co-op apartment is to see tree-lined streets, a nice park, and well-dressed families. "My neighbors are schoolteachers, bus drivers, corrections officers, police officers," he explains. "They are basically civil servants, lower middle class, working for the post office and making a decent living." For a time the co-ops could boast a resident congressman and a police chief, people the kids could look up to. Albert and his second wife have lived in this quiet, stable, family-oriented complex for eight years.

Three blocks over and across a wide boulevard, however, lies a different world. Crack vials started appearing on the sidewalks near the housing projects almost as soon as the epidemic gathered force. Petty street crime grew by leaps and bounds "over there," and parents on Albert's block started warning their kids to stay away from the trouble zone.

> Over in the projects, the people are mostly on public assistance. I mean, I guess they are doing the best they can do. I'm not knocking them for being on welfare, but you know, basically that's what [they do]. They are not working—they are hanging out on the street, finding drug activities.

The literature on segregation explains that even upwardly mobile middle-class blacks are likely to have poor neighbors.[19] They do not outrun poverty, since as soon as comfortable African Americans arrive in a community, their poorer counterparts move in next door,[20] taking up the space left when whites retreat to the suburbs. Fathers like Albert are well aware of the challenge this presents when their kids hit the teen years. They try to micromanage the whereabouts of young men and meet a wall of resentment because the heavy hand of discipline is at odds with the mission of growing up and becoming autonomous. Moreover, achieving a physical separation between a middle-class family and a drug-riddled neighborhood may be possible at home but it doesn't prevent kids from mixing elsewhere. School districts span good blocks and bad and bring kids into contact with all kinds of peers. As Mary Pattillo McCoy has shown in her book *Black Picket Fences*,[21] middle-class parents have to put in long hours on the job if they are going to maintain themselves in higher-income neighborhoods. Until Albert retired, only a year or two before we met, that pretty well described his family life. He and his wife worked regular shifts and then overtime to put aside the money they needed for their kids' college education. They were not around to keep a constant watch over their son. When middle-class enclaves are located hard by drug zones, parents may fight a losing battle to keep their kids apart from the bad guys.

This is the dilemma Albert finds himself in now.

I have a fifteen-year-old son. I try to stay on top of him. Get him involved in different programs. Have him belong to the YMCA, play basketball. I mean if you are in that outside environment, things are going to happen. I mean, he had little problems. He has gotten in trouble with the police.

I tend to be forceful with him, try to dictate what he should do. He goes against it. We're always at [logger]heads. We sit down and discuss, and I explain why you can't stay out past a certain time because I don't feel it's safe. [My son] says, "I'm all right; I'm not a kid."

The police problem was minor, but as Albert well knows big trouble starts out as little troubles. It catalyzed the family to redouble their efforts to make sure their teenager doesn't fall off the straight and narrow. Only time will tell if they have been successful.

The moral of this story is that family background is not a guarantee. It helps to have two parents; it makes a big difference if they have stable jobs and good salaries. Yet if they live in an area that is surrounded by drug zones, as many middle-class minority families do, they may not be able to pull a teenager through without incident. If two police officers in one family cannot ensure that their teenage son stays free of trouble, it should not surprise anyone that Missy, a single mother without any family nearby to help her, could not protect her own sons from the same kind of difficulties.

The older generations in this book passed into adulthood and the years of raising kids during a particular moment in New York's history where ups clashed with downs. The opening of civil service jobs, particularly in the 1960s, provided a much needed shot in the arm for the African-American community, whose middle class was composed in part of preachers, teachers, and other professionals, and in part of post office workers, Metropolitan Transportation Authority employees, and hospital jobs. Their occupational mobility placed them well above their own parents who were typically blue-collar workers or migrants from the South and the Caribbean who had been agricultural laborers or domestic servants. Those who could afford to do so joined the suburban migration, fueled by cheap gas prices, federally financed highways to speed the commute, and the desire to join the growing mass of home owners.

By the mid-1970s, however, New York's fiscal condition began a devastating period of deterioration in both the private and public sectors. Manufacturing industries began to flee the northern cities. Many black and Latino neighborhoods saw the job base evaporate, leaving in its wake high unemployment and idleness. Welfare rolls began to climb and long-term joblessness spread. Inflation picked up and then climbed to all-time highs in the wake of the 1973 oil embargo. Tax receipts began to plummet. The city came close to declaring bankruptcy and was, instead, put under the management of a "financial control board" that mandated sharp cuts in the size of the public sector. None of this helped the quality of schools in places like Bedford-Stuyvesant. Fire stations closed, and not in the rich neighborhoods. Parks fell apart. Heroin and other pernicious forms of the drug trade began to creep in where the legitimate economy had failed.

For the families in this book, who stood their ground in the inner city, this downward spiral had very personal consequences. They watched their solid working-class neighborhoods become crime zones. They had to worry about the kind of climate their sons and daughters were exposed to at school, walking home, playing in the playground. It was an affront to their newfound status as members of the middle class, for it threatened their capacity to claim a permanent upward trajectory for their families. And indeed, in many families, that is exactly what happened. Fathers who were police officers, mothers who were career civil servants, ended up with kids who dropped out of school, ended up in jail, or married young (or had kids out of wedlock). Not a few of these errant children found themselves back in the laps of their parents when they were in their twenties and thirties, often with the next generation in tow.

While this turn of events was more likely to happen in single-parent households like Missy's, such things were not unknown in two-parent homes with two good jobs like Albert's. And for families that never knew this kind of income, like those who worked in factories for $3.25 an hour, the prospects were even dimmer. If they were able to call on extended family, by bringing their mothers over from the Dominican Republic, they could maintain a closer watch over their teens. If they couldn't do so, then it might take a miracle to see the next generation over the hurdles. For many African-American and Puerto Rican families, these potholes in the road to a stable family life grew deeper as the crack epidemic spread throughout the 1980s.

From the vantage point of the turn of the new century, this sounds like ancient history. New York City has been awash in good fortune, with crime falling to all-time lows. Unemployment is down. The parks are sparkling, though more so in rich neighborhoods than in the poorer ones. The schools are still in trouble, but they are not as violence-prone as they were even ten years ago. Former Mayor Rudolph Giuliani presided over a turnaround that will garner him lasting praise as the man who helped save the city (though, of course, this is not his only legacy). Still, the trail of the downturn left its mark in the generations that came of age in the inner city in the 1970s and '80s. And that matters as their parents grow into middle age, and even more so into their elder years. For unless they have been blessed with the kinds of resources that far more affluent families can rely on—savings accounts, pensions, nursing home insurance, and good health care—they are going to have to depend on some of the kids raised in those dicey neighborhoods to help take care of them in their old age. They will not be able to purchase supports, they will need "in kind" assistance. Instead, for the most part, the folks growing gray in the inner city find that the path is reversed: they are pressed into service once again, raising the third and fourth generations.

4–Men and Women: Together and Apart in the Later Years

"King, you don't understand. I don't want everything. That's not why I'm living . . . to want things. I done lived thirty-five years without things. I got enough for me. I just want to wake up in the bed beside you in the morning. . . . Your job is to be around so this baby can know you its daddy. Do that. For once, somebody do that. Be that. That's how you be a man, anything else I don't want."
—Tonya, speaking to her husband, King,
in August Wilson's play *King Hedley II*[1]

In the backyard of a run-down tenement in the Hill District, August Wilson's fictional Pittsburgh neighborhood, two African-American couples are wrestling with the history of their relationships. Elmore wants to reclaim his relationship with Ruby, now in her sixties, after a long absence. King (Ruby's grown son) wants to please Tonya, his thirty-five-year-old wife who is pregnant with his child, though she loudly proclaims that she does not want to bring a baby into a world—or a marriage—like this. King and Elmore have both been in and out of jail as a consequence of hotheaded murders, outbursts against men who wronged them in the past. Tonya and Ruby are fed up with the excuses, the absences, and the disappointments. They have learned the hard way how to live without men.

Ruby makes it clear that Elmore needs to make up for lost time if he wants to win her affection. She wants new dresses, some jewelry, and twenty dollars for some food, right now. Then she'll think about marrying Elmore. Tonya wants nothing of the kind from King. She knows he will do something crazy in order to "be a real man," something that will land him in jail. She cautions him, pleads with him, begs him not to sacrifice their lives together for the sake of "things." "I don't need things," she tells him. "I saw what they cost. I can live without them and be happy." Most of all, Tonya does not want to hear that King is stealing on her account. Her first husband followed that pathway to the penitentiary. Her teenage daughter, Natasha, hardly knows her father because he has been in jail for half her life. Like King, Ruby's first husband robbed in order to provide for his family, but this brought them nothing but grief. She wants King to abandon that destructive path.

> [Natasha's] daddy been in jail for half her life. She wouldn't know him if she saw him. For what? The same stuff you be talking. How he gonna get his. He don't want it all. He just want his little bit. What he got now. He ain't got nothing... Natasha don't even know what a daddy is. I don't want that for my children.

It is not the fate of black women, Wilson's plays tell us, to hold their men for long. Whatever happiness they can cobble together is sure to be temporary, cut short by the ambitions of men who have few options for making something of themselves. Hemmed in by racism, by disappearing jobs, by the erosion of the old black middle class and the ascendance of new generations who reject their values, these fictional men are waging a losing battle to find themselves in the world. As King explains to Tonya, he has to claim a place in a world that defines manhood in material ways.

> I ain't gonna stop living. The world ain't gonna change and all of a sudden get better because I be somebody's daddy. I can't go and get no job just because I'm gonna be somebody's daddy... I'm just trying to do my get. Get you the things you want.

Tonya and King are more eloquent than ordinary people, but this is all that separates Wilson's characters from very real New Yorkers. Surprisingly, though, we see very little in social science about how men and women in poor, minority communities think about their relations with each other in later life.

Virtually all of the research literature focuses instead on "disrupted" patterns of family formation, and with some reason. The sharp increase in single-parent households, always at greater risk for poverty, attracts the attention of anyone concerned with the fate of adults and the children they raise.[2] Yet the consequences of single parenthood do not end when the children are grown. What happens to the men who father children and then "disappear"?

Where do they go when they hit their fifties? What are their lives like when they are no longer young enough to live a high life? To what extent, if at all, do they maintain ties to the women they have loved, to the children they helped bring into the world? If these men come looking for their families, asking to be let into their lives, will they be welcomed? Or are they shown the door, cut off from their children and the women they have known because it is less risky to leave the past behind than to open up to future disappointment?

And what of the women, who have soldiered on, raising children by themselves, often on the most meager of incomes? How does the experience of single parenthood affect the way their lives unfold when they hit their sixties? Popular culture provides us with images of what ought to happen to men and women in old age: gray-haired couples living out their lives together, mutually supportive as physical decline inevitably intrudes. Does this happen in the inner city?

The scholarship that has been done would incline most experts to answer, "No." Once lovers break up—early on in the relational "careers" of young adults—they are finished, period. My research suggests this is not always so. Men and women *do* try to reconnect on the other side of the age spectrum. They engage in a complicated dance of longing and bad blood, of water that has passed under the bridge long ago, and fears of what the future might bring if a relationship falls apart again. That leeriness operates on aging adults and the adult children whom they have raised, who also have something at stake in reconnecting to fathers lost to them in their youth. It's a risky business, but one that unfolds often enough to make the question of relationships between men and women part of life in late middle age.

It doesn't happen to everyone, of course. Many poor women and men of color grow old by themselves. Widowhood arrives early. A rocky history of never-married parenthood, or serial divorce, leaves a void that is never filled. Old age may pass in the company of adult children and grandchildren, or with good friends who have stuck together through many years of difficult times. But the bond between husband and wife may not be part of the picture, even when a man has come knocking.

Some men establish new relationships in their later years, especially with younger women. Men are in short supply and can often rely on this scarcity to start over again rather than entangle themselves with former lovers or ex-wives. A goodly number, too, pass into their senior years without any romantic attachments, hanging on the fringes of their sisters' households or daughters' families.

The Father of My Baby,
the Mother of My Child

While the focus in this chapter is on midlife and the elder years, the trajectories of intimate relations begins much earlier. To understand how (and whether) couples re-form, we have to go back and look again at how they form in the first place. More to the point, we have to understand how men and women who have children together but never marry may nonetheless act like married couples for a period of time. That beginning, tenuous as it may seem, is often durable enough to lay a foundation that matters, that might be resurrected even twenty years after the fact.

These relations unfold along a continuum from short-lived, casual relations to marriage, with many gradations of commitment in between. On one end of the continuum, we find fleeting relationships that generate very little commitment from either party. Of course, one person's dalliance may be another's unrequited love. Yet especially among the very young, sociologist Elijah Anderson tells us, these are relationships born of the desire girls have to impress their girlfriends (or boys their male circles).[3]

Moving up in "connectedness" we find relationships that are more enduring, but may never develop into cohabitation. Girls with long-term boyfriends and boys with meaningful girlfriends may still lack the financial wherewithal to form a joint household, so they carry on from the distance of their natal homes. When children are born to such young parents, they often become the formal responsibility of the girl's mother.[4]

I have rarely seen relationships of this kind blossom into marriages, though it no doubt happens. More often than not, however, they dissolve as time goes by. Still, these are not one-night stands or short-term relations that crash and burn into bitter rejection within a month. They last, often for years, and they mean enough to the parties involved to generate a kin terminology of their own. Girls will speak of the "father of my baby," and mean something quite significant by that kinship tie. Boys refer to the "mother of my child" in return. Everyone in the community knows what they are trying to signify through these terms: a strength of attachment that may live on in the relations between father and child, long after the primary bond between lovers has broken up.

The "father of my child" is someone who knows his child, who provides for her when he can, who makes his own kin available as additional sources of support, and who publicly acknowledges that he is the father of this little girl.[5] The "mother of my children" is the person who is permanently responsible for their upbringing and someone with whom the partner has or once had a bond. To speak publicly about such a relationship is to cement its validity in the face of extended family or friends, to make a claim about the affection with which one holds this sometime partner. Acknowledging the presence of this partner means recognizing the ongoing contributions he/ she makes or made at some point in the past to the support and well-being of a child. It is, therefore, not a fleeting role but one that endures, at least for a time, particularly during the late adolescence of two young people.

When couples take the next step—generally reserved to people who are into their twenties or older—and move into a common household but do not marry, we must shift our focus to the literature on "cohabitation."[6] We know that this is an increasingly popular arrangement, across classes, races, and countries. Indeed, in some western European nations—particularly Scandinavia[7]—nonmarital cohabitation has become so widespread that marriage seems almost to be going out of style. Out-of-wedlock childbearing is increasing everywhere in the developed world.[8] But this doesn't necessarily imply that children are in classic "single parent" families. They may well have two parents who lack those rings and city hall licenses but who are couples nonetheless.

Among the families I describe in this chapter, cohabitation meant living together, sharing resources, bringing children into the world. In most instances, living under the same roof triggered contributions from other female kin, especially the grandmothers of the children in these long-term couples. Whether cohabitation is merely a form of marriage without the paperwork, or a qualitatively different kind of relationship between partners, is a matter of some debate among social scientists who study the family.[9] Often it is of short duration—though so are an increasing proportion of marriages. It may mean that monies are kept separate, with each partner giving the other amounts of money or in-kind contributions, rather than pooling their resources, but this pattern of separate finances is on the increase even among middle-class couples who are married.[10] What is important about cohabitation for our purposes is that these couples behave as though they are married. They pool their resources, make decisions together, and move in and out of the labor market in consort.

Reynaldo and his family illustrate the point well. When I first met him in 1994, Reynaldo was eighteen years old and working for the summer in a fast-food restaurant in a Dominican neighborhood of upper Manhattan. A tall, affable, and good-looking young man, Rey had a succession of girlfriends and an equally rapid turnover of jobs. While working in the formal labor market for the minimum wage, he also picked up odd jobs for cash under the table in drugstores and copy shops in Washington Heights. In one of his particularly successful periods, Rey took to selling cell phones to his friends and neighbors. This, too, was "off the books," and basically illegal, but it is a common practice in poor neighborhoods where the demand for these luxuries is as high as it is in any middle-class community, but where the money is insufficient for the licensed, aboveboard gadgets.

Four years later, I contacted Rey again to find out what he was doing with himself. Now twenty-two years old, he was in the process of settling down. In the interim he had been in and out of a community college where he was, in essence, completing the high school diploma he had abandoned in earlier years. He now had a steady girlfriend with whom he shared an apartment and they were expecting their first child. Rey's girlfriend, Margolita, was working as a cashier in a toy store, earning the minimum wage. Rey had graduated into a good part-time job as a porter in one of the high-rise apartment buildings on the upper west side of Manhattan. His job was unionized, paid the handsome sum of $14 per hour (in 1998), and, most important of all, carried health benefits. As the baby's birth approached, Rey dropped out of school and increased his work hours so that Margolita could stop working and stay home with the baby.

Reynaldo and Margolita were not married. For all we know, they may never marry. Yet one would be hard pressed to figure out why it matters very much in terms of their behavior. He is acting like a husband and she is behaving like a wife. They are moving in and out of the labor market in consort, pooling their resources, planning together. What more would a formally married couple do? In following this pattern, Rey may be partially mimicking the behavior of his own parents. His mom and dad had lived together for twenty years at the point I encountered them (when Rey was eighteen). They were formally married for about eight of those years, but divorced (only in the eyes of the law) so that his mother could collect welfare benefits. She relied on public assistance when her children were small, but eventually used them to support her own further education as a medical records technician, which she hoped would pay off in a good job. Rey's dad maintained a fictitious address elsewhere so that there would be no challenging his "wife's" right to the assistance, but the fact is the family lived together under one roof and were as permanently wedded to one another as most formally married families I have known.

Rey's father comes from a different, and perhaps more traditional, generation where childbirth outside of wedlock was considered a scandal. Having a child without the benefit of marriage is increasingly common[11] and now carries little stigma. This bothers conservatives because they believe it is immoral and it worries liberals because they can see that children of single parents face an uphill struggle where educational attainment, labor market prospects, and poverty pathways are concerned. There is little question that children who have only one parent to look after them and provide for their needs are at a disadvantage. Yet as the case of Reynaldo illustrates, not all "single parent families" are single in quite the same way. Some children live with parents who are, for all intents and purposes, truly married.

What little we know about cohabitation suggests that these relationships survive for a shorter period of time than does the average marriage.[12] But when one looks at marriages among people of equivalent economic standing, age, and race (that is, young, working-poor minorities), few differences are evident between those who are married and those who cohabit.[13] Indeed, those who live together for a period of time are likely to turn into couples with wedding bands. Yet even those who never take that step have formed families that look and behave like marital families.

As we turn our attention to men and women at the other end of the age continuum, those entering their fifties and sixties, why do patterns of family formation matter? They are important because the quality and intensity of the links established in those early years has an impact on those relationships as they unfold over time. This seems to be particularly true if a major rupture, like an acrimonious divorce, does not figure in the dissolution of a couple. For many of the couples discussed in this chapter, devastating splits were not part of the picture. Rather, they drifted apart, or were prevented by other relatives (especially disapproving mothers) from becoming a solid couple in the first place, even when they had kids. Circumstances like these may provoke disappointment and a sense of failure, but not the kind of hatred that drives divorcing couples as far as possible from each other. Thus when it is the case, rapprochement is possible.

Case in point: Alvin and Lizzie, African-American residents of Harlem, now in their late fifties. Lizzie has worked as a domestic all her life and raised one stepdaughter and two daughters of her own. The two daughters share a father, Alvin, who began living with Lizzie when she was in her mid-twenties. He already had a young daughter—Latoya—by that time, but he was on the outs with her mother, Ilene. Ilene raised Latoya until she was about ten years old and then took seriously ill. Alvin brought Latoya to live with Lizzie and she grew up alongside her stepsisters. Alvin lived with Lizzie and the children until he developed a serious drinking problem. Lizzie put up with the booze for a time but ultimately decided Alvin was too much trouble, so she put him out. For the next decade and more, Lizzie carried on raising her daughters and stepdaughter on her own. By the time I came to know them, they were all working girls and mothers in their own right.

Together these half sisters, some of whom had steady men in their lives, took turns going out to work and caring for the children they had between them. Lizzie, now a grandmother, took her turns baby-sitting as well. Between the four women, round-the-clock child care was available, as long as nobody got sick and no one's boss insisted on changing the shift schedules.

During the years I was in close contact, this family of women and children celebrated holidays together, packed a church pew, worked out their complicated day-care arrangements, helped one another get jobs—mostly of the low-wage variety—and held a nonstop gossip fest about the men in their lives. Lizzie continued to bend her back, cleaning the houses of well-to-do whites on Manhattan's east side, where she was regarded as a reliable and craftsmanlike housekeeper. Alvin surfaced every so often, especially around holiday time. But he didn't live in Lizzie's house and his appearances were largely without warning.

About a year after I first began getting to know Latoya and her sisters, Alvin started to make more frequent guest appearances. He would show up for Thanksgiving and Christmas. Sunday dinner, something of a ritual in Lizzie's house, began to include him more often. Slowly, but steadily, Alvin seemed to be coming back, reclaiming a position in the family, and he was accepted, although tentatively at first. Worries were voiced about whether his drinking would be a problem, but Alvin was making efforts to dry out. In fact, after many years of only sporadic employment, he had found a job driving a truck and was making decent money. Time and poor health had taken their toll, and Alvin was clearly looking for a real home, for some stability in his life.

The girls—now women—were pleased to see him (especially since all but one of them had homes of their own nearby and so were not, themselves, living with Alvin). A void of sorts was slowly filling up, even if only on a trial basis. They had never entirely lost touch with Alvin, so this was not like encountering a long-lost prisoner of war or shipwrecked father. Yet for many years Alvin had been no more than an occasional presence, so his return, signified by an increasing number of personal items sitting on the shelf in the living room, was a good sign. Lizzie was considerably more closemouthed about her feelings on the subject, but judging by her actions she, too, seemed content for her man to be back. No one was rude enough to ask her if she thought this would last over the long run. Besides, at this age, the distant future didn't seem to matter all that much. If the present situation works, then count your blessings, or so Lizzie would maintain. As for Alvin, he seemed relieved to have a home to be a part of. Living on his own had been no picnic, especially so once he started feeling his age.

Thick Skins and Hard Shells

The distinguished sociologist of race, Orlando Patterson,[14] has issued a challenge to romantic—or, at least, benign—portraits of African-American families. Conventional wisdom, he argues, posits either that black families have remained strong even in the face of overwhelming numbers of never-married mothers and high divorce rates or that there is nothing race-specific about these patterns. Scholars rushing to the defense of black single mothers have argued with great conviction that there is nothing pathological or debilitating about these families.[15] Or, if there is something broken about broken families, it is a consequence of poverty and the economic marginalization of black men rather than of poisonous gender relations.

Nonsense, answers Patterson. Slavery hammered the self-respect of black men and undermined the stability of African-American families. Poverty creates pressures of its own, but the black working and middle classes look only marginally better where marriage is concerned. Survey evidence presented in Patterson's work offers a blistering portrait of distrust between men and women in the black community. Women seem to believe men are generally no good: irresponsible, self-absorbed, looking out for number one. Men spit back that women are domineering, calculating, and manipulative. It's a catastrophe, Patterson tells us, and one that has lasting consequences, particularly for the more than 50 percent of black children growing up in single-parent households today.[16]

By many measures, marriage is in rocky condition in the United States, and not just among minority families. The divorce rate doubled in the 1960s and '70s, owing in part to the expansion in women's labor-force participation and the more generous provision of welfare benefits, both of which freed women from financial dependence upon men and from relationships they deemed destructive. A million children experience a parental divorce every year.[17] Yet Patterson suggests that more is at stake in the case of African Americans than these secular, cross-race trends. The preexisting tensions that he argues hold sway over men and women in the black community are so bad that they don't even get to the point of divorce; they don't marry in the first place.

Patterson makes important points based on survey research, but as with all work of this kind there is more to this than meets the statistical eye. First, as I noted earlier, this "never married" designation is a multifaceted category. Many of the people in it are what we might call "behaviorally married," even when they lack the paperwork. Others are closer to the object of Patterson's scorn: the one-night-stand relationship, resulting in a child, which can never progress because it is steeped in bad blood. And like the 50 percent of marriages that dissolve into divorce, some of these never-marrieds begin at one end of this continuum—acting in consort as full partners—only to dissolve into something that looks a lot like divorce, often of the bitter variety. We are poorly positioned to examine these patterns given the current resources of survey research. They cannot accurately capture the nuances. This is unfortunate because much of the Western world is in the midst of a fundamental change in patterns of marriage that we do not yet understand. We won't make much progress if we cannot figure out how to describe the "semimarriages" that characterize cohabitation with children that is so evident in, for instance, inner-city New York.

These patterns are mainly of interest to those concerned with family formation. They matter a great deal, however, throughout the life course and come home to roost when men and women reach their mature years. Brief encounters, even those that bring children into the world, rarely resurface when former partners reach their elder years. Men don't try to reconnect and women usually have no idea what has become of them. Relationships of greater duration often take a different path. Cohabiting mothers, like Lizzie, both permit and encourage ongoing contact between dads and kids. These are the cohabitations that are more likely to reemerge in middle age or the elder years, albeit with many of the reservations and worries that August Wilson's fictional women express. But for every Alvin, who remained in contact with his kids, there is another man who makes the effort only to face a slamming door. They are rebuffed by their former partners, who are bitter about being abandoned or convinced the fathers will be a bad influence in their kids' lives.

Ironically, older women often realize too late that cutting their ex-partners out has hurt their (now adult) children. When they see the pattern recur in the next generation, they often try to make up for lost time. They encourage their cohabiting daughters who suffer a breakup to let their grandkids maintain some kind of relationship with the errant fathers. This is delicate ground, for the adult daughters are often looking to their mothers to take sides, to validate their own damaged feelings by ratifying the daughter's decision to sever her ties with her partner. Yet from the vantage point of their own mature lives, these grandmothers often risk the ire of their daughters and tell them to let the children keep in touch with their fathers. Such grandmothers are trying to repair, at a distance, wounds that opened up in the course of their own adult lives.

*   *   *

Cheryl Naylor's experience illustrates the ways in which relationships that come and go in the space of early adulthood come back to have an impact on a woman's mature years. Elegantly thin, Cheryl is now nearly sixty years old, her features worn by time. A chain-smoking fan of Kool 100s, she is most at ease stretched out on the long, black leather sectional couch that sits in the living room of her two-bedroom apartment. The housing project where she lives is one of the better-known public developments in central Harlem and she has been a resident for nearly twenty years now. The walls are festooned with baby pictures and posters of rap groups she likes.

Cheryl met her first serious boyfriend in the neighborhood where she grew up. She was eighteen when she first noticed him, sitting on the stoop of the apartment building next door.

> He was nice looking all right. He had just came from the South, I think. He was likin' one of my girlfriends, but she didn't like him and me and her used to be together all the time. And he asked her who I was and it just started like that. So I met his mother and his brothers. By being right across the streets I used to always go up to his mother's house.

They started hanging out on the sidewalk outside the apartment building, leaning against the cars on the curb, and graduated to going out to the movies together. Cheryl's mother was wary of Lucas; she didn't think he was right for her daughter, and she took to looking out the window, watching over them, telegraphing her disapproval.

> She just kept saying he wasn't no good. You know how them mothers was back then. He wasn't no good; he wasn't no future for me and stuff like that. I don't know what made her say that because she never really saw that much of him. I guess she heard what the neighbors were saying about him.

Mama's dour gaze did not dissuade Cheryl from pursuing her relationship with Lucas, but it did convince her that she had to keep at least one big secret: she was pregnant. Even as a teenager Cheryl was tall and slender; her figure helped her to conceal the baby. She was nearly eight months along when her mother finally discovered the truth.

> I worked in a hospital at the time and didn't used to get home until about 1:00 A.M. Lucas called me at about 3:00 A.M. one day and [my mother] picked up the other extension. I answered the phone, but she could tell [something was up] because he kept saying, "Did you tell your mother yet? You told her?" I said, "No, I ain't gonna tell her." And she said to me, "Who's that, that black snake!"

Things went from bad to worse thereafter. Cheryl went crying to her brothers, asking them to intervene. Then Lucas's mother came calling to try to reason with Cheryl's mother. She wanted to see a marriage take place, but Cheryl was somewhat reluctant herself and Lucas seemed resistant. The truth of that interchange is buried in the past. Whatever the intentions and desires were, no wedding took place. Instead, Cheryl carried the pregnancy to term for the "whole, miserable nine months." They stayed together as girlfriend and boyfriend from the distance of separate houses for a time, but they never did try to form a family. Eventually their relationship unraveled, mainly because Cheryl was disappointed in the meagerness of Lucas's own contributions toward their daughter's care. Nonetheless, Lucas "recognized" his daughter, meaning he made it public that he was the father and extended the helping hands of his own mother toward her granddaughter.

> His mother, every week, used to send cases of Carnation milk and baby food and stuff like that. And I told her that I appreciated it, even though I was working. I said, he's not gonna never do anything, and I took him to court and everything. But he always somehow bailed out of it or something for child support. I never got child support from him.

Cheryl appreciated the way Lucas's mother "did the right thing." But she was annoyed that Lucas himself had been let off the hook. Lucas's own contributions were limited to occasional donations of cash over the two or three years that followed Yvonne's birth. Sensing that this was the most she was ever going to see out of him led Cheryl to reject the idea of marrying him in the first place.[18]

Eventually, Lucas took up with Robin (a friend of Cheryl's) and they had four or five children together. Because Cheryl and Robin were friends, they didn't fight over Lucas. In fact, Robin admonished Lucas about the importance of taking care of baby Yvonne. Robin and Lucas managed to make a go of things. They still live together in a big house in Queens where Robin has established a real estate business. They have grandchildren whom Cheryl knows. "They really doing all right. They come over here every now and then. Robin calls me; we talk on the phone and it's just like it was way back there in the sixties and seventies."

Cheryl is more comfortable maintaining her friendship with Robin than any semblance of her former relationship with Lucas. Even so, over the years he has been an occasional figure in his daughter Yvonne's life. "He'll come and see her every now and then. You know, he'd give her money to give me or something like that, but really he never was into her life [in a big way]."

Cheryl's experience with Lucas was the norm as she remembers it. A few of her more fortunate friends married Prince Charming and rode out of Harlem. But this was the exceptional case, not the rule. Most of the time, boys would get together with girls until the babies started coming and would disappear thereafter.

Some of my friends was all right. They went off and got married. And they lived happily ever after. The other ones was in predicaments like I was. They had babies and the guys stepped off; they never saw them anymore and they had to fend for theirselves. They had to get up and start going to work for theirselves to take care of their children.

This pattern stands in contrast to Cheryl's own childhood and the experience of her own parents. Her mother and father both grew up in intact families and Cheryl was, by her own admission, much closer to her dad than her mom as she grew up. It was not a matter of long-standing custom that men were rotten deserters. In Cheryl's own generation, though, expectations for a happy marriage, or even a long-lasting partnership, receded sharply, to be replaced by low aspirations for intimacy. After Lucas, who was a disappointment, Cheryl has experienced mostly short stints when she felt she mattered to her man. The father of her second child did not work out any better than Lucas.

He was never here; he was always back and forth, in and out, in and out. Him and his mother had a terrible relationship. He always hated his mother and used to tell me [so]. I said, you not gonna have a good life, you hate your mother.

Cheryl moved in with her own mother and went out to work to support herself and her two children. She would hear periodically about her ex-partner's "career" in jail and the other relationships he started (and finished), but she didn't give him a lot of thought.

The third—and last—of Cheryl's men turned out to be a more durable presence in her life, but for that reason an even more profound disappointment. By this time she was in her mid-thirties. She was working as a waitress in a bar and met Rodney on the job. It was, perhaps, not the most propitious of circumstances for beginning a new relationship, but Cheryl was looking for someone to love, and Rodney seemed to be in search of a new home, and a stepmother for his own children. She fell into the role, almost without thinking. Rodney would call her up and ask her to come over to his mother's house and she took him up on the invitation. She braved the hostility of Rodney's then-girlfriend, the mother of his children, and gradually established a relationship with him, and perhaps even more so with his children.

Rodney moved in slowly, but eventually he became a fixture in Cheryl's life. More than anything, though, Cheryl grew attached to his children. They were the magnet that drew her into the relationship.

> His kids started coming. That's just how it was. But I love kids and I just fell in love with his kids. His daughter had that thick hair with the wave in it that comes down her back. I'd love them kids; I still love them.

Rodney and Cheryl were together for nearly a decade. The early years were wonderful, despite the tensions with his ex-lover. Cheryl felt she had found a man who not only loved her, but who would help her care for Yvonne and her younger daughter, Janet. She set limits on his authority over them and he adhered to them, while doing the same for his kids.

> The first three years was beautiful. . . . He had good rapport with my kids. I told him, "You're not their father, but they're goin' to have to respect you. Don't hit my kids. You can chastise them but don't put your hands on them." And they loved Rodney to death. They called him Daddy and everything. We went to dinner all the time. Every weekend he would take us up to Sammy's [a well-known restaurant]. One week he would just take me, the next week he would take Yvonne and Janet and some of the kids from our building. We went to amusement parks. You know it was just really good.

As Cheryl looks back, this was just about the happiest part of her life. Her kids had a dad; his kids had a more responsible mom in Cheryl than they did in their own mother; Rodney and Cheryl had each other. But it didn't last. Simultaneously, Yvonne went off the rails and Rodney's daughter Quanda sank into total rebellion. Yvonne started running away from home, indulging in drugs, and storming through the apartment in defiance when Cheryl tried to discipline her. Quanda was worse, as Cheryl discovered by prying into her diary.

Cheryl turned to Rodney, warning him that Quanda could not continue her weekend visits if she was going to dabble in drugs and sex. No change. Quanda continued to indulge, particularly since she met no resistance from her own mother who was, by this time, a crack cocaine user and a heavy drinker. The mother neglected Quanda and her siblings, who would turn to Cheryl, calling to complain that there was no food in the house. Cheryl did what she could from a distance and earned the enduring love of Rodney's sons, and the equally permanent enmity of Quanda. Telling them they should respect their mother, no matter how badly she behaved, Cheryl stood up for what she thought was a better model of child rearing. To be truthful, the model wasn't working very well with her own daughter Yvonne.

Coincident with these traumas, Rodney began to insist that Cheryl stay close to home. Cheryl's cousin had offered her a job working as a teacher's aide in a Muslim school in Queens. The job required that she travel from Harlem to Jamaica Bay, but she enjoyed it since it was a step up from working in the bar where she had met Rodney. Cheryl couldn't understand why Rodney was losing his temper over her whereabouts, because she was always home by six o'clock to cook dinner. He issued an ultimatum: "It's me or the job." She turned him down.

Rodney's insistence was particularly irritating because he was becoming a less dependable figure himself. He would disappear for a day or two without explanation. Rodney ditched the construction job he had held down for most of their years together. Cheryl wasn't sure where the money was coming from, but she began to hear from other women in his life who wanted some. They would call, ask for Rodney, and hang up when Cheryl said he wasn't there. The calls grew a bit bolder: women demanding Rodney pay their rent, or buy Pampers for their children. One showed up on Cheryl's doorstep holding a baby she claimed, loud enough for all the neighbors to hear, was Rodney's child. That was the end for Cheryl. She issued an ultimatum of her own: get out. Cheryl gave Rodney thirty days to pack up and leave. The next week, his belongings disappeared from her house and that was that.

The disappointment she felt was powerful enough to convince Cheryl that there really are no good men in this world. Women should be suspicious of men's intentions, she says, and ready to treat them instrumentally. She does not want any man in her house or her life.

When that box [of Rodney's belongings] was gone and all his stuff was outta my house, I knew that he was gone. And that was that. He just left. And after that I said I wouldn't even let [repair]men come into my house. I used to just hate men. To this day, I don't want any of them in my life. I'm getting over it now, gradually. The first year, it was hard. I'm not gonna lie to you. . . . Now I don't want nobody to come back in my house and put no shoes under my bed.

Cheryl "got over" Rodney, and now after many years on her own she wants nothing to do with men at all. She has become the kind of woman Orlando Patterson bemoans when he writes about poisonous relations between black men and women. Yet she did not start out from that position. For many years she believed that love was possible and she acted on that assumption through several relationships. Belatedly, and bitterly, she has concluded she was wrong about all that.

Cheryl knows that her youngest daughter Janet has inherited some of this ill will. Much as Cheryl bears these internal scars, she did not wish them on her daughters. Hence she has tried to make amends by encouraging Janet to keep her own ex-partner in touch with the son they share. Janet was resistant, having also learned through her own bad experience that men are not to be trusted and that women have to make do on their own. It fell to Cheryl to try and maintain the links between her grandson and his father.

Janet told me that she was glad her father wasn't in my life because it made me a stronger woman. And her son's father is the same way. My daughter has been taking care of her own son for sixteen years on her own. You know, she don't ask [that man] for anything. But when [the father] Tom comes around my house, her son sees his father. Like Janet said, there will never be no real relationship there because he don't even know how to converse with this kid because he's never around him. But they sit outside, they play basketball.

Janet said, "Ma, take [my son] upstairs when [he comes around]." And I said, "No, Janet. He don't see his father, so let him stay out there and play." They stayed outside until like two or three o'clock in the morning. I looked out the window and there they was out there playing [basketball]. I said, "Tom, don't you think it's time for that boy to come upstairs?" And he said, "Okay Miss Cheryl, I'm gonna bring him up. And he sent him up." And the boy looked so happy that day because he really loved his father. He knows his father.

Tom is not the perfect father or son-in-law. Yet his son knows him and his lineage. He doesn't have a dad he can rely on for steady advice or support, but he does not suffer the confusion of not having a clue about where he comes from. As Cheryl explains, he has a set of kinship coordinates, a sense of location.

He knows his father. He know his grandmother. He [knew] his [other] grandmother before she passed away and his aunts and uncles. Whenever they come and get him, or ask Janet [if] he can go, she always let him go.

Getting Janet to this point, moving her beyond bitterness, has not been easy either. Cheryl has had to pull her over that hurdle.

Years ago, Janet would say, "Ma, if Tom ever died, my son is not going to his funeral." And I sat her down and said, "Janet, you can't do that; it's not right. He'll never forgive you for doing that. He know now, he's sixteen. He understand. He know that his father never did anything for him. But when [Tom] do come around, he try to be with him. So you can't do that. If he pass away today or tomorrow, that still his son. You can't deny that. Maybe he wasn't nothing, but that's still his son and that's still his father. And that wouldn't be right. I might not be here to see it, but you will regret what you did because he would tell you about it in years to come."

Bringing Janet around to this way of thinking took some courage because Cheryl could easily have been defined as a hypocrite, unwilling to admit the mistakes she made in raising her own two daughters. As it happens, she does recognize the error of her ways and regrets much of the pathway she herself took as a mother. She blames herself for the tension between her two daughters, the jealousy that pitted them against each other and hurled Yvonne into such a state of fury that she lashed out physically at Janet and then turned around and hurt herself. She blames herself for the drug habit Yvonne developed, which landed her on Rikers Island and bequeathed to the next generation a twisted life of acting out, flunking out, and striking out in retaliation for neglect and abuse.

The only real pride Cheryl takes in surveying her family is vested in Janet.

The younger daughter has made her own mistakes and fallen off the deep end more than once. But Cheryl worked hard to rescue this one and turn her around. Today she has a regular job as a beautician and earns a decent living. She has raised her son, without his father but with enough of a backbone to keep him out of trouble. Janet has become a new woman and a solace to Cheryl, the mainstay of the family. She is the person Cheryl knows will keep her company in her own old age.

Thousands of African-American women in inner-city neighborhoods have known this kind of disappointment in their lives. They are reaching their late fifties, as has Cheryl, with a rocky history of broken marriages or no marriages at all, with sons and daughters who go on to repeat their experience. They have learned to fend for themselves as the sole workers in the household, to lean on their mothers to help them raise their children, and to return the favor to succeeding generations when they become grandmothers themselves. Emotional satisfaction endures less in the bond that ties men to women than in the vertical link that binds mothers to children. The company they keep is only episodically punctuated by lovers or husbands, brothers and fathers. Mostly, it is a community of women.

From the perspective of the middle class, including its African-American members, this is a poor substitute for a real family, which is supposed to have, at its core, a couple. From an economic perspective, there can be no doubt that families like Cheryl's are disadvantaged in almost every respect. They are poorer, the children who grow up in them often have problems in school or get in trouble with the law. Girls, like Yvonne and Janet, are "at risk" for repeating their mothers' experience. All of this is true. Yet there is another truth that bears observation as well: there is strength in these women and they are, in many respects, better off than the men whom they have cast off or who have let them go. They *do* have family to lean on. There are constants in their lives, alongside the hardship. Cheryl does have Janet and together they have Janet's son.

When Cheryl was thirty, she felt badly about the men in her life. She was reconciled to a cordial, though distant, relation to Lucas, but felt burned and resentful toward Rodney. Now that she is nearly sixty, she has come out on the other side of this stress. Yes, she wishes it might have turned out more like the storybook weddings she dreamed about as a young girl. But no, she is not living out her life as a sob sister. On the other side of middle age, that couple-centered existence doesn't matter as much to her. So many of the women she knows never had it either. They are the norm in her inner-city neighborhood, not the exception. Hence what matters to her most is not the lack of marriage but the presence of her daughter and her grandson. She knows that Janet will be there for her over the long haul and feels blessed that she has someone to rely on. The people she feels sorry for are the ones who don't have such a daughter, who only have kids like Yvonne out on Rikers Island. Everyone needs to have at least one person they can count on and that much Cheryl has for sure.

From the Men's Side

Sociologists focus their attention on poor families primarily from the viewpoint of women and children. Men are present in scholarly writings only peripherally, often because they have absented themselves from the families they helped to create. But they don't just disappear. How do *they* think about the trajectories of their relations with the womenfolk? Virtually everything we know about this subject from the man's angle is really about boys, or rather adolescents. Elijah Anderson's provocative essays[19] provide key insights into the competitive psychology of young men, intent mainly on proving their mettle to their fellow males using the currency of female attention. As he tells it, the boys are not interested in what one might call a relationship. They are interested in "getting one over" on the girls, on getting the sexual goods from as many admiring girls as possible for use in bragging rights.

Journalists and social scientists have seized on this kind of instrumental behavior as a prime mover in the story of broken families. The disinterest that men show in "settling down" or being "responsible fathers" leads directly to female-headed households, increased risk of family poverty, the absence of role models for children (especially male children), and a growing suspicion among women that men are just no good.[20] To be fair, women often come to the conclusion that two can play this game and, like Cheryl, decide they are the ones who want out of binding commitments. In the main, though, it is men who are seen (both by women and by themselves) as free agents. But for how long? Is this a pattern of disconnection that lasts throughout the life cycle? What happens when men begin to feel their age?

Some men we interviewed who have now reached sixty-five look back on their wilder days as something of a burden. Living up to an image of virility, performing in bed or on the streets, often to impress other men, left them exhausted, and not particularly satisfied or proud of themselves. They don't claim to be looking for sympathy, nor would they deny that their high-living days weren't fun at times, but they also note (quietly and not for public consumption) that there were times when they just wanted to go home, relax, and forget about posturing for anyone else's sake.

Geoffrey Powers certainly sees his life in this light. Now in his late forties, Geoffrey comes from a South Carolina farm family. He moved to New York to join his older brother, the first of his seven siblings to move north in the 1970s. They had heard there were good jobs in New York and the opportunities for young, black men in the rural South were not very appetizing. Geoffrey did not get much of an education. The GED he acquired after dropping out of high school was not nearly as important as the carpentry he learned in the Job Corps. With these blue-collar skills in his back pocket, Geoffrey made a solid living in the building trades. These days he works as a shipping manager for a firm in Queens, where he hopes to stay until he turns seventy. Geoffrey has come a long way and he knows it. He grew up in a house with no inside toilet and not enough food on the table. Today he can look forward to retiring on his pension in the rent-controlled apartment he now lives in.

In his youth, Geoffrey did his share of "acting foolish," running around on the streets and getting into trouble. Job Corps training came his way because he was regarded as "at risk" and it did the trick in terms of providing him with skills. But Geoffrey had a field day in New York. He partied, drank more than he should have, had lots of girlfriends. He finally found a girl he really treasured and they had a child together, even as he was living at home with his older sister.

> My biggest problem was, well, I had no real job at the time. And I didn't know nothing about really raising no kids. I didn't know how to keep money to take care of my kid.

This saga sounds quite familiar by now, except that in Geoffrey's case he finally did settle down and marry (a different woman). He had a second family with his new wife and they now have two adolescent children, a girl and a boy. They are not problem-free kids and Geoffrey often finds it a challenge to separate them from the untoward influences of the poor neighborhood where they live. He lectures his son about drugs and his daughter about boys and is never entirely sure that either sermon has hit its mark. They are latchkey kids because Geoffrey is a working man and so is his wife.

Yet there is a lot of pleasure in such a stolid, settled life, with basic rhythms that change very little from day to day. Among them is the knowledge that he no longer has to walk on the wild side. Indeed, Geoffrey takes satisfaction from raising his second set of teenagers with more care that those he had when he was not much more than a teenager himself.

I'm proud of my family, proud of my kids. I'm proud of being able to get up and go to work every day. I'm proud of just being still alive! My family, though, that's the best part, the proudest part of my life. I really ain't got too much in my life but my family. Failure is when you sitting in the street being a wino. You ain't got no job, you don't have a place to live. That's a big failure. But me? I mean, I got an apartment, I go to work every day. That's a blessing in disguise.

Most of all, Geoffrey is glad that he lived long enough to outgrow the pathways that he followed when he was a young man without much sense of obligation toward anyone else. Those wild days might have been fun for a while, but they got to be wearing.

I don't hang on the street like I used to, you know. I don't run around. When I come home from work, I [am] tired. I go to bed. There's a big change in me. I used to be on the street all night long. Can't do that no more. I'm at the middle age time when you just come from work, go home and take a bath, eat your supper and get to bed. 'Cause I have to work every day now.

These days he can let all of the pressures of that macho stereotype flow off his back. Geoffrey's focus is on planting his feet in one place and making sure his family is secure.

When you get to be forty . . . that's the time you're supposed to be done, situated, ready to just . . . watch your kids grow up and be help- ing your kids out. You go to work and sit back and relax and pay the bills. And take care of your family. Life changes for the better. No more hotdogging. No more running around. I think it's time to settle down and just look after family.

On occasion Geoffrey regrets that it took him so long to come around to this settled version of himself. He left a lot of trouble in his wake before he figured out that the old street-gang lifestyle wasn't for him. There is that lost daughter and a lost common-law wife and no amount of excuses can really make up for those errors of judgment. Like the other men we interviewed, Geoffrey has come to a belated recognition of the collateral damage done when he was "young and foolish." By the time it registered in the life of his first child and her mother, it was really too late for Geoffrey to remedy the past. What he could do was to try again and that is exactly what he did.

Middle-aged men in the inner city who have not managed to stabilize as well as Geoffrey also seek some kind of home life in their later years. More often than not, they look to settle down at last with a new and untainted woman or someone they've known as an acquaintance for a long time but were not romantically involved with in the past. Their "new" partners are beyond the childbearing phase, though they may be responsible for someone else's kids off and on. Like an old married couple, they mainly attend to each other. Old men try to find some peace and comfort in the arms of the one kind of woman they may not have had for a long time: a wife.

Clark is a case in point. A brown-skinned, muscular man whose body has seen better days, Clark is now fifty-seven years old. He lives in a one-room studio apartment in a housing development in Harlem that was once a middle-class enclave but is now inhabited mainly by the working poor. The whole apartment is about 300 square feet, with a kitchen in one corner and a computer in another. A nice-looking man, whose 5 foot, 9 inch frame is overburdened by muscle that has gone to seed, Clark has had a rocky road since adolescence. Like many other men he knows, Clark comes from stable, working stock. But his own life has not been so stable, and his downward drift crisscrossed the lives of several women.

Clark was born in Brooklyn, one of six children. Both of his parents were from South Carolina and came up to New York as teenagers, in the river of African Americans that flowed out of the Deep South during the Great Migration.[21] They met as teenagers in the Bronx and married in their early twenties. Clark's mother was an educated woman who found a job as an elementary schoolteacher, and his father worked as an auto mechanic. Together they made a good living, but with so many children to provide for the household was always a bit chaotic. Misbehavior brought forth spanking from their father. Mother took a different tack: she would "brow beat" the kids, urging them to buckle down, get an education, work hard. With hindsight, Clark says, he recognizes she was right. In his youth, though, he wanted to have his own way. He saw his mom as old-fashioned, out of touch, with "ideas that were for her time," while he wanted to "pursue what [he] wanted to pursue." Clark humored his mother by heading off to school, and then pleasured himself by cutting classes. Ultimately, he skipped school, playing hooky.

Clark's parents drifted apart emotionally in their later years. They remained under the same roof until the day his dad died, but the tight bond between them loosened and Clark knew it. "When I was younger," he says casting his mind back to childhood, "everything was hunky-dory. Clark could just see that his parents did not seem to share very much with each other after a time. "The relationship was strained," he says. "They didn't speak as much and my father spent a lot of time out of the house. . . . They just grew apart."

Clark's interest in the opposite sex kindled at thirteen or fourteen, but wasn't serious until he was sixteen. That was the year he met Sandra. Sandra and Clark lived in the same neighborhood and passed each other on the way to school. But Clark wasn't the only guy in the picture. "All of the guys wanted to be with her," he says smiling broadly. She was "hotsy totsy," he remembers, but she was also widely known as a "good girl," who was respected for her virtues.

> You know how guys are, right? They will stand around and brag [about girls] even when they have no basis in fact to do so. And you never heard [Sandra's] name come up in those kind of conversations. She always carried herself well. She was somebody you could take home to your mother.

And he did. Clark's mother, the schoolteacher, liked Sandra a lot. Clark was in a slight state of shock since he didn't expect to gain approval for any of his relationships. "It was scary," he says with a laugh. "Scary when your mother likes someone . . ."

Her churchgoing family, especially her father, a deacon, ensured Sandra's standing. Accorded much respect in the neighborhood, Sandra's kin took it for granted that she would only go out with a "good boy," and Clark—son of a schoolteacher and a steadily employed father—fit the bill. No fool he, Clark joined the church choir, even though "you know, I can't sing at all." With this fiction, he "got past her father," and they started dating under the watchful, and approving, eyes of both sets of parents. They went to movies, dinner, and long walks on the promenade facing the magnificent harbor alongside Brooklyn Heights. Clark and Sandra were an item for nearly three years, although they saw other people as well (or at least Clark did). But he knew his mother did not approve of anyone other than Sandra.

> My mother was a mental disciplinarian. [I would see girls in between] and you would know immediately, immediately how my mother felt about it. She didn't have to say a word. She could be standing at the refrigerator with her back turned. If I brought somebody into the house that she didn't like, a young lady, especially while I was Sandra's [steady], she didn't say anything. And you know what, the girl could

feel [the chill]. My mother might not say a word. You might not even see the expression. It's just like the whole house got cold.

Though not one to keep his mother happy, Clark tended to stick with Sandra. And she returned the affection, giving him the one gift that really signaled how much she loved him: her virginity.

Given this praiseworthy young lady, he might have felt on the top of the world were it not for the troublesome influence of his peers. Boys in Clark's neighborhood were impressed that he "got Sandra," but having one steady girlfriend was not exactly their idea of success. Just in case something happened with "your main girl," you should always have some action on the side. The point, as Elijah Anderson would say, was to compete.

It's not even cheating, really. It is, but we're talking at the time as a young guy. You're gonna try to, as many young boys do, try to meet as many women as you possibly can. Whether or not anything happens between you and the young lady [as a consequence] is kind of irrelevant. The thing is to meet as many as you can. That was the attitude at the time.

What the boys were interested in was not the occasional churchgoing, good girl so much as the number of conquests they could brag about to one another. Hanging out on the stoop of their Brooklyn flats, Clark and his buddies gathered in groups to take in the perpetual show of women "on parade." They compared notes on a girl's body, her walk, the way her clothes fit. "Typical, ridiculous stuff," he laughs, the stuff of short relationships and temporary commitments. "We didn't want to hear about marriage at that age. Marriage? Please!"

Truth be told, Clark was happy enough to bask in Sandra's attention. But all around him he saw a different model of men and women together. Even his father, loyal spouse that he was, was constantly the subject of sidelong glances and inappropriate attention from other women. "Women used to speak to my father," Clark remembers, "and it was probably a source of tension between him and my mother." As far as Clark knows, his dad never acted on impulse and declined to pursue whatever it was that was "on offer." His attractiveness, Clark thought, might have been a "weapon against my mother, because she could be quite intimidating mentally." Smart, professional, and respected, Clark's mother cut a higher-class figure than her auto mechanic husband, at a time when it was not "done" for wives to be superior in status.[22]

When Clark ventured out into the territory of boy/girl relations, he was operating with contradictory "instructions." He had his parents to look to, a long-married couple, but one where temptations from the outside were visible even to the children. And he had his friends, none of whom were lucky enough to find a girl of Sandra's caliber and who substituted a numbers game for relationships of any great meaning. For them, masculinity was a matter of conquest, and a deliberate eschewing of the kind of "go steady" commitment that Sandra expected.

Competing models finally got the better of Clark, and not just with respect to Sandra. He started to lose face because he was acting too much like the good boy her deacon father admired and too little like the badass his friends put some store in. So Clark started cutting school more often. He dabbled in the drug trade for a bit of fast cash. Clark started going out with other girls in a secretive, evasive fashion. Worst of all, he was hard-hearted in the face of Sandra's extreme disappointment and played the big man, the tough guy. He became the one that was "hard to get" and impossible to keep.

> We just grew apart. Yeah, she didn't like the direction some parts of my life was going in. I wanted to do what I wanted to do. And you know, at that age, there's a lot of ego involved. So it was like, "You can't get with my program." We eventually just drifted apart.

It didn't take long for Clark to find another lady and this one was different than Sandra. Tricia was easygoing, independent, and didn't hang on Clark. She had long legs and tight shorts—all the requirements. Clark had felt a bit burdened by Sandra's middle-class expectations about high school, church, and loyalty. Tricia was different.

> She didn't try to pressure [me] on a lot of stuff. She had an attitude like . . . she was always secure in herself. You know, you do your thing and I'll do my thing. A lot of women want you to account for every second of your time. Tricia wasn't like that. She was secure enough I guess by herself to let [me] go off without pressing [me] about where I was gonna go. And trust in you and herself enough to know that [I was] gonna come back.

Other girls—Sandra included—were possessive, annoyed by the flirtatious behavior of other young girls with boys who were spoken for. Clark found the flings fun and the jealousy of girlfriends a drag. Tricia never pulled that chain; so as far as Clark was concerned she was the perfect girl, and they became an item.

Indeed, they saw each other fairly steadily for about three years. Out of the blue one day, or so Clark remembers, Tricia went into the bathroom and came out leaking water. She had a full-term baby on the way.

> Up until my daughter was born, the day she was born, neither one of us thought about kids. I didn't even know [Tricia] was pregnant. . . . [Tricia] didn't grow at all. She had no stomach . . . her face was a little fat and her butt got big. The day her water broke, we were going crazy. We took her to the hospital and she had the baby, who was about four or five pounds. . . . She was underweight. But, no, we never planned on anything.

Clark moved in with Tricia and her parents after Sonya was born. Despite their reservations about Clark, Tricia's parents seem to have accepted his role in their grandchild's life. Even though she was not the result of careful planning, Sonya was loved, "a happy addition to the family," he says with satisfaction. Tricia looked after the baby for a time and then went to work in a hospital, leaving her mother on child-care duty. Clark got a job in shipping and receiving and began making his "little money" contributions to the coffers of the extended household. He took Sonya out for walks, and while he admits he wasn't one for the diapers, as he looks back on her infancy he sees himself as a dutiful and attentive father, within limits. Tricia and her mother were the full-time caregivers for Sonya. What he did was play a part that was, from his perspective, far more involved than many other men who had children in his peer group. At twenty-two, he was helping to support his daughter and living with her mother. He was not an absentee dad.

Clark and Tricia talked about getting married off and on, but seem to have felt little urgency about the prospect. More important to Tricia was just the fact that Clark was still there and still hers. They were managing financially, with the pooled resources of the several generations in Tricia's household, and Clark's steady job was part of the equation. But whatever they learned from the accidental birth of Sonya didn't stick because, within a year or so, another baby girl was on the way. Now the pressures on Clark to form an independent household began to grow. To make matters worse, both Clark and Tricia boosted their drug use from an occasional indulgence to a more serious habit. Money started to become a big problem.

I used drugs casually before we met. But during the time I was with her, that's when I started indulging heavily. Heavily. I got in with a group of guys who were also making money and it looked good, wearing glamorous clothes. Always had a bunch of money in their pockets. But with all of that stuff came a whole lot of other stuff. I was out there [selling]. The lifestyle, everything. I went for it.

Space was very tight in Tricia's parents' house and her parents were distraught about the erratic behavior that Clark began to display. Tricia was working, drugs notwithstanding, but Clark started disappearing without warning, flashing leather jackets they knew he couldn't afford on his clerk's income. They didn't get mad, they just got worried, and tried repeatedly to talk sense into Clark. He couldn't hear them.

I was like a son to them. They tried to talk to me as you would to a son, but my mind was in the streets. My own mother was going crazy too. I had a lot of opportunities that I passed by, that I blew through stupidity, not staying in focus and know what my goals were supposed to be.

My mother says I'm scared of success. She said, "Every time you get close to something, you find a way to blow it."

Her views were pretty far from Clark's mind at the time, though. He was fixed on "the streets" and Tricia was focused on moving out on their own. With two baby girls and the uncomfortable, prying eyes of his "in-laws" watching them, the couple was desperate for a little privacy.

She really wanted to get out of [her parents' house]. We wanted to get out of there. We wanted to get our own place, naturally. And I felt like I wasn't making enough money. I guess you never make enough money. And whatever little money we made, we spent on drugs, too. So there's never enough money in that situation.

They didn't move out. Clark blew the chance by diving headlong into the drug trade until he attracted the attention of the police.[23] In some respects, he was relieved. Clark was not exactly the king of the mountain. He was trying to make it in a business for which he was temperamentally unsuited. "I am not a killer-type guy, you know. I am not ruthless." Ruthless is what you have to be to become a successful drug dealer. In retrospect, he realizes he was terrified of the trade. "They committed heinous crimes and hurt people." "Thank God there are prisons" for people like that because, as Clark sees it, "I would never want to see those guys on the street or to be near my daughters." He did not have the fortitude to follow in their footsteps.

Busted under Rockefeller's draconian drug laws, he started cycling in and out of jail. After eight years of life with Tricia, he found himself doing some serious time, leaving his "wife" at wit's end. They broke up in 1989, during Clark's third stint in jail. With a lot of time on his hands, and the benefit of hindsight, he knows now that she didn't have much choice but to break it off. She had just had enough of him, and probably of her own drug troubles. Tricia had two kids to take care of and parents to whom she needed to prove she could be trusted. Clark had to go.

> She told me that she would always love me, but that she was not making jail a part of her life. That threw me for a loop 'cause it wasn't like I didn't love her. But she cut me off. I was still in love with her and tried to hold her. But if a woman's fed up, don't you try to hold on. That was one of the lessons she taught me. That took a lot of my self-esteem. 'Cause she had to be brutal with me to get me to under-stand that it was really over. I used to call the house. . . . She used to hang up on me. You can't keep a person there who doesn't want to be there.

It took many years for him to work his way toward some kind of rec-onciliation with Tricia. They were never together again as a couple, but they found some kind of peace between them that enabled Clark to reconnect with his daughters in middle age.

> I wasn't there for them as a father. They never had the opportunity to be around me and I didn't have the chance to be around them as much as I would have like to, or as much as they would have liked me to.

To Tricia's everlasting credit, she did not prevent Clark from connecting with his daughters even when he was in jail. She made sure they sent him cards and kept in touch with him no matter where he was and no matter how recalcitrant he became.

> I stayed in touch off and on. Guilt kills, though. When you're wrong and you know it, you sit up in the cell sometimes and think. . . . I won't even bother them. I would stop writing to them. I stopped writing to

everybody for years. I just wouldn't even call home. The correctional officials would tell me to call home and I wouldn't.

Reverting to his father's "strong, silent" mode of noncommunication, Clark closed himself off from everyone in his family and cut his links to his children before they had much of a chance to develop in the first place. Yet Tricia persisted in trying to keep a line open.

I'm grateful to Tricia for that. She never tried to keep my daughters from me. She never talked bad about me. And I will always respect her for that because she could have. She never talked bad about me. None of that. My mother, other people told me, "[Tricia] never [bad-mouthed] you."

Clark's family was brought into the circle and kept close so that the girls would know their kin on his side.

She let the children know my mother, my sisters. You understand? She knew that the loss of her relationship with me affected her [ability to] integrate the children with all aspects of the family.

When Clark got out of jail, Tricia cultivated his affection, not for herself but for her kids. Eventually he came out of his shell and shed some of the shame he'd built up in prison.

He found some joy in reconnecting to the kids, though he never tried to push the father/daughter relationship very far. Instead, Clark kindled a quiet kind of friendship with his children and through it hoped to make up for some lost time. Perhaps his take is self-serving, but today he believes they understand—in ways they could not have known in their childhood—that he made big mistakes in his life. The crater that opened up where a father was supposed to be developed not because he didn't care about them, but because he cared more about himself.

They understand that I love them. Yeah, [they think], my father did some stupid things. He's been in prison. He's done it on more than one occasion, but he loves me. And now they're able to understand that. They understand it's not nothing that I specifically did to them, you know. Daddy didn't leave you because Daddy didn't want to be with you. You understand. Daddy left because he was an asshole. Okay.

Clark expects no sympathy or understanding for this destructive drift. He just feels better knowing that his kids realize it was indeed his self-absorbed mistakes and not any disregard for them that left a big zero where a father should have been standing. That recognition cleared the way for him to reconnect with his daughters as a friend. "I call them up, 'Watcha doin'?' You know, I'm knowing my daughters now. We are rebuilding our relationship now. They are pretty cool about it."

Clark might not have been able to reconstruct his family life years later if it had not been for Ramona, the woman he ultimately married. She gave him new hope and some of the emotional reserves that he needed to put his life back together after his jail term. Clark and Ramona met in Phoenix House, the drug-rehab program where he got a job as a staff counselor. Clark's job involved designing and monitoring treatment programs for as many as ten and twenty people at a time, running encounter groups where all kinds of hostilities and fears are aired, and young drug addicts are "busted down," their egos battered into submission. Only then will they accept their responsibility for treatment, or so the Phoenix House philosophy goes. Clark was seen as a successful graduate of the program, a veteran of more than a year's worth of tough love.

When Clark arrived in the Bronx facility to collect a group of new drug-treatment "clients," he found Ramona standing on the steps, looking quite fetching. "I swear to God," Clark says with a slightly sheepish grin, "this might sound corny, but when I looked at her I knew she was gonna be mine." He didn't say a word to Ramona, but his heart skipped a beat or two and he scurried around looking for her records. Clark managed to get Ramona assigned to Phoenix House where he knew he'd get a chance to get a bit closer. They spent weeks circling each other. Ramona was suspicious of his attention and Clark, well, he was too cool to let on about his intentions. They sparred over her treatment, with Clark taking advantage of the authority his counseling position afforded.

She was leaning against the wall when she came in, and in Phoenix House you are not supposed to lean against the wall. No. You stand up straight. You're not supposed to have your hand in your pocket or nothing like that. Right? So I'm a counselor, so I give out "haircuts" on the floor. A haircut is when you verbally chastise somebody. So Ramona is leaning on the wall. "Get up off my wall!" I let her have it. She was just coming out of induction [intake] and knows the basics, but she don't know [exactly] where this guy's coming from.

Clark started visiting her "encounters," group counseling sessions designed to get the anger out. He would "let her have it" some more and then walk out. Eventually, for reasons known perhaps only to Ramona, they started having more civilized conversations. They fell for each other to the point where all Clark wanted was to get Ramona out of Phoenix House and into his house. She obliged by dropping out of the program and joining him at home.

They lived together for the next eleven years or so and then finally tied the knot. Their wedding day was one of the high points of his life, Clark says. They have been together now for sixteen years, though their lives have hardly been trouble free. Clark's drug problems always linger in the background and threaten to erupt, despite the fact that he was once a poster boy for Phoenix House, praised for having overcome his habit, his prison record, and his bad attitude. He has been in and out of jail during his years with Ramona, most recently for posing as a janitor and stealing laptop computers and pocketbooks from midtown offices. Ramona sticks by him and is always waiting for him upon his return, but it has not been an easy ride. She faces a lot of criticism from her family for putting up with Clark. They are right, lord knows, that he has serious problems. He doesn't blame them for being worried. "They want to see her happy," he says, "but with someone who is doing something with his life." Unfortunately, and with cause, "they don't see it coming from me."

> I don't want to be responsible for anybody's happiness in that way because I have a history of letting people down. I build people up to the point where they depend on me for a lot of things. I deliver up to a certain point and then I just . . . [blow it]. I carry a lot of guilt because I have disappointed a lot of people . . . a lot of people, and myself as well. I have seen people cry over me. I don't like to disappoint people. So don't make me responsible for your happiness. I like a woman who have lives other than me . . . who have their own job, own career and their own interests other than me.

The last time we interviewed Clark, he had been on release for a month and swore that this time it would be different. For better or for worse, though, Ramona and Clark remain a couple. It is more than he deserves, as Clark is all too quick to point out.

Entering middle age with a rocky biography and limited prospects for an economically feasible "retirement," Clark is almost entirely dependent upon his wife's fortunes. He has no money, no job, and no serious prospects for one. What he has is Ramona. To a more limited extent, he also has his daughters, thanks to Tricia's desire to keep their father in the picture. Most men with prison records of this kind are not so fortunate; they lose everyone.[24] It is hard to know the degree to which necessity has been the mother of invention in Clark's case.[25]

If we want to know what growing old is going to mean for Clark and Ramona, we can see at this point that it is probably going to be shared. At least if the past sixteen years is any guide, Clark will most likely remain "coupled," while Cheryl will not. Older men, even those with very complicated pasts, are "in demand" in communities where so many men have disappeared from women's lives.

Pulling the lens backward from the details of these individual lives, it seems clear that the story of men and women in the inner city remains complex throughout middle age and the elder years. For some, like Reynaldo's parents, it is a story that looks to a census taker like a marriage that dissolved into divorce, even though the divorce was "in name only," to protect welfare benefits. Those on the inside know that this is a long-"married" couple that can now dandle a couple of grandchildren on their knees.

For others, like Lizzie and Alvin, the ups and downs of the past that separated them for many years have now been largely forgiven. They are spending their fifties together under the same roof and have reconstituted their family, replete with children, stepchildren, and now a number of grandkids as well. Clark, too, has found a family in Ramona, and has tentatively reached out to the children he left behind through his many bouts in jail and the end of his relationship with their mother. Though he hates to admit it, his relationship with Ramona is really "her call," since she is the one with steady employment and he is, for all intents and purposes, dependent upon her. That is rarely a recipe for stability and his history does not suggest much stability in his future. Yet he would retort that he and Ramona have been together for sixteen years now and if that is not evidence of staying power, what is?

It is a long run that women like Cheryl have not really known in their lives, sometimes by choice and other times by default. They are without much male company nowadays and have not been active in the romance department for some time. Still, they are hardly alone in any other sense. For years now they have had their children and now their grandchildren for company. It is not always quite what they wanted. At times they would have been just as happy to be alone, or at least free from obligation, especially from their teenage grandchildren, who are often a source of trouble in their lives. Yet each of them has one special child who has managed to hang in there and made their elder years more worthwhile, and certainly not bereft of company.

During the 1970s, minority families—particularly "the black family"—came under heavy attack as deviant, destructive, and the source of our poverty problem. Liberal social scientists rushed to the rescue, pointing to the resilience of single-parent households, the creative use of social networks and private safety nets to shore up a poverty-stricken community, the essential dignity of mothers and the struggling, and morally culpable, absent fathers. From the vantage point of a new century, it seems only fair to note that the resilience and heroic effort is real enough. *A Different Shade of Gray* is filled with stories of women (and sometimes men) who have shouldered burdens that would break most people. They are the only safety net under their children, the main caretakers who look after the elderly, and even the final safe haven for men who may have been an irregular presence for twenty years. Their steadfastness in the face of adversity is to be admired.

At the same time, the costs of problematic family life are enormous and should not be cast aside in a rush to avoid "blaming the victim." The emotional toll that failed relationships take, particularly on women, can be devastating to self-esteem and foster a hard shell as they try to shield themselves from future disappointments. Children are damaged by the loss of their fathers, and even if they reconnect when they are all grown up, they are less trusting and more likely to repeat the family breakdown in their own lives. Finally, the financial costs, to which we return in the conclusion, are enormous. Without two incomes to support a household, it is increasingly difficult to escape the clutches of poverty; if they had had more money in the bank, they would probably have departed along with the millions of others who took to the highways and headed for the suburbs. Lacking income, they were stuck in deteriorating neighborhoods, unable to amass the equity in housing, the savings in bank accounts, or the social security that comes to married people. As inequality has grown in the United States since the mid-1970s, single parents have fallen further and further behind married couples in financial terms. The consequences for their children, in school performance, in health outcomes, and in risks of poverty, are severe and lasting.

August Wilson's fictional character Tonya knew all this without cracking the cover of a sociology textbook. That's why she wanted King to stay with her, whatever the cost to his manhood. "Be there," she said. But by the end of *King Hedley II,* Tonya's worst nightmare comes to pass: King dies, killed accidentally by his own mother. It is a sorrowful and sobering tale without even a semblance of a happy ending. We come away respecting the sacrifices Tonya and Ruby have made to raise their kids, acknowledging the noble aims King and Elmore have for wanting to make something of themselves. We know as well that those many years of separation and disappointment have taken a huge toll on everyone onstage—and in the real world, too.

5–Old Before Our Time

Creaky bones, a twinge of arthritis, puffing up the stairs. Anybody over the age of forty is familiar with the way the body marks the passage of time. Few of us expect to be able to do pushups or run the mile the way we did at twenty. But cancer at forty-five, diabetes or dangerously high blood pressure at fifty—these are diseases we don't expect to encounter until we've had a longer run. Yet medical research[1] tells us that poor people, especially poor minorities, face these burdens at much younger ages than their more affluent counterparts.[2]

Why is this the case? The best available explanations suggest a link between persistent stress and bad health outcomes. The more the burdens, the more we indulge in stress-induced, but possibly damaging, behaviors: smoking, overeating, drugs, inadequate sleep.[3] Those who are poor may be less aware of the importance, or just have fewer opportunities, to exercise, eat healthy food, and truly rest and relax. Consequently, the body does not wind down and recoup. Instead, it is running at full tilt, always vigilant. And like any other biological system under constant pressure, it begins to show the wear and tear much earlier than organisms that have the luxury to take life a little easier.

Arline Geronimus, a noted social epidemiologist at the University of Michigan, has argued that poor minorities run their bodily engines at such a pace and have so little respite that they actually age faster than those who are better off. The "weathering hypothesis" is the term she has coined to describe the ways in which cumulative burdens mount to produce early onset of chronic illness and, ultimately, hasten death.[4] Her studies of African Americans have convinced her that this is why blacks suffer from heart disease and hypertension at greater frequency and in earlier years than is typically the case for other members of our society. They are weathering quickly, running down the biological clock at a faster pace. This is one of the reasons, she argues, that black women have children at younger ages than white women: they don't live as long. If they want their mothers to be there to help them, if they want to live long enough to see their children mature, they will have to begin childbearing young. Their life expectancy is so much shorter than their more fortunate counterparts that they will not enjoy these experiences at all if they don't get started at what our society deems a young age.[5]

The weathering hypothesis is controversial, but the basic facts are incontrovertible: minorities suffer greater morbidity and earlier mortality than the rest of the population.[6] Is this because they are black and brown or because they are disproportionately poor? It turns out that middle-class African Americans also suffer from earlier onset of chronic disease and higher death rates than their white counterparts, even at high income levels.[7] Could it be that the mere experience of being a minority—even when not poor—is a sufficiently stressful condition such that these patterns should be explained by discrimination, for example, rather than economic disadvantage? David Williams, a sociologist also at the University of Michigan, has examined this question and he concludes that this is the case.[8] Even when the respondents to surveys report that they themselves have not directly experienced discrimination, merely knowing (and experiencing the psychological consequences) of lower expectations or less than a full welcome in social institutions may be enough to mark African Americans for heart disease and high blood pressure. Whether this constitutes premature aging is another matter, but it is an explanation that must be taken seriously.

Later on in this chapter we will look closely at what the premature arrival of serious health problems does to make inner-city minority men and women feel old before their time. We will consider the ways that health-related disabilities influence their capacity to participate fully in their own community and in society at large, how it complicates the task of caring for other family members and interrupts a productive working life. Stress is a feature of inner-city life that we should not overlook either, hence an ethnographic encounter with what kinds of stresses and how little relief from them the average Latina mother or African-American father in poor communities experiences will be an important part of this discussion.

For the moment, though, it is instructive to ask how inner-city minorities compare with those surveyed in national studies of middle-aged and elderly Americans in terms of health. Armed with this broader understanding, we can depart from the numbers and ask how they matter in the daily lives of real people. The MacArthur Foundation's national study of midlife Americans asked nearly 5,000 people questions designed to capture their perceptions of their own health and well-being. While this survey reached few minorities, it did reach a broad cross section of whites in the United States. We asked the same questions of the African Americans and Latinos in New York City and the comparison between the two populations is instructive.

When asked about their physical health in general, about 50 percent of the national sample said they felt that they were in good or excellent health. Only 35 percent of our minority sample had the same opinion. The differences were evident across all age categories of adults but were most pronounced among the oldest people in our study. Nationally, about 38 percent of the respondents who were over sixty-six years old felt they were in good or excellent health, but only 11 percent of our inner-city dwellers said the same. This dramatic difference suggests that the conditions of life, and the pathways to aging, really are harder for poor minorities. Is this a question of race or income? It is clearly both, for at virtually all age levels, the African Americans and Dominicans report worse health outcomes than the national sample, which is predominantly white. Yet when we look at the national respondents who *are* poor, we find that they look very much like their minority, poor counterparts. The fact that poverty is disproportionately experienced by people of color in the United States means that they are more likely to feel in poor health, but this may be as much because they are poor as it is because they are people of color.

Similar patterns are in evidence when we shift the focus from physical health to mental health. A clear majority of Americans[9] regard their mental health as good or excellent. Among the minority adults we interviewed, however, only 38 percent agreed with this assessment, with the differences being most pronounced when we look at the oldest age group (sixty-six and older). Here the numbers are quite striking. Only 11 percent of the oldest African American and Latinos said they were in good or excellent mental health. More than half of the national sample in this older age group were at the high end on mental health. This is a stark difference, reflecting the disparate life experiences that lead to old age in these racial and ethnic groups. Yet, as was true with the physical health measures, the ethnic difference all but disappears when we look only at the poorest people in both studies. Among those with annual earnings of below $10,000 (in 1995), 32 percent of the minorities and about 40 percent of the majority gave themselves low marks for mental health. For both populations, mental health issues seem to be troublesome, reflecting the toll that poverty takes on people regardless of color. At the top of the income distribution, the disparity reappears, with majority respondents more likely to say that their mental health is in good condition as compared to their minority counterparts.

Depression is a common problem, but interestingly enough it seems to be more prevalent among the largely white national sample than it is among the New York–based minorities we interviewed. At every income level, depression is reported with greater frequency among the respondents to the national survey. This is consistent with other data that show blacks have lower suicide rates than whites.[10] In both instances, depression is more pronounced among those who are poor, but it is not a trivial problem for the income groups that are just above the poverty line and the working-class families that earn less than $25,000.

All of us experience stress in our lives. Pressures cascade from our jobs, our families, the communities we live in, the commutes we endure, and the uncertainties of our own health or economic prosperity. But the resources we use to buffer ourselves from these pressures vary quite dramatically. Some Americans are well positioned to cushion the blows of daily life: they can buy help, they can look forward to vacations, they live in places that permit quiet rest, and they have enough steady income so that they do not have to worry about paying the bills at the end of each month. These resources are crucial "shock absorbers" that give the better off a chance to wind down, regroup, and soldier on. Others have no one else they can rely on and many people depending upon them at the same time. They don't have enough extra cash to respond to an emergency need—a transmission that blows up, a roof that leaks, a child who needs an operation. Their engines keep running all the time and they have few effective buffers to help them manage their burdens. Clearly, this pattern of inequality has implications for how easily any given individual can cope with life's curveballs. It also matters in determining the extent to which they feel they are in control of their lives.

Perceived control is very important—indeed, almost as important as resources. If you believe you are in charge of your life, your sense of psychological efficacy becomes a rock to stand on. If, at the other extreme, you feel like a leaf in the wind, blown about by powerful forces beyond your capacity to influence, the result is debilitating. Perceptions of control over health are particularly important, not only for what they say about feelings of efficacy or helplessness but because they may determine how actively individuals seek preventive care, engage in exercise, or eat healthy diets. If fate is in the hands of the gods, ordinary mortals may feel it is futile to try to reverse the course of bad health.

Table 5.1 shows that as one ascends the income ladder the perception of

Table 5-1

Perceived Control Over Physical Health
by Race and Annual Individual Income
(where 0=no control and 10=the most control)

	<$10,000	$10,000–$24,999	$25,000+
Minority Sample	7.36	8.06	8.47
National Sample	7.21	7.36	7.74

control grows. Conversely, moving down, the sense of control slips. The pattern holds within minority and majority groups, but interestingly enough, our New York sample seems to have greater confidence in the ability to control health at each income level than is true in the national sample. This is the first of a number of clues I discuss in this chapter that suggest that minority men and women in poor communities are often more resilient and optimistic than one might expect given the comparatively limited material resources they possess.

What role does access to health care play in ensuring the health of the wealthy and the vulnerability of the poor? The most knowledgeable experts on the subject argue that this issue is overblown as a policy matter and in political debate.[11] This is not because medical care is unimportant. It is largely because patterns of morbidity depend far more upon who gets sick in the first place than they do on who can get in to see a doctor. Medical care is critical once one is ill. But the forces that determine who contracts serious diseases in the first place are more important in the overall scheme of things.[12]

Only 28 percent of middle-aged adults nationwide report that it is hard to get good medical care. Over 40 percent of the minority New Yorkers make this complaint. Not surprisingly, those at the bottom of the income distribution in both samples think it's hard to find good medical attention, hence income is probably the controlling factor here. Since minorities are disproportionately poor, however, it will not surprise anyone to discover that as a group they have more trouble securing medical assistance.[13] As we move up the scale in terms of income, a smaller proportion of the people find the access issues irksome, but it's not a trivial problem, even for those who earn up to $25,000. One-quarter of them see this as an issue in their lives.

Leaving aside the national respondents now, it is useful to look more closely at the health issues on the minds of the African Americans, Dominicans, and Puerto Ricans we interviewed in New York. There are some important differences between these ethnic groups in their assessments of

Table 5-2

Physical and Mental Health Assessments

African Americans, Dominicans, and Puerto Ricans combined

	Physical health	*Mental/Emotional health*
Poor	8%	2%
Fair	23	15.2
Good	34	44.4
Very Good	24	19.2
Excellent	11	19.2

physical and mental health; in the ways health problems interfere with the tasks of everyday life; and with the frequency of depression or worry they experience. The good news is that most of these ethnic minorities report that they are in good physical and mental/emotional condition. Still, over 30 percent think of themselves in poor or fair physical health, and 17 percent say the same about their mental health.

African Americans were more likely than Dominicans or Puerto Ricans to be feeling "very good" or "excellent," in part because they are actually better off economically.[14] Not surprisingly, within all three ethnic groups older individuals were much more likely than younger respondents to report poorer physical and mental health, a pattern that reflects the national profile of older Americans.[15] Sixty percent of the minorities in the New York sample who were over sixty-six years of age said they were in poor or fair health, compared to only 20 percent of those under thirty. Gender matters too. While men and women rate their physical health in a very similar fashion, women are more likely than men to rate their mental and emotional health poorly.

Education is another important dividing line. As Figure 5.1 shows, the college educated are far more likely to think of themselves as being in good health.[16] The pattern is very lopsided. It derives in part from the very close association between education and income. The slings and arrows are far less likely to come the way of someone who is well educated in the first place, and when they do, the educated person has more resources to lean on in responding, since they are also—on average—better placed financially, with more "margin for error." It is also the case that education provides its own protective effects, perhaps by providing individuals with knowledge they can put to use in improving their health (through exercise, avoidance of smoking, etc.).

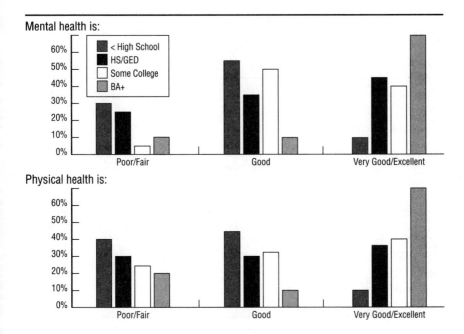

Figure 5.1
Physical and mental health by levels of education

Mental health is:

< High School
HS/GED
Some College
BA+

Poor/Fair · Good · Very Good/Excellent

Physical health is:

Poor/Fair · Good · Very Good/Excellent

One way of assessing the burdens that health problems put on adults in the inner city is to ask what kinds of chronic diseases they have to manage through medication. This is not a perfect measure, for it ignores those who have such poor access to health care that they are not being treated, even when they ought to be. Nonetheless, examining medication patterns gives us some purchase on the impact that disadvantage has on health.

How do these figures compare to the national sample collected by the MacArthur Network on Successful Mid-Life? Compared to the national sample, the minority adults in New York as a group are doing slightly better in the hypertension, high cholesterol, and anxiety departments. They are less likely to take medications for these serious conditions, but they are more likely to need medication for diabetes. Looking internally at the three ethnic groups, however, we see that African Americans look considerably worse than the national average in regard to hypertension and diabetes, as do Puerto Ricans where diabetes is concerned. Dominicans seem to be more likely to need medication for anxiety.[17] Cancer and heart attacks seem to be relatively uncommon in our New York minorities, at least in terms of medication regimes.[18] This finding should be treated with caution, though, because medication and incidence of disease are not the same thing. National

Table 5-3
Prescription Medication Taken in the Last Thirty Days

	Total NY	(National)	Puerto Ricans	Dominicans	African Americans
Hypertension	11.1%	(13.0%)	9.4%	9.1%	14.7%
Diabetes	9.0	(3.9)	12.5	2.9	11.8
High Cholesterol	3.0	(5.2)	3.1	5.9	0*
Anxiety	7.0	(10.2)	6.3	11.8	2.9*

*Difference from national sample significant at the 0.05 level.

	<$10,000	$10,000–$24,999	$25,000+
Hypertension	14.3%	12.1%	8.9%
Diabetes	4.5	12.1	8.9
High Cholesterol	4.5	3	2.2
Anxiety	18.2*	0*	6.7

*Difference between these two income groups is significant at the 0.05 level.

statistics indicate quite clearly that African Americans have higher mortality rates from heart disease and cancer than do whites of the same age and income.

These data tell us that chronic and serious disease is a problem for those growing old in the inner city. What they don't tell us is what kind of limitations these problems pose in their daily lives. Some people are laid low by health problems, including those far less serious than the ones mentioned here, and others push on without changing their daily routine. Hence if our interest is in how health affects the other aspects of one's life, it may be more instructive to consider a standard set of measures that public health officials often rely on[19] to assess the limitations people experience in performing routine activities.

It would appear that for the vast majority of these inner-city dwellers, health problems do *not* greatly impede their ability to take care of the basic tasks we must all attend to in living independently. Vigorous activity takes the largest hit as a consequence of health problems, but this is to be expected in an older population and does not differ significantly from the profile of the nation as a whole. In fact, our people are "looking good" in this respect, and in those domains where 10 percent or more have trouble–lifting gro-

Table 5-4

Limitations on Daily Activities as a Consequence of Health Problems
(African Americans, Puerto Ricans, and Dominicans in
New York)

	A lot	Some	A little	Not at all
Lifting/carrying groceries	10%	5%	5%	80%
Bathing/dressing	0	2	2	96
Climbing stairs	10	16	9	75
Bending, kneeling	10	1	10	79
Walking several blocks	5	6	8	81
Vigorous activity	16	6	11	67
Moderate activity	5	4	8	83

ceries, for example—big-city living may make things somewhat easier, at least in those neighborhoods served by larger food stores. Delivery services that bring the groceries to the door are not uncommon, for example. Elevators are the norm, even in poor housing (especially public housing), which obviates the problem of climbing stairs.

More significant, as least as far as impairment in daily life is concerned, are the figures on depression and worry. Researchers interested in the prevalence of depression often ask survey respondents whether they have experienced a depressive episode during any two-week period in the previous year. This is now a standard measure.[20] Among those we interviewed, nearly one-quarter said they had indeed felt depressed and reported classic symptoms: tired, low energy, trouble concentrating, feelings of worthlessness, loss of interest in things, loss of appetite, and so forth. Depression was more likely among women, individuals with low incomes (less than $10,000 per year), and those with little education, but it is a condition that surfaces in all income groups. However, it is also a problem that seems, if anything, more widespread in the nation as a whole. By a small[21] but nonetheless noticeable margin, every income group in the national sample showed higher rates of depression than their minority counterparts in New York.

Depression can be a very serious condition, hence the fact that nearly 25 percent of these minority adults experience it with some frequency is cause for concern. Yet there are other psychological conditions, for example, excessive worry, that are as important to recognize as actual depression. About 14 percent of the minorities in this New York population feel that they worry more than other people in "the same situation," and about 42 percent of

Table 5-5
Rates of Depression

	New York Sample	National Sample
<$10,000	31.8	36.1
$10,000–$24,000	28.1	35.7
$25,000+	15.6	24.8
Males	17.1	20.9
Females	27.6	34

those people think they worry quite a bit more than others like themselves. Just how bad, or debilitating, are these ruminations? More than half of the "worriers" (who are a minority, we must remember) find they can't put their worries out of their minds, can't control their worrying, become irritable because of their state of mind, and/or cannot concentrate or sleep properly. They feel on edge or nervous, have trouble remembering things, tire easily because they are tense, and find that their worries interfere with life activities. Again, these people are not the norm, but they constitute about 14 percent of our sample, which is not negligible.

Ironically, perhaps (given these downbeat statistics), middle-aged and elderly minorities are reasonably optimistic about what their lives will be like in the years to come. We asked them to compare their lives ten years previously with the present and to project forward ten years in the future. The answers were instructive. Overall, they are more likely to think things were better in the past but were pretty sure that things would get better in the future. This was not the case in the national study of midlife Americans. In the country as a whole, the middle aged believe that their lives have been improving continuously and will continue to do so for the foreseeable future. Exceptions to that rule included the lowest-income respondents nationally, who think their lives have been going downhill when compared to a decade ago. Low-income people in the New York sample tend to agree, and they consistently score their lives—past, present, and future—as lower than those of their higher-income counterparts.[22]

Standing back from this number-driven portrait, what we see is a population of minorities in late middle age and early elderhood that continues to face more than its fair share of health-related problems, particularly chronic diseases like hypertension, diabetes, and self-reported mental health issues. The differences are most pronounced, in a negative direction, when we look at low-income populations, whether in our New York sample or in the nation as a whole. But because minorities are disproportionately likely to be low income, we tend to see these problems cropping up in greater concentrations in minority households and neighborhoods. Elderly people, those over the age of sixty-six, fare better in the national sample than they do in our Latino and African-American households on most of these measures. This suggests both that they face burdens in their present lives that have more health consequences and, perhaps, that they are now experiencing the long-term impact of conditions that have plagued them for much of their adult lives.[23] This would be consistent with the "allostatic load" model[24] that posits a kind of cumulative "wear and tear" on people who are under consistent stress, with insufficient resources (time, money, quiet, space) to relax and recoup.

Yet we also see signs of resilience in the face of challenge. Minorities are less likely to suffer from depression, more likely to feel some control over their physical health, and less likely to be taking medications for serious, chronic diseases than their counterparts across the country.[25] Good news is also visible in the data on daily activities, where the vast majority of our minority respondents say that they can take care of business (bathing, climbing stairs, lifting, etc.) without any trouble at all. This kind of "behavioral" data is more convincing, perhaps, than self-reported assessments of health. It can be taken as evidence for the proposition that greater stress, brought about by lower income and less comfortable living circumstances, can provoke fortitude and resilience rather than decline and resignation. Perhaps it should not surprise us, then, that compared to the national norm these New Yorkers believe the future is more promising than the past, that an upward trajectory is possible or expected.

What the Numbers Don't Show

Surveys are very helpful for grasping the big picture, but they also leave gaps in our understanding of real lives. For those who confront limitations based on ill health, particularly those who are still relatively young, the story cannot be summed up in a line on a table. Frida Burton is a case in point. Her life has been turned inside out by the early onset of serious disease, and the ramifications are evident in the lives of her children. She has not been able fully to protect them from the psychological consequences of parental incapacity, but neither has she collapsed in the face of pressures that might defeat a less resilient person.

Frida was born in Panama in 1956, the daughter of a Costa Rican mother and a Panamanian father. She lived in a small, poor town in Panama until she was twelve, a place she remembers dimly now as a community where "the children respected all the adults that were around them." "Everyone knew each other," she says wistfully. "You couldn't do anything and your mother not hear about it because it was so small." The people in her town didn't move about very much since virtually no one had a car and buses were scarce. Frida walked to school; her parents walked to work, when they had work to go to. Women worked as housekeepers for the wealthier Panamanians and the Americans who came to town courtesy of the Canal Zone. Her brothers and father worked in transit, mainly on the railroads, and they made do. No one was well off. Indeed, by our standards (which are now Frida's standards as well), her family and town were dirt poor.

Yet poverty seemed not to wear the face of a racial divide, at least not in the same way it now unfolds in her Brooklyn housing project.

We had Indians and what we called Spanish people. Very few whites. There were different colors and different backgrounds. But there was no racial tension there. It was nothing, you know, like this. Everyone pretty much lived in the same neighborhood and sometimes in the same development and everybody got along. Everyone looked out for the other person.

Church formed the core of community life. She cannot remember a single family that did not participate and can recite by name the community leaders who were anchored in the church.

Frida and her eight siblings moved to New York in the late-1960s, when she was about twelve. Their mother had very little money and worked all day in the factory, seeing her kids only late at night. This was a big step up in the world, since her mom had been confined to domestic service in Panama, but the expense of living in New York was significantly higher as well. In the end, she couldn't earn enough to put a roof over all of their heads, so she farmed Frida out to the home of her oldest sister, then living in an immigrant enclave in East New York. Frida missed her mother and didn't get along well with her aunt, so as soon as her mother could manage to take her back she moved back home. It was a working-class neighborhood on its way to becoming a much tougher inner-city ghetto. By the time she reached her late teens it was a different story. Nowadays, she wouldn't walk the streets of that Bushwick neighborhood in broad daylight. "The place where I lived," she notes with resignation, "I wouldn't go there now. It's just nothing but crime. That's all there is now; it's just horrible."

Because she spoke only Spanish, Frida found the adjustment to New York difficult, the kids her own age frightening and unfriendly. She struggled in school and ultimately dropped out. It was a mistake.

> I could have done better than I have. I could have lived different that I have lived, in a lot of ways. I could have educated myself a little better than I did and I probably would have a better job than I have. I'm restless because I don't feel like I have accomplished the things I should have accomplished. I'm not satisfied.

Frida readily admits that no one else is to blame for this detour. Neither does anyone else deserve the credit she has coming to her for buckling down to the GED classes and completing her high school equivalency exam in her early twenties. Against the odds, she learned enough English to enroll in the local junior college where she could pursue her dream: a nursing degree and a shot at a professional job in health care. She met her husband-to-be, an African American born and raised in New York, in college. They married and she got pregnant at the age of twenty-four. Without child care, Frida found she had to leave college behind. Her husband, Jamal, had a steady job, though, and they could eke out a living from his salary as a unionized security guard while she took care of the kids.

One more son followed four years later and Frida realized that she would have to find work. They needed a larger place, and without a second income this was not going to happen. Without a college degree, but with a respectable educational track record up to that point, Frida was able to qualify for decent, nonprofessional jobs. Starting in her early thirties, she got a position as a security guard like her husband, standing watch over city-run hospitals, principally in the emergency room. Because it was a city job, it paid well—nearly $14 an hour—and it came with full benefits.

That was a particular stroke of luck, because as her third child became a toddler, Frida's marriage began to crumble. Jamal started seeing other women on the sly, something Frida simply would not tolerate. Their arguments became more strident as his deceptions became more blatant, and eventually he moved out and filed for divorce. In the beginning, he kept in close contact with his three sons, then ten, five, and two. Jamal would swoop in and take the two older ones off for the day, treating them to toys and candy that Frida could not afford on her lone salary. He was reasonably good about child support, contributing enough to make it possible for Frida to remain in the apartment they had found together. But when it came to the new shoes those growing boys needed or the uniforms required for parochial school, Jamal was not exactly Mr. Dependable. The presence of his girlfriends set the older boys off, making them more and more unruly as the permanence of their parents' breakup became clear. As Jamal's attention began to wander further, his financial contributions became more sporadic.

With child support an increasingly scarce resource, Frida found she had to economize on the rent. She packed up her three sons and moved them into the two-bedroom, section-eight apartment she presently occupies in a black and West Indian neighborhood in Fort Greene, in Brooklyn. By local standards, the apartment building is a fine place to live. It is about ten stories high, with long, narrow corridors of apartments that, while tiny, are modern and clean. The security guard that sits at the front desk has a bank of monitors that give him an unimpeded view of the parking garage, the front door, and the concrete "yard" that the apartments share. Frida's home would be regarded by many inner-city families as a real plum.

A closer look, especially through Frida's eyes, tells us that it is far from paradise. The guard cannot see the inside of the elevators or the stairwells, the hot spots where robberies take place on a fairly regular basis. He cannot hear the occasional bouts of domestic violence that take place behind closed doors, but which the walls are too thin to disguise. Frida and her sons have been menaced in the parking garage to the point where she, in particular, is scared to venture down there. Certain older boys are to be avoided at all costs, and Frida's youngest son, now about nine, is wary of them, particularly when his older brothers are not around to protect him.

When windows won't close, the heat doesn't come on, the plumbing breaks down, and the intercoms installed to increase safety no longer function, little action is forthcoming. The maintenance department doesn't really seem to care one way or the other how the tenants feel or what they want. The tenants are suspicious of one another, convinced that only those who have special pull will see the repairman. What one person gains, the others seem to lose; as a result there is little sense of community. You don't borrow a cup of sugar in this building. You watch your back and avoid public spaces that are not in full view.

These atmospherics became particularly burdensome when, at the age of thirty-seven, Frida developed relentless headaches, loss of balance on the stairs, and blurred vision. She ignored the discomfort at first and stuck steadfastly to her job, now needed more than ever since Jamal was providing less and less in the way of child support. When her symptoms took a turn for the worse, she finally relented and went to the doctor, courtesy of the health insurance she had from her city job.

The doctor was not happy with what he saw and referred her to an oncologist. Frida was terrified. She tried to push the most frightening thoughts aside and just concentrate on her job and her kids. Her worst fears were confirmed a week later when white-coated Dr. Parker sat her down and told her she had a brain tumor. He set up the X rays on the lighted wall and tried to show her the shadow of the beast, but she was too stunned to take it all in. Frida began a harsh regime of chemotherapy in the first of her never-ending weekly visits to Sloan-Kettering hospital, and prepared for surgery. When we first met, in her tidy apartment "decorated" with the high school graduation pictures of her oldest son, the surgery was several months past, and Frida was still in radiation treatment. Unfortunately, however, the prognosis was not encouraging.

Frida kept on working right up to the surgery date, but she had to take disability leave thereafter. Indeed, by the time we met, she had trouble walking and would find herself winded and exhausted in a brief two-block walk from the subway to her building. Nonetheless, she made that walk as often as she had to, particularly when she needed to visit her middle son's school. Her illness, the disappearance of his father, and the departure of his oldest brother for the Navy unhinged the boy and sent him into a spiral of misbehavior in school. At the age of nine he had begun moving around their neighborhood on his own, falling in with a group of boys who were up to no good. He started cutting classes, his marks plummeted, and ultimately he got caught in the crossfire when guns were drawn outside his middle school. Leroy was hit in the arm and was lucky it was nothing more serious, but ever since he has been a discipline problem, both at home and in the classroom. His mother's illness seemed to be the last straw. Running away from home, dabbling in minor criminal activity, and refusing to answer to his mother's authority followed close on the heels of her diagnosis. Thus in addition to coping with the anxiety, nausea, and exhaustion of her treatment, Frida had to do what she could to stop Leroy from going totally off the rails. She wasn't succeeding.

The contrast with his older brother, Robert, product of a more stable home environment in his own adolescence, could not be more pronounced. Robert's clean-cut, smiling face, dressed in his immaculate Navy uniform, looks down from its prideful place on the mantel. His portrait is surrounded by awards for "best attendance" and "most dependable student," conferred by his high school some years back. Frida makes a point of showing me these visible signs of his accomplishments and makes it clear that she thinks the Navy will provide him with a future. Leroy doesn't seem to find this inspiring. He stays in his room when I come to visit, pausing occasionally to bark at his younger brother.

Frida's youngest boy, Jamal Junior, seems largely unaffected by the tension that surrounds his middle brother. He loves to draw and spends hours at his mother's knee, coloring pictures on the living room table. She sits on the green couch, its arms covered with the kind of white lace doilies my own grandmother favored, trying to conserve her energy and recover from the exhaustion of radiation treatment. Junior keeps her company, crayons spread far and wide, his art notebook opened to reveal dozens of drawings of Power Rangers, imaginary worlds. Frida has tried to provide him with extras—art lessons, music, sports—that will insulate him from the downward spiral that has swallowed Leroy. She knows Junior loves his drawing and karate classes, but it is becoming increasingly difficult to transport him by subway from school to lessons. Frida pleads with Leroy to help her, to take his little brother to his various appointments. But on more than one occasion Leroy has left Jamal Junior standing forlorn on a sidewalk or forced him to walk home on his own in the dark, through neighborhoods that are not safe at night. Frida's failing health makes it almost impossible for her to be the kind of mother she wants to be.

Indeed, her condition is so serious now that she has had to go on permanent disability. "Thank god I have health insurance," she says with a knowing sigh of relief. "What I would do if I couldn't get treatment is beyond me." Compared to many of her Fort Greene neighbors, Frida is well off. Her housing cannot be pulled out from under her; she can see specialist doctors; and she can put food on the table with the income from her disability pension. Still, she cannot supervise Leroy and is tearing her hair out—what is left of it—over his erratic ways and angry outbursts. He is given to slamming doors, stomping out of the house, disappearing for hours on end, and bullying his younger brother. Frida thinks he is furious with his father, who pays him no mind these days, and takes it out on her when Jamal Senior disappoints them all by not showing up as promised. She despairs because she thinks Leroy lacks goals, misses the guidance that a father should provide, and then finds solace in the worst of places. Young people everywhere seem to her in danger of drifting away.

> They have no guidance, no one to coach them. It's just them. No one else is around. So, it's difficult when it's like that and most of the people I see today are like that: lonely. They don't have others to push them and if they do, they're not listening to them, they're listening to friends. They are into [going] here and there. I see very few young adults that are going forward. There might be some point when they come back [to their senses], but for now I see them drifting. Not focused.
>
> This generation has to deal with a lot of things I did not have to

deal with. . . . They have drugs, they have all this crime. They have a
school system now that doesn't give a damn whether they learn or not.
They just go from one class to the next and that's all right with the
teachers. When I was growing up, it was different. You respected adults
and adults helped. But now, the kids have no respect for adults,
therefore, the adults don't need them.

. . . Kids are not getting what they're supposed to get from the educational system . . . or from home. It's like they are lost, they are out
there in space somewhere.

Frida worries a lot about the space Leroy is lost in. It is full of temptations
and bad influences. But she is absorbed by her own battle with cancer and
has run out of the energy required to deal with him.

She is panicked about what will become of her children if she cannot beat
this disease. Who will take care of them? This nagging fear—which would
strike terror into the heart of any parent—is particularly pressing for Frida
because it is not an idle concern. No one in her family has the resources to
take on two children who still have many years left at home before they can
fend for themselves. Their eldest brother is too young, just starting out in
the Navy, and would not be able to provide for them. Swallowing her pride,
Frida has approached Jamal about whether he would take responsibility for
his sons if she passed away. His response has been noncommittal, almost
unhearing. He has not refused flat out, but neither has he said he would. He
acts as though she is putting him on the spot and, as Frida sees it, he is
searching for a way to wriggle out of the responsibilities she has shouldered
on her own since they divorced. Frida is thinking she should ask him to
renounce his parental rights altogether. Perhaps that way she could find another relative to be her children's guardian, and free them from the possibility
of a custody contest if she dies.

One of her five sisters, who has an apartment in western Massachusetts,
may be a candidate. When the kids were younger and she was in good
health, Frida piled the family into the car and drove them up to Dolores'
place once a year for the only vacation they could really afford. Crunching
through the New England leaves during those rare breaks, Frida caught a
glimpse of how the other half lives—all those vivid colors, that bright blue
sky, peace and quiet, the freedom to walk outdoors without crowds pushing
past or the need to keep one eye out for threatening pit bulls or their dubious
owners—all this was a refreshing change from their housing block in Fort
Greene. Indeed, if Frida could figure out a way to manage it, she would
move lock, stock, and barrel up to New England herself and just get away

from everything that winds her up. But Frida has to remain near her oncologists, so she will not be living in New England any time soon.

Frida's health has impinged on her life in so many ways. It has effectively ended what was a steady track record of employment and has pushed her family closer to poverty, since she must be content with SSI and a modest disability pension from her city job. The normal difficulties that beset single parents in poor neighborhoods are multiplied by her limitations. Her medical problems have exacerbated Leroy's already unruly behavior problems and left Frida with insufficient energy or will to try to hold him in check. She has little strength to deal with assault problems in the hallways, and the studied lack of attention she gets from the building's management when she complains about the dangers of the parking garage. All kinds of picky rules—those that outlaw the kind of air conditioner she has, those that require her to put in time at tenants' meetings or contribute to the patrols when she isn't up to it—seem designed to make her feel worse.

Were she in a better neighborhood, if she had a spouse to help, if she had money to use to lure Leroy into more productive activities (like the baseball camp he longed for at thirteen), she might not be facing the double burdens of illness and guilt over his lack of direction. As it is, she has to thank her lucky stars that she lives in subsidized housing and has health insurance she can count on. Things could actually be worse.

Even the strongest person might feel defeated by Frida's problems. Yet she does not dwell on them. She is not in a blue funk. She gets frustrated with the deck she has been dealt, particularly with respect to her health, but in visiting with the Burton family, you are just as likely to hear about how well her oldest son is doing in the Navy and how proud his mother is of him. The walls of her apartment are testimony to her capacity to look on the bright side and derive a sense of satisfaction from his life, as well as from the burgeoning artistic talents of her youngest son.

Frida spends a lot of time talking about what she would like to do in the future, about how she'd like to go back to school, and hers is not the voice of a pipe dreamer. She makes concrete plans for her children, thinks about enrolling in school to pursue that nursing degree she had always hoped to have under her belt. She makes plans for trips to see her sister in the months ahead. Frida has not given up. Indeed, she would be taken aback by my description of her life because I have focused here on the dark side. That is not her way. It seems to be a characteristic feature of many minority families in the inner city that they do not buckle under burdens or dwell on their misfortunes. The statistics we have seen that show noticeably lower levels of depression in the sample of New York minorities, compared to the national sample that is largely white, reinforce the point. Life throws a lot of curveballs at people like Frida, but she has a wellspring of resilience that keeps her focused on the future when many lesser people would just give up.

Daisy Carrasquillo shares this resilient quality. Like Frida, Daisy is in her early forties and has been battling cancer for almost a decade. Raised in both New York and Puerto Rico, Daisy is the daughter of a building super who worked two jobs to keep his family afloat. Because housing came with her father's job, Daisy grew up in safer and more comfortable neighborhoods than her dad's salary alone could have ensured. Nonetheless, when it came time for her to go to high school, Daisy headed back to Puerto Rico to live with her grandmother. She thought she would pursue a secretarial career, a significant step up as she saw it from her dad's manual labor job and her mom's occasional factory work, so a few years later Daisy enrolled in the University of Puerto Rico. In her senior year, Daisy began to experience chronic pain.

> I had cancer and I didn't know it. I was really very sick and living on my own. . . . Every day I had to drive the car to go to school and I would get these pains. I was studying like that for about six months, for the whole term. It was very hard trying to finish the semester. I don't know how I did it.
>
> But when I came to New York to visit my family, they told me it was all nervous tension and I got to believe it. It's all nervous tension because of your school, your studying. I had all kinds of tests in Puerto Rico . . . [but] they were just doing funny medicine. The problems just continued and I just started worrying something was really wrong. When I tried to get back into the university, I wasn't accepted back because my grades had gone down. So I just came back to New York for a semester recess and had a bunch of tests.

Daisy needed surgery. It turned out to be the first of many return visits to the operating table.

> [When I was first diagnosed], they took care of the problem. They were ninety-nine percent sure that I would never have to come back to the operating room. But that one percent came back to haunt me and I had to do it again. Then it came back a third time. They said, "Well, we hope it won't give you any more problems for maybe twenty years." But then it came back up again, for the fourth time. Now they

are telling me that there is a section that is inoperable. So it just keeps getting worse and worse and there is no way of stopping it.

Despite four surgeries in the last decade or so, Daisy finds the reserve energy to care for her two young sons. She does so with enthusiasm and an outpouring of love and affection. Indeed, Daisy fairly defines herself by her devotion to family, her almost giddy hopes for her kids' futures.

Because she has a happy family, a solid marriage, and a home in a safe and secure neighborhood, Daisy feels blessed compared to others she knows who are in Frida Burton's situation. Her husband can carry the family financially and their housing is guaranteed by his job as a building super, like his father-in-law before him. While they cannot put much money aside, they are not drowning in debt, and they have been able to put their children in good schools in middle-class neighborhoods that are well above their own economic station. The basic foundations for survival are, therefore, well in hand in Daisy's household, even though she is plagued by health problems.

Daisy's main problem involves finding doctors who will give her a straight answer and treat her like a human being, unlike the clinic-based physicians who "treated [her] like a dog." "They had a real attitude," she remembered. Looking down their long noses at these Puerto Rican patients, they refused to give her any information about her condition. "You asked them a question and it's like, 'Well, you are not paying so we will treat you like garbage,' " she says with bitterness. That was not her only brush with high-handed people who think themselves superior to her because she doesn't speak English. For a time, Daisy received vouchers for surplus foods through the welfare department's WIC (Women, Infants and Children) nutrition program. The checkout clerks in the stores shared with those haughty doctors a superior attitude that really stuck in Daisy's craw. As far as she was concerned, she is an educated woman with good values and well-groomed, well-behaved children to prove it.

Of course, like all children, they are not perfect angels. Truth be told, Daisy is relieved when they go off to school and leave her with a little private time to sit and watch her favorite soap opera, *All My Children*, broadcast in Spanish on one of New York's several cable channels. She fatigues easily, and when her sons can't get along she finds it hard to muster the energy to intervene. Her physical frailty interferes with her ability to plan for events that she feels are important markers of mothering—one son's Catholic confirmation, the other's first communion.

Problems of this kind would be hard for anyone to live with, no matter how fat their bank account. But for a family like Daisy's, which lives from week to week, paycheck to paycheck, the burden chronic illness imposes can be the last straw. Her treatments are covered by the health insurance policy of her husband's union. They are determined to provide their children with a good education and have enrolled them both in parochial school. Tuition is modest, but is manageable for them only if they are very, very careful about how they spend their money. Daisy is a careful shopper, coupon clipper, and avid bargain hunter. There is little margin for error in her budget, however, particularly because she doesn't avail herself of the public supports that others around her seem to embrace at the drop of a hat.

> When I go to the supermarket, I really have to stretch my dollars and compare prices. Then I go to the store and I watch these people buy huge, all sorts of stuff. You know, junk. And I just get upset. . . . People in my own family are collecting welfare without needing it. And it used to bother me because we didn't qualify for that and then you see people taking advantage of it, people who also didn't qualify but were taking advantage. They had second cars and stuff like that. I was really needing it, but didn't technically, correctly qualify. You have to be poverty-stricken.

The children receive reduced-cost breakfast and a break on the cost of school lunches and Daisy receives SSI disability payments. Saving money is an impossible goal. Perhaps she should be glad that her family isn't wallowing in red ink, but being a forward-thinking Mom, Daisy takes only minimal comfort from their technical solvency. She wants to know where the money will come from to send her teenager to college, particularly if the scholarships she has been counting on disappear. Surveying the world from her vantage point, Daisy doesn't hold out a lot of hope that the financial aid offered during her college years will still be available when her kids need it.

Daisy is not living below the poverty line. She no longer qualifies for means-tested benefits. But she is not on easy street, particularly because her illness renders her unable to work. Without two incomes in hand, the family is under financial pressure, though not nearly as severely as genuinely poor families, particularly lone-parent households. Knowing this to be true, Daisy is actually hesitant to complain.

Indeed, if anything, she is grateful for the resources they have, and not just from a checkbook perspective. Chief among her assets is an attentive husband, who puts a lot of time into supervising the kids, particularly when Daisy herself isn't up to the task. Together they set a strict regime for their sons, controlling their movements in nonschool hours, making sure they don't associate with troubled kids. They know far too many children who have fallen off the straight and narrow in their teen years.

> They can't even cross the street alone. My son is fourteen. He told me that he asked my husband if he could ride a bicycle and my husband said, "No, you can't cross the street." He says, "Mom, Dad, I'm fourteen years old! A lot of kids my age are hanging out, going to the movies. I can't even cross the street!" I told him, "That's the way it is."

Daisy's husband, Julio, chimes in from the kitchen, "We care!" Emerging with a bowl of potato chips in hand, Julio goes on to contrast their parenting style with those of other families they know.

> We are protective because we care. He tells us, "Other parents permit this or that." He's so smart! But I tell him, "Just because other parents let them do all kinds of stuff, doesn't mean they [are right.]"

Daisy nods at Julio and explains that their kids don't have much social time with other children except at school. They don't "hang out" at all.

> The only friends they have, they don't see very often. . . . They really don't speak to each other outside of school. On the phone they do. Once in a while I tell them, you can go visit, but only if you remain right in front of the house. That was the way I was raised, and that is the way I'm raising them.

The contrast between these two families tells us that the consequences of health problems depend a great deal on the context within which they unfold. Being sick and poor makes it hard to raise children successfully, almost no matter what else is going on. When the hardship is borne by two parents, though, the difficulties are much easier to cope with and the well-being of children is at less risk. Neither of these families has any extra money. One is getting by because of section-eight housing and a relatively generous disability plan, the other as a result of "tithed" housing and a unionized job. The differences between them in terms of standard of living are not massive, though Daisy lives in a better neighborhood than her family income alone would permit. Similarities of economic position notwithstanding, it is clear that the children in these two families are on different pathways. One house is buffered by the presence of two adults, the other is vulnerable because of the absence of a partner.

The same dilemmas beset single-parent households where the child is the sick one, rather than the parent. Children in poor neighborhoods often suffer from chronic physical illnesses,[26] particularly asthma and lead poisoning, not to mention hyperactivity and attention deficit disorder, which require a great deal of additional adult time in the form of doctors' visits and missed school days that have to be supervised by somebody.[27] These burdens are hard enough to manage when there are two parents in the household to cover for each other. For single parents—whether mothers or fathers—the difficulties are overwhelming and have almost immediate impacts on their own labor-force participation and therefore their reputations among employers as dependable workers.[28]

When possible, single parents with sick children look to their own siblings and parents for help, or to their older children (whose own school careers suffer as a consequence). They will do almost anything to protect their jobs so as to keep on supporting the family, particularly in the present context of welfare reform, which has removed any meaningful backstop. If they cannot find in-kind help somewhere, they are often forced to leave sick children at home alone.

The uneven employment patterns of single parents, especially mothers, owes a great deal to the impact of illness in their families. And this has cumulative consequences, for if they cycle in and out of the labor market, or simply lose jobs periodically, they will find it difficult to pull out of the low-wage sector into something better. Sick kids translates into long-term poverty, for what other choice is there? Few mothers, or fathers for that matter, will turn a blind eye to a child with asthma and surely, as a society, we wouldn't want them to. Yet we have done relatively little to help them with the task, by offering for instance paid sick leave or flexible work schedules that will make it possible for them to attend to these responsibilities without damaging their track records in the workplace.

These problems spread far beyond the inner-city women who are of "mothering age." It extends to elders who, for a variety of reasons, retain that role long after most of us have shed it for the empty nest. Rita Tilly, the African-American great-grandmother we encountered in chapter one, knows this all too well. Rita has worked all her life and is now in her seventies. She has her own health problems, the accumulated damage of many years of high blood pressure, for which she now takes medication. Retired now, she worked most of her life in law firms in Manhattan. Rita was fortunate to have a job that provided a modest pension and qualified her for

Social Security. Those resources were supposed to underwrite a comfortable retirement, and if all Rita had to do was take care of herself, they would be enough to live on modestly, without fear of major financial distress, particularly now that she is old enough to qualify for Medicare.

Rita has a lot more to worry about than just herself, however, and has been in this fix for nearly a decade now. Her savings have been used up taking care of the medical expenses for her daughter and the cost of raising her granddaughter. "That's what wakes me up in the middle of the night," she laments, twisting a handkerchief in her hands. "I keep wanting to throw all these bills on the table and say, 'See what you did to me? You made me poor and I don't have any money left at all because I've spent it all on you, paying your bills and everything.' "

Rita resents the sacrifices she has had to make. She is convinced this was the right thing to do, indeed the only thing she could do. But that doesn't mean she is happy about having been put in this position or even-tempered in the face of all this financial pressure and domestic tension. What bothers her the most is the fact that nobody in her family shows her any gratitude. Instead, they complain about her attempts to shape her adult children, nearly adult grandchildren, and teenage great-grands. They think she's bossy and out of bounds. She thinks they are ingrates.

> I just feel that I know what's goin' on and that they should try to do it my way, or even sit down and talk about it and we can see. We could do it this way and it would be better. But they won't sit down and talk with me. So that's where I get my anxieties and disappointments and not feeling good. I want to pick up and move and get away from all these people. And then I say, what can you do? Where [am I] going to go? I don't have money even to put down [on another home]. You have to pay a month's security to move. Where would I get the money to move? I live from day to day and have enough to meet my needs. That's it.

Anthropologists who have studied "sharing networks" marvel at the support these private safety nets afford poor families.[29] And indeed, they are critical for survival, particularly when so many family members are troubled, and the help they can expect from public sources is limited. Grandmothers like Rita are a real lifeline. However, health researchers have pointed out that people who are blessed with "dense ties" also show high levels of depression,[30] suggesting that altruists suffer significant stress from the strain. In Rita's case, the anxiety mounts not only because of the wear and tear but because the more she turns her pockets inside out to assist family members in need, the more trapped she feels. Should she decide at some point that she just can't take it anymore, she will have little recourse and she knows it. There will be no resources left to tap for her old age.

Rita has one child left who might "make it" and therefore be there for her if she gets sick. She is not sure this daughter really will come through for her and, without that security, she lies awake at night wondering what will become of her if she ever hits a serious health snag. Questions of this nagging sort plague many poor households, particularly those headed by aging single mothers. They spend hours with their siblings and cousins, rummaging through the family tree to find the one niece or nephew who might turn out to be the reliable one.

Yet precisely because their support structures are tenuous, men and women who are growing old before their time develop a thick hide, a quality of personal resilience that is unmistakable. Rita is often frustrated and tired of shouldering so much responsibility, but even in her seventies she is still an active problem solver. Indeed, some would argue that she is younger than her years precisely because the social role—as opposed to the chronological position—she occupies is closer to that of a middle-age mother than an elderly grandparent.

Illness is particularly disruptive in families with young kids still at home, but it is also a force to be reckoned with among inner-city dwellers at middle age whose parents now face the disabilities that come in the elder years. This, too, is a problem middle-class families recognize, for they are also caught in a kinship "sandwich," responsible for the well-being of children and ailing parents at the same time. Irene Mandel, an African-American school administrator, has recently come to understand how these commitments define middle age itself.

I found myself making four trips a year instead of three to see my parents. I anticipate those will become more. So, therefore, there will be less money that I will spend on myself. The things that were important are not as important anymore.

Would she be thinking this way if she were a man? Irene doesn't think so. She looks at her brother's response to their parents' needs and finds him more distant, willing to leave it to Irene to handle their needs.

Men and women differ in middle age. Women pay more attention to family responsibility. . . . It's just a perception of life. I look at the way my brother reacted to a family crisis and I was [telling him], you know you have to call. We have to find out what's going on [with Mom and Dad]. And his reaction was, "Do we have to do it now?"

Irene doesn't think she will be able to depend very much on brother Richard as time goes on for what, in theory, is a responsibility they share. She doesn't spend a lot of time worrying about it, though. She accepts, with reluctance, the fact that she will probably be able to badger him into helping from time to time, but the main burden will be hers to shoulder.

Parents are not the only people on her "to do" list. Irene's maternal aunt, now nearly ninety years old, is also the kind of close family that no one can abandon. Now quite elderly and alone, Aunt Ruth depends upon Irene to manage most of her affairs, even though she lives nearly eighty miles away.

She put me down for power of attorney when she made out her will. . . . Her husband died three or four years ago and there are no relatives where she [lives]. His relatives [came] out to write the checks for her, lining up the bills so she could sign the checks. An ex-daughter-in-law came out to help put out the garbage on Mondays. That was how they wanted to keep in touch with her.

For some years after her uncle's death, Irene could rely on a network of relatives to help care for her aunt Ruth. But as time went on her aunt developed symptoms of dementia, one of which was an intense suspicion of the intentions of her caregivers. She started pushing her relatives away, certain they were ripping her off.

As she got older, and more lonely, Ruth became more paranoid about them taking advantage of her. And she was very insulting to her niece who was writing checks. Chased off the former daughter-in-law who was coming out to make sure the garbage was out. Was beside herself when her granddaughter took the car keys. And so they [told me], "You have to have power of attorney and there are some things only you can do." So I had to step in and begin paying her bills. I had to get someone to go in three days a week to be with her.

Irene had hoped this would stabilize the situation, but she found that Ruth was increasingly uncomfortable and then belligerent with these caretakers she thought of as strangers. She didn't want the money to be spent on them; she

wanted to leave her money to her nieces and nephews. Irene pleaded with
her to remember why she saved in the first place.

> I'm telling her, "You worked hard for this, so you could take care of
> yourself in your old age. I'm just helping you do that. But I need you
> to be nicer to these people, who are here and who will be the ones that
> contact me if you ever need me."

Ruth grew more querulous as Irene imposed limitations (on driving, on
spending). What Irene saw as protection, Ruth defined as intrusions intended
to undermine her independence. Increasingly, as Irene saw it, Ruth was making decisions that made no sense. Her hands ached with arthritis, so she
spent $5,000 on new windows that weren't worth half the price, only so that
she could open them more easily. Predatory sales people started coming
around with various schemes designed to pry Ruth's money out of her hands
and she became less and less capable of sorting out the good deals from
the bad.

For a time, Irene was able to manage these complex responsibilities, but
finally she became convinced that her aunt could not be left in her home
alone. Though she felt guilty about it, Irene also realized that she was going
to have to take her own needs into account in deciding what had to be done
for Ruth. Irene has a demanding job and found she was exhausted by the
tension within the circle of relations who were trying to help. There was
nothing left at the end of the week, no reserves to draw on in soldiering on
with her own life. Agonizing over the right pathway, she finally confronted
her aunt with the need to find a better living situation, among people who
could offer daily care.

> I think she needs a lot more companionship. She says, "But I don't
> have a problem being alone." I have to explain to her that the human
> spirit needs companionship. And so, I've gotten her to fill out forms
> for assisted living. It was such a burden, at first, and I was over-
> whelmed. Work-related things just kept me so tired, so that on the
> weekend, I just didn't want to take a day to drive up and see her. I
> did get her to fill out the application.

This was a tough decision for Irene. In earlier generations, she would
have taken Ruth into her own home. Poorer families still do. Though the
saga of Ruth's care is hardly over, Irene can at least see a way out that she
genuinely feels will be better for her aunt. The whole experience, too, has

made her aware of what awaits her when her parents are no longer able to manage on their own. For now, she notes they are in fine shape. At eighty-seven and eighty-three, they are still able to drive and are still in good health, having had no heart attacks or strokes. This luck won't hold forever and Irene knows that, when the time comes, she will have to return to the care-taker role she has played with Ruth.

Midlife Americans confront the true meaning of aging when, like Irene, they have to deal with its consequences for a loved one firsthand. They take on special significance for someone like Irene, though, because she has no children who might reprise her role decades from now when she herself needs someone to lean on. She married and divorced before having any kids, so her support structure looks a bit thinner than the one that surrounds Aunt Ruth.

Fortunately, Irene has a number of treasured friends who care a great deal about her. This sisterhood has been close for many years now and is com-posed mostly of women in their forties and fifties who are educated and hardworking, just like Irene. They are churchgoing women with fairly tra-ditional, family-centered values, regardless of their marital status. Some of Irene's friends are divorced and a few are married, but they all count these female-centered bonds as among their most important sources of solidarity, friendship, and just plain companionship. They get together to share a meal at one another's homes about once every two weeks. These retreats permit them to relax, trade stories and gossip, chat about clothes or goings-on in their neighborhoods. Because all of them work hard, they look forward to these retreats as a solace and steam valve for the pressures that build up in their busy, city lives.

Irene became particularly aware of how important her friends were as a support structure when she hit an unexpected bump in the road and felt very vulnerable.

I have low blood pressure and if I get up too fast, or get too hot, I just pass out. So my friends and I were working on these Saturdays and we used to call each other to remember to get up, and of course, I was always the last one up. And as I hung up from one of those calls, I passed out [because I got up too fast]. It was very scary that I wasn't with anyone. If it hadn't been for the fact that my girlfriend was calling other friends, she wouldn't have known that I had passed out. The connection wasn't broken. What brought her to me was her saying, "Hello??" and trying to get the line to clear. And it was just—kind of scary.

Scariest of all was the parallel Irene suddenly began to draw between her own life and her aunt Ruth's. She could suddenly see the wisdom with regard to her own life that she had been trying to get across to Ruth.

A lot of people don't understand that if we were meant to be alone, God would have put us on different little planets. And they think that it's a great thing that they are independent and all the rest of that. I think it takes a toll on people.

Irene wonders whether her girlfriends will stay the course for one another and "be there" over the long run. Can a group of friends take the place of family? Will they do for one another what children would do for their parents? Perhaps her brother's family will think of her as someone special, in the same way she thinks of Aunt Ruth. Yet in this day and age of marriages that come unglued, she is not sure his marriage will hold or that she would be able to depend on his children in the future. Irene rarely gave these uncertain aspects of aging a passing thought until she had to devote so much time to Ruth's care. Irene doesn't dwell on them much now either, but she hears a voice in the back of her mind every so often that mutters something about how hard all of this could be if she had no one to rely on.

Many of the people we interviewed were tentative when asked about whether they could turn to family, friends, or neighbors to help them in a health crisis. Twenty-one percent of the African Americans, 31 percent of the Dominicans, and 34 percent of the Puerto Ricans reported that there really was no one to help them with their responsibilities and keep them strong and happy. Even among those who did report having a degree of "social support,"[31] many suggested that they believed they had to deal with problems on their own for the most part. They were not willing to depend on others or trouble these friends with their concerns. When asked whether they could turn to others for help, this is what they had to say.

- Helena Melendez, Dominican, age forty-five
  "I am a loner, I depend on me. I do the things I do because I don't want to depend on nobody. I feel [badly] if it ask somebody for something, so I try not to."
- Anita Saldivar, Puerto Rican, age fifty
  "I don't like to bother people. I prefer to do things myself. I just ask a person once. If they can't help me, forget it. I will do it myself. I count on my mother and my best friend, and nobody else."

- Missy Darden, African American, age seventy-something
  "Most of the time, I'm on my own. I've had to do it alone and you form habits of not involving other people with what you consider your own problems. I mean, I talk to people, but I don't depend on anyone but myself. I'm independent to a fault."
- Barry Howard, African American, age sixty
  "I don't need nobody. I don't need support from other people to keep me happy. I do what I got to do."

Is this just rugged individualism speaking? Americans think of themselves as weak if they admit to needing the care and attention of others. This cultural script is at work among inner-city minorities who embrace it as much as the rest of the society does. Yet few of us are totally independent. In the inner city, the lines of reciprocity between family members and unrelated neighbors run continuously. People are contributing many hours to the care and counsel of friends, relatives, the apartment dweller next door, the extended kin living on islands thousands of miles away.[32] They extend funds to them, take them in when they have nowhere else to go, loan them money, and lend them an ear. Yet it is striking, despite this clearly observable behavior, how an ideology of independence, an almost fierce defense of the idea of being alone and self-reliant, endures. And for some it is not just words, but a genuine description of how they understand their lives. Whether or not they are actually on their own, they feel they should be able to cope by themselves.

Social support makes a significant difference for health. Married people, for example, live longer and enjoy better health than do single people.[33] People who score high on measures of "network density," the extent to which they have close friends on whom they rely, are healthier than those with weak ties. "People who need people" are less susceptible to illness. Those with weak networks get sick at a much higher rate and recover more slowly than those who are embedded in thick social networks.[34]

Of course, one can have too much of a good thing. Many of the people we interviewed coupled their comments about the importance of being independent with self-portraits as "givers." They don't take the help of others, but they provide support to them because they are generous and independent at the same time. They don't want their friends to think they *expect* reciprocity. They extend themselves to others but do not want to be perceived as "rolling up credits" in some imaginary favor bank, to be cashed in one day when a crisis strikes.

*   *   *

Ill health contributes in powerful ways to the difficulty of managing the aging experience in inner-city communities. The stresses and strains that poor families face are magnified when their bodies begin to crumble, a crumbling that seems to develop at an earlier age than we might expect. Chronic conditions like diabetes, hypertension, and serious diseases like cancer or heart disease crop up with greater frequency and at an earlier point in the life span than they do in advantaged communities. When families confront these challenges armed with the resources of two parents who can support each other in the face of adversity, or from the safety of a calm neighborhood, they can manage with the least disruption. Extended families that pull together tap the "people resources" they can contribute to the care of their elderly aunts and uncles or sick children.

The hardest hit are inner-city dwellers whose family ties or friendships have withered or who are simply too burdened to step in and take on more. The difference between Frida—who is not sure that she has anyone she can count on—and Daisy—who knows she does—is not so much a matter of the severity of their disabilities or even the income at their disposal. It is the difference between a weak system of social supports and a strong one.

6–Does Race Matter?

For most people, reaching middle age is less about striving–that overdrive in search of a better job, a better home, a better life–and more about arrival and, to some extent, looking back to evaluate the meaning of the journey. For some the exercise is tinged with regret. Without that false step, that chance encounter with a malevolent boss, a mean-spirited teacher, or a girlfriend who turned out to be bad news, everything would have turned out better. For others, the retrospective gaze is a celebration of small victories, happy accidents, and deliberate choices that opened up possibilities that might otherwise have been closed.

American culture plucks out of the many conceivable explanations for an individual's fate those that center on individual decisions that we control, at least in theory. This is not a universal perspective. One can imagine cultures– and they do exist–where an individual's destination is not understood as the culmination of personal decisions over the life course. Rather, we could focus on the way the Great Depression or the Jim Crow era limited chances, or the way World War II created tight labor markets and jobs aplenty. We *could* focus on how history carved up the social landscape in ways that all but determined the fate of particular individuals. We tend not to, however. Instead, the culture of individualism and self-determination that has been the country's hallmark almost since its inception locates blame and credit in the character and actions of individuals and for the most part subtracts the history that has shaped their options.[1]

The suburban white families I have studied over the years had their own crosses to bear when it came to explaining to themselves (and my tape recorder) why they ended up in the condition I found them in. Unemployed executives, air traffic controllers who were fired en mass at the outset of the

Reagan presidency,[2] factory workers whose jobs evaporated—they all had disappointments they felt a need to account for. Yet in none of these interviews—and I did hundreds for my studies of middle-class mobility—did race figure. White people never mentioned, and as far as I know never thought, that being white made any difference in explaining what had befallen them, either for good or for ill. Race did not register.

This is what researchers who study the sociological phenomenon of "whiteness"[3] mean when they say that race is invisible to whites. Whites are largely oblivious to the ways in which race matters, because as far as they can see it does not for them. This is true not only for "personal fate" but for "group fate" as well. No one ever asks white people to account for the poverty that afflicts the members of their racial group, even though whites outnumber all other racial groups in the ranks of the American poor.[4] Whites do not constitute a group whose outcomes need to be explained.

Another reality shapes the experience of blacks and Latinos in this country. They *are* asked to account for the state of their poorest brethren. I am not suggesting that middle-class minorities are held responsible for what actually becomes of their lower-class counterparts. Only among the most nationalist of thinkers, bent on creating a sense of guilt and allegiance among middle-class minorities, is there ever a suggestion that the actions of upwardly mobile blacks have shaped the misfortune of fellow ethnics. Nonetheless, explanations are demanded by researchers, church leaders, and ordinary citizens who feel a sense of responsibility, a tinge of shame, a need to account for the distressing condition of inner-city ghettoes, the disproportionate imprisonment of minority men, or high rates of out-of-wedlock pregnancy. Race is presumed to have something to do with these outcomes. Liberals argue this on the grounds that racial prejudice and discrimination have structured the outcomes by limiting job opportunities or consigning poor children to lousy schools. Conservatives argue that the welfare state has preconditioned poor minorities to think the country owes them a free ride and therefore opened the doors to loose behavior that leads people to jail, single parenthood, or crime-ridden streets. Either way, race matters. And because this is understood on all sides of the political spectrum, race becomes central to the scripts that explain why differential outcomes are everywhere to be seen.

I hasten to add that when minorities, or for that matter whites, invoke race as a means of understanding why some people are poor or have lousy jobs while others are driving BMWs, the central tendency of individualism still resonates. Race explains the presence of hurdles. For some it accounts for particular burdens, psychological or cultural. It does not absolve people from the demand, which everyone in this society save very committed radicals issue, to leap over those barriers.

Individuals are supposed to "get over" the road blocks, despite the fact that those obstacles may be inherently unfair or excessively debilitating even for very talented and driven people. It is a tribute to the power of mainstream American ideals that we hold ourselves to such a high standard of performance and cut one another so very little slack when we overlook the structural pressures that shape group outcomes. We are quick to point to the counterexample, the person who has managed to surmount incredible barriers, and claim that success as evidence that everyone should be able to follow suit. Those who don't have only themselves to blame.

This is not just a "white" point of view. Indeed, I have found it a more powerful subtext among African Americans and Latinos, even those who can explain in painful detail how poverty has limited their options, how their neighborhoods have been trashed by landlords who didn't care or by police who swaggered into their midst with trouble in mind, or how gangs have roamed the streets and swept up their children and their friends. Even under these conditions, the insistence that individuals make a difference, that they can make choices and that they should be held responsible for the consequences of poor judgment, is nearly universal among these New Yorkers. Whites, ironically, are much more likely to give minorities the benefit of the doubt, to at least articulate the ways in which systematic disadvantage might explain poor outcomes. Blacks, by contrast, will explain in detail what those disadvantages are and then go on at great length with those exceptions that prove the rule: the man who made it, the kid who excelled in school, the young lady who did not get pregnant and graduated as the valedictorian. Exceptions tell us that personal responsibility counts and that when a hurdle rises, respectable people will practically kill themselves to get over it.

Nonetheless, there is much to ponder in the nonrandom nature of bad outcomes, both among youth and among the aged. It escapes no one's attention that poverty afflicts people with dark skins more often, that the kids hanging on the street corner are mainly minorities, that graffiti is not tolerated on Park Avenue but is ever present on the central thoroughfares of Harlem. The connection between race and destination is everywhere. How, then, does it influence the perceptions of older African Americans and Latinos when it comes to accounting for their own lot in life and the pathways of the generations they have helped to raise? It registers as part of an imagined hierarchy, a list of groups that are doing well and groups that are doing poorly, and some "folk explanations" for who sits where.

If this amounted to nothing more than the conclusion that racism holds minorities back it would hardly be worth reporting here. The story turns out to be far more complex. Elders in minority neighborhoods have quite nuanced views on the virtues of other racial groups—principally Jews, Asians, and nebulously defined whites—mixed, in some cases, with resentment or envy. As we will see shortly, though, they are far more likely to turn a critical eye on "their own kind," finding fault in the conduct of members of their own racial communities who, they feel, have squandered opportunities to advance as other, admittedly more favored, groups have done.

We tread here on delicate ground. The relations between blacks and Jews, Puerto Ricans and Dominicans, Asians and blacks have been fraught with tension for years. The race riots that followed the trial of Rodney King in East Los Angeles, for instance, underlined the depth of antagonism that separates Koreans and blacks.[5] The outrage that accompanied the police assault on Abner Louima in New York and the marches sparked by the police shooting of Amadou Diallo in the vestibule of his apartment building are testimony to the depth of mistrust and fury that African Americans and immigrant blacks feel toward the police, and perhaps toward the white world the police generally represent.

Minorities have been on the receiving end of racial prejudice, but they are also known to harbor biases themselves. Anti-Semitism among followers of the Nation of Islam is well documented.[6] Puerto Ricans and Dominicans in New York have long been antagonists, separated by their citizenship status, access to state benefits, and command of English, as well as by the racial divisions that crisscross their nationalities. On a bad day, one can elicit something close to the bitterness that characterizes the most damaged of black-white relations among these Latino groups. Dwelling at length on these feuds is not my purpose, here, however. Instead, we engage this territory in order to understand how late-middle-aged and elderly minorities invoke race as an explanation for the fate of their own groups, how they see the pecking order of privilege that surrounds their own, relatively powerless, neighborhoods. Only with this template in hand can we understand the dynamic tension that underlies assessments individuals render of their own lot in life, now that they have reached their mature years and no longer see for themselves major change on the horizon. For these inner-city New Yorkers straddle competing explanations of personal fate: those that emphasize forces larger than any individual and those that stress the choices individuals make that shape their own future.

Table 6.1

Who Is Hard Working?*

On a scale of 1 (not true at all) to 5 (very true),
this ethnic group is hardworking.

Group in question	Mean rating	% of sample giving this group a 5 (very true) rating
Immigrant blacks	4.11	50.5
Dominicans	4.01	48.0
American whites	3.83	39.4
Puerto Ricans	3.65	34.7
American-born blacks	3.36	25.3

*Using a p-value cutoff of $<.01$, the following differences are statistically significant: the difference between Dominicans and American-born blacks; whites and American-born blacks; immigrant blacks and American-born blacks; and immigrant blacks and Puerto Ricans.

Values Matter

Hard work, ambition, and drive—these are qualities Americans invoke when they explain whom they admire in this world. As Max Weber explained long ago in his classic tome, *The Protestant Ethic and the Spirit of Capitalism*, religious devotion to good works transmuted itself into a secular preoccupation with what we commonly call the "work ethic." It now suffuses a very mainstream conception of what makes for a respectable adult. Hence, when we say that a group has the reputation for being "hardworking," we mean much more than a simple statement about how they spend their time. We are noting, too, that they approximate the ideal to which all social groups should aspire, regardless of whether they end up poor or rich.

As Table 6.1 suggests, among the minority groups we queried, there is a distinct perception that the foreign born are the hardest-working members of our society, independent of race. Black immigrants are given the highest mean rating of all the ethnic groups in our survey. Close on their heels are the Dominicans, the only other true immigrant group in the survey, since Puerto Ricans are in fact U.S. citizens. Whites are the middle group, appearing to be in a neutral position. Both Puerto Ricans and American-born blacks are at the bottom of the list.

If this were just a matter of one group casting a slur against another, we might chalk up this finding to the permeation of stereotypes. Immigrants are popularly understood as hardworking and African Americans often charac-

Table 6-2

Perceptions of Work Ethic by Ethnic Group

On a scale of 1 (not at all true) to 5 (very true),
this ethnic group is hardworking.

Ethnic group in question	RESPONDENTS		
	Puerto Ricans	Dominicans	African Americans
Immigrant blacks	4.09	4.00	4.24
American whites	4.22	3.82	3.47
Dominicans	3.53	4.45	4.03
Puerto Ricans	3.69	3.27	4.00
American-born blacks	3.22	2.97	3.88

terized as lazy in unflattering explanations for their disproportionate poverty rates. We might imagine that the people who answered our survey are merely reflecting what the society as a whole has come to believe about the drive to work among different groups. Table 6.2 should give us pause, however. While each group generally views members of its own ethnicity in slightly more favorable terms than does the whole sample of respondents, the rank order changed only a bit.

Blacks believe that immigrant blacks work the hardest, while Dominicans see themselves as the hardest working of these groups. All three put native-born blacks near the bottom of this continuum. They vary to a degree about who occupies the middle ground. African Americans don't think very much of the work ethic of whites, in large part (as we will see shortly) because they believe the "breaks" routinely go to whites who, as a consequence, don't really have to work very hard in order to stay on top of the social system. Puerto Ricans don't agree with this conclusion, however, since they put whites ahead of Dominicans, the only other immigrant group on the list besides black immigrants.

Working hard is a key virtue, but it may be one that can be displayed only by people who have work in the first place. Who makes the most of the opportunities that are available? This question puts a little more "spin" on the work-ethic question because it asks the respondent to go beyond scanning the social horizon to note who is working and how hard. It forces some reflection on whether the groups in question are bothering to take advantage of whatever opportunities there might be in the labor market, in school, or in general. Here, too, African Americans see themselves in a negative light.

Table 6-3

Opportunity Ethic

On a scale of 1 (not at all true) to 5 (very true),
this ethnic group does not take advantage of opportunities.

Ethnic group in question	Puerto Ricans	Respondents Dominicans	African Americans
American-born blacks	3.25	2.97	3.12
Puerto Ricans	3.03	2.76	2.64
Dominicans	2.97	2.58	2.67
Immigrant blacks	2.53	2.73	2.59
American whites	2.00	2.00	2.41

Table 6.3 shows that they believe that American-born blacks are perceived as the least likely of the five ethnic groups mentioned to take advantage of opportunities, while whites are most likely to do so. Puerto Ricans hardly disagree at all, placing themselves close to the bottom too. Dominicans are the only group of respondents who grant themselves credit for making the most of what is "out there."

During the period when the New York survey was conducted, welfare reform was in the air. Indeed, the Personal Responsibility and Work Opportunity Reconciliation Act was passed in 1996, only a few months before our survey was launched. Debates filled the airwaves about why AFDC had become such a problem, why the country was burdened by generation after generation of "welfare queens" who were content to raise one child after another on the public purse. The fact that only a tiny fraction of welfare recipients could even conceivably be described in these terms seemed to escape notice. Instead, the whole "AFDC population" was vilified as a drag on the system, and liberal architects of the safety net were deemed responsible for creating a dependency problem that the honest taxpayer had to support year after year. Liberal defenders of those single mothers needing a helping hand tried in vain to point out that the vast majority of welfare recipients were short-term users with smaller families than the national average.[7]

The conservatives won the day, however, and in the course of the debate managed to shift the national conversation about what kind of safety net the country should offer its most vulnerable citizens. The casualty, along the way, was the reputation of social welfare as a legitimate stopgap. Then again, welfare was never a popular program.[8] It always suffered from the stigma

Table 6-4

Preference for Welfare?

On a scale of 1 (not at all true) to 5 (very true), this ethnic group
would rather be on welfare than work.

Ethnic group in question	Puerto Ricans	Respondents Dominicans	African Americans
American-born blacks	3.43	3.06	2.29
Puerto Ricans	3.38	3.09	2.35
Immigrant blacks	2.66	2.79	1.94
Dominicans	3.00	2.52	1.85
American whites	2.09	2.36	2.00

that attaches to those who do not work in a society where nothing less will do. How, then, did these attitudes filter down to our survey respondents? As Table 6.4 suggests, they generally did not think any of these ethnic groups preferred to be on welfare rather than to work for a living. Still, they were more inclined to think this was true of African Americans than of Latinos and rarely saw whites in this light. Each minority group tended to be harder, more self-critical, of their own members than those of other groups. On the whole, though, everyone rejected the assertion that any of the groups in question found welfare more attractive than working.[9]

This is an important finding. Without it we might have concluded simply that stereotypes common among whites have surfaced in minority public opinion as well.[10] The welfare versus work question tells us this is not the case. For while each of these minority groups leans on a consistent hierarchy of ethnic "desirability" (hardworking, opportunity driven), they equally clearly decline to see any of these groups as actively preferring dependency to self-support. Hence they may not work hard, but they prefer to work, and they may not seize all opportunities, but that is not because they like welfare.

How, then, might they explain the absence of the work ethic? Could education or discrimination play a role? The survey gives us some clues to this effect. As Table 6.5 shows very clearly, black people—whether native born or immigrant—are perceived as suffering the most discrimination of any ethnic group in the society. The degree of uniformity here is very strong. More than two-thirds of the respondents in our survey thought it was very true that African Americans and immigrant blacks were the victims of discrimination. No other question we asked generated this much agreement.

Table 6-5
Perceptions of Discrimination

Ethnic group in question	Puerto Ricans	Dominicans	African Americans
Immigrant blacks	4.03	4.52	4.47
American-born blacks	3.81	4.39	4.74
Dominicans	3.50	4.39	4.33
Puerto Ricans	3.38	3.70	4.0
American whites	1.16	1.39	1.82

In addition, all three subscribe to the view that American whites are free from this burden. There is an awareness of the roadblocks that minorities—especially blacks—face in the marketplace and elsewhere.

Education is an important part of the equation as well. Lack of a quality education is understood, even by people who are not well educated themselves, as a barrier to success in our society. It is one thing to have the opportunity to get ahead in school and refuse to pursue it. It is quite another to lack that chance. Survey respondents seem ambivalent about this issue. They may believe that blacks and other minorities face discrimination in a general sense, but they do not feel strongly that as a group they lack the opportunity to pursue a good education. That said, they are unanimous in seeing whites as facing no real hurdles in this domain and believe some kind of gap exists between the good fortune of the majority racial group and the more problematic access of minorities, including immigrants, to this key resource.

Thus far I have stressed the views that African Americans, Dominicans, and Puerto Ricans have about one another and, to a limited degree, the way they contrast these qualities with the corresponding characteristics of whites. A general portrait emerges from this survey exercise of minorities who agree across the ethnic spectrum that African Americans are the most disadvantaged group in their midst, but who also see them as somewhat deserving of this destination in the sense that it is lack of the work ethic or the drive to take advantage of opportunity that is placing them in this boat. Immigrants—both black and Dominican—are seen as having plenty of drive and as eager to take up new opportunities, yet facing an uphill climb in terms of discrimination. Whites are understood to be more like immigrants, though not as driven, and facing no barriers in their efforts to move up.

How do the views of New Yorkers compare to national surveys of racial

Table 6-6

Educational Access

On a scale of 1 (not at all true) to 5 (very true), this ethnic group doesn't have the same chance for a good education.

Ethnic group in question	Puerto Ricans	Respondents Dominicans	African Americans
Dominicans	2.06	3.06	3.70
Immigrant blacks	2.22	2.91	3.71
American-born blacks	1.91	2.67	3.65
Puerto Ricans	1.84	2.42	3.58
American whites	1.13	1.64	1.26

attitudes? The General Social Survey, a yearly effort to assess the attitudes of a nationally representative sample of Americans, asks a comparable set of questions. Sociologist Tom Smith at the University of Chicago published an important book, titled *Ethnic Images*, drawing on the 1990 GSS, and his findings echo the view of the New Yorkers in this book. Smith looked at data to understand how Americans view six different groups in our society: whites, Jews, blacks, Asian-Americans, Hispanic Americans, and southern whites. Each of these groups was evaluated along a set of dimensions similar to the ones we have just examined: wealth, work ethic, violence-prone, intelligent, dependent, and patriotic. Smith calculated a summary score that added up these dimensions, comparing each group against a base-line score attached to whites. Here is what he found.

"In groups" routinely score themselves higher than they are themselves rated by "out groups" on these dimensions, but the summary tells it all.[11] The rankings we see in our New York study are consistent with the national picture.

Group reputation is a small piece of the puzzle of race issues as they shape perceptions of outcomes. We must dig down a bit deeper to understand how racial structures translate into power and privilege for some and exclude others, partly for unfair reasons and partly because of the way the less privileged shoot themselves in the foot. It is the combination of these views—which stress personal responsibility and structural barriers—that gives us an uneasy and often contradictory sense of how race plays a role in who gets what in the city and, by extension, why growing older is harder on some people than it is on others.

Table 6-7
Group Differences in the General Social Survey
(1990)

Ethnic group	Summary Score
Jews	+.75
Whites	0
Southern whites	−2.32
Asian Americans	−2.65
Hispanic Americans	−5.70
Blacks	−6.29

The Ethnic Landscape

Who are the players, in terms of racial groups, as African Americans, Dominicans, and Puerto Ricans see it? Who is really in control of resources—
power, money—and in what ways are they visible to these minority groups?
Older African Americans could point to three ethnic groups of whites with
whom they had some contact, although the connection has grown increasingly distant: Jews, Italians, and the Irish.

When the survey respondents were young, the Jews were most often the
landlords and the owners of retail stores in black neighborhoods. African
Americans were tenants and customers. Before the 1960s, they might well
have been neighbors as well. After the great suburban exodus began, this
relationship became more distant, mutating from local business owner to
absentee owner and landlord. The distance may help to explain why today
distinctions between Jews and other whites are fading to the point where the
two terms are often used interchangeably in some areas of Manhattan and
the Bronx, where the actual degree of contact between the two groups is less
frequent. Brooklyn, where many of the African Americans in this book reside, is another story. Hassidic Jews, who are very clearly marked by their
nineteenth-century clothing, live side by side with African Americans and
black immigrants in the neighborhood near Coney Island called Crown
Heights.

American-born Jews were less interested in maintaining these family businesses in increasingly segregated black and brown neighborhoods and began
selling out to Asians, especially Koreans, Chinese, and South Asian Indians,
who continue to maintain much of the commercial infrastructure of the city's
poor minority neighborhoods. Relations between these Asian shopkeepers

and the customers they serve are fraught with mistrust[12] on both sides. Shop-keepers are wary of shoplifting in part because they work on tight profit margins. As recent immigrants, their command of English is often tenuous and their "tight" or subdued demeanor is apt to appear to an American observer as aloof or suspicious. Customers resent being watched and fol-lowed in anticipation of shoplifting since the vast majority of them wouldn't dream of taking something they hadn't paid for. The onus falls particularly on the shoulders of young men.

The Irish once dominated the police force and tended to live in their own residential enclaves in Hell's Kitchen on the lower west side of Manhattan until they moved en masse out to the suburbs of Long Island. However, the police force in the city is still heavily Irish, now commuting from some dis-tance to patrol neighborhoods that are sometimes resentful of their presence. Italians, too, joined the police force in large numbers, even after they departed their own ethnic neighborhoods. Friction between these whites and the mi-nority neighborhoods they patrol has boiled over on many occasions, with celebrated cases of police brutality capturing public attention and sparking angry protests by minority leaders.[13] Indeed, the fact that these cases have involved black immigrants (Haitian and Jamaican) who are indistinguishable on the street from African Americans has joined the two oft-separated communities—immigrant and native born—into a single political force in op-position to the cops and then Mayor Giuliani. Evidence of police corruption, which has been a special problem in the 30th Precinct, where many of our respondents live, has not endeared the police to the community either.

Under Mayor Giuliani's leadership, the police embarked on an aggressive campaign against crime in these neighborhoods, showering resources and attention on them that most residents felt was long overdue. For though they dislike the police they are even less enamored of the criminals who make life difficult and the streets dangerous to walk. The "community policing" cam-paign targeted these high-crime zones, saturating them with surveillance and arrests for "quality of life" violations (jaywalking, graffiti tagging, double parking) in hopes of netting the bad guys before they could cause serious trouble. Young men living in small apartments prone to overheating on a summer's day were accustomed to standing on street corners with a bottle of beer in a paper bag, shooting the breeze. This has become a difficult pastime in Washington Heights or Harlem because the cleanup campaign directs the police to break these groups up and hustle those young men off the streets.

Crime rates dropped precipitously in New York through the 1990s, to the vast relief of most city residents (of all colors).[14] While the same trend has occurred in other cities[15] that have pursued a different strategy of policing,[16] the operating assumption—at least according to some analysts—has been that intense surveillance and iron control are the reasons for this positive trend. Once crime rates fell, however, the police had to "fish" even more intensively to find the bad guys who were left on the streets. So many of them were already locked up that driving the numbers down even further meant combing the remaining residents even more thoroughly, looking for that (now more rare) needle in the haystack.

How do the elderly see this situation? Like many others outside the criminal ranks, they are of two minds. They are often the first victims of street crime, and in the days when the cops seemed to pay no attention whatsoever to their vulnerability, they felt abandoned by the authorities. It is a relief for them to be able to venture outdoors now without worrying as much about whether they will be knocked over by a purse snatcher or caught in the crossfire of a drug shoot-out. They are even willing to tolerate a high level of police harassment of their own sons and grandsons in service of the objective of making the neighborhood a safer place to live.

Yet the color of the policeman's skin does not go unnoticed. It is emblematic of an inequality in power relations that grates. Older people, particularly those who arrived from the South and remember all too well the occupying force of the "white man's army," are sensitive to the abuses of authority.[17] They resent mightily the ethnic slurs they hear coming from behind the badge and the closing of ranks that seems to accompany any investigation of police misconduct. It reminds them of a past that was none too happy and reawakens the sense of a racially defined "us" and "them."

These tensions are exacerbated, no doubt, by economic transitions that, until recently, worked to the disadvantage of minorities in the city. The flight of low-skilled job opportunities (particularly in manufacturing) and the increasing importance of education in accessing the remaining work opportunities[18] changed the occupational landscape in the 1980s and early '90s in ways that affected young adults and many mature workers as well.[19] Poverty rates did not change very much overall, but the geographic concentration of poverty increased, as the haves moved out and the have nots stayed put. Even now, as labor markets have tightened and employment rates have moved way up, an increasing proportion of the full-time work force is earning poverty-level wages.[20] This economic backdrop has increased the sense that a rising tide still leaves a lot of boats barely treading water, and exacerbates the view that whites have it easy while minorities are still in trouble.

Welfare reform, too, has had consequences for the perception that minorities do not get a fair shake. In general, the people whom we interviewed are harsh critics of the welfare system. They have been working people most of their lives and they don't particularly appreciate the way in which their paychecks are docked to support people who are not willing or able to take the kinds of jobs they endure. However, they also have adult children who have fallen on hard times, or have created hard times for themselves, who needed some of that assistance and no longer have it. When AFDC melted away into a much weaker TANF, the consequences changed the lives of many of the older women who appear in this volume. They were often the ones forced to pick up the child-care pieces, when they'd rather just put their feet up and let their daughters (and sons) join the labor force. Hence as much as they detest welfare and even denigrate their own kin for using it, it has not been lost on them that the powers that be, who are mainly white after all, seem to have it in for minorities.

That feeling has been exacerbated in recent years in New York as African Americans watched new Russian immigrants embraced by AFDC as part of their refugee assistance packages, while they themselves caught the brunt of the relentlessly negative image of "welfare queens." Particularly galling to those who were in the welfare system was the high-handed treatment they received at the hands of black caseworkers who were often in fact only a few steps above them on the income ladder. The juxtaposition of these two experiences—humiliation by "one's own" and open arms for white immigrants—did little to improve black/white race relations among the poor. Though only some of the people we interviewed were themselves caught in the jaws of AFDC, almost all of them have relatives who are or were. Whatever harsh views they have of people who depend on welfare, their feelings about those who run the system are even less sympathetic.

Ethnic discord is not limited to the black/white boundaries. Puerto Ricans and Dominicans are often tense along the dividing lines that separate them. The "older" of these two groups, Puerto Ricans have been moving to the mainland and back again to the island since the early 1940s, when they were actively recruited as factory labor.[21] Initially enclaved in tight, monolingual neighborhoods on the upper west side of Manhattan, succeeding generations of Nuyoricans have fanned out into other areas of the city (and other cities altogether). They speak English as a second, and often first, language at a much higher frequency than do Dominicans, who are the more recent arrivals. While both of these Latino populations are poor, the Dominicans are quite a bit poorer on average than the Puerto Ricans. Even so, where Puerto Ricans (as U.S. citizens) can avail themselves of public assistance benefits as well as any other Americans, Dominicans lack residency rights and any automatic claim to these vital sources of support for the poor.

The pecking order that places Puerto Ricans above Dominicans locally finds its origins off shore. Dominicans often migrate first to Puerto Rico before they come to the mainland United States and find themselves at the bottom of the labor market on the island.[22] They work as domestics, baby-sitters, and a host of other poorly paid jobs that mark them as low status. Thus long before members of either ethnic group arrived in New York, a status hierarchy had already colored their relations, with Puerto Ricans feeling a degree of class superiority toward Dominicans. The fact that both groups are poor and confined in large numbers to the Spanish-speaking enclaves of the Big Apple has not entirely wiped clean the distinctions that have shaped their relations far from these shores.

Racial differences also cleave these Latino communities. Dominicans often reflect their distant African heritage while Puerto Ricans typically look more Spanish. Color means something quite different in the Caribbean and elsewhere in Latin America than it does in the United States.[23] Recall (from chapter one) the shock that Darlene Cawley's mother felt when confronted by the harsh racial divide in Mobile, Alabama. Caribbean countries are not free of prejudice and it has long been the case that people of European descent are higher in status than are the more African or Indian populations of those countries. These distinctions, though not binary, have carried over to powerfully affect the relations between more African-looking Dominicans and the more Spanish-looking Puerto Ricans. Once the assimilation process kicks into gear, Dominicans often find themselves at arm's length from Puerto Ricans on account of a racial divide that does not function in the same fashion in either group's homeland.[24]

How People Get Power

This brief excursion into the sociological relations between different ethnic and racial groups in New York does not tell us very much about how these experiences inform the way people place themselves in the racial terrain. Yet there is no doubt that race matters in the way that minorities see the patterns of their individual lives, the fates of their family members, and the condition of the communities in which they live. Power and privilege elude them; their voices are rarely heard in the din of New York politics. They do not recognize much of a kinship in the people who claim to represent their interests. And they often look with a mixture of envy and admiration at the successes of other ethnic groups who occupy better jobs, safer neighborhoods, and live out their lives in greater comfort, with more social authority. Figuring out why life worked out this way is part of the process of growing old in the inner city.

Barry James was born in 1944 and raised in a poor black neighborhood in South Carolina. He now lives in Fort Greene, Brooklyn, not far from the public housing project where Frida and her two sons live. Fort Greene has been gentrifying at a steady pace as middle-class folk, black and white, flee Manhattan's ever-escalating housing prices. Long Island University is the largest institution nearby, and from its portals one sees thousands of students, mainly blacks and Latinos, pouring out the doors, backpacks loaded with books. Multicolored flags fly from the rooftop of the university's main building, located along the wide boulevard leading to the Brooklyn Bridge. A bustling commercial street with cafes, photocopying shops, flower stands, and business offices, the whole area is something of a success story of urban renewal.

Barry came to Fort Greene many years ago, when he was first starting his job in the post office. Back then he was an entry-level clerk just recently out of the army. He didn't make a lot of money, so he accepted a second job as a security guard at Macy's department store in Midtown, a few subway stops up the #2 express train that leads from Brooklyn into Manhattan. These two jobs combined put Barry and his wife, who worked as well, into an income bracket that gave them some security, a little extra to put in the bank and eventually contribute to the college education of their daughter. And it kept them living in a place where most people worked hard and the rest were retired. The riffraff kept across the way, separated from their neighborhood by a large boulevard that kept them out of sight and mostly out of mind.[25]

As the years went by, Barry became a postal supervisor and was able to quit the Macy's job. Thanks to the union, he earns a very respectable $35,000 a year with good benefits and can look forward to a reasonable retirement. A twenty-five-year employee now, Barry figures that day is about ten years into the future. In the meantime, he feels a sense of satisfaction in what he has accomplished for himself and sees the "proof of the pudding" in his daughter's career.

> I think I've made a lot of progress, you know, going back to the way I was raised. Everything was so different then. It was harder and a lot of things wasn't available where I born and raised at. And today, I've made great progress.
>
> The main thing I'm proud of is to see that my daughter finished college and she is going for her master's. She has another year to finish

it. Me, myself personally, I feel great. At the age I am, I think I'm in very good shape. Look good, feel good. I've been able to save money and living good, living very comfortable. I still have a few things I want to do, to accomplish, but the majority of things I have so that makes me satisfied up to this point.

With this history, one might imagine Barry would understand the world as a set of level playing fields where those who work hard pull ahead and those who don't fall by the wayside. Yet this is not how he sees the social universe: a lot of those playing fields aren't so level, he tells us.

It's not an equal situation between being Afro-American and being white in the United States. Whites are better off than the Afro-American or other minority groups in this country. They're favored more for just about everything. They make more; they have better incomes. They have better housing. Everything is in their favor.

As Barry sees it, privileged white "haves" confront black "have nots" who must struggle for every inch of ground. Other minorities, particularly new immigrants, learn from racist whites that they should look down on African Americans. Ignorant people generalize from the bad behavior of a few young toughs and project this onto the whole community of blacks, the vast majority of whom have even more contempt for juvenile delinquency in their midst than do distant whites. Barry believes that these reputational insults affect every African American who is trying to make it the hard way. Enclosed in a sea of competition for a decent education, good jobs, and housing, African Americans are routinely handicapped by the terrible public image unfairly handed them. He knows this firsthand.

Blacks are not seen the way they should be seen because a lot of other nationalities have been poisoned from the whites about blacks. I've experienced that when I was overseas [in the service]. We would have a conversation with other nationalities or different races and a lot of things that they have heard or thought of us wasn't true. So unless they actually dealt with us in some kind of way, they see us different from what we are. More of an underclass person or something like that, less fortunate.

It's what they was told, what they read from the news media or what not. Which don't always give the truth. I've found that to be a fact. And some of the things they [conclude] from a few incidents that happened [among] the Afro-American race, especially the young ones. And they take for granted that the majority of the race are like that.

These are not abstract attitudes that merely prevent people from getting to know one another. Barry believes that these underlying views influence decisions that powerful people make when they dole out the goods. Because they believe blacks are unworthy, they are inclined not to give honest workers a chance. That was the rule of the day in the South, where Barry grew up, and he will admit that much has improved since the Jim Crow era, when he first tried to find work. Even so, for every step forward below the Mason-Dixon line, Barry thinks he detects a step backward on the other side. "In the North," he says with conviction, "it's gotten a little worse." Equality is elusive, especially on the job.

Everyone is not equal on the job! Not in this country, anyway. Not in this city. I notice it on my job. Sometimes some nationality or some race gets promoted before the others or what not. And you can see where you go in different stores and you see more of certain nationalities than you see with some of the others, especially African Americans. Especially today in New York City. I visit stores, places, firms and a lot of them you don't even see Afro-Americans working. You see other nationalities that come from other countries.

New York has always been a magnet for immigrants. Over the last twenty years, Barry has noticed a change in the pace. Newcomers from poorer countries are flooding into the city. He has nothing against them per se, but he can see that the jobs that might once have been there for the picking, especially for black people who weren't well educated, became harder to access when Latinos and Asians showed up ready to work for very little.[26] Why were they able to displace native-born workers who, after all, could speak the language? On the plus side, immigrants *do* work hard. "It's just like when the Afro-Americans came up from the South," Barry explains. "They worked hard and then after a while everybody falls into the same boat." Driving oneself hard is a quality Barry sees in newcomers who have no choice, who know nothing different, who are not accustomed to the more relaxed attitudes of the American workforce as a whole. He doesn't believe we should all aspire to the immigrant orientation. They are, after all, coming here because they want something that isn't readily available in their own countries, including the opportunity *not* to work until you drop for a low wage.

There is another reason, he argues, why blacks are having a harder time in the labor market. Immigrants can trade on the inferior reputation of African Americans and snap up those jobs because employers would rather have almost anyone other than blacks, especially black men.[27] Even in the post office, a bastion of equal opportunity, Barry saw only a gradual evolution from a promotion system that privileged whites to something closer to a fair shake. But the glass ceilings are still there for old-timers to see.

I've been [at the post office] for thirty years now and I know many time, especially when I first started back in the sixties, there was a lot of favoritism. The whites got better breaks, better job positions, just plain outright. No ifs, ands about it. Things are a little different now than what it was then because, I guess, there's more involvement from other organizations to see that a lot of things should be more equal. But its still higher managers are more whites than Afro-American, Asian, Hispanics. It shouldn't be [like that] but it is.

Darlene Cawley lives in the same neighborhood as Barry James, but she has a different take on the race and opportunity question. She grew up in a more integrated setting that slowly became the racially segregated Willoughby Avenue she knew as an adult, with its descent into poverty. She is aware, of course, that race matters and that bias exists. Indeed, Darlene realizes that African Americans are among the least-liked social groups in the country, even by blacks who come here from other parts of the world.

A lot of minority groups dislike the [American] blacks almost as much as some of the whites do! They look down at them. I was in a car the other day talking to this black African driver. . . . He just looked down at American blacks as such a terrible [group]. You're from the West Indies, you're from Africa, you're from somewhere else. It's not half as bad as being born here in the United States. Blacks claim that foreigners are taking everything and that's why they can't go anywhere. It just a vicious circle. West Indians are more hardworking. I mean they could just get off the boat and two months later they've got a house. They have to borrow from every relative that they've got. And American blacks just feel that they [would have] to want nothing, work for nothing [to compete].

Tensions in the labor market that pit one group against another set up a social dividing line between people who look the same and are often confused for one another by outsiders.[28] When it comes down to it, though, Darlene thinks that people like Barry make too much of the whole issue of discrimination, that they think in groups rather than as individuals, failing to see how much personal character matters. Yes, there are these pernicious dividing lines between immigrants and the native born, between blacks and whites. You can get chewed up by the divisions and the aggravation they cause. We end up so sick with a sort of racial fever that we are blind to the opportunities that present themselves.

> As long as there's black [people], there's going to be discrimination. You can't stop a human being from thinking the way they want to think. There are means and ways to [combat] discrimination now. But people make too much of it. How do you know that employer's not going to hire you solely because you are not qualified? It's got nothing to do with this white girl or because you're black. I think what happens is we get so hung up on [thinking about discrimination] that we don't take the choices that we could do, the things that are open to us. We get so caught up in the [race thing] that it just gets out of hand. Like a sickness. It eats at us. After a while, we don't like nobody white, we don't like nobody Hispanic.

Darlene would not deny that racial divisions and conflicts between the native born and immigrants set up real divisions that have serious consequences. Even when these tensions derive from fictional stereotypes, they do their damage. She merely adds that focusing on those preexisting barriers leads people to dwell so much on racial division that they can no longer see past artificial distinctions to the individual characteristics that should (and actually do) matter.

Emphasizing personal qualities over structural barriers is both a matter of conviction and a consequence of a certain exhaustion or pessimism about the fate of race relations. As we learned in chapter one, Darlene got a firsthand look at what an apartheid-like system of racial exclusion does to people during her early years in Mobile. Her own mother was so stunned by the horrors of the Jim Crow South that she uprooted the whole family to get away from it. New York City was clearly a huge improvement over the extreme racism of Alabama. Indeed, Darlene's youth in New York was something of a genuine melting pot experience, since she lived in a racially, ethnically, and religiously mixed neighborhood for years until it drifted toward segregation. Yet perhaps because that youthful experience of integration did give way to separation and a downward spiral into neighborhood poverty, Darlene has come to think that race relations are stuck in neutral. Clearly, compared to the pre–civil rights days, there is much to be thankful for, but the pace of change has slowed to a crawl.

> Well, I'll tell you, at one point I thought it had gotten better. Now I won't say it's gotten worse. I don't think it's going anywhere. I think a lot of people are not making an effort. They're using little things to start a racial war in the United States. I mean anything, anything. You could call a cop because you've actually seen this child take a soda and it becomes a racial thing between the Koreans and the blacks, between the Arabs and the blacks. I think it's something that needs to be worked on constantly. I don't know what's going to cure it or if there's going to be a cure. I really don't. But I don't think it's gotten any better.

Darlene's pessimism reflects the tensions in black neighborhoods with commercial infrastructures that are in the hands of outsiders. Minority shoppers are objects of suspicion when they patronize stores owned or managed by members of other ethnic groups. On the rare occasion that something goes wrong—a child lifts a soda, a beggar reaches for an apple—the potential for violence in the streets flares like a bonfire. So much conflict, envy, and resentment attends the gap between seemingly prosperous store owners and their poorer customers that residents routinely expect outbursts of name calling and violence to follow. In the past decade, a number of incidents flared into monthlong boycotts of Korean merchants, stunned by the vehemence of local reaction to a simple shoplifting incident.[29] Asian shopkeepers have responded by trying to hire more local residents who can serve as cultural brokers, but the underlying inequality between the have nots in the neighborhood and the proximate representatives of the haves is hard to bridge. Resentment tends to smolder rather than dissipate.

This is, by now, an old story. The Jews and Arabs who managed these stores before the Koreans moved in were also targets of animosity. The repetition of conflict, moving as it does from one ethnic group to another, makes people like Darlene Cawley feel that nothing has changed for the better and causes her to wonder whether there aren't some people who want the warfare to continue.

Sheila Toft, a black woman in her early forties who grew up in a public housing project not far from Willoughby Avenue, is inclined to agree with Darlene that race relations are presently stuck in a rut. She agrees with Barry James that even immigrants, who ought to have a basic respect for all the people who inhabit the city they've come to join, arrive steeped in prejudice.

> Before any foreigner comes to America, they're taught that the black man and woman are very inferior . . . very negative. They feel that black people are less intelligent, less spiritual, less anything—just less. [Immigrants] just put them on the lowest [spot] on the totem pole. So any time somebody foreign comes here . . . they hate—most of the time they hate black people. And it's because of what they are taught.

No other group in our society is burdened by this universal condemnation, says Sheila. "When I'm in an environment with other ethnic groups, by the time they come out knowing me . . . they have a different view, a much more positive view on black individuals." Sheila enters a multiethnic arena knowing that the immigrants present already have convictions about her character. It falls to her to convince them they are wrong. The playing field is, never, level.

It is bad enough to suffer this reputational burden when it emanates from whites whose families have been in the United States for generations. But to realize that complete newcomers—those who have no automatic claim to the jobs, housing, schools, public benefits, and other emblems of good fortune the United States has to offer—start off their "careers" as New Yorkers thinking they are superior to the native-born African Americans they encounter is infuriating. After all, those native-born blacks are taxpayers, voters, and many generations deep in the United States, and they feel entitled to a little respect as part of the larger receiving culture that permits immigrants—including black immigrants—to come on board. To see instead that the cycle of prejudice is repeated before a new immigrant group even has any personal experience with African Americans tells Sheila that this deeply rooted bias may never go away. It awakes in every new generation.

An uncomfortable subtext lies beneath the subject of immigrant trajectories and how they compare to those of poor African Americans. As Sheila sees it, the success stories among immigrants merely reinforce the sorry truth that blacks are on the bottom of the social system, that almost anyone else is regarded as preferable for jobs or placement in elite schools. When a classic form of racial bias—white upon black—was the root of inequality, one could fight with legal remedies that forced a more equitable process of dividing the spoils. Racial groups could demand evidence of equal opportunity, and mount pressure for real results. With immigrant competition, however, it appears as though equally disadvantaged groups are milling about the melting pot, with blacks remaining at the bottom and immigrants clawing their way up the sides. If this is a fair contest, immigrant success becomes one more nail in the coffin of African-American attempts to claim a positive place in

American society. If this is a new prejudice (in favor of immigrants) emerging alongside an old racial bias, then the playing field is, as ever, not level. A new source of competition has merely entered the arena, one that may look the same on the surface of the skin but that capitalizes on another kind of unfairness: the superior reputation of immigrants. This, it would seem, is Sheila's worry.

I think it's going to become a much more visible thing in the future because we have a lot of foreigners here now. And because of that fact, we're able to see [where] blacks are on a scale. They're going to take these foreigners and make them to be what they want to be. The black race is slowly but surely going to be affected by this. There's going to be less of an opportunity for a black person to get, even if they are qualified, even if they are skilled.

You have many more ethnic groups here now. If you have these individuals [who] already have a concept that they are superior to the black person because of what they were taught before they got here. If they already have that, and you have the black person here still trying to make ends meet and getting somewhere in life, they're still going to be on the lower part of the pole because not only do you have white America thinking that the black person is inferior, you have now all these other ethnic groups who are feeling the same way.

If this was just a matter of atmospherics, of tension in the streets or in the local stores, it would be an irritation in a minor key. But as Sheila sees it, real policies that have an impact on life chances for African Americans are "decided" by these atmospherics. Affirmative action is a case in point. It was brought about, she believes, in order to promote opportunity for blacks long denied the good jobs, good schools, and good life in general. Affirmative action forced changes in promotion practices that used to exclude blacks like Barry James from opportunities in places like the post office. And it worked. Affirmative action *did* offer up opportunities that previously had been denied. Today, however, the whole policy is under attack from all directions and has been ruled illegal in many domains, including those of higher education and general employment. From Sheila's perspective, these attacks are not motivated by "race blind" convictions but by those who want to resurrect the days of the good ole boys, when all the best jobs were "wired" on behalf of whites. Why is this happening now? She argues that the bad attitudes toward African Americans never died. They just went underground and are now resurfacing in the form of sub-rosa efforts to dismantle the only policy that really stood a chance of changing the status quo.

> [Race relations] haven't improved. It think it's gotten worse. Affirmative action . . . them trying to do away with affirmative action is a classic example. It's more or less not done up front. It's done behind the scenes, in the background. . . . Affirmative action was clearly stated and put here for black individuals because we were . . . [not] treated up front. Affirmative action just said, "You can't do that no more." Now they're trying to take that away and let it go back to the old way again. And for people to justify this and say, "Well, if [affirmative action] wasn't here, maybe things could be better." It's false, it's false! We still have the same bad things happening. They're just done behind the scenes. There's still the KKK; there's still white supremacists. Things are still going on here, but they are kept under the cover.
>
> The black person is in more trouble than they have been in the last twenty, thirty, maybe even forty years because now they have to com-pete with other people who are telling them that they're nothing. . . . I feel bad for the generation's that's coming up. I think they will survive, but I think it's going to be a hard struggle.

How in the world is it possible that this struggle could be harder now than it was in the Jim Crow era, when official segregation was embraced and the power structure of white society was barely contested? Surely Sheila is exaggerating the alarm she feels, for by no reasonable score can it be the case that African Americans face hurdles like those of that distant, darker past. She would agree with this assessment at one level, and so would Barry and Darlene. They know that New Yorkers have elected black officials, that mi-nority kids are now sought after by elite universities, that bigots must actually go underground rather than be openly discriminatory because it is no longer socially acceptable to be a racist in polite society. Compared to the police state of Alabama in the 1950s, there really is reason to believe that the country has changed.

At least two reasons come to mind that help to explain why people like Sheila do not foreground the good news. First, the upward trajectory they have experienced over the course of their own lives seems to have stalled rather than continued the ascent. As economic inequality has grown, blacks at the bottom of the educational and skill spectrum—including many of their neighbors and their own children—were snared by a spiral of high unem-ployment and a proliferation of low-wage jobs. Those very jobs became the object of fierce competition precisely at the time immigrants from the poorer countries of Central America and the Caribbean descended on New York to compete for them.[30] Hence, in a very direct sense, the situation did get worse. And the attitudes of employers, which often favored immigrants who were indeed seen as harder workers, willing to take lower wages, left their nearest competitors—low-skilled blacks—at a disadvantage.

Second, the unraveling of so many inner-city families left many stranded without much of a support structure when times got hard. Liberal scholars argue that inner-city families came under extraordinary pressures because of increased economic hardship and declining opportunities, leading to collapsing marriage rates and increasing proportions of out-of-wedlock births.[31] Conservatives replied that a values collapse came first, spurred by governmental largesse that removed the disincentives to single motherhood and therefore encouraged erosion in the value of marriage. In this instance, it almost doesn't matter which of these explanations holds water. What does matter is that in the face of an economic situation that clearly did disadvantage inner-city minorities (disproportionately low skilled and poorly educated), the resulting stresses were borne by native-born black and Latino families.

The one category of people that seems not to suffer from this particular liability are the new immigrants. They don't stray very far from one another. When Sheila looks at them, she sees a strength that has all but evaporated among families in her own ethnic group. It might be a virtue that will not withstand the pressures of assimilation, but for the moment this is a genuine advantage that immigrants hold over more fragile American (and particularly American black) families, as Sheila notes.

> When you leave your house behind, other ethnic groups come and they take over the area. You may see an Asian person come—one family. Then you'll see two or three or four or five. You'll see Indians the same way. You'll see other ethnic groups the same way. It's because their concept of family is very important. Black people, because we have been brought up and raised to think like Americans, we're being divided. . . . [We're] tearing up a family structure within the black community and it's gone, it's gone. It's really sad because, you know, we really need to be grouped. As black Americans we need family, we need to regroup, and really start thinking about other generations.

Families are building blocks. With this as a foundation, communities emerge from collections of families. This is what immigrants seem to know and what Americans seem to have forgotten, as Sheila sees it. Prosperous

Americans may not care about this support, or need the backup, but black people are under pressure from all sides and the lack of solid family ties makes it much harder for individuals to manage. They are battered by a cascade of problems that even the strongest individuals cannot deal with by themselves. When Sheila catalogs this litany of obstacles, she fairly pushes herself over the edge of depression. The mess has so many dimensions: the labor market, the criminal justice system, the imploding family, the diminished ranks of the honorable black male. And the consequences come home to roost in the lives of the children, the next generation starting out with so many strikes against it.

> The labor market, it's sad because—well, what can we really say? Within the black community, most of the black men, half of the black men, and this is a fact, are locked up. Okay. So then you have most of the sisters out here compensating for the black men, and they're in the workforce. [But] a woman is not looked upon as being head of a household, as being head of the family; it's the man. We are—and I'm sorry to say this because the black family structure has been torn down. There's brothers in jail, there's brothers out here who's on drugs. And then you're working with [only] one-third of the black brothers here who have education, come from good families, or who just independently decided to do well on their own . . . You have all these black women having children from these men, and they don't have a family structure there. So what's going to happen? Who can they look up to?

Sheila is all too familiar with these problems. She was raised by a single mother who did her heroic best to raise her children right. A minister in her local church, Sheila's mother had a dense web of friends and fellow church members to rely on for support when she needed it, not to mention the kind of iron constitution for which so many black women are known. She was, and remains to this day, Sheila's "rock," the person she turns to for advice whenever she feels lost. Sheila knows that most women don't have those resources to lean on and cannot summon the strength of character that came naturally to her own mother. Few single mothers can fill the void of energy, time, and attention that a husband, working in consort with a wife, can give to a family.[32] The losses are written all over the children who are raised by struggling women who try, but fail, to do it alone.

> There's some very strong black women, like my mother, who basically did a good job with their families. But realistically, a woman shouldn't

be made to do that. . . . When a woman take on what they have to do plus what a man [should] do, it begins to break down, especially within the black community.

Partisans and advocates differ on the question of whether single parents can do as good a job as couples in raising kids. Feminists often react negatively to the notion that women cannot manage on their own; they fear that discussion of men's roles—as disciplinarians, providers, models of masculinity—will reinforce a patriarchal authority that subordinates women to male control. Sheila doesn't agree. She believes men ought to have a special portfolio within the family and that the absence of so many black men from the lives of their children has caused damage that mothers cannot compensate for. Other men can help, but that does not fully undo the mess.

Black children coming up need . . . positive male figures. I didn't have a—my father stayed away, but I had men I could look up to within the community. When I needed advice, I would go see these men. I had positive male images in my community.

When Sheila reflects on the state of her own ethnic community, she sees a battered population, felled by the pressures of prejudice that incline employers to choose almost anyone else before they hire blacks and by the animosity of immigrants who have been taught to believe that African Americans are the lowest of the low. At the same time, she sees the internal failings—whose origins are obscure to her—of black families, which are collapsing all around her as men go missing in action and women struggle to make up for their absence. Cracks have opened up in the foundation that is supposed to undergird the next generation. With nothing solid to stand on, they repeat the cycle of despair. Sheila is at one with the academics who point to the emergence of an urban underclass mired in long-term poverty, with broken families, high rates of out-of-wedlock pregnancy and incarceration, poor schooling, and weakened social control. The hardworking, God-fearing, churchgoing exceptions to these trends are too small in number, as she sees it, to overcome the drag caused by the sheer numbers of families in trouble.

The Jewish/Asian Question

Other ethnic groups who have faced similar challenges in the past managed to meet them and climb to the top of the power pyramid. How did the successful groups get there? What does their experience tell today's minorities about the solutions to their own dilemmas? Or is the skin-color barrier so formidable that these strategies will not readily work for others?

Much has been written about the attitudes of African Americans toward Jews[33] and vice versa.[34] Less is available about the feelings of blacks toward Asians, though the riots that followed the Rodney King beating in Los Angeles spurred a new wave of scholarship that explored this interface.[35] What literature we do have does not focus on how blacks understand the pathways to success these other ethnic groups have followed, but is instead largely about the experience of discrimination and hostility African Americans feel at the hands of these "outsider" merchants. There is a popular perception, supported by some research as well, of a rise in black anti-Semitism, an echo perhaps of a more general negative orientation toward Jews. When asked about how Jews climbed out of their own immigrant poverty toward the positions of influence they are perceived to occupy today, strains of anti-Semitism are indeed audible, particularly among some of the middle-class people we interviewed.

James Lane grew up in a small rural town in Alabama, bastion of the segregated South, and only later in his adolescent years moved to the more cosmopolitan environs of Nashville, Tennessee. James's family was middle class and well educated and tended to live in neighborhoods near college campuses where his was the only black family on the block. Basketball brought him together with the white boys in the area and, as he remembers it, the relations between the races were reasonably cordial, but not particularly close. Southern communities were starting to respond to the demand for busing about the time James was in high school. That blew the lid off whatever residential integration there was and slowly his block became blacker and blacker. A rash of "For Sale" signs spread all over the Nashville suburbs until, before long, there were only one or two white families left on James's block. The blacks who moved in were professionals, like James's professor father, on the lookout for good schools and green lawns. If anything, the class composition of the neighborhood shifted upward. The faces were all black eventually, though, and from this James drew a few lessons about the prospects for racial harmony. It didn't seem like a probable outcome.

Eventually, James took a BS and a JD at Southern University, a historically black school in Baton Rouge, Louisiana, and then joined the exodus north, landing in New York with his freshly minted law degree. He was able to find a good job working for a private charity that represents indigent families, until he was downsized. When that job disappeared, he went looking high and low for a public sector law job, especially in legal aid, but nothing worked out. James has his suspicions about why.

> Whites are favored more. Especially when I see them in a courtroom. A lot of court-appointed lawyers—a lot of times whites get more cases. They are given more cases. And a lot of times I could see white lawyers getting more favorable decisions from judges.

James allows that affirmative action has made a positive difference. "The doors are open a little more," he admits. His parents had nothing like this to assist them in their quest for upward mobility. "So it's easier for blacks to get jobs now," he says. But it's not all that easy. In fact, the older he got and the more qualified he became, the more visible racial barriers seemed to be. When he was "young and carefree," he didn't really notice these roadblocks, or at least not as he remembers those years now. When he reached middle age, however, it was a different story. White people seemed to be standing in his path, wherever he tried to go.

> Finishing law school, passing the bar—and whites absolutely see you more as a threat. [Now you] have the ability to accomplish something . . . to teach your children to carry on certain legacies or understand your history and the obstacles you had to overcome. You can do this and entitle blacks to move up more and to educate your people. And I think a lot of whites are trying to block you from doing that. And when they see you accomplish [something], they say, hey, you are on an equal footing with me right now and . . . they hate to see you on equal footing.
>
> You've got a family, you've got a home, you are raising your children, you are going to try to provide constantly the best for your family and you want to move up yourself. . . . I think that's when you really start experiencing a lot of racism.
>
> As I move up the professional field, I see whites that are less educated than I am and less experienced, and they are holding down these enormous jobs. Then you apply for a job not nearly as great as theirs and you get locked out for some reason . . . you are just constantly being slapped in the face.

Among the whites that bother James the most, Jews are singled out for special resentment. Jews have a lock on power and patronage, clout that he sees everywhere—from private sector jobs to the public sector employment system that he has tried to break into. Everywhere he looks, he sees Jews and blacks at loggerheads.

> Jews . . . they stick together, they control the job market, they help each other out. They have a lot of control on the welfare assistance. . . . They control the media. They are able to have more financially as well, and I think African Americans are locked out. They can't get businesses and loans—because, you know, because a lot of ethnic groups control banks.
>   Jews control so much . . . a lot is given to them. They have a lot of these jobs—they sit around doing nothing for these jobs. . . . Jews own more than half of New York. They would be more inclined to be more politically represented because even if they don't have a candidate to represent them politically, you have to answer to them. If you want to get ahead, you have to go to them, you've got to deal with them because they control everything. Whereas African Americans, they don't own anything, so you don't have to make any concessions.

James is particularly incensed about Jewish influence over the social service bureaucracy in the city. They occupy the highest managerial positions in the welfare system, he tells us, and from that vantage point can manipulate the system to benefit their own people. He doesn't think the Jews are actually using welfare, but rather are milking the system for the public sector jobs that it generates. What is left over after they have taken their cut? Not very much.

> The deck is against people of color in this city because there are so many obstacles they have had to overcome. Jewish people that control—whites that control this city are going to make sure they get their share first, and then they leave all of the minorities with whatever is left over. So when there are so many groups . . . fighting for a little bit, it is hard to make it.

How widespread is James's view? He was not alone. Nor was his the majority voice among our interviewees. When asked in a purely open-ended fashion who had the good jobs in the city, who had the assets, most of the African Americans mentioned Jews, alongside whites in general and, on some occasions, Asians. But James's more sinister explanations for the pattern did not surface among many.

Virtually all acknowledged that Jews had been successful and had therefore claimed good jobs and other coveted resources (housing, education, and the like). Yet most other blacks understood the road taken to this end point less as a matter of nefarious manipulation and more as a determined drive that should be admired and emulated. Jews had managed to circle their own wagons, support a collective bid for upward mobility, and boost themselves through the educational system into the professions. While the outcome of all this effort might well be visible in the form of unequal power, for many blacks the lesson to be learned from their Jewish neighbors is that they figured out a pathway that blacks would do well to copy. The message is one that Marcus Garvey and Malcolm X, never known for their embrace of Jews, might well have appreciated, for this is precisely the recipe for economic and cultural autonomy that they preached decades ago.[36]

Darlene Cawley grew up with Jewish neighbors, among other whites, and observed their practices at close range. She hasn't had Jewish neighbors in many years now, but she looks at their progress from afar and notes that they know how to get what they want out of the world.

> Because I think with the Jews, the Jews go for what they want. And they get what they want. They will march, they will go to the mayor's office and sit on his doorstep. We [blacks] might do that for two days with a thousand gathering, but after that, at the end of the week it's two, you know? [Jews] just go after what they want, you know? And they run the city. Like I said before, they control the banking. The judges. You know? How many black judges do we have? Most of them are Jews. They control the court system

Where James Lane sees this control as fundamentally unfair and the consequence of deception, Darlene argues it is the fallout from a successful strategy. The Jews know how to organize themselves to press for their needs. They don't take no for an answer.

Rita Tilly also had firsthand experience with Jewish families in the racially integrated Brooklyn neighborhood where she and her parents moved in the 1940s. She saw how Jewish families marched down to the schools and made sure their kids got the education they needed. By contrast, she says, people seem to have given up today. Teachers, parents, the whole community seem to think there is nothing they can do and so they don't try. There is a lesson to be learned, Rita tells us, about the ways the Jews got what they needed out of the very same public schools.

[Blacks] don't learn from school what they can do. And I guess our teachers are saying oh, Johnny can't read, he's not doing anything today. I don't care what he's doing. . . . Our teachers don't care. Our parents don't care because they don't go to the schools. When I went to school, it was a Jewish neighborhood. Those parents were there all the time and they went to see that everything was always running right. So, you didn't let the school run over you. You went up there and you ran over the school. But our parents today are not doing that.

Rita doesn't think the Jewish families were out of line in the old days. She thinks today's minority families ought to follow suit and demand that schools do right by their children. Nothing comes to those who are passive. Vigilance is the only way to achieve one's goals when you begin from a position of disadvantage. She knows that the Jews have done well for themselves and saw firsthand that this was not their birthright. They got to the promised land because they were demanding and united, willing and able to maneuver around the roadblocks put in their path. That resourcefulness, she argues, is a lesson for the disadvantaged today.

The WASPs I think, well, they've always been on top of everything because they discriminated against all the other groups, the Jewish group and everything. The blacks have always been working class, so WASPs have always discriminated against the working class. The Jewish group is still being discriminated against a lot, so they are almost alongside with the black and the Hispanics. But the Jewish group pulls themselves up and they work together and band together to get where they're going. They used to change their names—in my day, they changed their name from Goldberg to Mr. Gold or something like that, so they wouldn't know they were Jewish, because they couldn't get into schools. They have to have quotas for them to get into schools, until they bought the schools.

Instead, Rita looks at her own community in a state of near capitulation, attacking one another rather than turning their anger outward toward the institutions that are giving them short shrift.

The Jewish group work together and the blacks don't work together. Even the Hispanics are working together. Only the black group is the one that's not working together. Blacks are killing each other and doing our crime against each other mostly. We don't go outside of the community. We're not going over to Bensonhurst or somewhere else to rob others. We're staying right here and waiting for [our own] to get off the subway and hit us.

Rita's near neighbor Matilda has seen a similar history and has come to much the same conclusion. Now sixty-five, Matilda descends from her Mississippi farmer grandparents, by way of the Milwaukee foundries where her father worked. Today she lives with her sixty-four-year-old brother in a small apartment in Fort Greene. Her own "ethnic map" pointed to the ascendance of the Jews in comparison to her own community.

Who do you see as the powerful people in the city?
I'd say Jewish people. They've been down but you can't hold them down. I don't know what it is about them. I'd say Jewish people. Blacks are the ones who are down on the bottom.

Why is that?
Because we've always been there. I don't know. We don't work together enough to bring ourselves up. We always kind of hold each other down in our ethnic group. To me, I think that's the problem. Once we get like where we can work together and work with one another, then maybe we'll come up where we should be. . . . We just haven't made it up there yet. Like I said, we just don't pull ourselves together to reach the top. We don't try hard enough to reach the top with one another.

Matilda contrasts the problems of her own ethnic group with the Jews whom she sees as a success story. African Americans fight with one another, and in failing to pull together wind up stewing at the bottom. She thinks blacks could learn a lesson or two from the Jews who were also "down on the bottom" at one time but have managed to boost themselves as a collective up to the top.

Asians are similarly admired, but for a slightly different set of reasons. Lumped together with immigrants, Asians—particularly the Chinese, but sometimes South Asian Indians—are viewed as people who put the family, especially the extended family, at the center of their world. Individual autonomy is subordinated to family well-being: one for all, all for one. African Americans draw a sharp contrast between their own families' dilemmas and this stark example of the family "corporation," to which men are completely wedded. The Asian example holds a revealing mirror up to many inner-city black families that have floundered.

The contrast is particularly sharp for the older African Americans who have seen both sides of the black family themselves. The very oldest among them, now in their eighties, had hardworking blue-collar fathers and mothers who worked as domestics, the first generation to come up from the South. Single parents and out-of-wedlock children were less common in their day and they have observed, and sometimes experienced, the collapse in marriage patterns firsthand. They understand this as a tragedy that has befallen their community, one that has taken a toll on the young.

What is the "take home" message of these reflections? It is a self-critical one. Rather than condemn Jews for being successful or Asians for preserving their families, these African Americans argue that their own community needs to pursue the same course of action. Pulling together, supporting one another, keeping outsiders at bay, turning inward to work as a group for the collective advance of the group—this is how the work of mobility gets done. Never mind that this is a romantic perspective, belied to a large degree by the real truth of Jewish history in New York where internal class cleavages divided the poorer eastern European Jews from their better-educated and more re-fined German counterparts, for example.[37] When African Americans survey the ethnic landscape, they discern a hierarchy that is the result of decades of prior scrambling in which some groups prospered and others were kept, or kept themselves, "low down."

When the account of this sorting process is one that emphasizes discrim-ination, unfair treatment, and rigged games, then we find angry and embit-tered response. For some people, like James Lane, that is exactly the right way to think about why African Americans in the inner city live as they do nowadays. His people were, and continue to be, victims of forces lined up to prevent them from realizing their fair share. He sees blacks as especially vulnerable the minute they do constitute a serious competitive threat to middle-class white comforts. That's when the knives really come out and the racial exclusion cuts deepest. His is a compelling perspective, especially to the middle-aged generation among New York's African Americans who are familiar with calls to racial nationalism.

Their elders have a different point of view and one that is more self-critical than it is outward turning and angry. They lament what they see as the capitulation of the black community to its more predatory elements, its ina-bility to gather together in mutual support. These older black folk believe the better path would be a similar movement toward self-support and a ratch-eting up of demands on public sector institutions—particularly schools—to provide decent services. They counsel that minorities should be satisfied with nothing less and that to refrain from demanding more, in a united front, is to accept second-class status.

They advance an internal critique that trains a critical lens on parents, particularly men, who father children without regard to their welfare and walk away from the families they have created. Asian families, they argue, have prospered because of their intense devotion to the whole concept of the family. Working side by side; living in multigenerational houses; supporting new immigrants on the backs of those with little more to their name; pooling their resources, living frugally, and sacrificing today in the name of the future—these are the industrious habits of the Asians that explain their success. Above all, the integrity of the family and the willingness of members to put their own, individual needs "on hold" in favor of the group's well-being—these qualities have mattered for Asian-style Horatio Algers. They should be the model for black families today as well; so say the elders. The "fact" that these are not the lived values of inner-city families today, they claim, tells us most of what we need to know about why African Americans are where they are currently in the pecking order. Those who have made it out of the ghettoes, who emptied out of the neighborhoods where these families still live, are the ones who learned that lesson a long time ago. They put the emphasis on education, they made their marriages work, they were industrious, serious, and committed to one another. That is why they succeeded. QED.

Race and Class

The knowledge that many black families *have* succeeded in the same ways that Jews and Asians did before them underlines a lingering class division that is as important in explaining the plight of the poor as is race or ethnicity. Indeed, as Irene Mandel sees the matter, discrimination is only partly to blame for poverty. Middle-class blacks *have* moved into the middle echelons of many public institutions that hold sway over the lives of the black poor, from the schools' district offices and classrooms to welfare offices and hospitals. That is no longer an exclusively white world, as it once was. It is a middle-class black domain, and it is along the friction line that separates those with bureaucratic power from those whose lives they administer that we see a troubled division. It is not a race line; it is a class divide.

As we learned in the last chapter, Irene is an assistant principal in a Brooklyn middle school with a black and Latino student body. A veteran teacher who graduated into administration, Irene is the adult daughter of a Protestant minister and a housewife mother. She grew up in the seacoast islands of the Carolinas but moved to New York when her ex-husband, a Brooklyn native, finished law school, and wanted to live close to his family. Her mother and father are well into their eighties now and still live near the church from which he retired as the minister some fifteen years ago. It was a divided community of single-family homes and public housing projects, with blacks on one side of the tracks and whites on the other. Irene had the impression it was integrated, but looking back she realizes now that it wasn't. Her father's church was situated in the neighborhood with the projects behind it and the mansions occupied by whites in front. The division was repeated in the schools, as the public services were completely segregated. She could not go to the white school that was three doors from her house. Instead, she went to the all-black school eleven blocks away. "I don't think that [segregated] education deprived me any," she recalled, "simply because our teachers believed we could learn."

Indeed, if anything, growing up in the waning days of the Jim Crow South taught Irene the value of black control over institutions like schools. When integration arrived, black students were forced into white schools that didn't want them, their teachers and principals demoted in favor of the white leadership that accepted, begrudgingly, desegregation on their own terms. Before that moment arrived, however, the black community in this seacoast town had its own social hierarchy, its own leadership, and its own opinions about the black lower class. During World War II, when Irene was just a little girl, those working-class folk lived in the uptown public housing projects and held down blue-collar jobs in the shipyards. As long as the yards were humming, the money was fairly good. Black men, in particular, could make a good living helping the war machine to run smoothly. But when the war wound down, those jobs began to dry up and unemployment began to pull the poorer neighborhoods down.

Irene's world was entirely black, since desegregation came after she finished high school. Yet it was not an egalitarian society. Her father and the other well-educated, middle-class black families saw themselves as socially superior, not in a snobbish way but in the sense that they knew what was best for the black community. They were role models for the ordinary people living on the black side of the railroad tracks. And they had their own sense of decorum, which was not always forthcoming, as they saw it, among the less educated.

Irene is now part of a similar kind of class and she laments the passing of the social authority that the old elites possessed. When she looks around her

Brooklyn neighborhood now, she doesn't see the respect for authority that she remembers from the 1950s.

I don't think that authority is as clear now as when I was growing up. Of course, there's a lack of respect in general now.

Are there people in your neighborhood whom others look up to?

We have a large Baptist Church in the neighborhood, but I can't say that all of the folks . . . know those ministers. There are a couple of principals that live here, but they don't work in the neighborhood, so no one knows that. So you don't have the kind of leadership that was dominant in the fifties.

The public school where Irene works is in the heart of Bedford-Stuyvesant, an area of Brooklyn dominated by public housing projects that are very poor and completely black, as segregated as the community in which she was raised years before. But the social conditions are completely different. Here, the public services are overwhelmed by the demands placed on them. And the children are very, very needy.

We have one of the highest AIDS rates in the city. We have many foster children. When I worked in the junior high school, I think we had like 42 percent of the students in foster care. And, unfortunately, there are people who care for foster children who really are in it for the money. And are not really concerned about the children and the kinds of things that the school might have to call home about. . . . And the stories children tell you about their parents—their fathers being in jail. We have many children in need of some sort of counseling because they've seen things that are violent, that children shouldn't have to see. So, there is deprivation. There's real deprivation. It's hard.

It takes a hardworking and dedicated teacher to make a difference in the lives of poor children who are under such pressure and have so little support at home. Irene would like to think that teachers are drawn to these schools because they are highly motivated, attracted by the opportunity to make a difference. That, unfortunately, is not always what she has experienced. Instead, many teachers of all races—black and white—are burned out and irresponsible.

I prefer that teachers who aren't really willing to work just go elsewhere, where it will be easier. But, very often, they come in with attitudes that it will be easier for them, because [local] people don't care.
And it's sad, because it's not only teachers of other races, but teachers
of the same race, who have adopted the attitude.

That is not what Irene sees when she looks around the neighborhood
where she lives. The parents in her part of Brooklyn are engaged, they are
(as she put it) "in partnership with the school," there to see that their children
are learning and the atmosphere is conducive to achievement. In Bedford-
Stuyvesant, where she works, there is nothing of the kind. Though her skin
color is just the same, her class separates her from the parents of her students
and this friction often burns.

Where I work, we [teachers] are kind of seen as outsiders, as
authorities—part of the establishment—to be cut down and put in place.
It's often confrontational. I have to remember, or remind myself, that
I'm teaching two generations [parents and kids]. [I'm trying] to get
parents to understand that there are certain things that they do that
impact upon their children and things they don't do that impact upon
them as well. And that we are in a partnership. And that I see their
children doing something, being productive citizens.

The things [they think] are important might be a gold chain, or
expensive sneakers, or getting a patch dyed in the hair. . . . And sometimes that substitutes for what would be lap time. Spending time with
the child, imparting your values. Parents in my neighborhood . . . find
a way to take that time. Get their kids to little league, and whatever.
And there are so many parents where I work who, even though there
is a community center . . . don't take part in it. Don't have their children
take any part of it.

Race is not the explanation for this pattern. Irene is black, her fellow
teachers are black, and so are the kids they teach. This is about class, about
patterns of parental investment that sharply differentiate the black families
who live in her building, on her block, and those whom she serves as a
school administrator. When asked to reflect on her view as to why it is that
black people are struggling with high levels of poverty, where other groups
are not, it is the class divide that comes sharply into view for Irene. The
misplaced emphasis on giving things rather than giving time to children, the
lack of a dependable partnership between parents and schools, the acceptance

of mediocrity in the teaching ranks—this is class capitulation Irene's middle-class neighbors would never accept. Nor, for that matter, was it characteristic of the black elites among whom she grew up in the segregated South. They took responsibility for their own institutions and for their children's well-being, and in her own life's story Irene can trace the positive consequences of that moral rectitude.

She does not take a position on whether that capitulation is a symptom of moral decay for which the black poor should be held responsible, or a consequence of structural pressures of poverty that would cause any group to fold, for which society at large is primarily responsible. For Irene, it hardly matters which way those causal arrows point. The bottom line in her judgment is that there is a culture in place that is the chief reason why the children in the school she serves are not likely to come out with the same life chances as the children in her apartment complex. Again, that is not about race. It is about lifestyle, values, commitment, and the evaporation in poor circles of the culture of the church and the hold that black elites had over the conduct of the less fortunate when segregation ruled the land. That hold was broken, partly by integration, partly by northward migration, and in no small measure by the evaporation of steady work that stranded so many blue-collar black families. The old example of the church pastor and his flock seems more remote now and exerts less of a pull on the lower-class families she serves today as a middle school administrator.

The traces of this breakdown are to be found in chances not taken, in opportunities not imagined.

> We don't break from cycles. We haven't been part of the American dream so much. We're just becoming a part of that. I don't think that we even realize that there's a possibility for us to come out of welfare and go to college, and do something differently. Maybe own a mechanic shop. So we don't go to college. We don't get our own business.... We aren't considered good credit risks for getting that loan that's going to enable us to open that business.

Irene is not talking about her own family or the families of the other ministers she grew up with. She is lamenting the shortened horizons of the black poor in the inner city, the people whose children she teaches. The conditions of their lives and the culture it has produced has left its most profound traces, as she sees it, in a psychology of limits, a lack of confidence that a productive future is everyone's birthright. This in turn fuels a resig-

nation and an acceptance of a status quo that is manifestly leaving a huge
number of people behind.

Accountability

I have dwelt here on the explanations that middle-aged and elderly African
Americans offer for the condition of the black poor. They span the spectrum
from accounts that emphasize the impact of racial discrimination—directed
especially at those who are striving to move up—to those spotlighting the
cultural implosion that is eroding the stability of poor families, to a more
psychological account of limited aspirations. It would be completely consistent with almost any of these "models" to assume that the damage is so
significant that one cannot expect particular individuals—regardless of the
their drive, devotion, or motivation—to overcome the obstacles placed before
them. This is a problem for the society as a whole to attack; for government
to address; for pastors, ministers, rabbis, or priests to deal with; for grassroots
organizers to take as a priority. An organized response larger than any individual is required to move this mountain. That, at least, would be a logical
response to any of these laments, for they describe problems that are just too
complex for the average Joe to address in a meaningful fashion.

That is not how these older members of New York's black community
see the matter. It would be helpful, of course, if agencies could put shoulder
to the wheel, if politicians and philanthropists would put their weight behind
measures that would make a difference. These are not irrelevant contributions. The central responsibility, however, from their perspective, does indeed
rest with individuals. People cannot be let off the hook; they cannot point to
forces beyond their control and then wash their hands of the need to take
action. The individual is central to the solution. This does not signal a refusal
to recognize the structural barriers that impede progress, a total ignorance of
the ways that prejudice or competition obstruct the pathway. It means that
dwelling on the blockage and assuming that this is enough won't cut it. It
remains the task of each person to dust herself off and get on with the task
of getting through school or getting a job. As Irene Mandel puts the matter,
this unavoidably involves a certain amount of self-criticism.

> I think the deck is stacked against some people. But there are things
> that one has to open oneself to in order to get around the deck. How
> one thinks of oneself. Am I hostile? What language do I use [when
> seeking a job]? Am I prepared? Am I presenting myself as a person

who wants to work in this place? I think we can overcome these things. I'm not going to say it's easy. I'm not going to say that we don't overcome because there are quotas to be met. I think, every so often, that comes into play. But I think that if we have a person who speaks well, and looks like they're dressed for the particular part . . . they have a chance. The deck isn't always stacked as high for that person as for another one.

Barry James has seen African Americans in the post office break through glass ceilings that used to be unbreakable. Even so, he believes that the job market is a harder nut to crack than it once was because the competition is greater and the preparation of many young African Americans is less than optimal.

Even though you would think that [young people] would have it easier than what I had when I was growing up, right now it seems like the job market in this country is kind of hard. I don't think it's going to be easy for a lot of them as it was when we was growing up. Even though the money wasn't that great, [we] had more jobs available when I was growing up and you could do more with the money you made. But today the job market is very, very slow and due to the fact that you've got a lot of immigrants and foreigners coming into the country, which is absorbing a lot of the jobs, the small-paying jobs [are all that's left] and a lot of the young folks . . . especially African Americans and a few of the other minorities, don't have the education.

Nonetheless, Barry says, it is entirely possible to overcome these obstacles when you put your mind to it: "I think mostly anybody can really make it in this city. Even if they say the deck is stacked, it's not stacked that bad where they can't make it. I think most people could make it in this city, definitely."

Rita Tilly, who earlier remarked that she thought most African Americans dwell too long on race and too little on individual conduct, nonetheless realizes that nothing comes to minorities easily. They have to struggle against the odds to claim what should be theirs by right. Those who fail to put up the fight cannot shelter behind inequity. Rita charges them with the obligation to redouble their efforts to force those who will not otherwise perform. If they default, they have themselves to blame, not the society at large, which may well be responsible for the underlying inequality of opportunity. This is the essence of personal responsibility and it is a theme sounded loud and clear throughout most of our interviews.

Latino Perspectives

Benito Rivas was born in 1920 to a poor, single mother in a small town on the outskirts of San Pedro in the Dominican Republic. Schooled until he was about ten, Benito quit to work in manual-labor jobs that helped to support his mother and siblings. Carpenter, plumber, mason—he worked at whatever construction jobs he could find. At sixteen he had a child by a teenage girl-friend whom he offered to marry, but Benito could not get past her family's objections so he just continued to send what he could now and again to help his firstborn. By the time he was in his early twenties, he was married and looking for work that would support his new family. With six children to feed, he was drawn to New York as a place where he might earn enough to make ends meet.

His wife left the country first and he followed a year later. One by one, they brought their children over and raised them on a solidly Dominican block in Washington Heights. He had jobs in construction and in factories, repairing radios, and worked steadily for more than thirty years. "The factory," he says, "was a league of nations. There were people from all over. There were more Latinos than Americans!" There were a few American blacks, though, so Benito got a rare chance to learn a little English. But he never got further than learning the English names for various radio parts. Other than this brief opportunity, he has lived in a Spanish-speaking world throughout his time in New York.

Benito kept his factory job until he was in his early sixties, when he was disabled in an accident. His leg was broken in two places and he could no longer stand for assembly line work, so he retired; the factory packed up and moved to Texas. By now his children are grown and even have grown children of their own. By age seventy-five, he was a great-grandfather three times over. Benito and his wife get by on social security, Medicaid, a small pension from the union, and the food stamps they receive on account of his blind sister-in-law who lives with him. These are benefits, as he sees it, that he earned through a lifetime of honest labor. With them in hand, he is not well off, not comfortable, but he survives and survives better, he figures, than he would ever have done if he had stayed in the Dominican Republic. He has a roof over his head and is not worried about losing it. Knock on wood, he is reasonably healthy, though that leg injury returns to haunt him now and again.

What of the racial landscape in Benito's life? How does he locate himself in the ethnic mosaic of New York's neighborhoods? Simply understanding what race means is a complex task for its meaning is fused with ethnicity and tempered by a sense that there is a hierarchy out there that he grasps only in its bare outlines.

> Race is a concept we haven't known how to define. Those of the Chinese race, Haitian race, Dominican race, and American race are different but the same person. Because they are Chinese, they find themselves superior to Americans and Americans find themselves superior to the Chinese and to ourselves. And that is not [right]. We are all the same.

I noted earlier a tendency among African Americans to perceive others as bound in solidarity, while defining their own ethnic group as divided and dysfunctional. Latinos like Benito say the same thing about their own people. They sabotage themselves through in-group divisions.

> The Chinese ethnic group lives well because they do everything together, united. The Jewish ethnic group is united. The Latino ethnic group is the one that is dispersed. As Latinos, we should have unity. We don't have it. The Argentinean group, which is Latino, lives over there. The Puerto Rican group, which is Latino, is over there. The Dominican group, which is Latino, lives over there. They are all dispersed. However, Jews, Chinese, Irish, and Arabs, they all look out for their community.

Rivas's comments are interesting in two respects. First, he believes, as do his African-American age mates, that internal divisions retard the prospects of his ethnic group and that other groups have somehow managed to overcome this obstacle. They have moved ahead of Latinos because they have created forms of in-group solidarity. Second, he moves beyond his own ethnicity—Dominicans—to a pan-Latino definition when he explains the splintered path. It would hardly have made sense, in the Dominican Republic itself, to identify as a Latino. But in the U.S. context, he has come to see himself as at least theoretically able to join in an ethnic identity that is language-based and, to some extent, Caribbean focused, but disengaged from national origin per se.

Benito recognizes as well that others who are outside the fold–whites, African Americans, Asians–look upon Latinos as an undifferentiated group. The advantage gained is to magnify the numbers of any one of the constituent ethnicities in order to increase their leverage. The disadvantage, as he sees it, is that the behavior of a small group of miscreants tars the whole.

> There are many Latino groups who have done wrong things and done barbarities and then for one [group] we all pay. There are people who blame the Dominicans. No, stop there, let's see. Among Dominicans there are a hundred that are good for nothing but there are a million that are better than you.

While the language of race or ethnicity is familiar to Benito, he is equally alive to the distinctions of class that are meaningful in his native land, which often correspond to color.[38] Economic distinctions had pronounced political and cultural consequences in the Trujillo era and left their mark in a simmering (and sometimes explosive) resentment among the poor toward those who were higher up the class ladder.

> I worked in an office [in the Dominican Republic] and there were good opportunities for the "perfumed class." There were middle-class girls in those times who worked to support their luxuries . . . in order to dress well. And every two or three months they got a raise. Whoever had been working there longer and who were poor heads of families were paid miserably. . . . It was only the whiter ones, as they say.

Doctors and lawyers were the "light-skinned ones" favored under the dictatorship. Repressive regimes are not required for colorism to prevail, however. Throughout the Caribbean and in much of Latin America generally, the lingering traces of European colonialism and the institution of slavery are visible in the fusion of class distinctions and skin-color prejudice. Indeed, some have argued that the predominance of African heritage among Dominicans subjects them to greater racial rejection in the United States than Puerto Ricans, who typically look more Spanish than black. For Benito Rivas, however, class comes first. Society is divided into haves and have nots and he has been on the wrong side of that divide, color notwithstanding. He sees these boundaries as man-made, purposeful efforts to subjugate.

They are invented by a society who doesn't want poor people to do better. The rich one lives off the poor one. Do you understand? The poor one doesn't have a right to anything. Only to work for the rich one, to produce for the rich. . . . For the poor there are no holidays, nothing if he is sick. But the rich doesn't do things because he feels he has a little flu, or because it is raining a lot, they can't go out. The poor one has to go out and get wet because he has to go produce the rent.

These are sentiments born of a highly unequal third world country, where the gaps between the poor and the middle class (not to mention the rich) are enormous and enforced—for much of their history—by military repression. Do they persist when immigrants move to the United States, which, for all its own faults, does not come close to the degree of inequality that permeates the Dominican Republic? The story we like to tell ourselves (that immigrants repeat to their relations back home) is that things are very different here. Mobility, opportunity, freedom, the main chance—this is what the United States stands for. And, of course, relative to the Dominican Republic, this is largely true. But for immigrants like Benito, an ethnic and racial hierarchy comes into view here as well. Even though its consequences are mitigated by a higher standard of living for the American poor than for their counterparts in the Caribbean and greater protection for political liberty, he feels that those "streets paved with gold" are traveled mainly by other ethnic groups. Latinos are at the bottom of the hierarchy because they don't speak English and because (the foreigners, at least, among them) they lack access to basic social protections afforded by the welfare state. Hence they are relegated to the fringes of the labor market, without the backstop of public benefits to which American blacks, Puerto Ricans, and other native-born ethnic minorities can turn.

What becomes of Latinos under these circumstances? Denied power and opportunity as well as social protection, they form the bottom of the labor market and they work themselves into a frenzy.

The poorest group are the Latinos, the last group who got here. Us. They are the most hardworking, the Latinos—the Mexicans, Hondurans, Puerto Ricans. They all work very hard. From among those groups there are also drug dealers, bad people. But those who work are the Latinos. The least hardworking are the black Americans. Because they live only off welfare. I walk around the neighborhood and you see how indigents live, on the sidewalk. With that cold, they would wake up in the morning wearing only underwear.

African Americans can turn to the welfare system, as Benito sees it, but at the cost of a degradation that Dominicans, who do not have this option, do not face.[39] He does not see the legions of blacks who fill the low-wage labor system, even though they are hard at work in neighborhoods immediately adjacent to his own.[40] Even further removed from his experience is the African-American middle class. What he sees—and even more, what he hears about—are the visible signs of dispossession and poverty of the homeless panhandler, who is likely to be black.

Latinos are at the bottom of another, more important, ladder: that of the labor system. They are the ones that face active, daily discrimination because they are minorities who do not speak English and because they are foreigners (or are confused with foreigners) who have no rights or protections.

> The most discriminated against are the Latinos, specifically those who don't speak English. They catch everything that falls. The Irish do the most discrimination. The government also discriminates. They know that you [the Spanish-speaking interviewer] are Latino, and you speak good English because you need it. But if you slip just a little, you are worth less than any one of them. If I go to an office where Latinos work, they ask me to speak English to them. You can tell by the accent that they are Latinos. If you speak Spanish why do you make me speak English? "No, here we have to speak English." That is what bothers me.

Instead, Latinos battle it out on the bottom rung of the labor-market ladder where opportunity appears to be locked up in the hands of those who are savvy in the ways of the American system. Particularly for those who do not speak the language, or who lack the right work papers, the land of milk and honey can appear just beyond reach. And the difference between those who are on the inside and those who stand at the edge is not so much arbitrary as a consequence of ethnic hierarchies that cannot easily be budged.

> Italians have the high-paying blue-collar jobs locked up. Why? I don't know. But all of those jobs at the docks are controlled by the Mafia. Those are good-paying jobs. I worked once, for about a month and a half, in New Jersey in the navy yard repairing an oil tanker. That was the best job I ever had. I made nine dollars an hour and I didn't do much. It was all soldering and bringing a table back and forth, and I worked seven days a week. . . . I would come home with $650. The employers were Greeks.

Jobs like that one have been few and far between in Benito's working life. He has had to make do with much less for most of the time and his wife has had to put in her time as a "floor lady" in a clothing factory so that they could earn enough to raise their four kids. Benito worked night shifts, arriving home at 3:00 A.M., long enough to catch some sleep and see his wife out the door to her day job. None of those jobs put him in a position to learn English, and his obligations at home, to help care for his kids when the wife was out to work, also isolated him and ensured that he would not be able to communicate adequately with Americans.

Nonetheless, he made his way in the world and without much help from others, thanks to a stubborn streak of self-reliance and a dose of disdain for those who collapse back on the government or friends when they run into trouble. Benito would rather die first. He cannot fathom the ethnic groups that make a habit of relying on handouts. Nor could he comprehend the byzantine rules that governed the welfare system in the old days of AFDC. In such a rich country, with so many jobs—including the bad ones—neither the passivity of the jobless poor nor the seeming meanness of the government make much sense to him.

> In a country like this, which is the capital of the world . . . I don't even know how to say it. It is ahead of the whole world. They should have a system here for assistance to those single mothers. Instead of putting them on welfare, give them jobs. But the problem is that in this country, there are laws that just don't fit in. Instead of helping they do the opposite. Where I used to live, on the fifth or sixth floor, a woman lived. They would bring her a box of good food and that woman, do you know what she did with that food? She would throw it away because the inspectors would come over and check on the husband. The woman would put something in the window and if he saw the signal, he would keep on going. They had a system [of warning signals].

The "man in the house rules" that governed the old welfare system mandated inspections to investigate whether single mothers actually had live-in partners who were providers, and they would be cut off if a man was discovered on the premises. Benito could not understand why any government would force a husband and wife to run and hide in this fashion, or throw out food to avoid detection (undoubtedly a point of confusion on his part, but this is illustrative of his view that there was something quite crazy about the public assistance system).

The whole welfare conundrum is something that an able-bodied person should avoid anyway, as Benito saw it. Virtually any kind of work was preferable.

> A job is always better because it is the sweat of your brow. It is money earned honestly. But living off welfare is losing face immediately. I understand that welfare should be given to people who can't work, because of their age, or their health . . . but young men and women?

Benito tells many stories of welfare cheats who live high on the hog but take from the public coffers and he is quick to condemn the practice. Even when his family was burned out of their home in the midst of a bitterly cold New York winter, they avoided public assistance, relying instead on a short dose of charity from the Red Cross. Pride is part of this equation, but perhaps more important is Benito's sense of privacy and his desire to shore up the wall that separates his family from the outside world. He finds it hard to imagine that others do not share these priorities.

When we interviewed him, Benito Rivas was nearly seventy-five years old. He had traveled a long distance in his life, but for most of his adult years his world was contained inside the Dominican enclave of Washington Heights and the factory life that he had shared alongside other immigrant workers. Without being able to speak English, he was forced to peer out at the socially distant world of American culture, a world his children, grand-children, and now great-grandchildren inhabit with far more ease. He knows more about the Latino world, the great Hispanic melting pot of New York, where Spanish is the lingua franca and for many practical purposes the English-speaking world does not exist. Benito sees Latinos as a divided community, split by their national heritage, pushed away from better opportunities that are reserved by whites of varying ethnicities themselves—Italians, Jews, Irish—though he has had only minimal contact with one of these groups in the waterfront shipyards. For him, the African American is only slightly differentiated from Americans of other colors, for they have in common their English-speaking lives and he rubs shoulders only slightly more often with blacks than he does with whites.

Daisy Carrasquillo, the native Puerto Rican whom we met in chapter five, has a different view of the ethnic landscape. Though she is perfectly comfortable speaking Spanish, she came to New York at a much younger age than Benito Rivas and attended Catholic elementary schools in the city before going back to Puerto Rico to live with her grandmother. Most of her formative years were spent in Latino neighborhoods filled to the brim with second-generation Nuyoricans and their immigrant parents.

For Daisy's age mates, the transnational life was the norm. Moving back and forth between the island and the mainland, maintaining close ties with relatives in both places, families like the Carrasquillos had two meaningful homelands. Daisy attended school in New York until she was thirteen and then went back to Puerto Rico to keep her grandma company and to escape the rough world of New York's overcrowded public high schools. She completed high school on the island and studied for an AA degree in secretarial studies, while taking vacations with her parents back in New York. Given this pattern of movement, Daisy learned to navigate easily in both Spanish and English and was at ease working in the two cultures. In this respect, she differs from Benito, who is both considerably older and more typical of first-generation immigrants in his more circumscribed world.

The upper west side neighborhood of Daisy's youth was not an easy place to live in the 1970s. Once a stable working-class community, it cycled downward as the drug epidemic swept poor neighborhoods, a trend the Carrasquillos associated with the succession of poor Dominicans moving into Puerto Rican territory.

> The neighborhood changed so drastically. I just get so mad when I think about it. A lot of drug dealers moved in. I always go back there because I can see the place where I lived. My mother lived on the same block as my grandmother. We were always at my grandmother's house every Friday, every weekend. So that's what I consider really my second home. . . . Now it's just gunshots and people get killed and it's all over drugs; it's just so different. So depressing to see. Some buildings have been knocked down because they were drug infested and they wanted to get rid of the dealers, so they knocked the buildings down. Now the majority of the people living there are Dominicans. Before it was all mixed, Anglo-Saxons and Puerto Ricans. And now there are less and less [and more Dominicans].

The increasing poverty and ethnic friction between Puerto Ricans and Dominicans drove Daisy's father to move the family to Brooklyn Heights, where he worked two jobs, one in a hotel at night and one during the day as a building super in the apartment house where they lived. The peacefulness, good schools, and more upscale atmosphere of their new surroundings was a relief to the whole family, especially to Daisy's younger siblings who were still at home. It was also an ethnically and racially integrated neighborhood, closer in composition to the community she lived in on the west side before the Dominican influx arrived.

The lesson Daisy drew from this experience, which she applied to her own family when it came time to decide where to raise her children, was that mixed-race neighborhoods that have a substantial white population are better places to live. Although she counts herself as a devotee of Puerto Rican culture and is proud of her ethnic affiliation, she wanted to raise her kids in a neighborhood where they would not be restricted only to Latino schoolmates. Her husband was a working-class building super like her father and his job permitted them to live in an upscale neighborhood, but supers have tiny, first-floor apartments and not enough space for a growing family. When they made up their minds to buy a house of their own, Daisy set out to find a community that was not an ethnic enclave.

> I told my husband, I saw a lot of Jewish people [in the area where we were looking]. The house was not that great, but in my mind I thought, I want my son to go to school not where he is going to be picked at. He's going to be the only Hispanic. I want to be in a good area. I just looked and looked and came to this house. I called the [police] precinct and asked them how was this block because I want to buy a house and want to know how is the neighborhood. And he said, "You know what, of all the blocks, Harmony Avenue is the block where we get the least amount of calls." And I said, "Oh, that's pretty good." I told my husband and we moved here and I just love it.

Their Bronx street is a quiet, ethnically integrated, family neighborhood full of people Daisy describes as hardworking adults and well-behaved kids. Bangladeshi families, working-class whites, Hispanics, and blacks live together and look out for one another's property. They are close knit, so much so that when one disruptive family moved onto the block, the rest got together to wring their hands collectively and pray they would leave.

In the midst of this little UN, Daisy positions herself as a fiercely proud promoter of Puerto Rican culture, not to the exclusion of other people's traditions but as an act of cultural solidarity.

> I was raised in New York, but . . . I fully identify myself with Puerto Rico. I am into the folklore and music. I like the culture of the people. I have my kids going to music lessons at the barrio, they are getting free duadro lessons (guitar) and we all go on Saturdays. . . . I wanted

to learn the culture, my culture and my husband's. I believe strongly in [my kids] keeping up with their culture and identifying with it.

Daisy prefers to think of her community as defined primarily by this respectable, rich ethnic culture. Yet she understands that class and ethnicity are collapsed into a single heap by outsiders who cannot tell the low-lifes from the mainstream.

The wires that connect the Puerto Rican and Dominican peoples of New York are often stretched taut by these very images. Concentrated poverty significantly affects both ethnic groups.[41] Dominicans are particularly disadvantaged because they have been on the mainland for a shorter period and therefore have less experience with English, and also because as foreigners they have a more tenuous hold on benefits that stabilize the household incomes of many Puerto Ricans; without citizenship, they are excluded from most forms of public assistance.[42] Yet both Latino communities have experienced rapid growth due to increased immigration and high birth rates. The combination, when fused with the low-wage jobs that are on offer, ensures a high level of poverty. It also means that they are thrust into a competition with one another for the limited amount of jobs, housing, and schools that are on offer.

This tension is sometimes inflamed by the racial dynamics of the receiving society. Dominican teens that have African roots are mistaken for and often drawn toward native-born blacks living in the neighborhood who are also poor and disproportionately disadvantaged. Puerto Ricans are more classically Latino in appearance, reflecting their Spanish heritage. Patterns of "segmented assimilation"[43] influence the incorporation of these two ethnic groups, particularly in the second generation, and often set them at odds with one another along racial lines. Yet their common heritage as Spanish speakers, at least in the oldest generations, keeps them bound together as two of the more prominent Latino populations who share a migration experience from the Caribbean.

Race and ethnicity matter in the aging process because these characteristics have such a powerful influence over the opportunities that are available across the life span. As long as color or language define where someone lives, what schools they go to, what kinds of jobs they hold down, and what kind of income trickles across the threshold, these attributes will shape the resources available in the elder years. Race and ethnic origins operate on the neighborhoods people age in, the savings accounts they can (or cannot) draw upon when they no longer work, and even the personal safety they enjoy (or do not enjoy). These dimensions play a powerful role in determining the quality of life in elderhood.

Race and ethnic divisions also define a moral posture, albeit one that defies consensus, about who is responsible for the shortfalls, for the lack of power to turn the situation around, for the failings of the community itself. Economists and sociologists point to the structures of our society that tilt the playing field, that make race an unfair determinant of one's destiny. Ordinary people see these barriers as well but make a moral project out of contending with them. For some, racism and the discrimination it fosters must become the rallying cry of a social movement. For others, the hurdles become one more reason why minorities must work harder to "get over" the obstacles placed in their pathways. Concentrating on this personal mission is an obligation every person on the receiving end of poverty must be committed to. Nothing less will do and no excuses are acceptable.

Pointing to ethnic groups that seem to have made it against the odds, some minority elders see a history of unfair power and clubbishness that has robbed other downtrodden groups of their fair share of the good jobs, the decent neighborhoods, and now the benefits of old age. Others see the stigmatized groups that have devised the only solution: a united front, militant demands on the public sector, a refusal to accept subordination, and an inward-turning solidarity that has shed the criticisms as well as the company of outsiders. If this is what it takes to climb the ladder of success in America, they surmise, so be it. This is what we—the black and brown people who stand on the bottom rungs of that ladder today—must do.

These arguments saturate the moral universe of inner-city communities regardless of the age of their members. But it is a particularly poignant conversation among those who are older. They are the generation that asks itself why their lives, the lives of their children and grandchildren, neighbors and friends, turned out as they have. For those who look out on a sea of poverty, the answers are often elusive. We tend not to think about these issues when we imagine the aging process. Yet they are important frameworks for understanding why some people come into their elder years in comfort and others have much less.

7–Local Caring: Social Capital and Social Responsibility

With the publication of Robert Putnam's much discussed book *Bowling Alone*,[1] a burst of concern surfaced about the diminishing involvement of Americans in community organizations. Voluntary groups, churches, and parent-teacher associations are said to be evaporating before our eyes. Erosion of civic engagement has been blamed upon working mothers no longer available to staff the PTA, or working fathers running to stay one step ahead of the downsizing ax and therefore unable to coach in the soccer league. Excessive materialism has also been blamed, as Americans seem more concerned these days about the model of their cars than the health of local institutions. Even the lowly television has been blamed for privatizing recreation, drawing couch potatoes away from activities that would once have brought them into contact with their neighbors. Diminishing social ties, we are told, produce weak forms of solidarity and even weaker levels of trust or engagement in public institutions (e.g., government).[2]

Declining social capital has been identified as a particular serious issue in American ghettoes. Beginning with James Coleman's (1988) seminal article "Social Capital in the Creation of Human Capital," and continuing with William Julius Wilson's arresting portraits of neighborhood disintegration,[3] it has been suggested that poor minorities are suffering the consequences of an inward-turning withdrawal from public life. Coleman argued that declining parental participation in schooling reduces a child's human capital (individual skills or formal credentials) because parents lack the resources that would otherwise derive from social ties (especially with fellow parents and teachers), which are necessary to monitor and influence a child's educational performance.

Wilson points to the erosion of economic opportunity in inner-city communities, which opens up avenues for the dangerous trades (drugs and guns, and the violent behavior that goes with them), and forces families back into the privacy of their homes for safety's sake. The more law-abiding families withdraw, the more the institutions they once bolstered (from churches to stores) depart the scene. An empty "commons" signals the death knell of social capital in the inner city, and all its residents pay the price.

Why does this topic matter for understanding middle age and the experience of elders in the inner city? First, the generations we consider here are part of what Putnam has called "the long civic generation," men and women who came of age after World War II. However, they are not the people we typically think about when we consider the Elks Lodge, the bowling leagues, and the PTA, even when these individuals did their part for similar organizations. Those organizations are quintessentially suburban and white. Yet minority families have their own institutions, which have, if anything, been more important in sustaining inner-city communities. These neighborhoods have always been less able to rely on government and therefore more self-sustaining. Their infrastructure resides in the black church, in the activist Latino ministries, and more recently in the storefront organizations that advocate for community development, employment, child care, and the like. Growing old in the inner city, for these generations at least, has meant devotion to community life through these mechanisms.

Social capital is also important because community strength and internal trust is key to the well-being of older inner-city residents. Of course, everyone benefits from a healthy stock of social capital, but the most vulnerable people in a neighborhood—children and the elderly—are perhaps most seriously affected if the stock runs down. Coleman recognized this for children and wrote with great insight about how social ties influence educational performance. It is no less true for the older people, who are more likely to center their lives around their homes. Younger people move in and out of their residential communities and may not regard these locales as particularly important to their identities or sense of well-being. Integration into the work world or educational institutions gives them other venues within which to develop personal attachments and nurturing social networks. But for older people, the home place sets the tone for their daily lives.

The reputation of inner-city adults for apathy in the face of community needs turns out to be wide of the mark. Our research shows that, in many respects, minorities value civic engagement more than their national (mainly nonminority) counterparts. A large percentage of the New York sample believes that it is a very great obligation to be aware of national issues, to sacrifice their own financial resources for the greater good, and to volunteer their time and money to important causes. At least the ideals of participatory engagement are in evidence in these inner-city neighborhoods.[4] If we look at the proportion of the survey respondents who felt these obligations very strongly, the midlife New Yorkers seem more committed in many ways than do their national counterparts.

Though these data are comforting, they tell us nothing about how people actually behave, whether they actually *do* watch the news, vote, serve on juries, or collect funds for cancer research. The records we do have do not fully support this picture. Minorities, particularly those who are poor, are far less likely to vote than are their more affluent minority counterparts, or their equally poor white brethren.[5] This might incline us to assume that minority communities are weak in social capital. Participation in formal organizations, however, may not be the best barometer of social responsibility for the people whose lives are chronicled here. Measures that rely upon participation in such institutions—giving money, volunteering in some official capacity—define a form of social responsibility that may predominate among middle-class families. Among the comparatively well heeled, the financial resources to support philanthropic generosity are available, and participation in voluntary organizations is expected as a culturally approved signal of public engagement.

For urban minorities, particularly the aging poor among them, social responsibility is expressed in a different form, one that is paradoxically privatized and directed not at the general social good but at those defined as "one's own." Men and women living in problematic neighborhoods look to the daunting task of raising their children, or tending to the safety of the streets, as both a personal task *and* a contribution to the well-being of society as a whole.

In a society divided by race and class differences, social responsibility takes on a more privatized quality, directed at "the community." The borders of community are narrowly circumscribed by the men and women in this book. Drawing boundaries around the people to whom one owes selfless acts is a complex process, moving out from the immediate family to the surrounding neighborhood, and to groups of people who occupy similar positions in the racial or economic hierarchy. Formal organizations, particularly the church, can become a vehicle through which to express commitment to others. More often than not, though, private behavior and informal practices express the responsibility that ethnoracial or economically defined groups feel for their members.

The emphasis in this chapter lies only partly on socially responsible *behavior*. I focus here equally on the *subjective* or conceptual dimensions of obligation and belonging, on the ways midlife minorities define their position

Table 7-1

Dimensions of Civic Engagement

Comparisons Between New York and National Samples

On a scale of 0 (no obligation at all) to 10 (a very great obligation), how much obligation would you feel:

	New York Sample Mean (% rating "10")	National MIDUS Mean (% rating "10")
To keep fully informed about national news and public issues	7.81* (40.4%)	7.23 (19.8%)
To vote in local/ national elections	7.61 (42.4%)	8.16 (46.4%)
To volunteer time or money to social causes you support	7.14** (29.3%)	6.39 (10.7%)
To pay more for your health care so that everyone had access to health care	6.99*** (30.3%)	5.88 (11.2%)
To collect contributions for heart/cancer research if asked	6.98*** (35.7%)	5.66 (10%)
To serve on a jury if called	6.86 (35.7%)	7.31 (33.1%)
To vote for a law that would help others worse off than you, but would increase your taxes	6.56*** (24.2%)	5.50 (8.1%)
To testify in court about an accident you witnessed	6.51*** (31.3%)	8.08 (33.5%)

*Difference from national sample significant at the 0.05 level; **0.01 level; ***0.001 level.

in a stratified society. Any complete understanding of social responsibility involves a deeper sense of to whom that responsibility is owed, to the cultural compass that guides giving and receiving.

Mapping the contours of social responsibility is most easily and economically done by radiating out first from the most private sphere of the family, then to the neighborhood, and then to social groups defined by race and ethnicity. This is both a logical arrangement and, as it happens, the map that most accurately describes the social spheres of participation that matter most to inner-city New Yorkers. In each band of the concentric circle that begins with the family and ends with groups defined by national origin or race we must seek to understand how the men and women we interviewed define their social obligations, the community to which they owe whatever selfless commitments they feel.

Family Values: Socially Responsible Child Rearing

As sociologist Alice Rossi has suggested in her volume *Caring and Doing for Others*,[6] attending to family obligations, particularly those that bind the three living generations of child-parent-grandparent, is an important facet of social responsibility in most American communities. These are fairly universal definitions of intergenerational obligation, though they may be met by financial outlays among middle-class families (for elder care or child care) and by time outlays by those less affluent.[7] It would probably be fair to say that most middle-class, midlife Americans define these responsibilities as private obligations that are incumbent on families. They are, then, examples of social responsibility that are primarily oriented toward the quality of family life and the personal obligations generations owe to one another.

Among black and Latino New Yorkers, child rearing is understood both as a personal responsibility and as *public* obligation. They know this is so because they can point to a host of families who have not followed through, leaving neighbors and strangers to contend with the consequences of their parental failures. This is more than a subtle difference. Where middle-class families consider parental "work" as a serious moral obligation, its social character is not as well developed. Parents raise their children because their private lives are circumscribed by these responsibilities. In poorer communities, taking care of one's children or grandchildren is almost as much an obligation to the peace, security, and well-being of neighbors and fellow community members as it is to the success and comfort of the next generation in the family.

Rosa Picante is a thirty-eight-year-old Dominican immigrant living in a poor neighborhood on Manhattan's upper west side. She does not have the time for volunteer work. Nor does she have the resources or the inclination to donate money to charity, apart from an occasional contribution to her parish. If Rosa were to complete the standard questionnaire on civic behavior, she would score low on many indices of social responsibility. Yet she sees herself as a good citizen of her community because she has taken care of her private responsibilities and, in so doing, contributes in positive ways to the quality of life of her neighbors and friends.

> Bring your children up with an education, yes, you are helping the community. Helping the society, so that the area that you live in is not so bad. Because if everyone contributes his part to do something good on their own, they are doing something for the community.

Jason Norwald, a thirty-two-year-old African American who works as an assistant teacher, would agree that taking responsibility for family members is key to both personal integrity and public order.

> If something were to happen to my brother and his wife, there would be no question as to where their children would go. . . . [They] would be my responsibility. I don't have a problem with that. My parents would be largely my responsibility. . . . My brother and I would probably share the responsibility for my parents, for our parents. My aunt—there was never a question. . . . I think that's how we have to look at it. They took care of me when I was young, so I should take care of them now that they're old.

Jason expresses a social contract between generations that, at one level, has nothing to do with the world outside close kin. Yet he defines his obligations in contrast to the way he perceives more affluent families shuffling their older relatives off to nursing homes where they have no family ties. He rejects this path as an abrogation of a contract between generations, and in accepting his personal responsibilities to care for his own he also makes good on a commitment to keep his family business out of the "burden" column for the rest of society. In short, private acts—caring for the elderly, raising children, monitoring public behavior on the neighborhood streets, visiting with a child's teacher—take on a larger resonance as examples of commitment to the community.

The responses in Table 7.2 reveal some dramatic differences between our

Table 7-2

Family Obligations

On a scale of 1 (no obligation at all) to 10 (very great obligation), how much obligation would you feel:

	New York Sample Mean (% rating "10")	National MIDUS Mean (% rating "10")
To drop plans when children seem troubled	9.01 (61.6%)	8.86 (52.6%)
To be in touch with parents on a regular basis	8.88** (60.2%)	8.66 (51.9%)
To call/write/visit adult children regularly	8.55* (48.5%)	7.81 (29.7%)
To take divorced/ unemployed adult children back home	8.45** (51.5%)	7.40 (29.7%)
To raise the child of a close friend if the friend died	7.02 (32.3%)	6.95 (22.2%)

*Difference from national sample significant at the 0.01 level; ** 0.001 level.

minority sample and the largely white national sample. On the whole, African Americans, Dominicans, and Puerto Ricans in New York are more committed to remaining in close contact and providing support for extended family members. Indeed, their mean scores on these items are considerably higher than the averages for the questions about general civic engagement, a finding suggestive of a more inward-turning orientation when defining social responsibility. On both counts, the minority sample professes greater commitment to these obligations than does the national population.

Their normative ideals are further supported by the patterns of contact they maintain with members of their families who are not coresident. When asked "How often are you in contact with any members of your family—that is, any of your brothers, sisters, parents, or children who do not live with you—including visits, phone calls, letters or electronic mail?" our respondents are 20 percent more likely to answer "several times a day" than is the majority of the national sample. The pattern makes sense when we think about the importance of family for defining social networks, especially among the poor, who may be less able to draw upon friends from work than are the middle class. Among the more affluent, friends may come to assume a more important role than siblings, for example, especially as adults reach middle age. The opposite seems to be true for inner-city folk.

Communicating with family is one thing; supporting family financially is another. Here, too, our New York families are "givers": 55 percent contribute to the support of their parents, children, in-laws, or grandchildren. Nearly half provide support to other family members or close friends. Perhaps they do so in anticipation of reciprocity, but there is very minor evidence of "giving back," at least as our survey respondents tell the story. Only 22 percent say they receive material support from their kin and a very small group (7 percent) receives contributions from religious groups. With so many giving and so few receiving, it is hard to know whether we have just captured the more generous people in our survey or whether cultural norms encourage people to report giving more readily than receiving.

Taking care of children, keeping them under control, is seen by most Americans as a private duty that all parents should adhere to. In poor communities, these private obligations may take on a more public significance as a form of civic behavior. Families who do not do their part, who let their children run wild, sow the seeds of neighborhood decline. In communities facing a daily onslaught of petty crime, disorderly or belligerent conduct, graffiti, and broken windows, stable, law-abiding, respectable[8] families who dominate the local culture recognize that the environmental problems they face are "homegrown." Little credence is given to the liberal position that society has failed urban youth (through poor schools, cutbacks in social policy, and the like). Instead, as Mason Bradley explains, child rearing is defined as a family's social obligation.

> You can be responsible for the community just by taking care of things at home. This way the community is not bothered with some of your own home problems, things that can be stopped at home such as dealing with the children, curbing their attitudes, things such as that. So this way, if you trained your child correctly at home, when he comes out into the community someone else will not have to . . . curb your child.

The reverse argument also holds in ghetto life. Families bound by social norms, who raise their children to "do right," express a commitment to the social good, to the protection of their communities from behavior that would—absent their vigilance—degrade the quality of life in inner-city neigh-borhoods. The private *becomes* public in this very special sense. And the task of raising children becomes an expression of commitment to the well-being of the neighborhood as well as to the family. The well-behaved child is sub-tracted from the ledger of potential problem cases that residents of poor blocks must contend with. Since that ledger can be long, the source of much daily grief for families struggling to live in peace in the midst of run-down conditions, the positive kudos that accrues to the responsible parent is sig-nificant.

Middle-class families also hold themselves accountable for their children's behavior. But since they are blessed, on the whole, with orderly neighbor-hoods and stable social institutions, they are less likely to create a public problem if they neglect private family obligations. A child who grows up a stain on his family's honor in suburban America is a matter of personal shame. He is less likely to be a threat to his neighbors.[9]

Because the obstacles to a conventional adulthood are considerable, fam-ilies that navigate these waters successfully are looked upon as success stories, people who have surmounted the odds. Their efforts to leap those hurdles—to raise their children without succumbing to negative influences—are therefore culturally defined as an expression of social responsibility toward the sur-rounding community as well as a personal achievement.

The Complexities of Reciprocity

There is another reason why raising children properly is defined as a social obligation. Reciprocity across the generations, particularly in the more tra-ditional Latino communities, implies that the favor will be returned. When parents grow old, the children they have "raised right" will care for them in exchange. Yet this expectation is complicated by the influences of modernism, the intergenerational autonomy that is normative in the American middle class.

Lucia Noventa was brought to New York from Puerto Rico when she was six months old. A married woman with four children, ages three to nineteen, Lucia draws clear boundaries around her obligations. They stretch only as far as her own family.

> The only obligation that I have is to my kids and to my husband. That's it, and of course, God forbid, to my mama. My mother—first God, then my mother. My obligation is to my kids. They didn't ask

me to bring them into this world. I brought them in. So, as long as I am physically able, I am obligated to give them, to provide for them, so that they can grow up and provide for themselves.

Lucia sees her first task as ensuring her children's survival, making sure they have a roof over their heads. Next on the list is her own mother, to whom she is promised as a caregiver. But she would not want to depend on her own kids for the same care.

I am not asking for them, when I grow older, "Oh, you gotta give me something from your paychecks." "If you want to help me out, you help me out. If you don't want to, power to you."

Lucia's comments reflect the darker side of the immigration experience. Puerto Ricans and Dominicans who come from cultures built around the obligations that bind generations confront an American code that values autonomy, subtracting from the social contract between generations the duty to provide financially.[10] Affection and respect are meant to be unhinged from economic responsibility. These are truly foreign ideas in the eyes of these other cultures and they come hard to those who arrive on American shores.

Carol Stack's classic work *All Our Kin* (1973) explores much the same tension among African Americans in the neighborhood she calls "The Flats," a segregated and poor community in southern Illinois. Descendants of the generation that migrated out of rural southern towns in Mississippi and Alabama on their way to the northern metropolis of Chicago, the residents of The Flats confronted poverty with extended and fictive-kin ties that provided a private safety net. Goods and money circulate from one household to another, ensuring some protection against fluctuating resources (aid checks cut off, jobs lost). "What goes around, comes around," Stack's informants explain: givers become receivers, building up mutual obligations over time that ensure a modicum of security. However, the cost of such an arrangement is serious: it puts a brake on the upward mobility of individuals enmeshed in a web of dense ties, for they cannot hoard resources against the claims of "partners" if they expect to be able to ask for help in the future.

Social responsibility in The Flats extends outward from the natal household to encompass extended family and close friends, but it is always crosscut by the thoroughly American desire to break free and prosper independently. The tension is ever present when good fortune shines on one individual and he or she must decide whether to break from the leveling power of the social network or rest within, an insurance policy against future need. Those who decide to hoard their resources and make a move toward a better neighbor-hood, or a Catholic school for their children, will not be able to distribute their savings to friends and family in need. There isn't enough to provide for both directions. Thus making the choice to do for your family imposes some restrictions on your participation in the sharing networks you may need to rely on for survival when things get tight.

For many immigrants and native-born poor in New York, a similar drama plays itself out as families contend with the shifting social norms that define the relations among their members. For Lucia Noventa, the tide has shifted in favor of independence, of grooming her children to make it on their own, with the hope that they will not forget who made their good fortune possible.

> I want to instill in them a sense of family, the sense of self-confidence in themselves. Otherwise, who am I going to be obligated to? I am looking for my best work if I can [get it]. I will give it my best effort, but I am not going to be obligated [to the workplace]. My obligation is to my kids, and once they grow up then they are obligated to make sure that they can take care of themselves.

What Lucia hopes is that her children will not have to take care of her and that they will be able to survive on their own so that her elder years will not be consumed by their needs. She cannot be confident of either out-come. Men and women who have spent a lifetime in irregular employment or the nontaxed economy (e.g., black and Latina women who worked as domestics) often lack pensions, access to social security, and medical care. Moreover, as we saw in chapter five, poverty leaves its traces in poor health that descends early.[11] Demands for care fall on the shoulders of family members both in accordance with custom and because there are few other alternatives. The resources that permit middle-class and wealthy families to buy services—home aids, nursing care, assisted living—are not available. It may well fall to Lucia's children to care for her when she cannot manage on her own.

To the extent that we believe that society bears some obligation toward the support of the elderly (expressed through social security, Medicare, pen-sions, and other benefits), it should be clear that the substitutional character of family labor among the poor is more than a private act. If Lucia's children have to respond to this call, they will be doing more than providing for their mother. They will also shoulder burdens that the rest of the society might otherwise have to contend with. This is surely what Irene Mandel has already done in taking care of her elderly aunt (as outlined in chapter five). If it weren't for Irene's efforts, Aunt Ruth might have had to resort to a nursing home at public expense. With Irene's support, she was able to retain her independence for many years beyond what many people would have experienced in similar circumstances. Irene carefully guarded Ruth's funds so that there was enough left over, when the family finally couldn't care for her on a daily basis, to support the expense of a private, comfortable facility.

Neighbors

Poor neighborhoods in New York have no shortage of problems. Almost everyone in our study complained of robberies, drug users and drug pushers, unemployment, and families that do too little to control their children's behavior. Under these circumstances, the natural response is to withdraw into private spaces, ceding the public domain to the negative elements.[12] In some of the nation's tougher housing projects, this isolation strategy may predominate,[13] hardly a recipe for social responsibility.

Yet in the barrios and black ghettoes of Harlem, the South Bronx, and Bedford-Stuyvesant, more communal efforts have developed that reflect an outward-turning commitment to the stability and safety of the neighborhoods. Housing projects have established tenant patrols, self-imposed curfews, and escort services for the elderly in an effort to reduce the burdens of crime. These informal activities take time, energy, and an underlying social solidarity that transcends the privacy of households.

Missy Darden has been mugged a time or two. The experience motivated her to do something to help herself and others.

> I tried to start a civilian patrol and a buddy system within the neighborhood or the complex I live in. People [who have to come home from work] late at night get together and have a telephone chain of people who are coming in at the same hours so people come in together. A person wouldn't have to walk down the street by themselves.

Neighborhood watch groups, informal escort services, and the like provide a vehicle to educate residents about the best way to avoid victimization. As Missy explains:

> You can wear certain items or walk a certain way. Having been a victim of muggings more than once, I've noticed that on those occasions [I was broadcasting], "Here I am." I had to learn to walk like I was nuts,

talking to myself and waving, and that sort of deterred people from bothering me. I really try to warn people or make them aware that certain things they do, certain things they can avoid, like walking in dark places or places that happen to be deserted, being aware of who's around you. That doesn't always work, but it's a start.

Missy was confident this would make her neighbors less vulnerable and saw it as her obligation to educate them in protective strategies. She also saw the local patrols as a vehicle for rallying the troops. Missy realized that the only way she would see more cops on the beat in her neighborhood was to amass public support and pressure that would be hard for officials to ignore.

Missy has also organized a yearly fair in her housing complex that brings the neighbors together in an effort to raise some money.

Every year I have this [event] on the plaza where we sell table space. I even include the young people. . . . Once people pay for their table space, whatever they earn after that belongs to them. I have culture groups come in dancing. . . . It's not a big moneymaking thing, but it's something to have people doing something together within the complex and the neighborhood.

Missy follows up by taking groups of young people to local African festivals. "Last year," she remembers, "I had about fifteen of them with me, teenagers, young people that are hanging around." Missy prefers to have them involved in things around their community, "Cultural things," she says, "rather than just hanging out."

Missy is not alone in her efforts. Juana Herrera, a Dominican immigrant in her early sixties, has many of the same concerns and has moved toward the same neighborhood-based solutions.

[What we have to do is] unite and have reunions with the community and the police. Now we are doing that because [robberies] were occurring here. The Mexicans were being assaulted when they came from work late at night. The poor things, with all the working hard they have to do, so that others try to take it away from them!

In studies of Chicago neighborhoods, Robert Sampson and his colleagues have found that, controlling for median income and ethnic composition, neighborhoods that exhibit high levels of social capital—dense networks and social trust—suffer considerably lower levels of crime and disorder than those where residents are more anomic.[14] Social responsibility, expressed in the form of neighborhood-based solidarity, works. This lesson has not been lost on Jason Norwald, who has observed the idea in practice.

> There are floors that have break-ins, and there are floors that don't, simply because the neighbors watch out for each other. Not necessarily an organized kind of thing, but hey, "That doesn't sound like Rose at the door. So let me see who's out there." With, of course, you being aware of the possibility of putting yourself in danger, but still looking out for the neighbor.

There are forms of social responsibility at the neighborhood level that are not expressed in organizational form. Sentiments of solidarity surface as personal practices of reciprocity, as Henry Montez, a native New Yorker of Puerto Rican descent, reports.

> I think neighbors should look out for one another, for the elderly. My neighbors love me. Whenever they ask me for something, I will try to help them out. [Some people] will try to take advantage of me. But if you are nice people and I see you need help, well . . . what goes around comes around. Today you have money and tomorrow you have nothing. Today you are healthy and tomorrow you are sick. [So you have to help others.]

Henry's work brings him into contact with many of his neighbors. While he always hopes to be paid for his work, he also provides pro bono services to elderly Puerto Ricans in his Brooklyn neighborhood who cannot afford to pay for the plumbing help they need. Henry knows that the good he does will be rewarded in the future and considers this kind of reciprocity both a cultural obligation and a good investment.

Rita Tilly, the seventy-one-year-old African American featured in chapter one, sees the same advantages in being considerate and outgoing toward people she knows mainly by sight.

> You can be friendly to people as you see them. When I go to school [with my great-granddaughter], I see these people every morning and I try to say hello and good morning to them, because they're taking the kids. I don't know them but they're going the same way taking the kids to school. This way you get to know people. . . . And it's good to know people in the neighborhood because when you're walking down

and something [bad] is happening, someone will say, that's Miss so-and-so, the lady I know who lives on this block. And they'll sort of help you and protect you.

This kind of reciprocal giving is a form of personal insurance, expressed in the ongoing ties between neighbors. The instrumental and strategic aspects of local ties are mixed in with sentiments of solidarity and time-honored kinds of self-help. It "takes a village" to ensure the viability of a neighborhood in these inner-city communities and the investment in building social capital requires effort.

While the village is made up of people of all different ages, these older members of the community are among the most active contributors. This is partly a generational phenomenon: they come from a cohort of people who have volunteered their time, worked in their church soup kitchens, helped out at Sunday school, organized the tenants' watch groups, and generally given of themselves. This is the inner-city version of the "long civic generation" Putnam discussed in his treatise on social capital, *Bowling Alone*. But it is also a tradition defined by age that earlier generations enacted and, presumably, younger ones will mature into as they approach old age. Once they no longer work, they put their time into the village, even if the village is defined simply as their apartment building. Part of being an elder, or what Eli Anderson calls an "old head," in an inner-city neighborhood is adopting this service ethic. It is partly self-interested, for it improves the quality of life for the giver as well. It is motivated just as much, however, by a genuine desire to help others and thereby sustain the community.

We see some striking differences in levels of neighborhood social integration when contrasting the New York sample and the national experience. As Table 7.3 suggests, these big-city dwellers are very connected to the people who live around them.

Those who believe that neighborhoods are characterized by a high degree of social interchange will be heartened by these findings. Those who worry about social isolation may find them less encouraging. For the flip side of spending a lot of time with your neighbors may be loss of interchange with the wide world outside of poor enclaves. In any case, we see that the Dominicans, Puerto Ricans, and African Americans are much more likely to spend time with their family members and neighbors than seems to be true of the national sample.

Of course, constant interchange does not necessarily lead to social trust, the outcome social scientists most hope to see grow out of personal contact. Indeed, poor minority neighborhoods often are described by journalists and

Table 7-3

Social Integration in the Neighborhood

How often do you have a real conversation or
get together socially with any of your neighbors?

	New York Sample	National Sample
Almost every day	43%*	8.2%
Several times a week	13%	13.2%
About once a week	9%*	20.6%
1–3 times a month	9%*	16.9%
Less than once a month	6%*	17.8%
Never/hardly ever	20%	23.4%

*Difference from national sample significant at the 0.05 level.

social scientists as wary, suspicious places, largely because of crime problems. We don't have direct observations of trust, but we do know how our New Yorkers feel about the people they live near. On the whole, they are quite satisfied by the sense of belonging and fellowship that surrounds them.

I have characterized neighborhoods as arenas within which social responsibility is expressed by poor minorities who recognize the redeeming, protective consequences of reciprocity and engagement. Yet these same enclaves can be divided by race and ethnicity. The poor are forced into areas with low housing costs and poor job opportunities, pitting groups against one another in the scramble for scarce resources. Where these conditions produce deep cleavages, solidarity develops inside ethnic and racial lines rather than across them.

Indeed, the MacArthur Network's MIDUS survey shows that even after controlling for total household income, educational attainment, and home ownership, African Americans report lower ratings of safety and social cohesion in their neighborhoods than do all other racial groups. This undoubtedly reflects the toll that racial segregation is taking on neighborhoods and the relative lack of trust that characterizes poorer neighborhoods. MIDUS also shows, however, that African Americans have more frequent social contact with their neighbors than do other ethnic groups, even when controlling for levels of neighborhood safety, income, home ownership, and family size.[15] This suggests a level of in-group interaction in the national sample that is consistent with the New York–area findings.

Table 7-4

Social Solidarity in Minority Neighborhoods

How much does each statement describe the way you feel?

	A lot	Some	Little	Not at all
I feel I belong to this neighborhood	68%	20%	6%	6%
I feel loyal to the people in my neighborhood	58.6%	19.2%	14.1%	8.1%
A feeling of fellowship runs deep between me and my neighbors	53%	17%	15%	15%
Living in this neighborhood gives me a sense of community	56%	17%	13%	14%

Circling the Wagons

There is, of course, a long-standing tradition of self-help and inward-turning social responsibility in the African-American community. Starting with Marcus Garvey and extending to Malcolm X, the notion that helping one's own—through a racially bounded church, a program of "buying black," or an organization like the Black Panthers—is a primary obligation. It contrasts with a more universal definition of civic commitment.

Similarly, immigrants are known for their habit of taking care of their countrymen, beginning with the chain migration patterns that bring related individuals or former neighbors from their nations of origins to the receiving communities in the United States.[16] Suspicion of outsiders is all too common and is exacerbated when the market (for housing, jobs, etc.) thrusts immigrant groups into competition with one another or with the native-born. These conditions do not foster interethnic harmony. Instead, as we've seen, competition for resources enhances in-group solidarity and generates wariness toward outsiders.

These forces surface in the form of strong and abiding sentiments that one's primary social responsibility lies in addressing the needs of the ethnoracial group. This definition of social responsibility must be distinguished from that which fosters engagement in the neighborhood, even though co-residents may also be defined by their common racial or ethnic heritage. Here I refer to the ways in which individuals identify themselves as members of a racial group that transcends neighborhood, city, or even personal acquaintance. Obligations flow between people who share a skin color, a national origin, or a common heritage of discrimination on account of language or appearance, whether or not they are known to one another personally.

Social responsibility toward one's race/ethnicity can be expressed as a hierarchy, leaving room for more universal commitments as well: first I serve my own, and then I can turn my attention toward outsiders. For others, the attitude is more exclusionary: I owe a great deal to my own and little to others. Either way, the racial and ethnic groups turn inward toward the protection, sustenance, and promotion of the life chance of their members.

Irene Mandel expresses this hierarchy of social responsibility. She is frankly nationalistic in her commitments, noting, "I feel responsible to African Americans." Her racially defined sense of social responsibility led her to change jobs so that she could act on this bounded commitment.

> I left the school district that I taught in—Sheepshead Bay. I was sent there when they were balancing racially. And I felt like I had a responsibility to come back to my neighborhood or a neighborhood similar to mine, and share my expertise for the children, and my attitude toward children's learning and the possibilities for [black] children.

Irene does feel a general commitment to children as a whole; this is her motivation for being a teacher. Still, she sees the world in terms of racial groups and conceives of her responsibilities as flowing first to African-American children.

Aida Gonzalez, a forty-six-year-old Dominican, shares Irene's feelings.

> I feel responsible to my own group. Like for instance, if I can open a day care [home care] on a corner in a little apartment, I would try to get my own people to employ and to take care of. Even though I have Chinese and Indians and white. I would try to get more of [my own].

The primacy of self-help is often driven by the view that ethnic communities, particularly inner-city enclaves, are uniquely plagued by (or even targeted for) social pathologies like drug abuse and violence. It does not escape the notice of ghetto dwellers that drug dealers ply their trade in their neighborhoods and not on predominantly white Park Avenue. They resent the fact that police corruption and abusive treatment is endemic in their communities and absent in middle-class white enclaves. Hence, while a "race conscious" nationalism can produce an inward-turning sense of social responsibility, so too can a feeling of victimization—indeed the two sentiments are not unrelated.

As Mason Bradley put the matter:

> We [speak] to kids, underprivileged kids, that is white, black everybody under the rainbow. But I want to especially reach out my hand to people of color, those children, and let them know. Listen, you can do better. . . . We have to stop promoting a lot of [bad] things that go on. This guy, sells drugs, but [they think] it's okay. No it is not okay. That is wrong. And we will not tolerate that in this neighborhood. . . . You take those drugs somewhere else! I love my people. I am a black man; I am going to stand up for the black woman and the black man. How can I truly call myself a black man and you are out here poisoning my people, poisoning my children.

Immigrants share the preoccupation of African Americans with self-help and racial solidarity. When asked to whom he felts obligated, Fred Moreno, a twenty-six-year-old Dominican college student, was quick to answer: "My Dominicans. I want us to have a power. I want us to have a say. I want us to be better than we are. That is something that motivates me, that drives me." Fred moved to New York from the Dominican Republic when he was eight years old and has lived inside the barrio ever since. His closest ties, from the family to peers, are contained within this ethnic enclave. The barrio of Washington Heights, where he has lived most of his life, is surrounded by other ethnic groups that are competitors for housing, jobs, and most other forms of opportunity. Fred has learned from this ethnically segregated milieu that he should define himself in terms of his own people rather than a pan-ethnic or American identity.

Cleaving to one's own is a natural response in neighborhoods that are divided by race or national origin. Even when residents face common problems, and locate themselves (sociologically) by neighborhood, these divisions can be hard to surmount. Edna Carson, a black woman whose parents migrated from North Carolina to Brooklyn, is raising a family of her own in a mixed community. Solidarity based on common location has proven elusive in her neighborhood.

You got to think where you're living in the neighborhood when people are from different places. A lot of them don't have their green cards, a lot of them don't have immigration cards, so you don't have a real lot of unity. You're just American black and you've got your papers because you ain't never went nowhere, so you don't have that kind of unity with them because they're scared. You have Mexicans, you got Hispanics, and a lot of Dominicans, they don't have their papers. So they're not going to help you protect anything because they just want to stay by themselves and they don't want immigration bothering them. So, you lost it, you lost that bridge to come together because there's so many gaps in between.

The Missing Poor

The inner-city households in this book span the class range from the working poor to members of the lower middle class. There are teachers, accountants, and professionals among them, but the majority have spent their working lives as blue-collar operatives, or in hospitals where they were employed as lower-level white-collar workers. More than half of the qualitative sample had household incomes below $25,000, even with multiple earners in the family. They do not think of themselves as impoverished, though they live in low-income neighborhoods from which the more affluent have fled.

In their world, as in most middle-class communities, race is the most visible marker of social position. Class, by contrast, is a missing category. That is not because they do not recognize that they live in a poor community. It is because if they attribute this fate to any cause, it will almost always be race or ethnicity that trumps class as the force behind their social and geographic location.

Perhaps for this reason it is striking how questions about social responsibility fail to elicit much commentary on the needs of "the poor." One hears lengthy discussion about the obligations individuals have to their families, to their community, and to their group, but not to those who are poor. Part of the explanation for this gap may lie in the commitments some have made to the church, an institution that provides services to the poor in New York's barrio neighborhoods. Indeed, over 42 percent of this sample said that they contribute money, food, clothing, and other goods to their churches.

It may also be that living so close to the poverty line themselves, the working (or retired) poor tend not to feel as much sympathy toward those less fortunate than do others who are socially distant and looking for a target for their charitable impulses.[17] So much publicity has been given to AFDC and its problems that my informants often equate "the poor" with "welfare mothers" (as do middle-class supporters of time limits and the end of "welfare as we know it"). The working poor see finer gradations of status at the bottom of the social hierarchy and do not confuse themselves with the homeless, the hopeless, or the welfare dependent. Indeed, the welfare dependent come in for a great deal of criticism among them.[18]

At the same time, our interviews contain consistent references to the "truly needy": young children, the indigent beggar on the corner, young mothers over their heads with family responsibilities, and the like. Hence while the category of "the poor" is little discussed, particular poor people are the objects of sympathy and charity. In this, our respondents mirror the attitudes discussed in Herbert Gans's powerful book *The War on the Poor*. Gans explains that while sympathy is shown toward specific individuals, the poor are demonized as a social category. Indeed, the negative attribution toward the category of the poor is a powerful source for antipathy directed at welfare and other programs that ameliorate poverty. To the extent that social responsibility is politically defined, these New Yorkers embrace the mainstream view that distinguishes the deserving poor from the rest.

The Missing Nation

Equally absent from local conceptions of social responsibility was the kind of abstract idea of the nation, the society as a whole, as an entity toward which commitment must be expressed. Of course, the interviews discussed here were conducted several years before the bombing of the World Trade Center, which catalyzed an outpouring of patriotism that, at least temporarily, bound the nation across racial lines. But before (and probably after), the importance of the nation as a primary bond or an inspiration for sacrifice had been (is) weak. This is partly explained by the immigration status of the Dominican respondents in our study. Puerto Ricans, in turn, draw upon a mixed and wary view of the United States as a place that has incorporated them, but not on their own terms.

Earlier waves of immigrants, who entered the country when the economy was on an upswing, achieved their economic mobility over time. Waves of Americanization, molded during the course of World War II and consolidated by postwar affluence, generated attachment to "the best country in the world." Rapid suburbanization fostered a break from the ethnic enclaves of the cities, and sped the process of cultural assimilation. The nation became an identity and a source of solidarity among, for example, American-born descendants of Italian and Irish immigrants. Civic or communitywide conceptions of social responsibility developed over time, as relative newcomers gradually became privileged members of the middle class.

Few of these conditions held fast by the mid-1970s, as waves of Puerto Rican and Dominican migrants settled into cities like New York. Like the African Americans who had preceded them in the Great Migration out of the rural South to the industrial North, the "new" immigrants had to find their way into the urban economy at a time when high-paying industrial jobs were rapidly disappearing. The service jobs that replaced unionized, blue-collar jobs were distinguished by low pay and dead-end job ladders.

Upward mobility has become far more problematic for the new generations of immigrants in our time.[19] Under these economic circumstances, identification with the nation has become more tenuous, and abstract ideas of social responsibility are equally strained. Solidarity with "one's own" has greater appeal when barriers to mobility are firm and persistent, precluding the development of subjective and moral commitments to the larger community. Ironically, the greatest attachment to common institutions is probably found among sports enthusiasts, who cross ethnic lines to a greater degree than any other form of civic participation.

When we investigate the contours of social responsibility, we are asking powerful questions not only about what people do to "make good" on their conceptions of obligation, but about the boundaries they draw around their identities. How do they situate themselves in a moral sense? What are the forms of community that exert a powerful enough influence to produce a moral claim on their time, their resources, and their sense of social location?

Inner-city minorities are often described as socially disengaged isolates who have pulled back from wider social obligations in response to safety problems in the neighborhoods where they live. That portrait is misleading. The migration experience, urban segregation, and limited economic mobility have all conspired to create a strong sense of belonging. The same forces have bound minority groups into enclaves that breed both solidarity and division. Loyalty is owed to those who are within the boundaries, though the lines are themselves fluid and shifting according to time and circumstance. Neighbors may see themselves as locked together in a struggle for survival or protection against fellow residents who do not share their values. Co-ethnics confronting racial barriers may separate themselves from fellow residents of their neighborhoods who belong to another racial group or nationality.

The lived reality of these boundaries, however, is created in part by the social responsibilities insiders feel toward one another. Parents who raise their children "right" do so not only out of a sense of family values but out of the conviction that they owe this effort to others in their community. They fault irresponsible parents not only for what they have done to destroy their children's futures, but for what they have wrought upon the neighborhood in the form of antisocial behavior. Neighbors band together to watch over one another, forming block watch groups, youth parties, and other types of support as measures with which to battle the social decay that threatens their peace of mind and the safety of their children. Dominicans and Puerto Ricans think about what they should do to foster the well-being of their own people, putting them ahead of the demands of others who may be equally needy, but who must be someone else's responsibility. The ethnic "mosaic" expresses a racially fractured understanding of the community to which they belong. Yet within the boundaries these divisions create, a sense of social responsibility is clearly expressed and acted out in people's daily lives.

8–A Different Shade of Gray

Middle-aged inner-city dwellers are aging faster than their more comfortable counterparts who now dominate the news regarding what it means to grow into maturity and old age in America. They don't have the bank accounts, houses gaining equity, private pensions, or gated retirement villages that cushion more affluent Americans. As a consequence, middle age and elderhood involves "a different shade of gray" from what we are accustomed to seeing across the rest of the country. Those dramatic differences—economic, social, and environmental—are a consequence primarily of the strikingly different pathways that lead up to middle age. No one arrives at age fifty a new kind of person, but as the sum of a personal history. And as a result of the histories of Latinos and African Americans in inner-city New York, this has left them with unique burdens coupled with diminished resources.

The problems surrounding aging in the inner city are not limited to women with another round of youngsters to raise. Mortality figures among blacks and Latinos, who get sick earlier and die younger than their white counterparts, are telling as well. We are losing valuable years of productivity from middle-aged minorities, and their families are burdened by chronic illness that disrupts the work lives of younger members. Men and women who have managed on their own—especially those living alone in public housing projects—have often had no choice but to remain behind closed doors in high-crime enclaves. They can't run, so they have to hide. Because there are thousands of American families living with these burdens, it makes sense to ask whether there is anything we can do as a society that will make their middle-aged and elderly years more comfortable, safer, less insecure.

The most serious of their problems are traceable to inadequate income, hardly a new facet of life for most men and women in poor families since they have cycled in and out of poverty over the course of their adult lives. If they had come into their later years after a long period of rising income, blessed by intact marriages, living in safe neighborhoods during their child-rearing years, they would not be staring at old age with so few resources. If their adult years featured decent diets, no smoking, and the security that comes from a savings account or regular access to a doctor, they would be a lot less stressed nowadays. That long history catches up to people in their mature years, making them old before their time. It is something of a patch-work solution to address the holes such a life course produces in the end game. We would do better to encourage more stability and security all along.

Yet it is not the aim of this book to discuss solutions to the poverty problem over the whole of the life span. Instead I want to bring it to a close by drawing attention to barriers that are of greatest concern to the aged. So eager are we to debate solutions to the difficulties of poor teens, single parents with young children, gangs, and the like that we forget they have grandfa-thers and grandmothers. Policies we set in motion decades ago are taking their toll on the way that the older generation is faring, and there is work to be done to adjust our safety net so that it addresses their needs more effec-tively.

Social Security Reform

Before the economy weakened in 2001 and the attack on the World Trade Center diverted attention from budget wrangling in the first year of the Bush administration, the airwaves and op-ed pages were filled with discussion of social security reform. The aging of a baby-boom generation bound for re-tirement has increased anxiety about a "crisis" of solvency in our national retirement accounts. The booming stock market of the late 1990s convinced many that the answer to the dilemma lies in privatizing social security by investing those contributions in the stock market. Giving individuals more control over their portfolios sounded very appealing to those swimming in profits from an unprecedented bull market.

Liberals worried out loud that a shift toward private accounts would leave those unfamiliar with the intricacies of investing out in the cold. They decried privatization plans as a ploy to capture a huge market for Wall Street through an artificial panic over the system's viability. The left suggested that only unrealistically pessimistic projections of economic growth would produce a deficit in these accounts, and that if it happened at all it would be nearly seventy-five years in the future.[1]

Conservatives beat the demographic drum and warned about the need to cut benefits or raise taxes in draconian fashion if something drastic wasn't done to increase the returns.[2] With the ratios of active workers to retirees due to shift dramatically, those who favor privatization insisted the whole system would go belly up without it. Their entreaties found sympathy in the millions of baby boomers with no memory of the Great Depression and little confidence in government at all. It was also persuasive to many Latinos, who differ from African Americans in their higher rates of marriage, less divorce, and more conservative values. They, too, seek higher rates of return on their retirement.[3] Many Americans agree with the view that individuals can do a better job managing their own money, that the private capital markets are a better investment, and that time for corrective action is running out.[4]

The privatization debate is consequential for many women and most poor people, who are right to be anxious about how they would fare if a universal entitlement instead becomes a variable benefit, dependent upon their investment expertise. They might very well do much better under privatization, but the risk that they would do significantly worse looms.[5] As the Economic Policy Institute stated the matter, "No one gets rich on their Social Security benefits, but most everyone gets by. With private accounts, some people would do very well, but others would fare quite poorly." The risks became more visible in 2000–01 when the stock market nose-dived and private pensions invested in everything from technology stocks to the blue chips plummeted. The Enron fiasco of 2002 further underlined the vulnerability ordinary workers and investors face when their retirement is tied up in the market.

It is hard to forecast how this debate will be resolved. One thing is for sure, though: the millions of elderly poor—including widows of all colors, and men and women in the inner-city neighborhoods described in this book—cannot afford a social policy that tampers with the absolute certainty of that monthly check. Having spent years working in jobs that did not offer private pensions, they confront old age uniquely reliant on the resources social security provides. One in five elderly women receive all of their income from social security. An even larger proportion (nearly one-third) get 90 percent of their income from this source. They don't need a roller-coaster ride, even if the upswings might provide them with more resources. What they need is to be sure that the money they have coming to them keeps arriving in their mailboxes each and every month.

For many advocates, however, the debates over privatization are secondary to the more urgent need to address the basic benefit structure of social security. Our rules were designed in another era, a period when women virtually always married, where marriages lasted until "death do you part," and men were the chief breadwinners. These assumptions were built into the basic architecture of social security and have remained, even as large numbers of women entered the labor market, though on terms that fell short of those men have enjoyed. Increasing divorce rates and single motherhood have been the lot of millions of American women, particularly African Americans, but the system cannot easily accommodate these realities and preserve a basic fairness in retirement. The gender divide is particularly pronounced: the average benefit received by women is only 62 percent of that received by men because female lifetime earnings are lower and an increasing proportion of women have not been married long enough to access benefits accruing to men.

During the 2000 presidential campaign, a number of proposals to reform the benefit structure of social security surfaced. Vice President Gore outlined several initiatives that would have made for significant improvements in the lives of the elderly in the inner city.[6] The first of his proposals involved eliminating the "motherhood penalty," a provision that is largely responsible for the difficulties facing poor people with irregular attachments to the labor market. Currently, when a parent leaves her job to care for her children, she receives no credit from Social Security for the years during which she worked at home and had no earnings. When retirement comes, all those "zero years" are averaged into her earnings and her benefits are set by that average.[7]

The same problem besets workers who have to leave their jobs to care for elderly relatives, a problem common to women and especially visible in minority communities, where the resources for nursing homes are often nonexistent. Leaving the work world to care for an elderly mother or an aunt will leave that caretaker with a big hole where full-time earnings would otherwise be. And she will feel the pain when she retires. About 75 percent of the elderly poor are women, who average fourteen years out of the workforce because of their family responsibilities.[8] The Older Women's League released a report on the consequences of the current benefit rules for elderly women on Mother's Day, 2001. They concluded that "those who look after the elderly lose about $2,100 a year in Social Security benefits." That is a lot of money when you live in the vicinity of the poverty line.

Vice President Gore argued that society should recognize the work parents do in raising kids by crediting their social security accounts for time spent out of the labor market in service of those familial responsibilities.[9] Specifically, he argued that credits toward social security benefits be extended for up to five years for those who are out of the workforce or working part-time and would have counted those years as if the caregiver earned half of the nation's average wage ($16,500 in 2001). If this were to become law, there would be many fewer zero years for caregivers. Part-time workers would be topped up too. This would automatically increase social security benefits and protect millions of elderly women from poverty. It is a policy that would help everyone—from middle-class housewives who don't work to low-income workers who have interrupted careers. Indeed, Gore argued that about 8 million Americans, most of them women, would benefit from this policy change. For the Latinas and African Americans in this book, such a policy would make an enormous difference.

The motherhood penalty will become increasingly important as more and more women claim social security based entirely on their own earnings, as is true of so many women who appear in this book. About 37 percent of American women receive benefits based on their own earnings, rather than on their husband's earnings. Since so many women are in the workforce now, that percentage is expected to rise to about 60 percent by 2060. If they earned as much as men, all would be equal. They don't, not only because their wages are lower but because they are more likely to "stop out" to take care of kids and elders. It is imperative that we find a way to recognize the value to the nation of this caregiving activity and stop punishing women through an impoverished retirement.

The 1999 Working Conference on Women and Social Security went a step further and argued that benefits need to be increased for divorcées. At the moment, divorcées receive only 50 percent of their former spouse's social security benefits, and can access that account only if the marriage lasted for at least ten years. Those whose marriages end before that magic period of time are completely out of luck. Advocacy groups all over Washington have argued that the benefit package must be improved and eligibility relaxed to seven years of marriage. Representative Nita Lowey, congresswoman for the Westchester area of New York, picked up on these ideas, along with a plan that would eliminate waiting periods that force divorced spouses to delay receipt of their benefits if their "ex" is still working. Given the fragile nature of wedlock, particularly in the inner city, this would help to increase the resources coming to those whose marriages were short-lived.

Improving survivor benefits for widows is another way of improving the lot of the elderly. Poverty among elderly widows runs at 18 percent, compared to 5 percent for elderly women who are still married. These figures flow naturally from the rules that cause household social security benefits to decline by between a third and a half when one spouse dies.[10] This is likely to be the case among black women, whose earnings are often as high or higher than their husbands'. The Gore campaign proposed that the survivor benefits be increased to give the remaining spouse at least 75 percent of the benefit received by the married couple. Nita Lowey also argued that widows between age sixty-five and seventy be allowed to supplement their benefits with earnings from employment without losing any of their social security. All of these policy changes would be helpful to inner-city minorities in their elder years.

We tend to think that social security is the province of the elderly. Yet millions of American children[11] either receive social security benefits or live in households where someone else does and are therefore dependent upon it as an income source. The Social Security Administration notes that of the 6.6 million American children living in these households, nearly 2 million of them are poor. Most of them are children of deceased or disabled workers, while the rest receive the benefit because they themselves are disabled. In this fashion, we make a commitment to the care of children whose parents die or become disabled and a promise to help families who have disabled kids, on the theory that their caregivers will have to leave the labor force to help them.

Families in the inner city are heavily represented in all of these groups. Given the poor health profile of so many minority adults, they are more likely to be disabled or die, leaving behind kids whom we help to provide for through this program. But it is not exactly generous by contemporary standards. The average monthly stipend for the nearly 4 million children who receive this benefit was $406 per month in 2000. That is considerably below even the most conservative estimate of the monthly cost of raising a child under the age of eighteen.[12] The more we can do to increase this benefit, the less likely it will be that children, and the grandparents who are raising them, will be hobbled by poverty.

The social security system's regulations need to be changed so that marital history and family responsibilities do not play such a powerful role in determining who is poor and who is not in old age. Our western European counterparts figured this out a long time ago and moved to protect women, widows, and those who earn low wages through government pensions that are not as earnings-dependent as is our own system. In a number of countries, the income that accrues to a household in any given year is split between the husband and wife, regardless of who earned it, so that credits flow to both parties even if one of them is at home taking care of children or the elderly. It is time to unhinge our social security system from the social histories of recipients so that all Americans, particularly those who are poor, are not at risk for poverty in their elder years. We have shown that dramatic changes of this kind can be enacted in the past. After all, prior to the 1930s, to be old was virtually always to be poor. Social security largely broke that connection. But it needs to be updated to reflect the present state of marriage and the realities of family life. This, above all, would make a positive difference for the inner-city poor.

Social security is not the only federal program that matters. Supplemental Security Income (SSI) is also critical. SSI is a federally administered means-tested cash benefit for needy aged and disabled persons (inner-city recipients often refer to SSI as "disability" to distinguish it from TANF and social security). Unlike social security, which pays out based on past earnings, SSI is a "targeted" policy that transfers resources to individuals based on their income and assets at the time of benefit receipt. Federal benefit levels for SSI are below the poverty line and it is possible that increasing the resources that flow to the poor through the SSI program might be the single most important thing we could do for elderly inner-city families, because they are disproportionately recipients of these funds.

Kathleen McGarry, an economist at UCLA, has estimated that SSI benefit levels could be raised to the poverty line for $12 billion per year. Even with this policy change, some elderly families would still be poor, however, because the take-up rate for SSI is significantly lower than for other transfer programs.[13] Thus, folding the SSI guarantee into social security or substantially expanding outreach efforts would be necessary to come close to fully eliminating poverty among the elderly. Even more modest expansions of SSI could make an important dent in elderly poverty. Under the current rules, SSI benefits are cut by $1 for every $1 in "countable income." The first $20 of monthly unearned income is not counted, a threshold that has not been altered in the past twenty-five years, despite increased inflation. Harvard economist Jeffrey Liebman's analysis for the Gore campaign points out that if we simply increased that income disregard to $55 to account for past inflation, an additional 100,000 elderly Americans would be lifted out of poverty.

A case can be made that we owe it to poor minorities to make these kinds of adjustments because early death robs them (and their families) of the opportunity to collect on the full social security benefits they are owed, even under current rules. The hard facts of mortality reverse the progressive nature of social security, which, by design, is supposed to pay out more to the poor than to the rich. Because the poor and minorities die young, they get back a great deal less than they would receive if their life expectancy equaled that of their middle-class counterparts.

The way we pass wealth on from one generation to the next also tends to disadvantage the families in this book. Social security is not "heritable": it cannot be converted into a resource that can be left to help support children left behind. By contrast, middle-class families generally do have significant savings (houses, stocks, life insurance benefits) that can be inherited.[14]

These two facts—differential life expectancy and divergent asset profiles— spell problems for the inner-city elderly. Jeffrey Liebman[15] has identified two policies that would go some distance toward redressing both. First, he recommends recalculating the benefit formulas to make them more progressive, that is to increase the redistributive function of social security by paying out more to those at the bottom of the income distribution, perhaps through a tax on high-income earners. Second, in families where death visits early, he recommends that a proportion of the foregone benefits be passed along to the next generation. Heirs whose parents collected social security for fewer than ten years before death would be able to inherit what their parents did not receive in retirement. Both of these proposals would cost us. Funding would have to come from somewhere, possibly from individual accounts with higher rates of return. The road to a more equitable system is rocky, politically speaking, because unless we can increase the size of the social security pie every move to equalize is likely to rob a richer Peter to pay a poorer Paul. Yet in focusing on aging Americans in the inner city, we can say without question that increasing the resources that flow to their families in the ordinary course of retirement or in the event of early death will make a huge difference.[16] Additional social security in the hands of a middle-class home owner might be icing on the cake, but for a poor woman who lives on nothing else it spells the difference between a cupboard full of food and an empty stomach.

Health Care and Health Insurance

Health issues are among the most vexing of all the challenges facing inner-city minorities who are in middle age and older. Educational campaigns are needed to spread the word about the things that the average citizen can do to avoid crippling health problems like diabetes or lung cancer. Weight control, exercise, and smoking cessation are all critical tools in the fight against the major diseases that disable and kill minority adults. Public health officials, schoolteachers, and doctors all have an important role to play in spreading the word from the youngest children to the oldest of the old about risk behaviors they can control. The alarming increase in childhood, or type I, diabetes tells us that waiting until adulthood is a mistake. Nutrition and exercise are life patterns that are set and must be taught early.

While our best bet is to prevent poor health conditions from developing in the first place, once they are set in motion it is critical that they are caught early. This is far less likely to happen in poor minority communities. Instead, the poor lack access to the medical community, obtain their medical care in emergency rooms when disease is advanced, and fail to get treatment when intervention would have provided the greatest payoff. Inadequate health insurance is part of the problem. The rising number of uninsured Americans is not a random problem: it predominantly afflicts low-wage workers, part-time employees, and the unemployed, all of whom are more likely to be inner-city minorities than any other demographic group.

The distribution of medical facilities is also a factor: poor people are often poorly served. Educating more minority doctors, who may have greater access, understanding, and willingness to serve in disadvantaged communities, would help in providing more comprehensive preventive care. The Older Americans Act, renewed by Congress in October of 2000, contained a support package for the historically black colleges and universities that will help to increase their output of minority medical students. Loan-forgiveness packages for any medical student willing to serve in persistently poor neighborhoods will help to get medical care to the poor when it can make the greatest difference.

As the United States ages, we confront the need to do much more than we have to provide home-based assistance to the "old old," so that they can remain in their own homes and avoid the punishing expense of nursing homes. Bathing, dressing, eating—all of these daily activities require the strong arms of younger people when the very elderly can no longer manage for themselves. Among Latinos and African Americans, it has traditionally fallen to women alone to provide these supports for their elders. We celebrate the commitment these women display to the care of their aging relatives. But we should recognize that this kind of work is exhausting and never-ending. It robs middle-aged women of the opportunity to work, something they need to do if they are going to keep their social security on track and not face an impoverished retirement themselves. Ironically, though African Americans have a much shorter life expectancy than whites, those who make it beyond the age of sixty-five live for quite a bit longer than nonminorities. These survivors are resilient, but they are not superhuman. When they hit their eighties they will need help, and for the most part they lack the financial resources to purchase it. Discrimination and high costs keep them out of nursing homes, which puts their families at a disadvantage as they struggle to keep themselves afloat.

The least-expensive way to address their needs is to provide additional federal and state support for the Medicare system so that they it can cover these services. Enforcing antidiscrimination laws already on the books is an important part of this picture. By the year 2020, we can expect to see about 12 million elderly Americans in need of long-term care. Those who are well off will probably be able to buy it, though it will drain their resources to do so. And those who are the poorest of the poor will be covered, at least to some extent, by the Medicaid system. As Judith Waxman, director of Health Care Advocacy for the Families USA Foundation, noted in her congressional testimony, it is the people in the middle who will be out of luck.

> The people who do not qualify for Medicaid find that they really cannot afford these services. Nursing home stays can be anywhere from $30,000 to, in some States, $40,000 or more per year, and in-home care generally costs somewhere between $50 to $200 a day. So just think about that family that has the elder person in the home, who wants to stay in the home, and is trying to support that person in the home. There is literally no public support for help of that kind.[17]

Medicare falls short in other ways as well. It does not cover annual physical exams, out-of-hospital prescription drugs, eyeglasses, hearing aids, dentures, and chronic long-term nursing home care. For those services that Medicare does cover, the elderly must pay premiums, coinsurance charges, and deductibles, costs that have climbed steadily higher as medical care has become more expensive.[18] Medicare generally pays only 80 percent of the "reasonable charges" billed, but the remaining 20 percent can be costly, particularly for those who have no fat in their monthly budgets. Again, the very poor are relieved of these burdens because Medicaid picks up the costs and those who can afford a private "Medigap" policy to cover the difference can manage. Yet this still cuts across their personal bottom line in ways that cause many poor elderly Americans to forgo care altogether.

Medicaid, "health insurance for the poor," is meant to be the solution to many of these problems for the inner-city families we are concerned with in this book. For those who really are at the very bottom, who live in public housing, have no savings and no pensions, the system is workable. Anyone who rides just above the poverty line or who has assets of any kind will find themselves ineligible. The bureaucratic requirements for getting onto the benefit system defeat many others. As a consequence, only about half of all poor minority elders are covered by Medicaid.

Congress has taken constructive steps in the past to prevent extreme financial hardship as a consequence of the rising cost of health insurance premiums. In the late 1980s, they required Medicaid to "buy in" to Medicare, that is to pay the premium, deductibles, and out-of-pocket costs for covered services for Medicare eligible, low-income seniors who are disabled. The contributions Medicaid was to make to this "gap closing" plan increased steadily in the 1990s. However, despite these efforts, the "buy in" benefits are not well understood by impoverished elders. They simply do not know about the provisions and often refrain from enlisting in Medicare at all because they fear the costs associated with it, costs that are now covered by Medicaid. A 1991 study showed that 2.2 million poor seniors, just over half of those eligible for this buy-in protection, did not have it at all.

This is not the place for a truly comprehensive treatment of the health insurance situation in the United States. Whole political campaigns have been built around it and many books have been written by experts in the field advocating policies that will do a better job of encouraging positive health behaviors, preventive care, early detection, routine medical care, and insurance for catastrophic and chronic illness. Still, when we think about what kinds of policies would make a difference for the inner-city poor, health care rises to the very top of the list, right alongside the protection and enhancement of social security. What is clear enough is that the systems we have put in place are not reaching enough of the people who need to hear the message and receive the services. They are getting sicker earlier and dying younger as a consequence. We need to do far more than we have done up to now to extend public health education campaigns, and provide for routine care so that elderly inner-city dwellers can remain in their homes and enable their younger relatives to stay in the work world. Anything we can do to encourage early detection of chronic disease will ultimately save the country money, enhance the quality of later life, and ease the burdens on families with elders who need their help.

Dilemmas of Kin Care

The crack epidemic carved its way through inner-city families in the 1980s and early '90s, leaving in its wake thousands of children whose parents could no longer care for them. Where did these children go? By 1998 more than 2 million kids, about 3 percent of all the nation's children, were living in some kind of "kinship care" situation, living with a relative or someone else emotionally close to them. These numbers swelled over the last two decades for at least three reasons: the number of unrelated foster parents has not kept pace with the demand; extended family members are now given first priority by child welfare officials when kids require placement; and the courts have recognized the rights of relatives to act as foster parents and to be paid for doing so.[19]

When kin care arrangements develop without the involvement of the child welfare system, the government refers to the situation as *private*. If the government has to step in, providing public assistance or foster care benefits, the term it uses is "*public* kinship care."[20] About 200,000 of the 2 million kids met the latter definition, because they were living with extended family and receiving public assistance of some kind. It is no easy task to describe how this "system" works, though, since every state administers its own program. However, as a general rule, kinship care givers receive public assistance benefits because they are generally poor, while nonkin foster parents receive services from child welfare agencies. The two different systems—welfare and foster care—are like parallel universes. The first, now part of the Transitional Assistance for Needy Families, or TANF, has been the subject of dramatic reform since 1996. Grandparents and other kin who receive TANF benefits on account of their grandkids are subject to the same rules that single moms live by: time-limited welfare and benefits that have declined over time. Nationwide, TANF stipends provided to adults providing care for their grandchildren average $150–$225 per month for a child under the age of eighteen.[21]

Unrelated adults who care for foster children receive their benefits through an entirely different system, the child protective services administration of their respective states. Technically, the children in foster care are wards of the states in which they reside. Their foster parents must consult with social workers about the education and medical care of the child. Intrusive regulations were put in place on the theory that the state is the child's real parent, while foster parents merely deliver the services and provide a home environment. The stipends foster parents receive average three times as much as TANF allowances: approximately $500–$600 per month.

At first blush, the difference seems market driven: it costs more to attract unrelated people to care for someone else's children. But the widening disparity owes more to the accidental intertwining of kinship care with the welfare system, particularly in its reform mode. TANF was aimed at one group—single mothers—but it snared another: custodial grandparents. As a consequence, the declining value of welfare stipends, intended to push recipients into the labor market, is taking its toll on middle-aged and elderly grandmothers who are trying to raise their grandchildren. The responsible elder, trying to save grandkids from the foster care system, has little choice but to raise them on inadequate stipends. TANF recipients, no matter what their age or station, are subject to the same work requirements and time limits as a young, single mom—the person welfare reformers had in mind when they designed the user *un*friendly TANF system.

It is hard to see how the enormous financial difference between foster care and kinship care can be justified. Extended kin and unrelated foster parents both are shouldering a responsibility on behalf of society. It costs both kinds of foster parents just as much to raise the youngsters they have taken in. We should close this gap immediately by providing grandparents with custody of their young relations stipends equivalent to what we give foster parents. Kinship care should be extricated from the TANF system entirely so that the complex politics attending welfare reform do not adversely affect these extended families. It will also be necessary to revisit the reporting systems that currently require foster parents to clear every detail of their child-rearing practices with state authorities. While it may be a good idea to maintain such a system where foster parents are concerned, grandparents should be accorded more freedom to act as the real parents that they are. It should not be necessary, as it currently is, for Grandma to seek a social worker's permission to take her charge on an out-of-state trip or to regulate how many beds or bathrooms they have on hand. For the protection of children "in care," however, some level of supervision may be necessary in planning for the educational and medical needs of kids in kin care, if only to make sure they are in school and covered by Child Health Plus, or some other insurance system.

One out of every four grandparents caring for a grandchild lives in a household that is below the poverty line. When we look just at grandmothers who are sole caregivers, that number more than doubles. Children growing up so disadvantaged are at grave risk for repeating the cycle of poverty. If we can lift some of the financial burdens from their grandparents' shoulders, at least up to the level we already provide for unrelated foster parents, we will be making a worthy investment in the life chances of those kids. At the same time, we would be taking some of the pressure off their grandparents who do not deserve to be even poorer than they would otherwise be because they have stepped forward to solve a serious problem in their family. Increasing the resources they have to work with would make their own old age less stressed and undoubtedly diminish the health problems they face as a consequence.

In the waning months of the Clinton administration, Congress reauthorized the Older Americans Act, which had lapsed and been left dormant for nearly five years previous to that. It is a critical piece of legislation for many reasons, but one of its new provisions is particularly important where grandparent caregivers are concerned. The National Family Caregiver Support Act, championed by Senators DeWine (Ohio), Jeffords (Vermont), Kennedy (Massachusetts), and Mikulski (Maryland), provides for counseling, support groups, training, and respite care—and not just for the "old old."[22] For the first time, the act includes support for people under the age of sixty. While this legislation does not address the key issue of direct financial support, it recognizes other important needs of the 2.5 million families headed by grandparents who are caring for more than 5 million children. We need to follow up on this legislation with federal and state provisions that will close the gap between foster care and kinship care, so that the financial needs of these families will be addressed at a minimal level.

Safe Streets

Declining crime rates in cities like New York have been a blessing for everyone. As street hooligans have fled into the shadows, residents of the barrios and the black ghettoes breathed sighs of relief. It would have been more to their liking had this positive turn come about through less intrusive methods. Older men and women who would like to walk down the street without fear are not particularly happy to know that their increased safety comes at the expense of their grandsons' freedom to move about or congregate with their friends on a hot summer night. Those whose children and grandchildren have been harrassed or brutalized by the police do not approve of hyperaggressive crowd control or blatant discrimination against black or brown young men.

Even so, because elderly minorities are the first victims of crime, particularly street crime, they swallow hard and sometimes look the other way when New York's finest get the job done. After all, the most vulnerable crime victims are not affluent whites but poor minorities, who tend to live side by side with the criminal element. We are accustomed to hearing about juvenile violence and its impact on peers, but if it is dangerous for kids to be in the vicinity of the bad guys, it is worse for their grandmothers. Elderly people are very vulnerable to street crime. They make easy targets for purse snatchers and home burglars. Those who live alone—which includes a very high proportion of the "oldest old" Latinos and African Americans—are particularly at risk.

No one knows exactly why crime rates have dropped so precipitously. Criminologists point to demography (smaller numbers of teens) and the positive consequences of economic prosperity and low unemployment (providing better options for those who might otherwise turn to crime). Conservative politicians are more inclined to single out the "get tough" policies that have swept so many into jails (particularly on drug charges). No doubt all of these forces play a role in driving crime rates down. Whatever the ultimate cause, the trend is salutary, especially for middle-aged and elderly men and women in the inner city.

Though we tend not to think about crime control as an "aging policy," it is clearly an important part of what we must continue to do if we want to ensure that these elders fare well over time. Indeed, we should probably go further than we have to use our police force proactively, to make sure they pay attention to elderly minorities on their beats in addition to the young people who may claim more of their time. For many years, high-crime neighborhoods were almost devoid of old people walking the streets. They were too afraid to venture out and spent their time barricaded behind security locks. The situation has improved but continued vigilance is necessary to keep poor neighborhoods as free of crime, particularly violent street crime, as possible.

Finally, we should recognize that middle-aged and elderly people are a resource in the fight against crime, not just a population in need of protection. Social scientists who have studied the relationship between crime and the density of social relations among residents are beginning to understand how important the latter is for combating the former. Among equally poor neighborhoods in Chicago, those that boast high levels of social trust, of people who are willing to intervene when they see public disorder, are much lower in crime.[23] What makes the difference between neighborhoods that are high in trust and those that aren't? The density of social ties between people seems to be key. In neighborhoods where there are churches, schools, and community centers, that density is high. Architectural features that encourage communication and socializing—the front porch, the urban stoop—also make a difference. Many of New York's poorest communities are hemmed in by gigantic public housing projects that afford nothing of the kind. If we build neighborhoods that foster "social capital," we will find that they cost us less in police overtime. They yield self-regulating enclaves that develop fewer serious crime problems in the first place. These are the kinds of communities where "old heads," those graying grandfathers and grandmothers, have a special place.

*   *   *

What does aging mean to people who have spent most of their adult lives in the racially segregated enclaves of the inner city? The ways in which experience adds up to a sense of satisfaction or disappointment can be understood only against the backdrop of their generational histories, an important consolidation of a trajectory whose curves may have been hard to discern earlier in life, and that is colored by economic conditions, political climate, and cultural changes. For the people we have been thinking about in this book, the backdrop is shifting and discontinuous.

Ironically, many of them would regard themselves as fortunate, when compared to their own parents. Those who grew up in the South as the Jim Crow era was ending and the civil rights movement gathered steam have lived long enough to see real progress in race relations and improved job opportunities for minorities. They may remember Bull Connor in the distant past, but can look to David Dinkins in their later years. Their own parents were often poorly educated, working in menial jobs, living in tenement houses. Those who benefited from the commitment to equal opportunity, particularly in the 1960s and early '70s, claimed their place in the post office, the transit authority, the hospitals, and the school system, with the pensions and health insurance that came with "city jobs." Even those who did not see such prosperity, who worked as security guards or cleaning ladies, were often better off than their parents, who were lucky to find backbreaking jobs in rural southern food processing plants.

This is not to say that this younger generation could rest on their laurels and collect fat retirement checks. These families always had to watch their pocketbooks. Most were (and are) renters, rather than home owners, and have long been subject to the pressures of the New York real estate market. Security and stability proved illusive for many, with the civil servants among them by far the most advantaged in this regard. For many others—the factory ladies, the security guards, the cleaning ladies—the job market waxed and waned in what it provided.

Perhaps the most profound problem in their midst was the increasing crime and disorder in poor neighborhoods that grew out of control in the 1970s and '80s. The deterioration had serious consequences for middle-aged men and women in the inner city, whose children got swept up in it. Sons ended up with criminal records and daughters ended up as single moms, often unable to care for their children. These unfortunate pathways are not entirely attributable to the drug trade, of course. But the trends escalated at the same point in history and had the cumulative effect of making it more likely that young people raised in inner-city neighborhoods at the time would come into their own adulthood in problematic condition. The "troubles" drove wedges between the generations. Parents were stunned, frustrated, and helpless to stop the descent of their own kids. "Tough love" sometimes meant throwing their children out of the house or calling the police to come and take their kids away as a protective measure. Others pleaded with their kids to walk a straighter path or banged their heads against the wall trying to get them treatment.

I do not mean to argue that every single kid raised in Bedford-Stuyvesant turned into a dangerous drug addict. I have written books about the majority, who went to school, took low-wage jobs, and did what they could to help their families.[24] They would be the first to agree that they had to battle a status system on the streets that took them to task for taking "chump change jobs." Challenged constantly for "staying straight," they had to defend their choices in the community, in school, and among their peers. Summoning the strength to withstand that onslaught was not easy for teenagers in Harlem, even as their own parents appreciated the contributions they made to the household coffers.

Of course, rising crime had its own, independent impact on middle-aged and elderly folk in the inner city. Fearful of being victimized, they often found themselves having to withdraw from the stoops, walk quickly to the subway, and stay home after dark. Their communities suffered as businesses pulled out, taking jobs with them. The downward spiral that was particularly evident in New York in the '70s and '80s left its traces in the stress it caused, and the children it took, many of whom were unable to care for the children they in turn bore, leaving them to their elders to raise.

All of this was hard on happily married parents. It was many times more taxing for single parents, especially mothers, who were often left to contend with the destruction tearing through their families on their own. Out of this turmoil came many a valued friendship. Kin came to the rescue too, moving in to pick up some of the pieces when men disappeared from the scene. Divorce is hard on all classes and colors. When it is compounded by teens running off the rails, neighborhoods that are falling apart, or jobs that do not provide enough income, the life of a single parent can be stressful in the extreme.

By late middle age or the early years of their elder lives, many women can add loneliness to their list of troubles. They have often spent many years without men in their lives, in a country where couplehood is expected. If the path that led in this direction is one strewn with disappointment, abandonment, or double-dealing, an understandable hardness sets in. "I don't want no man's shoes under my bed," becomes the refrain, one part truthful re-action to bad experience and one part defensive distance because there are no men in the picture, whatever the women may want.

Men have more options, as they always have had. We don't like to speak in terms of "tournaments" where personal life is concerned, but in fact the marriage market provides more options for minority men than women.[25] Even men who have prison records may find an open door if there are women who really long for company. These men have their regrets too, often revolving around the loss of respect, affection, and even connection to their children. And they often come knocking when their youthful days are over, sometimes because they want back into the original family fold but perhaps more often because fatherhood has become important to them.[26]

The final straw for many growing old in the inner city is the impact of illness. Chronic diseases (diabetes, heart disease, cancer) crop up earlier in the lives of the poor and are discovered at more advanced stages than is true for the middle class. Bad habits—or "risk behaviors," as scientists call them—are more widespread in this population. Medical insurance is scarcer, partic-ularly for people who are "near poor," which is what many of the people in this book might be called. The well-off have private doctors; the very poor have Medicaid; and the very old have Medicare. But the not-quite-poor who are in middle age get very little. Black and Latino elders are particularly at risk. Indeed, minorities look worse in terms of their health profiles at every age and in every economic category than other racial groups. Illness derails the productive work lives of those in middle age, creates financial hardships because of reduced earnings and medical costs, and destabilizes the lives of others, especially younger relatives, if they are available, to help care for sick family members.

Race has a lot to do with how this unfolds. Yet is it not a straightforward story of racial oppression, blocked opportunity, nationalism, and "us versus them" thinking. On the contrary, the men and women we interviewed do not see the world this way. It has not escaped their attention that they live in the poorer parts of town. Some have experienced the sting of rejection on racial grounds, glass ceilings that have limited their advancement in the work place. Yet just as many were what we might call "strong individualists," who don't believe all this race talk makes sense. They often see their own "in group" as its own worst enemy, looking to place blame on other shoulders that belongs "in house." Particularly striking was the sentiment that other oppressed groups have made their way up the ladder through solidarity, organizing to make their demands known, never settling for second best.

From a social science perspective, there are many bones to pick with this view. The history of racial bias against African Americans, the rules and informal practices that were applied to this group in ways that no other ever experienced—from segregated housing to overcrowded schooling—go much further in explaining differential fortunes. But we are less concerned here with those "facts" and more with the subjective perspective that middle-aged and elderly people in the inner city bring to bear on the problem. I find them quite resistant to explanations that "blame the system" and more inclined toward a critical appraisal of their own. They do think an individual is responsible for his or her own fate and that groups have to take what worked for some (e.g., Jews or Asians) and apply it to their own problems. Of course these sentiments can shade into resentment or racism of another kind, but most of the time it is more a matter of sober assessments of why the poorest of the nation's minorities—including their own friends, neighbors, and family—have ended up where they are. Those assessments are not always flattering, but are rather self-critical (or group critical) in ways that would cause most liberals to flinch.

What, then, must they do? The first lesson of "social responsibility" is to keep one's house in order. Raising decent kids, for example, is not just a personal responsibility, but a contribution to the well-being of the whole community. Not everyone has done this much and that occasions some bitterness coming from people who have had to live in neighborhoods with dangerous characters whose parents "did not do their job." Radiating out from this inner circle, being responsible to the extended family is a serious obligation. Indeed, the evidence shows that minorities are very likely to take their elders in and care for them rather than send them to nursing homes. This is partly a function of resources: poor people, and even more so the near-poor, often lack the money to pay for nursing homes. But it is also cultural tradition. You don't send Grandma off to be cared for by strangers. If your sister dies young, you take her children. If your son ends up in jail, you do what you can to help his children, even if he is not married to their mother. Safety nets are woven from the stuff of kinship and friendship. Finally, you look to the members of a community to pull within and address the needs of the neighborhood, the ethnic group, or the race before you expect the rest of society to do very much and before you consider your obligations to some abstract notion of "the nation."

This, of course, is an overgeneralization. The events of September 11, 2001, which saw New York's World Trade Center towers buckle under the blows of terrorists, powerfully affected everyone: white, black, Asian, Middle Eastern, South Asian, and Latino. The firefighters and police officers who died trying to save people in the disaster and the Emergency Medical Technicians who tended the wounded were of all colors. Tragically, so were the dead. Military personnel who left on aircraft carriers not long thereafter included many fiercely patriotic minorities. In times of national crisis, the divisions that turn us inward toward our own are suspended in favor of a broader sense of belonging, catalyzed by the threat of a common enemy— whomever that may turn out to be.

Would that this unity would last forever, even as the reasons for its emergence fade from view. Past experience suggests this is not likely. We are all bearers of a particular history, as it unfolded in specific spaces. The time and the place leave their marks on us as we pass through middle age and into elderhood. We do wear different shades of gray because the pathways that take us there are not the same. Some are much easier than others, in part because of damage we inflict on ourselves and in larger measure because inequalities in resources affect our options at every step of the way. Yet we need not shrug our shoulders and conclude there is nothing to be done to smooth out the rough spots and make the aging process a more equitable one. That is what public policy is for.

We should remember how much of a difference policy has made in the past. Before the social security system was created in the 1930s, to be old was almost a guarantee of poverty. Only those who were truly fortunate could look forward to an old age of comfort. Everyone else was either destitute or beholden to the charity of their families, given in varying degrees. While we did not solve this problem in its entirety, no one with any credibility would maintain that social security made no difference. It made an enormous difference. Medicare did so as well. Where there is a political will, there is usually a social policy that will lead the way.

Some would argue that our greatest need now, having dealt with the elderly, is to address the problem of child poverty. There is much truth to this for nearly one-sixth of all American children live in households below the poverty line. Poverty is rarer among the old, but that does not mean that we should turn a blind eye to the problems of the inner-city poor as they head toward elderhood. Many of them are shouldering burdens on behalf of the rest of society that they did not create. Millions have worked all their lives, only to find themselves disabled before they can collect retirement benefits. Others spent their lives flipping our burgers or selling us toothpaste in jobs that provided no private pensions at all. If we have a commitment to seeing that the elder years are among the best years of any American's life, we must finish the job.

Appendix

Three data sets figure in *A Different Shade of Gray* and a word is in order about their contents. The first was a nationally representative survey sponsored by the MacArthur Foundation. The second was a special companion survey of minorities in midlife in New York City. The third was a set of in-depth interviews with a random subsample of the New York survey. Below I describe the data sets and then refer the interested reader to other sources for more background information.

The MacArthur Foundation Midus Survey[1]

In 1995, the MacArthur Foundation Network on Successful Mid-Life Development launched the MIDUS SURVEY (National Survey of Mid-Life Develoment in the United States), a nationally representative sample of non-institutionalized, English-speaking adults, aged twenty-five to seventy-four, living in households with phones in the coterminous mainland. There were 3,323 respondents who completed the telephone interview, for an estimated response rate of 60.8 percent.

The MIDUS respondents were, on average, better educated than the nationally representative samples collected by the Current Population Survey in a roughly similar time frame. African Americans were underrepresented as well; 11.2 percent of the October 1995 CPS were black, while only 6.1 percent of MIDUS respondents were black.

Table X-1
Selected Demographic Characteristics of the
MIDUS Survey Respondents (Unweighted)

Sex			
	Male	48.5	
	Female	51.5	
Race			
	White	87.3	
	Black	6.1	
	Other	6.5	
Age			
	25–34	20.8	
	35–44	24.2	
	45–54	24.0	
	55–64	19.9	
	65–74	11.1	
Education			
	Fewer than twelve years		10.0
	Twelve Years		29.3
	More than twelve years		60.8
Marital Status			
	Married		64.0
	Not married		36.0

Ethnic and Racial Minorities in Urban Areas Survey[2]

The MacArthur Network was aware at the outset that its national survey would probably be "high end," that it would underrepresent low-income and minority Americans. Hence they commissioned a companion study of ethnic and racial minorities in Chicago and New York. The Chicago study gathered data on Mexican Americans and African Americans, while the New York Survey gathered data from African Americans, Puerto Ricans, and Dominicans. The instrument was developed by Dr. Diane Hughes, Department of Psychology at New York University, on behalf of a group of scholars that I directed for two years under the auspices of the Social Science Research Council, also in New York.

Interviews were conducted face-to-face for a period of approximately two hours. Interviewers recorded the responses.

Qualitative Sub-sample of New York Minorities

Since the New York survey was limited to a fixed-choice questionnaire, I developed a qualitative, interview-based study of 100 respondents who were chosen at random from the subjects who completed the ERMUAS survey described above. All data reported in this book, which refers specifically to *interview* responses given by African Americans, Puerto Ricans, and Dominicans, are drawn from this subsample study. However, when I present *survey* data that refer to these minority groups (and compare them to the national study), I refer to the responses this subsample provided to the items on the ERMUAS survey instrument. The subsample is a true random sample of the whole New York survey population (in ERMUAS); I have checked their responses to all reported items and report them only when they match those of the survey. Readers interested in further findings from the New York survey will want to consult the publications of Dr. Hughes, who is responsible for that larger analysis.

For descriptive purposes, I present the demographic characteristics of the ERMUAS survey and the qualitative study in Table X-2

The qualitative interviews that the subsample respondents participated in covered a wide range of topics, including migration history, employment, education of the respondent and family members, attitudes toward welfare, opportunity, and race relations, visions of middle age, and health and well-being. These focused life-history interviews were tape-recorded. Each interview took approximately three hours.

Important Features of the Qualitative Sample

About half of the people discussed in this book—and virtually all of the African Americans[3]—were born in the United States. Among those who identified themselves as Dominican, almost three-quarters were born on the island and are therefore relatively recent migrants to the United States. Puerto Ricans began mass migration much earlier in the twentieth century, so that only half of those we interviewed were born on the island. The rest are New Yorkers who grew up in Puerto Rican enclaves of the city. Among those who were born outside the U.S. mainland, most came to these shores when

Table X-2

Comparative Characteristics of the New York ERMUAS and Qualitative Samples

	NY ERMUAS survey (n=900)	Qualitative Sample (n=100)
Average Age	44.2	43.6
Gender (% male)	50.6	41.8
Ethnicity		
% Black	37.6	34.7
% Dominican	31.1	33.7
% Puerto Rican	31.3	31.6
Employment Status		
% currently employed	45.9	52.1
% currently unemployed	11.9	8.2
Immigrant Status		
% U.S. born	53.2	53.1
% immigrated <18 yrs old	10.4	9.2
% immigrated 18+ yrs old	28.7	27.5
Neighborhood Type		
% living in neigh. 30% or more white	10.5	9.2
% living in ethnic enclave 51%+ own ethnic group	35.0	36.7
% living in mixed neighborhood	54.3	54.1
Mean Neighborhood Income	$27,306	$27,016
Public Aid		
% receiving AFDC in household		
African Americans		15
Puerto Ricans		27
Dominicans		22
% receiving SSI in household		
African Americans		15
Puerto Ricans		24
Dominicans		22

they were teenagers or young adults.[4] Hence they have vivid memories of their communities of origins and nearly all have family members who still live in their homeland with whom they continue to share resources, though on a more episodic basis now.

The ages of these New York minorities range from twenty-five to seventy-four, a wide span set deliberately in order to capture all phases of the aging experience. We interviewed more African Americans over the age of sixty-five than we did in the other ethnic groups, but we were able to talk with Puerto Ricans and Dominicans who were also in this cohort. Across all three ethnic groups, a substantial proportion are between forty-one and sixty-five years of age, and thus are suspended somewhere between middle age and their elderly years, a limbo zone determined more by their health and perceptions of vigor than by years per se.

Sixty percent of the respondents are women, largely because a disproportionate number of Dominicans (74 percent) were women. The other ethnic groups are more evenly split along gender lines. Roughly two-thirds of the whole sample have no education beyond high school and only 10 percent have bachelor's degrees.[5] Not surprisingly, African Americans are the most educated, in part because they faced no language barriers and had more resources than the immigrants we studied. This also tells us that they are not the poorest of the poor inner-city blacks (who are often hard to capture in surveys to begin with). Forty-three percent of the African Americans in this book have at least some college education, while only 25 percent of the Puerto Ricans do. Educational differences in our sample are a function of age as well. The younger generations are more likely to have completed high school and gone on to get some college education. Only 10 percent of those who are older than sixty-six have any college, and none of them have college degrees.

Family formations reflect most of the national currents described earlier in this chapter. Less than half of the people we interviewed are presently married.[6] Nearly 20 percent of these New Yorkers are divorced and small proportions are either widowed or separated. African Americans are more likely than either Dominicans or Puerto Ricans to have never married and so are less likely to be married now.[7] Still, among those who are married, relationships are durable. Two-thirds of the currently married people have been married for more than ten years and two-thirds are in their first marriage. Surprisingly few of the single people in the sample are currently cohabiting.

Nearly half of the people, particularly the older African Americans, no longer have children (under the age of eighteen) living in their homes. Yet

Table X-3
Ethnic Density of Respondent Neighborhoods

	Puerto Ricans	Dominicans	African Americans
Low Density	43.8%	35.3%	29.4%
High Density	56.3%	64.7%	52.9%
Hypersegregated	0	0	17.6%

10 percent of the elders who are beyond retirement age do have children to care for, as do the middle-aged minorities. Virtually all of those in their thirties have kids at home to care for, and almost half of those forty-one to sixty-five do as well.

Context matters a great deal in the aging experience, a point I have made with respect to generational history. Other contexts are important as well, particularly that of residential neighborhood. When we first set out to look for minorities growing older in the inner city, we realized that the enclaves within which they live vary along many dimensions. Among the most important are the racial composition and the economic profile of the neighborhoods. We wanted to know whether it makes a difference if one grows toward old age in a community that is racially segregated or more integrated, and how much it matters if the enclave is largely poor or more mixed income. Toward this end, we looked for a random sample of Puerto Ricans, Dominicans, and African Americans who were living in "High Ethnic Density" neighborhoods, where at least 30 percent of their own ethnic group resides, or "Low Ethnic Density" neighborhoods that lacked this threshold level of "in group" residents.

As Table X-3 shows, African Americans are by far the most racially segregated of the groups surveyed in this book. They are the only race group with any members living in hypersegregated neighborhoods (surrounded by 70 percent or more of their own racial group). Yet these neighborhoods are not necessarily poor. Indeed, the poorest communities in New York are not well represented here (e.g., East New York or the South Bronx). Instead, the black New Yorkers we hear about in this book live in more stable enclaves that are often set cheek by jowl with poorer communities. While neither the Dominicans nor the Puerto Ricans live in such segregated conditions, over 40 percent of each group live in neighborhoods where there is a sizable representation of their own ethnic community (over 30 percent).

Residence is a reflection of both cultural affinity and the income that families bring to the table in their search for housing. The families who appear

Table X-4
Income of New York Respondents Compared to
National Sample

Income Level	New York	National
<$10,000	22%*	5.6%
$10–$24,999	33%*	16%
$25,000+	39%*	78.4%

*Differences from national sample are significant at the 0.05 level.

here are considerably poorer than those captured in the national survey conducted by the MacArthur Foundation to study the experience of middle age.

The median income of these New Yorkers is roughly $18,500; the median for the national sample is more than twice that amount: $45,000. Low income is particularly problematic in a city where living is as expensive as it is in New York. Even those families that approach the national median find themselves in difficult circumstances unless they have secured rent-controlled or public housing. It is not uncommon to find one-bedroom apartments costing $1,500 a month, even in fairly dilapidated and segregated parts of the city. The high cost of living is especially burdensome for single parents and for those with multiple dependents (children or elderly), conditions that are common among our respondents.

Notes

Introduction

1. *Newsweek*, "The New Middle Age," April 3, 2000.
2. Furthermore, Americans age eighty-five and older make up the country's fastest-growing age group; this is also the age group facing the most serious health concerns. Federal Interagency Forum on Aging Related Statistics, *Older Americans 2000: Key Indicators of Well-being*, cited November 29, 2000, p. 2. URL: www.agingstats.gov/chartbook2000/default.htm
3. In 1999, 86 percent of whites age sixty-five to seventy-five were home owners, as were 69 percent of blacks and 67 percent of Hispanics in the same age bracket. Across all age groups, the home ownership rates were 73.2 percent, 46.7 percent, and 45.5 percent for whites, blacks, and Hispanics, respectively. Joint Center for Housing Studies, *The State of the Nation's Housing: 2000*, cited November 29, 2000, Table A-10. URL: <www.gsd.harvard.edu/jcenter/ Research %20Page/SON%20intro%20page.html>
4. Beginning in the mid-1960s, more blacks were being hired and actually recruited by major corporations as professionals and managers. Sharon M. Collins, *Black Corporate Executives: The Making and Breaking of a Black Middle Class* (Philadelphia: Temple University Press, 1997), pp. 45–50. Richard B. Freeman found "the proportion of black male graduates obtaining jobs as managers roughly tripled in the decade following the 1964 Civil Rights Act, while the fraction of white graduates was roughly stable." Richard B. Freeman, *The Over-Educated American* (Academic Press, 1976), p. 146. In addition, black men's upward mobility, from blue-collar to white-collar jobs, increased markedly from 1962 to 1973. Dennis Gilbert, *The American Class Structure in an Age of Growing Inequality* (London: Wadsworth, 1998), pp. 154–55. Freeman argues that the increased demand for black college graduates in the late 1960s and early '70s resulted in black men earning income comparable to their white counterparts. As for black women, by the early 1970s, their income was greater than their white peers. This is attributed to the fact that black women tended to work full-

time and year-round, and black women showed more commitment to the job
market than did white women. Freeman, *The Over-Educated American*, pp. 139–
46. Scholars attribute this increase of blacks in managerial and professional
positions to pressures companies faced from protests and federal policies against
discrimination. Blacks who were accepted into corporate America were those
who were very educated and already assimilated into mainstream white culture.
Richard L. Zweigenhaft and G. William Domhoff, *Diversity in the Power Elite*
(New Haven: Yale University Press, 1998), pp. 79–80. Zweigenhaft and Domhoff believe that although the number of Latinos in the upper echelons of the
corporate world is not in line with their percentage of the nation's population,
"It is clear that Latinos have come a long way in thirty years: some are in the
corporate elite, and the number is increasing." *Diversity in the Power Elite*, p. 129.

5. Title VII of the Civil Rights Act of 1964 mandates that all companies with
fifteen or more employees cannot discriminate against a potential employee or
current employee based on race, color, religion, sex, or national origin. The
U.S. Equal Employment Opportunity Commission, *Title VII of the Civil Rights
Act of 1964*, cited July, 6 2001. URL: www.eeoc.gov/laws/vii.html. Executive
Order 11246 prohibits contractors who have federal contracts of over $10,000
annually from discriminating against potential employees on the basis of race,
color, religion, sex, or national origin. Additionally, contractors with equal to
or more than fifty employees and contracts of over $50,000 annually must
create a written affirmative action program to help "the contractor identify and
analyze potential problems in the participation and utilization of women and
minorities in the contractor's workforce." U.S. Department of Labor, Employment Standards Administration Office of Federal Contract Compliance Programs, *Executive Order 11246 Fact Sheet*, cited July, 6 2001, p. 1. URL:
www.dol.gov/dol/esa/public/regs/compliance/ofccps/fs11246.htm. With respect
to enforcement of these mandates, Richard B. Freeman asserts, "Court inter-
pretations of federal and state laws tended to favor active intervention in the
employment process." Freeman *The Over-Educated American*, p. 138.

6. During the 1970s, many blacks moved from the central city to suburbs due to
a preference for the less dense outskirts. William H. Frey, "Mover Destination
Selectivity and the Changing Suburbanization of Metropolitan Whites and
Blacks," *Demography* 22 (1985), pp. 223–43. Although the number of blacks in
the central city increased from 1970 to 1980, the proportion of blacks living
in the central city decreased. By 1981, one-fifth of all blacks lived in the suburbs.
Larry Long and Diana DeAre, "The Suburbanization of Blacks," *American Demographics* 3 (1981), pp. 17–44. Many scholars note that while blacks may be
moving to the suburbs, they are not necessarily integrating with white subur-
banites. Through the 1980s, blacks continued to move to suburban neighborhoods, but "still were channeled into a relatively few suburbs." Mark Schneider
and Thomas Phelan, "Black Suburbanization in the 1980s," *Demography* 30
(1993), p. 278. Blacks moved into older suburbs that were being deserted by
whites in search of newer housing. These suburban neighborhoods that previously had been predominantly white became black enclaves. "The Suburbanization of Blacks." See also Phillip L. Clay, "The Process of Black
Suburbanization," *Urban Affairs Quarterly* 14 (1979), pp. 405–24. Although this

experience is common for blacks moving to the suburbs, some are integrating with whites. While many blacks occupy older suburbs, their share of new development grew in the 1970s. "The Suburbanization of Blacks." Blacks with high incomes are moving to white suburban neighborhoods. "The Process of Black Suburbanization." Avery M. Guest identified growing suburbs, those in which absolute numbers of blacks and whites increased, and noted that these suburbs had the characteristics of a dominant white neighborhood. Avery M. Guest, "The Changing Racial Composition of Suburbs 1950–1970," *Urban Affairs Quarterly* 14 (1978), pp. 195–206. However, as compared to other minority groups, blacks experience more segregation after suburbanization. Hispanics and Asians are more suburbanized and more integrated within suburban communities than are blacks. Of the three groups, Asians are the most suburbanized and most integrated. Blacks in the suburbs are more integrated, however, than are blacks in the central city. Douglas S. Massey and Nancy A. Denton, "Suburbanization and Segregation in U.S. Metropolitan Areas," *American Journal of Sociology* 94 (1988), pp. 592–626.

7. See Elijah Anderson, *Code of the Streets: Decency, Violence, and the Moral Life of the Inner City* (New York: Norton, 1999).

8. Mobility is often conceptualized by sociologists as a measurement of individual movement through the labor market (intragenerational) or the difference that characterizes parents (mainly fathers) and children (usually sons) in terms of occupational prestige. The term "mobility project" refers to the ways in which families understand the positions of their members as evidence of a collective or corporate movement of the whole kinship group through the pecking order of social classes. See Katherine Newman, *Declining Fortunes: The Withering of the American Dream* (New York: Basic Books, 1993).

9. For an overview of the breadth of the gerontology literature, see John C. Cavanaugh, "Theories of Aging in the Biological, Behavioral, and Social Sciences," in *Gerontology: An Interdisciplinary Perspective,* John C. Cavanaugh and Susan Krauss Whitbourne, eds. (New York: Oxford University Press, 1999), pp. 1–32. As Cavanaugh acknowledges, the theory that informs most current social science scholarship on aging is the "life course perspective." Glen H. Elder Jr. and Lisa A. Pellerin, "Linking History and Human Lives," in *Methods of Life Course Research: Qualitative and Quantitative Approaches,* Janet Z. Giele and Glen H. Elder Jr., eds. (Thousand Oaks, Calif.: Sage, 1998), pp. 264–94, note that the life course approach lends itself particularly well to the integration of historical evidence with social science data but argue that such connections between historical change and individual lives are too rarely found in the literature. For a recent example of how ethnography and social history can be linked in the study of aging, see Judith Noemi Freidenberg, *Growing Old in El Barrio* (New York: New York University Press, 2000).

10. The MacArthur Foundation Network on Successful Mid-Life Development sponsored a national survey of midlife adults, the MIDUS (Midlife in the United States). A special survey—the survey on "Ethnic and Racial Minorities in Urban Areas"—using many of the same questions was developed in New York City and Chicago to study the experience of minority aging. Finally, a random sample of the New York respondents formed the core of an in-depth interview

project from which all of the interview data quoted in this book were taken. For further details on survey methods, sampling design, and demographics of the national and local samples, see the Appendix.

1: In the Shadow of White Flight

1. An important corrective is Steven Gregory, *Black Corona: Race and the Politics of Place in an Urban Community* (Princeton: Princeton University Press, 1998). Gregory's study of political organizing in two Queens neighborhoods from the Great Depression onward stands as one of the few accounts of tireless efforts of black men and women to preserve jobs, protect wages, and protest developments (such as LaGuardia Airport) that threatened their quality of life. He shows quite clearly that in Corona and East Elmhurst, church leaders, community activists, mothers in the PTA, and fathers in unions gathered in large numbers to claim, protect, and defend their neighborhoods.

2. The economic well-being of older people depends not only on income but also on assets. Once they reach retirement, many African Americans find themselves in a more precarious financial position than do their white counterparts, due to sharp racial disparities in wealth. Melvin L. Oliver and Thomas M. Shapiro, in *Black Wealth/White Wealth: A New Perspective on Racial Inequality* (New York: Routledge, 1995), argue that discriminatory government policy, barriers to black business development, and America's long history of racial inequality have resulted in wealth differentials so large that, materially speaking, whites and blacks live in different countries. These disparities are self-perpetuating, since the top predictor of net worth is the net worth of one's parents. See Dalton Conley, *Being Black, Living in the Red: Race, Wealth, and Social Policy in America* (Berkeley and Los Angeles: University of California Press, 1999), pp. 47–53.

2: The Big Picture

1. While the aging of America is not a new phenomenon, it is becoming more rapid and more prominent. In colonial times, for example, half the population comprised children (under the age of sixteen). By 1987 less than a quarter (22.6 percent) were were younger than sixteen, and half the population was age thirty-two or above. If levels of fertility, mortality, and net migration remain the same as current levels, half the population will be over the age of thirty-eight by 2010. If the levels of these social indicators actually drop, half the population could be fifty or older by the time we reach 2050. Scott A. Bass, Elizabeth A. Kutza, and Fernando M. Torres-Gil, eds., *Diversity in Aging* (Glenview, Illinois: Scott, Foresman and Company), p. 2.

2. Looked at another way, a person who reached age sixty-five in 1950 could expect to live another 13.9 years; the same individual reaching this milestone in 1997 could expect another 17.7 years of life, an increase of more than 27 percent. U.S. Department of Health and Human Services, National Center for

Health Statistics, *Health, United States, 1999* (Hyattsville, Md: U.S. Government Printing Office, 1999), Table 28.

3. In 2000, about 1 in 7 Americans was over the age of sixty-five. By 2030, 1 in 5 Americans will be a senior citizen. U.S. Department of Health and Human Services, National Center for Health Statistics, *Health, United States, 1999* (Hyattsville, Md: U.S. Government Printing Office, 1999), Table 1.

4. In the technical language of the U.S. Census Bureau, three-quarters are "non-Hispanic whites," a designation intended to distinguish whites of Latino heritage from whites of European origin. Throughout this book, I will use the term "white" to mean "non-Hispanic white" and "black" to mean "non-Hispanic black."

5. (52.8 percent). The population of non-Hispanic whites is expected to increase by only 10.2 percent between 1990 and 2050. U.S. Bureau of the Census, *Population Profile of the United States: 1987*, Current Population Reports, Series pp. 23–194 (Washington, D.C.: U.S. Government Printing Office, 1998), p. 8–9.

6. Non-Hispanic blacks.

7. (82.3 percent). U.S. Bureau of the Census, *Population Projections of the United States by Age, Sex, Race, and Hispanic Origin: 1995 to 2050*, Current Population Reports, pp. 25–1130 (Washington, D.C.: U.S. Government Printing Office, 1996), Tables I and K.

8. (328 percent). Ibid.

9. Ibid., Table M.

10. Research suggests that poverty can put children at risk intellectually, emotionally, socially, and physically. Preschoolers from low-income families, for example, exhibit poorer cognitive and verbal skills. Some studies contend that this is due in part to the fact that they are generally exposed to fewer toys, books, and other stimulating experiences in the home. Poor parents also tend to rely more on home-based child care, where the quality and amount of attention children receive is often inferior to that provided at professional centers. Jeanne Brooks-Gunn and Greg Duncan, *The Consequences of Growing Up Poor* (New York: Russell Sage, 1997). See also David R. Williams and Chiquita Collins, "US socioeconomic and racial differences in health: Patterns and explanations," *Annual Review of Sociology* 21 (1995), pp. 349–86.

11. Donna L. Franklin, *Ensuring Inequality: The Structural Transformation of the African-American Family* (London: Oxford University Press, 1997), p. 59.

12. According to data from the Department of Labor and the U.S. Public Health Service published in 1935–36, "while 66% of white families had over $1,000 a year to spend, only 31.8% of black families had even this much." Donna L. Franklin, *Ensuring Inequality*, p. 60.

13. Defined as under age eighteen.

14. U.S. Bureau of the Census, *Historical Poverty Tables—People: Poverty Status of People, by Age, Race and Hispanic Origin: 1959 to 1998* (Washington D.C.: U.S. Government Printing Office, 1999).

15. The U.S. Bureau of the Census did not begin tracking data for Hispanics separately until the 1960s.

16. Gaylene Perrault and Gilbert L. Raiford, "Employment problems and prospects

of older Blacks and Puerto Ricans," in *Aging in Minority Groups*, R. L. McNeely
and John L. Colen, eds. (Beverly Hills, CA: Sage Publications, 1983), p. 189.

17. Michele Wucker, *Why the Cocks Fight* (New York: Hill and Wang, 1999).
18. This rate is higher than that for Mexicans (32 percent), Cubans (14.8 percent),
and all Central and South Americans. The corresponding poverty rate for Dominican children would likely be considerably higher than this figure. Data from
1990 show that the poverty rate for Dominicans in the United States was 33.7
percent, the highest rate among immigrants from any of the countries in the
Americas (includes Argentina, Brazil, Canada, Colombia, Cuba, the Dominican
Republic, Ecuador, Guatemala, Haiti, Jamaica, Mexico, Panama, and Trinidad
and Tobago), and double the average rate for all of these countries (16.8 percent). Sheldon H. Danzinger, Gary D. Sandefur, and Daniel H. Weinberg, eds.,
Confronting Poverty: Prescriptions for Change (New York: Russell Sage Foundation,
1994), p. 349.
19. Defined here as sixty-five years and older.
20. 16.5 percent and 7 percent, respectively.
21. U.S. Department of Education, *Digest of Education Statistics, 2000* (Washington,
D.C.: National Center for Education Statistics, 2001), Table 9.
22. Signed into law on June 22, 1944, the "Servicemen's Readjustment Act of
1944" (commonly known as the GI Bill of Rights) provided several important
benefits to veterans, including education and training, home and business loans,
unemployment pay, and job-finding assistance. By the time the program ended
in 1956, 7.8 million veterans—a total of half the veteran population—had received some type of educational training. Many prominent African Americans
cite the GI Bill as a critical factor in the growth of the black middle class and
the education of a generation that spurred the civil rights movement. The bill
expanded black attendance at institutions of higher learning considerably. While
enrollment in black colleges accounted for 1.08 percent of the total college enrollment in 1940, by 1950 this figure had more than tripled to 3.6 percent of
the total U.S. college enrollment. Similarly, African-American enrollment at predominantly white schools rose as a result of the GI Bill. Some estimates maintain
that black enrollment increased from roughly 1 percent of the student body to
upward of 5 percent at some colleges. Subsequent GI Bills were enacted in 1952
(the Korean GI Bill) and 1966 (the post–Korean-Vietnam era GI Bill), but both
programs offered relatively fewer benefits. "The GI Bill of Rights," updated
1998. URL: <cw.prenhall.com/bookbind/pubbooks/burns3/medialib/docs/
gibill.htm>; Ronald Roach, "From combat to campus: GI Bill gave a generation of African Americans an opportunity to pursue the American Dream,"
Blacks in Higher Education 14.3 (August 1997): 26–28.
23. The typical male college graduate in 1958 took home $35,095. In contrast,
the average male high school graduate brought in less than three-quarters of
that amount ($25,516) in the same year. By 1968, the typical man with a
high school degree earned only 68 percent of the college graduate's income
($32,913 vs. $47,924). All income figures are in 1997 CPI-U adjusted dollars.
U.S. Bureau of the Census, *Measuring 50 Years of Economic Change*, Current
Population Reports, pp. 60–203 (Washington, D.C.: U.S. Government Printing Office), Table C-8.

24. While researchers have focused a significant amount of attention on racial inequalities in earnings and income, until recently comparatively little has been written about the black-white gap in wealth. Yet this is where the disparities appear to be greatest. Data from the late 1980s show that while the black-white ratio of median household income was 0.62, the black-white ratio of median wealth was a startling 0.08 (8 percent). Similarly, more recent research points to racial discrepancies in property ownership, which translates into serious black-white differences in long-term wealth equity. Melvin L. Oliver and Thomas M. Shapiro, *Black Wealth/White Wealth: A New Perspective on Racial Inequality* (New York: Routledge, 1995); Dalton Conley, *Being Black, Living in the Red* (Berkeley: University of California Press, 1999).

25. In fact, in 1954, the year the court decision was handed down, "the proportion of black pupils attending schools with whites in 11 Southern states was less than 1 tenth of 1 percent; 10 years later it had only increased to about 2 percent. Legal change, persuasion, and national public opinion had not produced any significant level of desegregation." Gerald David Jaynes and Robin M. Williams, Jr., eds., *A Common Destiny: Blacks and American Society* (Washington D.C.: National Academy Press, 1989), p. 75.

26. As Gary Orfield has long argued, segregated schools are not simply schools separated by race. They are also, and perhaps most important, schools divided by class and background: "Segregated black and Latino schools are fundamentally different from segregated white schools in terms of the background of the children and many things that relate to educational quality. Only a twentieth of the nation's segregated white schools face conditions of concentrated poverty among their children, but more than 80% of segregated black and Latino schools do . . . this means that when we talk about racially segregated schools, they are very likely to be segregated by poverty as well. There is strong and consistent evidence that high poverty schools usually have much lower levels of educational performance on nearly all outcomes. . . . This is because high poverty schools are unequal in many ways that affect educational outcomes. The students' parents are far less educated—a very powerful influence—and the child is much more likely to be living in a single parent home which is struggling with multiple problems. . . . High poverty schools have to devote far more time and resources to family and health crises, security, children who come to school not speaking standard English, seriously disturbed children, children with no educational materials in their homes, and many children with very weak educational preparation. These schools tend to draw less qualified teachers and to hold them for shorter periods of time." Gary Orfield, Mark D. Bachmeier, David R. James, and Tamela Eide, "Deepening Segregation in American Public Schools," URL: www.bamn.com/resources/97-deeping-seg.htm

27. See Catherine Ellis, *The Legacy of Jim Crow in Rural Louisiana*, Ph.D. dissertation, Anthropology Department, Columbia University, 2000. See also Leon F. Litwack, *Trouble in Mind: Black Southerners in the Age of Jim Crow* (New York: Knopf, 1998).

28. Note that the use of the term "Hispanic" is misleading, for it masks ethnic differences that matter a great deal in education. Middle- and upper-class refugees from Castro's Cuba were positioned very differently than Mexican mi-

grants who came across the Rio Grande River by night. Puerto Ricans and Dominicans are also very different, not only in terms of culture but also with respect to the schooling systems in the areas from which the immigrant generation derived, prior exposure to English, and the economic resources with which they began the emigration experience. Nonetheless, official census statistics use the term "Hispanic," and because they report the data this way we will follow suit. According to the U.S. Census Bureau, " 'Hispanic' refers to persons who trace their origin or descent to Cuba, Mexico, Puerto Rico, South or Central America, or other Spanish cultures. Hispanics can be of *any race*." As of the 1997 revisions to the standards for classification, the terms Hispanic and Latino may be used interchangeably. U.S. Bureau of the Census, "Revisions to the Standards for the Classification of Federal Data on Race and Ethnicity," Federal Register, vol. 62, no. 280 (Washington D.C.: U.S. Government Printing Office, 1997), 58782–58790.

29. U.S. Department of Education, *Digest of Education Statistics, 2000* (Washington, D.C.: National Center for Education Statistics, 2001), Table 9.

30. Frank D. Bean and Marta Tienda, *The Hispanic Population of the United States* (New York: Russell Sage Foundation, 1987), p. 238–39.

31. Latino students were first granted the right to desegregated education by the Supreme Court in 1973. While recent studies warn that they are now more racially isolated and more concentrated in high-poverty schools than any other group of students (including African Americans), this trend was evident decades ago in the dense Puerto Rican communities of the Northeast. Gary Orfield, et al., "Deepening Segregation in American Public Schools."

32. *Our Nation on the Fault Line: Hispanic American Education*, White House Initiative on Educational Excellence for Hispanic Americans, 1996, URL: www.ed.gov/pubs/FaultLine/who.html

33. Glenn Hendricks, *The Dominican Diaspora* (New York: Teachers College Press, 1974).

34. Sherri Grasmuck and Patricia R. Pessar, *Between Two Islands* (Berkeley, CA: University of California Press, 1991), p. 37.

35. In 1981, more than 46 percent of New York–based Dominican migrants had received only nine years of schooling or less, and fewer than a quarter had completed between ten and twelve years of schooling.

36. Geoffrey Fox, *Hispanic Nation* (Secaucus, NJ: Carol Publishing Group, 1996), p. 90.

37. Per-pupil spending in Puerto Rico is 55 percent of the *lowest* amount spent by a state in the United States, and only *one-fifth* the national average. *Our Nation on the Fault Line: Hispanic American Education.*

38. Defined here for females ages sixteen and older.

39. Women's labor force participation jumped from 16 percent in 1900 to roughly 60 percent today.

40. African-American women have always had strikingly high labor force participation rates, hovering around 40 percent throughout the first half of the twentieth century before increasing to nearly two-thirds (65 percent) today. Teresa Amott and Julie Matthei, *Race, Gender and Work* (Boston: South End

Press, 1996), p. 412. U.S. Department of Labor, *News: The Employment Situation: January 2001* (Washington D.C.: Bureau of Labor Statistics, 2001).

41. In 1990, for example, 60 percent of U.S.-born Puerto Ricans were in the labor force—a figure that puts them on par with the rates for women of other racial and ethnic groups. In that same year, however, only 45 percent of island-born Puerto Rican women were in the labor force in the United States. Maria E. Perez y Gonzales, *Puerto Ricans in the United States* (Westport, CT: Greenwood Press, 2000), p. 68.

42. Franklin, *Ensuring Inequality*, p. 77.

43. See Kathy A. Kaufman *Outsourcing the Hearth: Immigration and the Strategic Allocation of Labor in American Families* (Ph.D. dissertation, Sociology Department, Columbia University, 2000) for a discussion on minority female employment in domestic services.

44. Franklin, *Ensuring Inequality*, p. 104–5.

45. Bean and Tienda, *The Hispanic Population of the United States*, pp. 344–45.

46. Adriana Marshall, "New Immigrants in New York's Economy," in Nancy Foner, ed., *New Immigrants in New York* (New York: Columbia University Press, 1987), p. 93.

47. Grasmuck and Pessar, *Between Two Islands*.

48. Marshall, "New Immigrants in New York's Economy," p. 93.

49. U.S.-born Puerto Ricans were a notable exception. Their comparatively better English skills in large part allowed them to escape the manual factory work assigned to their island-born peers.

50. Jaynes and Williams, eds., *A Common Destiny*.

51. See Nicholas Lemann, *The Promised Land* (New York: Vintage Books, 1991), and Douglas S. Massey and Nancy A. Denton, *American Apartheid* (Cambridge, MA: Harvard University Press, 1993) for more on industrial development and the employment of black men.

52. Bean and Tienda, *The Hispanic Population of the United States*, pp. 344–45.

53. Similar to their female counterparts, a number of U.S.-born Puerto Ricans were able to establish a foothold in clerical occupations.

54. Grasmuck and Pessar, *Between Two Islands*.

55. Hendricks, *The Dominican Diaspora*.

56. Bean and Tienda, *The Hispanic Population of the United States*, pp. 344–45.

57. From 1960 to 1980, the earnings of Puerto Rican women fell from 99 percent of that of their white peers to only 63 percent. Earnings of Puerto Rican men likewise decreased relative to their white counterparts—from 63 percent in 1960 to 57 percent in 1980. See Bean and Tienda, *The Hispanic Population of the United States*, pp. 368–89.

58. U.S. Bureau of the Census, *Measuring 50 Years of Economic Change*, Current Population Reports, pp. 60–203 (Washington, D.C.: U.S. Government Printing Office), Table C-22.

59. Amott and Matthaei, *Race, Gender and Work*, p. 350.

60. Bean and Tienda, *The Hispanic Population of the United States*, pp. 368–89.

61. There is an important difference between legal and undocumented Dominican workers. Documented Dominican immigrants are more likely to locate jobs

that pay at least minimum wage and have some Social Security benefits. Sherri Grasmuck and Pessar, *Between Two Islands*, p. 182.

62. In contrast, 44.1 percent of the legal immigrants—compared to 28.8 percent of the undocumented immigrants—earned $200 or more per week. While the disparity between the two groups is not as large among the women, the trend is the same. Grasmuck and Pessar, *Between Two Islands*, p. 180.

63. Grasmuck and Pessar, *Between Two Islands*, p. 163.

64. 26.4 percent vs. 8.9 percent.

65. 21 percent vs. 8.9 percent.

66. While 7.2 percent of white Americans between the ages of thirty-five and sixty-four reported 1998 incomes below the poverty line, 17.6 percent of blacks and 17.9 percent of Hispanics in this age group were officially poor. U.S. Bureau of the Census, *Poverty in the United States: 1998*, Current Population Reports, pp. 60–207 (Washington, D.C.: U.S. Government Printing Office, 1999).

67. Among those over sixty-five, black and Hispanic men were nearly three times as likely to be poor than whites of the same age. The situation for elderly women who live alone is even more stark: in 1998, 18.8 percent of the nation's "solo" elderly white women were low income, while 48.1 percent of black and 52.7 percent of Hispanic women were living below the poverty line. U.S. Bureau of the Census, *Poverty in the United States: 1998*.

68. In 1998, 20.7 percent of nonworkers aged fifty-five to sixty-four were poor in 1998, as compared to 11.8 percent of elderly nonworkers.

69. While 4 percent of whites aged thirty-five to fifty-four who reported any employment at all in 1998 had incomes below the poverty threshold, twice as many working blacks (8.1 percent) and three times as many working Hispanics (11.9 percent) in this age cohort were poor.

70. In a similar fashion, the financial situation of *unemployed individuals* differs dramatically by race. Whereas 25 percent of whites aged thirty-five to fifty-four who did not work in 1998 were officially poor, 49.3 percent of unemployed blacks and 42.5 percent of unemployed Hispanics in this cohort reported incomes below the poverty threshold. U.S. Bureau of the Census, *Poverty in the United States: 1998*.

71. It is important to note that for many people, including some of Dominican immigrants whose stories are chronicled here, public assistance has been curtailed recently. Under the Personal Responsibility and Work Opportunity Reconciliation Act, legal immigrants will no longer be eligible for public assistance under SSI and therefore are ineligible for Medicaid. About one-fourth of SSI recipients are noncitizen legal immigrants. Marcia Bayne-Smith, ed., *Race, Gender and Health* (Thousand Oaks, CA: Sage Publications, 1996).

72. Agricultural and domestic workers were not considered part of the system of workers who were covered under the Social Security insurance program and therefore were not eligible for coverage. John J. Corson, Bureau of Old-Age and Survivors Insurance, Social Security Board, Federal Security Agency, *Legislative History: 1939 Amendments*, cited 13 July 2001, URL: <www.ssa.gov/history/reports/1989no3.html>

73. I am indebted to Ira Katznelson for alerting me to this point in his lecture, "Legacies of 'Universalism': Reflections on the ironic precursors of affirmative

action" (presented February 7, 2000, for the Wiener Inequality and Social Policy Seminar Series, Kennedy School of Government, Harvard University). Southern legislators pressured Roosevelt to exempt their black labor force and threatened to vote against the New Deal if he did not comply.

74. Robert B. Hill, "Income maintenance programs and the minority elderly," in *Aging in Minority Groups*, pp. 201–2.

75. Valentine M. Villa. "Aging Policy and the Experience of Older Minorities," in *New Directions in Old Age Policies*, Janie S. Steckenrider and Tonya M. Parrott, eds. (Albany: State University of New York Press, 1998), p. 213.

76. The gap in asset income between whites and minorities is considerable. While 67 percent of whites over the age of sixty-five receive income from assets, only 33 percent of elderly blacks and 27 percent of elderly Hispanics do. Again, given a history of educational disadvantage, fewer skilled jobs, lower salaries, and long periods of unemployment, blacks and Hispanics have been less able to accumulate savings and other assets.

77. As Garfinkel and McLanahan point out, mother-only families are both more likely to be poor than other groups, and more likely to experience poverty differently—poverty among single mothers lasts much longer and is more severe than the poverty experienced by other groups. This has significant implications for the children of these women—affecting school performance, attendance, and graduation rates. A poor single mother has less money and time to invest in her children's educational and extracurricular activities, is likely to experience frequent unemployment that places undue stress and burdens on her children, and is more likely to live in dangerous neighborhoods, where the quality of schools is questionable at best. Irwin Garfinkel and Sara S. McLanahan, *Single Mothers and Their Children* (Washington, D.C.: The Urban Institute Press, 1986). A study by Susan Mayer highlights a slightly different perspective on the issue. While the effect of parental income on any one relevant child outcome is not significant, she notes, the cumulative impact of higher income across all outcomes may be more substantial. Equally important, however, may be other, nonmonetary factors, such as unmeasured parental characteristics. Susan E. Mayer, *What Money Can't Buy* (Cambridge, MA: Harvard University Press, 1997).

78. For more detailed information on marriage and divorce trends throughout the second half of the twentieth century see, Andrew J. Cherlin, *Marriage, Divorce, Remarriage* (Cambridge, MA: Harvard University Press, 1992).

79. For example, in the 1960s, women married at twenty and men at twenty-three. Nowadays, people are waiting a bit longer: twenty-five for women and twenty-seven for men. National Marriage Project (2000:22) *The State of Our Unions 2000: The Social Health of Marriage in America.* Publication of Rutgers University, State University of New Jersey.

80. R. Kelly Raley, "Recent Trends and Differentials in Marriage and Cohabitation: The United States," in *The Ties That Bind*, Christine Bachrach, Michelle Hindin, Elizabeth Thomson, and Arland Thornton, eds. (New York: Aldine de Gruyter, 2000).

81. Cherlin, *Marriage, Divorce, Remarriage*, p. 92.

82. Ibid., p. 94.
83. Larry Bumpass and Hsien-Hen Lu, "Trends in Cohabitation and Implications for Children's Family Contexts in the U.S." CDE Working Paper No. 98-15, Center for Demography and Ecology (Madison: University of Wisconsin, 1998).
84. See Patricia Smock, "Cohabitation in the United States: An Appraisal of Research Themes: Findings and Implications," *Annual Review of Sociology* 26 (2000).
85. As Frank Furstenberg Jr. notes, "Young adults in low-income populations feel that they don't have the wherewithal to enter marriage. It's as if marriage has become a luxury consumer item, available only to those with the means to bring it off. Living together or single-parenthood has become the budget way to start a family. Most low-income people I talk to would prefer the luxury model. They just can't afford it. Marriage is both a cause and a consequence of economic, cultural, and psychological stratification in American society. The recent apparent increase in income inequality in the U.S. means that the population may continue to sort itself between those who are eligible for marriage and a growing number who are deemed ineligible to marry." Frank F. Furstenberg Jr., "The Future of Marriage," *American Demographics* 18 (June 1996).
86. Table reproduced from *The State of Our Unions 2000: The Social Health of Marriage in America*, figure 6, p. 25. Source data is U.S. Bureau of the Census, Current Population Reports, Series pp. 20-514; Marital Status and Living Arrangements: March 1998 (Update) and earlier reports.
87. From 22 percent to 36.2 percent. Bean and Tienda, *The Hispanic Population of the United States.*
88. In 1980 more than 11 percent of Puerto Rican women over the age of fourteen were separated from their spouses—more than six times the rate for whites. They were also twice as likely as their white peers to be married with an absent spouse (2.5 percent vs. 1.0 percent). While the reasons for such discrepancies are not entirely clear, some scholars have speculated that the Catholic faith, which actively discourages divorce, is an important reason why Latinos stay married in the face of marital problems.
89. Women of all races are considerably more likely then men to go through the aging process alone. Source data for the table is U.S. Bureau of the Census, Marital Status and Living Arrangements: March 1998 (Update), Current Population Reports, pp. 20-514.

Percent of Individuals Who Are Married with a Spouse Present, 1998

| | Aged 55–64 | | Aged 65+ | |
	Male	Female	Male	Female
White	79	68	74	42
Black	53	37	53	24
Hispanic	71	56	67	37

90. Kathleen Gerson, *Hard Choices: How Women Decide About Work, Career, and Motherhood* (Berkeley, CA: University of California Press, 1985). Howard V. Hayghe

and Suzanne M. Bianchi, "Married mothers' work patterns: the job-family compromise," *Monthly Labor Review* (June 1994).

91. In 1970, 60.6 percent of black married mothers with children under the age of six worked. In contrast, 42.8 percent of white married mothers with young children were in the labor force that year. Perhaps even more telling is the fact that 21.1 percent of these black working mothers—as compared to only 8.4 percent of the white working mothers—worked full time year-round. This gap still exists, although white women have closed it somewhat over the years—in 1992, 66.4 percent of white mothers with young children worked (29.1 percent year-round, full time), while 76.1 percent of black women (44.9 percent year-round, full time) were employed. Rates of employment among Hispanic mothers appear to be lower. In 1992, just over half (51.8 percent) of Hispanic mothers with children under the age of six worked. Hayghe and Bianchi, "Married mothers' work patterns," pp. 24–30.

92. At least they were married by the time they gave birth. Statistics on premarital pregnancy are a bit harder to come by, but we certainly know anecdotally that "shotgun" weddings were not uncommon.

93. A similar story holds for births to teenagers: from the 1930s to the 1970s, black girls who gave birth were considerably more likely than their white peers to do so without the support of a spouse.

94. All data from: U.S. Bureau of the Census, *Trends in Premarital Childbearing, 1930–1994*, Current Population Reports, Series pp. 23–197 (Washington, D.C.: U.S. Government Printing Office, 1999).

95. Ibid.

96. Sociologist Alejandro Portes attributes the failure of some immigrant families to pass on their values to the next generation to "segmented assimilation": "Adapting to the United States is not what it used to be. The general trend at the turn of the century was to find a blue collar job and stay within the ethnic community for the first generation. Then, the second generation gradually moved up to the supervisory jobs, and the third generation joined the middle classes. Today, the society is far more differentiated than it was at the turn of the century. We have increasingly an hour-glass economy with a lot of minimally paying low-level jobs and a lot of well-paying professional jobs. At the same time, there are greater expectations for consumption and achievement. The new immigrants are in a very real race against time to jump from the entry level jobs, pass through that narrow center of the hourglass, and reach the professional mainstream. But, increasingly, many second-generation children do not make it because of the shape of that economy. They are frustrated because they are Americans and have in a sense already assimilated the aspirations and the patterns of consumption of the society. . . . That gap [between expectations and reality] creates processes of relative deprivation which, in turn, evolve in different directions. The native-born Americans with long experience in the country have developed different lifestyles as a way to selectively adapt to these messages and to navigate a complex society. The immigrants arrive for the most part with the belief that they streets of America are paved with gold, that they are going to make it here. What they find is a very different reality. Their fate is often problematic in terms of the resources they can bring to bear on these issues.

For that reason . . . sociologists [use the term] segmented assimilation. No longer do we have assimilation to one society; we can also have assimilation to different segments of it." Alejandro Portes, "America 2050: Immigration and the Hourglass," *Crosscurrents* 1 and 2 (winter and spring 1994–95).

97. Amott and Matthaei, *Race, Gender and Work*, p. 413.

98. Ibid., p. 314.

99. U.S. Bureau of the Census, *Child Support for Custodial Mothers and Fathers: 1997*, Current Population Reports, pp. 60–212 (Washington, D.C.: U.S. Government Printing Office, 1998).

100. Payments: $3,539 for whites, $2,461 for blacks, and $2,507 for Hispanics. Data includes all women aged eighteen and over who received child-support payments—whether divorced, separated, or never married—in that year. U.S. Bureau of the Census, *Child Support and Alimony: 1989*, Current Population Reports pp. 60–173 (Washington, D.C.: U.S. Government Printing Office, 1989).

101. These differentials reflect the high rates of unemployment and poverty among men, and the comparative inaccessibility of the legal system for poor women going through divorce. They are less likely to seek child support, less likely to receive it when they have asked, and somewhat less likely to get the money they have been promised than white women who have the resources to fight for child support and whose ex-husbands have higher salaries with which to pay.

102. U.S. Bureau of the Census, *Child Support and Alimony: 1989*.

103. Doubled to 5.5 percent of all children under age eighteen.

104. U.S. Bureau of the Census, *Coresident Grandparents and Grandchildren*, Current Population Reports pp. 23–198 (Washington, D.C.: U.S. Government Printing Office, May 1999). For more on the role of black grandmothers, see Eli Anderson's and Linda Burton's writings.

105. (57.2 percent)

106. 14.4 percent of grandmothers in two grandparent/no parent families, and 26.9 percent of those in grandmother/some parent families live below the poverty line.

107. 26.5 percent of grandmothers in two grandparent/some parent families, 28.9 percent of those in two grandparent/no parent families, and 36.4 percent of the grandmothers in grandmother only/some parent families are in poor/fair health. U.S. Bureau of the Census, *Coresident Grandparents and Grandchildren*, Table 1.

108. Racial disparities in death rates are particularly pronounced in large urban areas like New York City and Chicago. While the annual death rate for blacks in rural areas is 1.44 times greater than that for whites, and 1.50 times greater in large suburban areas, it is 1.65 times greater in large core metropolitan regions of the United States. U.S. Department of Health and Human Services, Centers for Disease Control and Prevention, *Deaths: Final Data for 1998* (Hyattsville, Md: National Center for Health Statistics, 2000), Table 2. Hispanics fare far better than their African-American counterparts. The death rates for Hispanic males and females are similar to—and in some cases less than those for—non-Hispanic whites.

109. U.S. Department of Health and Human Services, Centers for Disease Control and Prevention, *Deaths: Final Data for 1998*, Table 2.

110. I use the term "middle age" here to denote people who are aged between forty-five and sixty-four.

111. Death rates from heart disease and diabetes among black men forty-five to sixty-four are, respectively, 1.8 and 2.5 times higher than those for their white peers. Blacks between the ages of forty-five and sixty-four are three times more likely than whites to suffer from diabetes.

112. Researchers have a difficult time explaining "the Mexican paradox": the poverty rate is high for Mexican Americans and many have no health insurance (both are factors related to higher rates of disease and death), yet they are less likely than either blacks or whites to die from common illnesses. Brigid Schutte, "Solving the puzzle of why minorities fare poorly," updated August 16, 1998. URL: ohio.com/bj/projects/healthgap/doc/025868.

113. U.S. Department of Health and Human Services, Centers for Disease Control and Prevention, *Deaths: Final Data for 1998*, Table 8.

114. 19 percent of white women, and 24 percent of white men suffer from hypertension. Rates for Mexican Americans are closer to those for whites—22 percent of females and 25.2 percent of males suffer from hypertension. Figures are age-adjusted, representing the time period from 1988–1994. U.S. Department of Health and Human Services, National Center for Health Statistics, *Health, United States, 1998*, Table 62.

115. 33.7 percent of white men and 34 percent of black men are overweight; 40.1 percent of Mexican men are carrying too much weight.

116. U.S. Department of Health and Human Services, National Center for Health Statistics, *Health, United States, 1998*, Table 70.

117. 28.5 percent of black males vs. 14.1 percent of white males.

118. Data from 1995. U.S. Department of Health and Human Services, National Center for Health Statistics, *Health, United States, 1998*.

119. *The Journal of the American Medical Association* (JAMA) reports that "lower levels of education and income are associated with a significantly higher prevalence of health risk behaviors, including smoking, being overweight and being physically inactive. The results also show that lower income leads to a significant increase in mortality risk, yet the influence of major health risk behaviors explains only a modest proportion of this relationship. . . . Socioeconomic differentials in mortality are due to a wider array of factors [than to just behavioral risk factors], including exposure to environmental health hazards and inequalities in the access and use of preventive and appropriate therapeutic medical care." Paula M. Lantz, James S. House et al., "Health Behaviors Don't Explain High Death Rates Among Poor," *JAMA* 279 (June 3, 1998): 1703–38.

120. Forty-five to sixty-four years of age.

121. Blacks are nearly twice as likely as Hispanics and three times as likely as whites to lack medical insurance. U.S. Department of Health and Human Services, National Center for Health Statistics, *Health, United States, 1998*, Table 62.

3: Work and Neighborhood

1. In the 1930s, Hortense Powdermaker conducted an ethnographic field study of Indianola, a Mississippi Delta town she called "Cottonville." She found that blacks in that community had class distinctions as did whites. The black upper class made up a small percentage of the black population while the middle class held the majority. While there were similarities between the class structures of blacks and whites, Powdermaker stresses, "The Negro classes are by no means to be equated with the White classes in the same relative positions" (p. 60). Upper-class blacks were on a lower economic level than middle-class whites. In addition, the way that classes were delineated was different for blacks. Powdermaker notes that the degree to which a black person emulates behavior "formerly restricted to Whites, particularly those which center in marriage and sex life, family life, education, occupation, and forms of religious worship," was directly related to that black person's place in the class system (p. 61). The black upper class behaved most like whites and attached similar meanings to their behavior. The middle class imitated white behavior but were less likely to accept the meanings whites gave to actions. The black lower class neither acted nor thought like whites. Hortense Powdermaker, *After Freedom: A Cultural Study in the Deep South* (Madison: University of Wisconsin Press, 1993), pp. 56–71.

2. The mechanization of cotton farming, coupled with the Great Depression, made it difficult for African Americans to find work in the South. As a result, many African Americans left the region, especially its rural areas, searching for jobs in cities. Lemann calls this "one of the largest and most rapid mass internal movements of people in history." Nicholas Lemann, *The Promised Land: The Great Black Migration and How It Changed America* (New York: Random House, 1992), p. 6. African Americans competed with white immigrants for the few jobs left. Hortense Powdermaker commented on the change in the labor market of Cottonville during the Depression. During those harsh economic times, jobs once seen as below white men were desired by African Americans. This competition bred hostility and contempt, especially in those white men who believed that their applications should be given precedence over those of African Americans. Hortense Powdermaker *After Freedom*, pp. 111–16.

3. During the war, many economic opportunities previously closed to African Americans were available to them for the first time in America. Between 1942 and 1945, African-American employment tripled. African-American employment in manufacturing grew by 150 percent, reflecting the move from farm to city. Sally M. Miller and Daniel A. Cornford, *American Labor in the Era of World War II* (Westport, CT: Greenwood Press, 1995), pp. 2–3. As an example of tight labor markets during the war, James B. Atleson notes that Detroit "lost 30 percent of its predominantly male workforce, and half of the new workers were engaged in factory work for the first time." James B. Atelson, *Labor and the Wartime State: Labor Relations and Law During World War II* (Chicago: University of Illinois Press, 1998), p. 158. These new workers were African Americans, women, and people from rural areas. It is important to note that although African Americans were given new opportunities, they were "primarily found at

the bottom of the occupational ladder, in jobs which were not only unskilled but often hazardous." Atelson, *Labor and the Wartime State*, p. 169.

4. Home care workers for elderly are a cost-efficient alternative to nursing home care. Many home care workers are low-income, minority, and immigrant women. The cost efficiency of this arrangement is a result of the undervaluing of the work done by these women. They not only have very low wages, but also have few or no benefits and little job stability. In a study of 404 home care workers in New York City, 96 percent were minorities. Almost half of the workers were immigrants. Their median annual income ranged from $5,000 to $7,000. Rebecca Donovan, Paul A. Kurzman, and Carol Rotman, "Improving the Lives of Home Care Workers: A Partnership of Social Work and Labor," *Social Work* 38 (1993), pp. 579–85.

5. In 1965, amendments to the Social Security program gave divorced wives benefits if their marriage had lasted at least twenty consecutive years. Beginning in 1977, if a woman was married to her ex-husband for at least ten years, she is eligible to a share of his Social Security pension. Geoffrey Kollmann, *Summary of Major Changes in the Social Security Cash Benefits Program: 1935–1996*, Congressional Research Service, The Library of Congress (CRS Report for Congress, December 20, 1996), pp. CRS9–CRS14. However, many older women today were divorced before this 1977 amendment was enacted. As a result, women in their late fifties and early sixties are seeking or continuing employment. For women in their early sixties, labor force participation was at a record-high 40.1 percent in 2000. In 1981 this figure was 32.6 percent. On the other hand, the percentage of older men in the labor force has declined over the past thirty years, despite a recent, small increase. Louis Uchitelle, "Lacking Pensions, Older Divorced Women Remain at Work," *New York Times*, June 26, 2001, p. A1.

6. In 1954, Social Security extended coverage to self-employed farmers, most self-employed professionals, and most home workers. Two years later, most previously excluded self-employed professionals and additional farm owners and operators were covered. Kollmann, *Summary of Major Changes in the Social Security Cash Benefits Program: 1935–1996*, pp. CRS5–CRS7.

7. Evaluation of Work Situation

Using a scale from 0 to 10, where 0 means "the worst possible" and 10 means the best possible, how would you rate your work situation?

	*New York Sample**	*National Sample*
These days?	5.59	7.22
10 years ago?	6.40	6.88
In 10 years?	7.40	7.64

*Mean score

8. The same pattern is evident in the data on health (see chapter six) where, despite some significant problems, our informants show lower rates of depression than do their more advantaged counterparts.

9. The national sample is fairly "high end," overrepresenting people of higher means than the average American family as the U.S. Census Bureau defines it. Using data from 1998, at which point household median income in the United States increased for the fourth consecutive year, it is clear that the MIDUS respondents' median income is well above that of the average American household. In 1998, the median income for all households in America was $38,885, more than $6,000 below the median income for the MIDUS sample ($45,000). Broken down by race of the householder, the figure from the MIDUS group remains high. For the non-Hispanic white householder, the median income was $42,439, still considerably less than the MIDUS group's. U.S. Census Bureau, Current Population Reports, P60–206, *Money Income in the United States: 1998*, Washington, D.C.: U.S. Government Printing Office, 1999.

10. The figures for New York were calculated by summing respondents' personal income, spouse's personal income, other family members' income, household social security benefits, household government assistance, and other family income. The comparable variable for the national sample just asks the respondent to provide the "total family income from all sources, before taxes, including everyone who lives in the household."

11.   Family Income by Age of Respondent

Age	Median Family Income	% <$10,000	% <$40,000
<30 years			
NY	$20,000–$24,999	14.3	28.5
National	$36,500	6.7	43.3
30–40 years			
NY	$20,000–$24,999	23.7	10.5
National	$45,566	4.2	61.0
41–65 years			
NY	$18,000–$18,999	18.4	18.5
National	$50,850	5.1	63.0
66+ years			
NY	$15,000–$15,999	40.0	0.0
National	$34,500	10.7	39.8

12. These figures are *not* adjusted for family size and thus must be treated with caution in terms of the poverty line.

13. Missy is referring here to the fact that lunch counters had not been desegregated. Her arrival in New York predated the civil rights movement by several decades.

14. In a study focusing on public sector organizations, Michael Diamond explains the factors that contribute to employee dissatisfaction in the workplace. Supervisors may show disregard for the individual, emotional lives of their subordinates, fail to include subordinates in important decisions, and be overly controlling. In addition, employees may feel as if acceptance of dominant values, norms, ideology, and identity are rewarded. This can cause resentment because of perceived infringement on personal freedom and independence. Others may perceive it as indoctrination. If employees accept these controls, they may feel

betrayed if rewards are not forthcoming. Michael A. Diamond, "Administrative Assault: A Contemporary Psychoanalytic View of Violence and Aggression in the Workplace," *American Review of Public Administration* 27 (1997), pp. 228–47. In a report by the U.S. General Accounting Office, the U.S. Postal Service was reviewed. The culture of their working environment was described as highly structured and autocratic. The report also described unsatisfactory working conditions and adversarial relationships between labor and management. General Accounting Office, *U.S. Postal Service: Labor-Management problems persist on the workroom floor (Vol. 2)*. Report to congressional requesters, created September 29, 1994. URL: <frwebgate.access.gpo.gov/cgi-bin/useftp.cgi?IPaddress=162.140. 64.21& filename=gg94201b.txt&directory=/diskb/wais/data/gao>

15. See Figures 3.1 and 3.2 and Table 3.3.
16. As Jennifer Hochschild notes in *Facing Up to the American Dream* (Princeton, NJ: Princeton University Press, 1995), the higher up the occupational structure, the more these frictions come into view. Higher-income minorities are more likely to feel that racial barriers are blocking their progress than are lower-income people who lead such segregated lives that black/white friction is less of a daily occurrence.
17. African-American men's median income has historically overshadowed that of their female counterparts. In 1950 African-American women earned less than one-third of African-American men's income. Through the years, this disparity has decreased. In 1960 African-American women's median income was 37 percent of African-American men. This figure continued to rise and was 71.8 percent in 1999.

Median Income of Blacks by Sex (in 1999 dollars)

Year	Men	Women	Women's median income as a percentage of men's
1999	$20,579	$14,771	71.8
1990	$16,403	$10,615	64.7
1980	$16,213	$9,271	57.2
1970	$16,777	$8,322	49.6
1960	$11,693	$4,331	37.0
1950	$9,354	$3,014	32.2

Despite these gains, African-American women on average still earn less than three-quarters the income of their male counterparts. U.S. Census Bureau, *Race and Hispanic Origin of People by Median Income and Sex: 1947–1999*, created February 7, 2001. URL: <www.census.gov/hhes/income/histinc/po2.html> Until the mid-1970s, a larger percentage of African-American women than African-American men finished high school. These figures rose modestly for both groups, but men did not completely catch up to women until 1977, when 45.4 percent of African-American women and 45.6 percent of African-American men had gone to high school. To this day, these percentages remain comparable. In 1990 they were 65.8 percent and 66.5 percent of African-American men and women, respectively. And in 2000, those figures were 79.1 percent and 78.7 percent. U.S. Census Bureau, *Percent of People 25 Years Old and Over Who Have Completed High School or College, by Race, Hispanic Origin, and Sex, Selected Years 1940–2000*, Internet release date: December 19, 2000. URL: www.census.gov/population/socdemo/education/tableA-2.txt

Percent of Black People* Who Have Completed High School by Sex

Year	Men	Women
2000	79.1	78.7
1990	65.8	66.5
1980	51.1	51.3
1970	32.4	34.8
1962	23.2	26.2
1950	12.5	14.7
1940	6.9	8.4

*25 years old and older

As evidenced by the table below, with respect to college education, there is more similarity historically between African-American men and women. U.S. Census Bureau, *Percent of People 25 Years Old and Over Who Have Completed High School or College, by Race, Hispanic Origin, and Sex, Selected Years 1940–2000.*

Percent of Black People* Who Have Completed College by Sex

Year	Men	Women
2000	16.4	16.8
1990	11.9	10.8
1980	7.7	8.1
1970	4.6	4.4
1962	3.9	4.0
1950	2.1	2.4
1940	1.4	1.2

*25 years old and older

18. Administered by the Department of Labor, the Comprehensive Employment and Training Act (CETA) was created in 1973 and abandoned in 1983. It consolidated job training and economic opportunity programs that had been under the Manpower Development and Training Act of 1962 and the Equal Opportunity Act of 1964. CETA gave block grants to states and local communities in order to get unemployed and underemployed people into training programs and public service jobs so they could later get permanent jobs. Diana Etindi, Andrew Bush, and Laura Kaye, Welfare Policy Center of the Hudson Institute, *Lessons From CETA*, cited July 19, 2001. URL: <www.welfarereformer.org/articles/ceta.htm>

19. Using simulated models of four cities, Massey and Denton were able to illustrate

how racial and class segregation can concentrate poverty in certain areas, even when these factors are independent of each other. "With or without class segregation, residential segregation between blacks and whites builds concentrated poverty into the residential structure of the black community." Douglas S. Massey and Nancy A. Denton, *American Apartheid: Segregation and the Making of the Underclass* (Cambridge, MA: Harvard University Press, 1993), p. 125. While both African Americans and whites may be ideologically in favor of integration, whites tend to have a different view of integration than do African Americans. African Americans view a 50–50 mixture of white and African American as an integrated community, while whites consider a much smaller proportion of African Americans to be an acceptable amount. "If whites accept integration in principle but remain fearful of living with blacks in practice, then blacks are more likely to be tolerated as neighbors when they constitute a small share of the population than when they are a relatively large proportion." Massey and Denton, *American Apartheid*, p. 111. African Americans are kept out of affluent, predominantly white neighborhoods by a variety of subtle exclusionary practices. A realtor can control which properties their African-American clients have access to. They can lie about availability or costs of properties. Audits of realtors in St. Louis, Palo Alto, Baltimore, and Chicago show that these practices are in effect. In addition, financial institutions can practice racial discrimination, lowering the chances of African Americans securing mortgages even when they can afford to live in an affluent community. Through these practices, "blacks remain the most spatially isolated population in U.S. history." Massey and Denton, *American Apartheid*, p. 114.

20. If an African-American family moves into an all-white neighborhood, "at least one white family's tolerance threshold is exceeded" and that family will move. Massey and Denton, *American Apartheid*, p. 96. The departing white family may be replaced by another African-American family, raising the proportion of acceptable integration beyond another white family's threshold. This could result in a "self-perpetuating dynamic . . . that leads to rapid racial turnover and inevitable resegregation." Massey and Denton, *American Apartheid*, p. 96.

21. Middle-class, African-American parents are concerned with ensuring that their children's lives are better, or at least comparable, to their own. However, they live in neighborhoods that are more economically diverse than the neighborhoods of middle-class whites. Thus, middle-class, African-American parents do not have as much control over their children's environment as do parents who live in more homogeneous communities. Middle-class status is accordingly more precarious for African-American children than for their white counterparts. "While parents do try to control their children's interactions, other avenues continue to be alluring and enticing for their children." Mary Pattillo McCoy, *Black Picket Fences: Privilege and Peril among the Black Middle Class* (Chicago: University of Chicago Press, 1999), p. 92. Middle-class, black parents employ certain strategies to keep their children from deleterious influences, such as encouraging enrollment in after-school classes, participation in sports teams, and involvement in church youth groups. However, normal adolescent rebelliousness undermines these plans. In addition, African-American parents may find themselves working long hours to continue earning their middle-class incomes.

Pattillo McCoy, *Black Picket Fences*, pp. 7, 91–105, 210–214. Single-parent households, especially those in which the mother is the only parent, are reflected in increased incidents of violence victimization. This has racial implications because "percentage black and percentage female-headed families are positively and significantly related." Robert Sampson, "The Community Context of Violent Crime," in *Sociology and the Public Agenda*, W. J. Wilson, ed. (Thousand Oaks, CA: Sage, 1993), pp. 266–27. The rate of violent victimization is two to three times higher in areas with predominantly single-parent households. Sampson, "The Community Context of Violent Crime."

4: Men and Women: Together and Apart in the Later Years

1. All quotations taken from August Wilson, *King Hedley II: A Play in Two Acts* (1999). Performed May 24, 2000, by Huntington Theatre Company, Boston.
2. See Andrew J. Cherlin, ed., *The Changing American Family and Public Policy* (Washington D.C.: Urban Institute Press, 1988); Frank F. Furstenberg Jr. and Andrew J. Cherlin, *Divided Families: What Happens to Children When Parents Part* (Cambridge, MA: Harvard University Press, 1991); Andrew J. Cherlin, *Marriage, Divorce, Remarriage* (revised and enlarged edition) (Cambridge, MA: Harvard University Press, 1992); Irwin Garfinkel, Sara S. McLanahan, Philip Robins, eds., *Child Support and Child Well-Being* (Washington, D.C.: Urban Institute Press 1994); Sara McLanahan, Irwin Garfinkel, and Dorothy Watson, *Family Structure, Poverty, and the Underclass* (Madison: University of Wisconsin-Madison, Institute for Research on Poverty, 1987); Sara McLanahan and Gary Sandefur, *Growing Up With a Single Parent: What Hurts, What Helps* (Cambridge, MA: Harvard University Press, 1994); Sara McLanahan and Karen Booth, *Mother-Only Families: Problems, Reproduction, and Politics* (Madison: University of Wisconsin-Madison, Institute for Research on Poverty, 1988); Irwin Garfinkel and Sara S. McLanahan, *Single Mothers and Their Children: A New American Dilemma* (Washington, D.C.: Urban Institute Press, 1986).
3. Elijah Anderson describes the formation of "baby clubs" in Northton, a pseudonym for an urban community located in the eastern United States. Baby clubs grow out of a social group of closely knit girls with weak ties to other networks. The peer group initially functions as a play group that often fills a "social, moral, and family void in the young girls' lives." Elijah Anderson, *Streetwise: Race, Class, and Change in an Urban Community* (Chicago: University of Chicago Press, 1990), pp. 123–24. The girls have very little adult supervision and are subject to few restrictions. Once a few girls in the group become pregnant, other group members aspire to become mothers in large part because a group norm rewarding this behavior develops. The girls derive status from having a baby: they have now become adults. Motherhood becomes the basis of the peer group and in these baby clubs the teenage mothers receive support and praise from one another. The girls also use their babies to compete with one another "on the premise that the baby is an extension of the mother and reflects directly on her." Anderson, *Streetwise*, p. 124. The young girls spend large amount of money buying their babies expensive clothes that will be worn at social gatherings. The

mothers "lobby for compliments, smiles, and nods of approval and feel very good when they are forthcoming." Anderson, *Streetwise*, p. 126. See also Elijah Anderson, *Code of the Street* (New York: W.W. Norton and Co., 1999), pp. 162–67, for a discussion of baby clubs; Elijah Anderson, "Sex Codes and the Family Life among Poor Inner-City Youths," *Annals of the American Academy of Political and Social Science* 501 (1989), pp. 59–78; Elijah Anderson, "Neighborhood Effects on Teenage Pregnancy," in *The Urban Underclass*, Christopher Jencks and Paul E. Peterson, eds. (Washington, D.C.: Brookings Institution, 1991), pp. 375–98.

4. Carol Stack discussed this pathway many years ago in her classic book *All Our Kin: Strategies For Survival in a Black Community* (New York: Harper & Row, 1974).

5. In poor, urban neighborhoods where many women are not married before they have children, the issue of paternity has always been (and continues to be) complex. Carol B. Stack finds that there can be a difference between what is generally accepted in the community and what a man decides. When a couple is involved and the woman becomes pregnant, the community generally identifies her boyfriend as the father. The man, however, has several options open to him. In some cases he can deny paternity (and any obligation) altogether. This is usually accomplished by implying that the woman has several partners simultaneously. Alternatively, the man can accept paternity. This can be done by telling his friends and relatives that he is the father, by "paying part of the hospital bill," or by bringing necessary baby items to the mother after the birth of the child. Paternity can also be established by the man's family. If the man's mother or female kin take an active role in the caring and support of a child, the community generally accepts him as the father, regardless of his assertions. Carol B. Stack, *All Our Kin*, pp. 50–57. Not all fathers that accept paternity have the same rights. A father who accepts paternity but provides no financial support "retains practically no rights in his child." Stack, *All Our Kin*, p. 52. Elliot Liebow, *Tally's Corner; A Study of Negro Street Corner Men* (Boston: Little, Brown, 1967), makes similar findings in his book. More recent accounts tell a similar story. Elaine Bell Kaplan finds the same pattern nearly three decades after Stack and Liebow conducted their studies. In her study of teenage mothers Kaplan finds that many of the boyfriends denied paternity by suggesting that the woman slept around. Indeed, Kaplan suggests that this is made easier by a "culture of protection" around the man whereby his friends assert that the baby belongs to another man. Elaine Bell Kaplan, *Not Our Kind of Girl: Unraveling the Myths of Black Teenage Motherhood* (Berkeley CA: University of California Press, 1997), pp. 99–102. However, as in Stack's work, paternity can be established through female relatives of the man. Kaplan finds in several instances that the mother of the man acknowledges the baby, usually through citing a physical resemblance, even though the man continues to deny any obligation. For a historical discussion of paternity in the United States see Kristin Luker, *Dubious Conceptions: The Politics of Teenage Pregnancy* (Cambridge, MA: Harvard University Press, 1996).

6. Cohabitation, which is generally conceived as a heterosexual, unmarried couple living together, has become increasingly prevalent in American society. Such arrangements were quite uncommon fifty years ago, but they have dramatically

increased over the past few decades. The number of cohabiting households increased from 1.1 million in 1977 to 4.9 million in 1997. Lynne M. Casper and Philip N. Cohen, "How Does POSSLQ Measure Up? Historical Estimates of Cohabitation," *Demography* 37 (2) (May 2000), p. 244. The change has been so dramatic that cohabitation has almost become the rule rather than the exception. Most young men and women can now be expected to cohabit some time in their lives. Patricia Smock, "Cohabitation in the United States: An Appraisal of Research Themes. Findings, and Implications," *Annual Review of Sociology* 26 (2000), p. 1. The proportion of all first unions that began as cohabitation rose from 43 percent in 1980–84 to 54 percent of unions formed in 1990–94. Larry Bumpass and Hsien-Hen Lu, "Trends in Cohabitation and Implications for Children's Family Contexts in the United States," *Population Studies* 54 (2000), p. 33. By 1995 half of all women in their thirties had cohabited. And the proportion of current unions that involve cohabitation has increased dramatically. About one-third of all unions to women under twenty-five and one-fifth of those between twenty-five and twenty-nine were cohabitation unions. Bumpass and Lu, "Trends in Cohabitation and Implications for Children's Family Contexts in the United States," p. 32. Cohabitation does seem to vary systematically with certain individual characteristics, although it must be stressed that cohabitation is common in nearly every subgroup. Younger people are more likely to cohabit than the elderly. Indeed, the group of people sixty-five years and older are the only group that does not show a decline in the proportion of unmarried couples in relation to heterosexual couples at a given point in time. Rebecca Gronvold Hatch, *Aging and Cohabitation* (New York: Garland Publishing Inc., 1995), p. 18. People of lower socioeconomic status (in terms of income or education) are more likely to cohabit. Steven Nock, "A Comparison of Marriages and Cohabiting Relationships," *Journal of Family Issues* 16 (1) (January 1995), p. 65. See also Arland Thornton, William G. Axinn, and Jay D. Teachman, "The Influences of School Enrollment and Accumulation on Cohabitation and Marriage in Early Adulthood," *American Sociological Review* 60 (October 1995), pp. 762–74. Similarly, people who express less religiosity and more liberal values are more likely to cohabit. Arland Thornton, William G. Axinn, and Daniel H. Hill, "Reciprocal Effects of Religiosity, Cohabitation, and Marriage," *American Journal of Sociology* 98 (3) (November 1992), pp. 628–51. Cohabitation does not seem to vary substantially by ethnicity, however. By 1995 there were no significant racial differences in the proportion that had cohabitated. Among women aged between nineteen and forty-four, 45 percent of whites and blacks and 39 percent of Latinos say they have cohabited. Bumpass and Lu, "Trends in Cohabitation and Implications for Children's Family Contexts in the United States," p. 32.

7. Western European nations along with Canada and the United States have seen a large increase in cohabitation over the past several decades. Cohabitation has become almost universal in Scandinavian countries. Judith A. Seltzer, "Families Formed Outside of Marriage," *Journal of Marriage and the Family* 62 (4) (November 2000), p. 1249. Since the 1970s, nearly all Swedish women who have married cohabited prior to the marriage. Britta Hoem, "Sweden," in *The New Role of Women: Family Formation in Modern Societies*, Hans-Peter Blossfeld, ed. (Boul-

der, CO: Westview, 1995), p. 44. In 1991, 78 percent of women aged twenty to twenty-four who lived in conjugal unions were cohabiting. Hoem, "Sweden," p. 47. Moreover, Swedish law does not distinguish between married and unmarried couples. Unmarried cohabiting couples receive the same tax assessment, child benefits, and housing allowances as married couples. Hoem, "Sweden," p. 40. By 1987, nonmarital cohabitation had become the preferred type of second union in Sweden and Norway. Ann Klimas Blanc, "The Formation and Dissolution of Second Unions: Marriage and Cohabitation in Sweden and Norway," *Journal of Marriage and the Family* 49 (May 1987), p. 398. See also Stephen Parker, *Informal Marriage, Cohabitation and the Law, 1750–1989* (New York: St. Martin's Press, 1990); Zheng Wu and Michael S. Pollard, "Economic Circumstances and the Stability of Nonmarital Cohabitation," *Journal of Family Issues* 21 (3) (April 2000), pp. 303–28; Hans-Peter Blossfeld and Götz Rohwer, "West Germany," in *The New Role of Women*, pp. 56–76; Henri Leridon and Laurant Toulemon, "France," in *The New Role of Women*, pp. 77–101; Jenny de Jong Gierveld and Aart C. Liefbroer, "The Netherlands," in *The New Role of Women*, pp. 102–25; Kathleen E. Kiernan and Éva Leièvre, "Great Britain," in *The New Role of Women*, pp. 126–49; Hans-Peter Blossfeld and Achim Wackerow, "United States of America," in *The New Role of Women*, pp. 150–73; Margarita Delgado, "Spain," in *The New Role of Women*, pp. 191–210.

8. The United States has seen a huge jump in out-of-wedlock childbearing over the past sixty years. In the 1940s, 10 of every 1,000 women had a child out of wedlock. By the 1990s, 45 of every 1,000 women had children without a husband. Mark Abrahamson, *Out-of-wedlock Births: The United States in Comparative Perspective* (Westport, CT: Praeger, 1998), p. 124. Rates have also increased in other developed countries over the past half century. By 1992, the out-of-wedlock birth rate for the United States fell in the middle range of that for other industrialized countries. Thirty percent of births in 1992 were to unmarried women in the United States. The rates for Sweden, Denmark, United Kingdom, and France are 50 percent, 48 percent, 31 percent, and 31 percent, respectively. Abrahamson, *Out-of-wedlock Births*, p. 36. See also Sara McLanahan, Irwin Garfinkel, and Dorothy Watson, *Family Structure, Poverty, and the Underclass* (Madison: University of Wisconsin-Madison, Institute for Research on Poverty, 1987); McLanahan and Sandefur, *Growing Up with a Single Parent*.

9. See Casper and Cohen, "How Does POSSLQ Measure Up? Historical Estimates of Cohabitation," pp. 237–45; Patricia Smock, "Cohabitation in the United States: An Appraisal of Research Themes, Findings, and Implications," *Annual Review of Sociology* (2000), pp. 1–20; Bumpass and Lu, "Trends in Cohabitation and Implications for Children's Family Contexts in the United States," pp. 29–41; Steven Nock, "A Comparison of Marriages and Cohabiting Relationships," *Journal of Family Issues* (January 1995), pp. 53–76; Judith A. Seltzer, "Families Formed Outside of Marriage," *Journal of Marriage and the Family* (November 2000), pp. 1247–68; Elizabeth Thomson and Ugo Collella, "Cohabitation and Marital Stability: Quality or Commitment?," *Journal of Marriage and the Family* (May 1992), pp. 259–67.

10. A study done by Judith Treas finds that while pooling money in marriages is the preferred method, a large minority of couples chose to keep at least some

part of their money separate. Thirty-three percent of couples report at least one separate account. Of the couples who have at least one separate account, half have separate accounts and combination accounts while the other half has no joint accounts. Several factors are related to whether or not a couple holds a joint account. If the husband or the wife has previously experienced some kind of marital disruption, the couple is less likely to own a joint account. Couples with longer marital durations are more likely to have joint accounts as are more educated men and nonblack couples. Moreover, those with high income are more likely to have joint accounts. Judith Treas, "Money in the Bank: Transaction Costs and the Economic Organization of Marriage," *American Sociological Review* 58 (October 1993), pp. 723-34

11. In 1989 one of every four children in the United States was born to an unmarried mother. Larry Bumpass and Sara McLanahan, "Unmarried Motherhood: Recent Trends, Composition, and Black-White Differences," *Demography* 26 (2) (May 1989), p. 279. The rates have not been the same for every subgroup. The rates for blacks have always been higher than the rates for whites (even though both groups have seen an increase in out-of-wedlock childbearing). In the 1960s one in four black children and one in twenty white children were born out of wedlock. By the 1990s two-thirds of black children and 25 percent of white children were born to an unmarried mother. Herbert L. Smith, S. Philip Morgan, and Tanya Koropeckyj-Cox, "A Decomposition of Trends in the Non-Marital Fertility Ratios of Blacks and Whites in the United States, 1960-1992," *Demography* 33 (2) (May 1996), p. 141. Latino women have also seen an increase in out-of-wedlock childbearing. In the early 1960s the rate for Latino women was around 20 percent; by the 1990s the rate had increased to around 40 percent. Abrahamson, *Out-of-wedlock Births*, p. 31, figure 2.2. Moreover, the rise in nonmarital births has increased in all age groups; it is not a phenomenon limited to never-married teenage girls. In 1989 half of the nonmarital births were first births and only one-third of the births were to teenagers. In 1984, 41 percent of the nonmarital births to whites and 53 percent of the births to blacks were not first births. Bumpass and McLanahan, "Unmarried Motherhood," p. 280. The increase is also not limited to women of one particular socioeconomic class. However, more educated women have much lower rates than less educated women. See Abrahamson, *Out-of-wedlock Births*, p. 33, table 2.1. Researchers have found several factors that affect the risk of an out-of-wedlock birth. Parental economic resources and family structure are two important factors that appear to affect nonmarital fertility. Women whose parents have few economic resources and women from single-parent families are more likely to bear children out of wedlock. Scott J. South, "Historical Changes and Life Course Variation in the Determinants of Premarital Childbearing," *Journal of Marriage and the Family* 61 (3) (August 1999), pp. 752-63. Out-of-wedlock childbearing did not abate throughout the 1990s but the trends changed slightly. Most notable among these is the closing gap between blacks and whites. While the rate for black women has remained stable, white women's nonmarital fertility has increased markedly, thereby diminishing the distance between the two groups. Moreover, the rate among Latino women has actually increased over

time. South, "Historical Changes and Life Course Variation in the Determinants of Premarital Childbearing," pp. 752–63.

12. Despite its prevalence, researchers have found cohabitation to be a relatively short-lived arrangement. About half of cohabiting couples end the arrangement (either through a separation or through marriage) in one year or less. Only about one-tenth of cohabiting relationships last five years or longer. Bumpass and Lu, "Trends in Cohabitation and Implications for Children's Family Contexts in the United States," p. 33. A survey conducted in 1987–88 found that of the cohabiting relationships that do not end in marriage, only about 2 percent lasted ten years. This is in sharp contrast to married couples that did not cohabit: 27 percent lasted ten years. Conversely, 59 percent of cohabiting relationships that did not end in marriage ended within one year while only 4 percent of marriages (that did not begin as cohabitation) ended within one year. Larry L. Bumpass and James A. Sweet, "National Estimates of Cohabitation," *Demography* 26 (4) (November 1989), p. 620, table 4. Moreover, cohabiting relationships that do end in marriage seem to be less stable than marriages that were not preceded by cohabitation. See Thomson and Collella, "Cohabitation and Marital Stability: Quality or Commitment?," pp. 259–67, and Smock, "Cohabitation in the United States: An Appraisal of Research Themes, Findings, and Implications." This instability has increased over time. Between 1980–84 and 1990–94 the proportion of couples that had separated by five years increased from 45 percent to 54 percent. Bumpass and Lu, "Trends in Cohabitation and Implications for Children's Family Contexts in the United States," p. 33.

13. See note 4 and note 8 from this chapter.

14. Orlando Patterson, *Rituals of Blood: Consequences of Slavery in Two American Centuries* (New York: Civitas/CounterPoint, 1998), writes: "Afro-Americans are the most unpartnered and isolated group of people in America and quite possibly in the world. Unlike any other group of Americans, most of them will go through most of their adult lives without any deep and sustained attachment to a non-kin companion" (p. 4). Patterson argues that gender relations in the black world are as bitter and dysfunctional as they could be. Patterson cites a study conducted at Temple University in which working- and lower-class blacks were asked if there was distrust and even hatred between black men and black women. Sixty-six percent of men and 74 percent of women answered affirmatively (p. 5). Patterson traces much of the problem to the legacy of slavery. He argues that while other groups in the United States have faced similar economic and social problems, such as "rural and urban poverty, ethnic persecution, and economic discrimination," only blacks exhibit such strained gender relations and the high rate of paternal abandonment (p. 159). What sets Afro-Americans apart is the historical fact of slavery and no explanation of Afro-American families is complete without a discussion of the slave system. The slavery system conducted an "[assault] on the roles of father and husband" and produced a hostile environment for "pregnancy, women, childbirth, infancy, and childrearing" (p. 159).

15. See Robert William Fogel and Stanley Engerman, *Time on the Cross: The Economics of American Negro Slavery* (Boston: Little, Brown, 1974); Eugene Genovese, *Roll,*

Jordan Roll (New York: Pantheon Books, 1974); Herbert G. Gutman, *The Black Family in Slavery and Freedom, 1750–1925* (New York: Pantheon, 1976); Paul J. Lammermier, "The Urban Black Family in the Nineteenth Century: A Study of Black Family Structure in the Ohio Valley, 1850–1880," *Journal of Marriage and the Family* 35 (August 1973), pp. 440–56; Charles Vert Willie, *Black and White Families: A Study in Complementarity* (New York: General Hall, 1985).

16. This pattern refers to children in any single-parent family. Patterson, *Rituals Of Blood,* writes: "Sixty percent of Afro-American children are now being brought up without the emotional or material support of a father" (p. 4).

17. Andrew J. Cherlin, "Generation Ex-: Review of the Unexpected Legacy of Divorce: A 25 Year Study by Judith S. Wallerstein, Julia Lewis and Sandra Blakeslee: Hyperion Press," *The Nation*, December 11, 2000, pp. 62–64. Divorce rates have skyrocketed over the past century. About half of all marriages contracted in 1967 will end in divorce. Of the marriages contracted a hundred years earlier, only about 5 percent ended in divorce. Steven Ruggles, "The Rise of Divorce and Separation in the United States, 1880–1990," *Demography* 34 (2) (November 1997), pp. 455–66. See also Cherlin, *Marriage, Divorce, Remarriage*; Teresa Castro Martin and Larry L. Bumpass, "Recent Trends in Marital Disruption," *Demography* 26 (1) (February 1989), pp. 37–51; David Lester, "Trends in Divorce and Marriage Around the World," *Journal of Divorce and Remarriage* 25 (1–2), pp. 169–71.

18. Kathryn Edin, "What Do Low-Income Single Mothers Say About Marriage?," *Social Problems* 47 (1) (February 2000), pp. 112–33, provides a discussion of women's reluctance to marry. She interviews 292 low-income single mothers and finds that several factors contribute to the women's reluctance to marry. The economic position of potential husbands is very important. Most of the women believe that the man should earn considerably more than minimum wage before he becomes marriage material. The women assess a man's economic position by looking at the regularity of his earnings, the effort expended to keep his job, and the sources of his income. Irregular earnings, illegal sources of income, and little effort in maintaining or looking for work all disqualify potential mates as spouses. Other studies substantiate Edin's findings. See Pamela J. Smock and Wendy D. Manning, "Cohabiting Partners' Economic Circumstances and Marriage," *Demography* 34 (3) (August 1997), pp. 331–41, and Wendy D. Manning and Pamela J. Smock, "Why Marry? Race and the Transition to Marriage among Cohabitors," *Demography* 32 (4) (November 1995), pp. 509–20. Kathryn Edin, also finds that women are also reluctant to marry for nonmonetary reasons. The respondents believe that a woman's social standing is tied to that of her husband. Thus, only a man who can bring a woman "respectability" is viewed as a good match. If the man is not able to maintain a job then his class standing disqualifies him from consideration. Issues of control also enter into marriage decisions. Many women are unwilling to enter into marriage if they believe they will have to fulfill a subservient role. Finally, many women avoid marriage because of their distrust of men in general and because of their fear of domestic violence.

19. Elijah Anderson, *Streetwise*, suggests that "sexual relations, exploitative and otherwise" are as common among middle-class teenagers as they are among the

lower-class adolescent respondents. In contrast to the middle-class youths, however, the young men see "no future to derail" by having a child (p. 113). Thus sex, and the offspring as the result, becomes a source of status for the boys. Anderson finds that the young fathers who maintain strong links to their peer group, often "congregate on street corners, boasting about their sexual exploits and deriding conventional family life" (p. 112). This boasting is important because it provides proof of the man's sexual prowess. Finding willing female partners requires men to have good game: gaining a girl's confidence and favor enough for her to sleep with him. Seducing many different women garners the boy more respect from his friends while continued rejection by women earns him strong ridicule. See also Anderson, *Code of the Street*, pp. 142–78; and Anderson, "Sex Codes and the Family Life among Poor Inner-City Youths," pp. 59–78.

20. Timothy Nelson, Kathryn Edin, and Susan Clampet-Lundquist, " 'Doin' the Best I Can': How Low-Income Non-Custodial Fathers in Philadelphia Talk About Their Families," unpublished manuscript (May 16, 2000), find in their sample of low-income, noncustodial fathers that few of them provide consistent financial support to all of their offspring. Many of the men are highly involved when the children are initially born yet this involvement tends to drop off sharply as the children get older. This is particularly true if the relationship between the man and the child's mother is not amicable. Despite this fact, Nelson et al. find that fatherhood has strong symbolic meaning for the men. Indeed, the authors assert that "low-income non-custodial fathers generally ascribe tremendous importance to their children and firmly believe that their lives would be infinitely less meaningful without [them]" (p. 2). Many of the men in the study describe their lives in "before and after": before having children and after having them. Contrary to what the researchers expected, most of the men said that becoming fathers changed their lives for the better. Many of the men describe fatherhood as their salvation: having children had prompted them to change their ways or at least cut back on dangerous behavior. Many also describe the "irrevocable nature of one's status as a father" (p. 22). Unlike other relationships, this bond could not be broken. The authors suggest that fatherhood holds such a cherished position in these men's lives for several reasons. First, children provide the only opportunity for the men to experience social advancement. Secondly, children provide a means of achieving "immortality" (p. 23). Having children leaves some evidence that you were "on the planet" (p. 24). See also Kathryn Edin, Timothy Nelson, and Rechelle Paranal, "Fatherhood and Incarceration as Potential Turning Points in the Criminal Careers of Unskilled Men," unpublished manuscript (May 5, 2001).

21. The Great Migration began between World War I and World War II and gathered steam as the factories pumped out munitions for the war effort. Altogether, some 5 million African Americans decamped from the rural South and journeyed first to the southern cities and then to the northern cities where booming factories were short of labor. See Nicholas Lemann, *The Promised Land: The Great Black Migration and How it Changed America* (New York: Knopf, 1991).

22. Research has shown that people of similar socioeconomic status usually marry one another. This is commonly measured using education: the spouses have

equivalent levels of education. However, persons with dissimilar amounts of education do get married. During the 1990s, when marriage (or cohabitation) occurred between people of dissimilar educational attainment, it was more likely for the woman to be better educated than the man. Zhenchao Qian, "Changes in Assortative Mating: The Impact of Age and Education, 1970–1990," *Demography* 35 (3) (August 1998), pp. 279–92. Moreover, these dissimilar unions were more likely to take place between people of lower educational attainment. Robert Mare, "Five Decades of Educational Assortative Mating," *American Sociological Review* 56 (February 1991), pp. 15–32. See also Matthijs Kalmijn, "Assortative Mating by Cultural and Economic Occupational Status," *American Journal of Sociology* 100 (2) (September 1994), pp. 422–52; Matthijs Kalmijn, "Status Homogamy in the United States," *American Journal of Sociology* 97 (2) (September 1991), pp. 496–523; and Robert Mare, "Five Decades of Educational Assortative Mating," *American Sociological Review* 56 (February 1991), pp. 15–32.

23. See Bruce Western and Katherine Beckett, "How Unregulated Is the US Labor Market?: The Penal System as a Labor Market Institution," *American Journal of Sociology* 104 (4) (January 1999), pp. 1030–60. The number of people incarcerated in the United States has risen dramatically since 1980. In 1980, 500,000 people were in prison. By 1996 the number of people had risen to more than 1.6 million, (p. 1034–35). Moreover, an increasing percentage of inmates are black. Afro-Americans accounted for 22 percent of the prison population in 1930. Sixty-two years later blacks comprised more than half of the country's inmates (p. 1035). Prison time has become part of many black men's lives: one out of every three black male youth "was under some form of state supervision" and about 7 percent of black male adults were serving time in 1995 (pp. 1035). This situation is not found with whites. While the incarceration rate (incarceration per 100,000) for blacks in 1992–93 was 1,947, the rate was only 306 for whites (p. 1036, Table 2). The United States has a much larger prison population than other industrialized countries. Western and Beckett argue that this is not a product of higher crime rates in the United States. Instead they suggest that incarceration rates have risen because of "more aggressive prosecutorial practices, tougher sentencing standards, and intensified criminalization of drug-related activity" (p. 1037). The United States imprisons more drug and property offenders than other industrialized countries. In 1994, for instance, about 30 percent of state prison inmates were convicted of nonviolent drug offenses. In contrast, nonviolent offenders made up only 6 percent of the state prison population in 1979 (p. 1037). Se also Bruce Western, Jeffrey R. Kling, and David F. Weiman, "The Labor Market: Consequences of Incarceration," *Crime and Delinquency* 47 (3) (July 2001), pp. 410–27.

24. Edin, Nelson, and Paranal, "Fatherhood and Incarceration As Potential Turning Points in the Criminal Careers of Unskilled Men," conducted a study between 1995 and 2001 of 300 low-income noncustodial fathers living in Philadelphia and Charleston. The researchers find that many men who are incarcerated attempt to reconnect with their families after they are released. However, this process can be quite difficult and in many cases incarceration severely damages relationships that were fragile to begin with. Nearly all of those respondents who had a romantic relationship before going to prison saw their relationship crumble

due to incarceration. Their girlfriends either broke it off and/or began a relationship with someone else. After the men were released, their former partners often refused to reestablish the connection. This refusal to let the men back in their lives also caused problems in the relationship between the father and the child. "[Mothers] are generally the conduit through which communication with children flow"; thus the men had a more difficult time remaining in their children's lives (p. 8). The researchers even found some cases in which fathers attempted to reconnect with their girlfriends/wives and children but were unable to because they could not find them. The women had moved away without notifying the father (p. 22). U.S. law can also make it more difficult for fathers to reunite with their children. The 1997 ASFA adds more criteria to a previous law, which enables the state to terminate the parents' rights if the child has been in foster care for fifteen or more months out of the last twenty-two months. John Hagen and Juleigh Petty Coleman, "Returning Captives of the American War on Drugs: Issues of Community and Family Reentry," *Crime and Delinquency* 47 (3) (July 2001), pp. 352–67. See also C. F. Hairston, "The Forgotten Parent: Understanding the Forces that Influence Incarcerated Fathers' Relationships with their Children," *Child Welfare* 77 (5), pp. 617–39; Sara McLanahan and Bruce Western, "Fathers Behind Bars," *Contemporary Perspectives in Family Research* 2 (1996), pp. 309–24; Robert J. Sampson and John H. Laub, "Crime and Deviance Over the Life Course: The Salience of Adult Social Bonds," *American Sociological Review* 55 (1990), pp. 609–27.

25. Economic necessity, and the need for caretaking services, keeps many a middle-class couple together too. Data collected since 1860 show a general rise in divorce rates over the past 150 years. However, the divorce rate has fluctuated with economic expansion and depression. Cherlin, *Marriage, Divorce, Remarriage*, finds that the annual divorce rate increased after every major war. In contrast, it decreased during the Great Depression. There is no reason to believe this is the case because somehow people get along so much better under conditions of economic stress. More likely, men and women who would be even more vulnerable apart stick together out of necessity. Indeed, Cherlin argues this very point: because jobs and housing were scarce, many couples chose to stay together (or at least to postpone their divorce). Cherlin, *Marriage, Divorce, Remarriage*, pp. 21, 23. By the same token, it has been suggested that welfare freed up poor women from a degree of dependence and that divorce rates rose in response to their freedom. That freedom can evaporate, as it has in Clark's case, when there are no good options for economic independence. Indeed, he has to hope that he and Ramona stick with their relationship, because without it he would be in deep, deep trouble.

5: Old Before Our Time

1. The relationship between socioeconomic status and mortality and morbidity has long been established. People with low incomes have shorter life spans and experience poorer health than their middle- and upper-class counterparts. This finding holds for each socioeconomic group, not just the very rich and the very poor—that is, each group along the socioeconomic ladder has incrementally bet-

ter health outcomes than the group below it. This socioeconomic gradient is steepest in societies with the highest levels of inequality. But access to health care fails to adequately explain these disparities; rather, investment in human capital—especially education—and the level of social cohesion and social capital within a society appear to be more important determinants of health outcomes. While it is true that overall mortality rates have been decreasing for all members of society in recent decades, the disparity in mortality rates between socioeconomic groups has increased. See especially Norman Daniels, Bruce Kennedy, and Ichiro Kawachi, *Is Inequality Bad for Our Health?* (New York: Beacon Press: 2000); Jonathan S. Feinstein, "The Relationship Between Socioeconomic Status and Health: A Review of the Literature," *Milbank Quarterly* 71 (2) (1993); Michael G. Marmot, "Social Differentials in Health Within and Between Populations," *Daedalus* (Fall 1994); Gregory Pappas et al., "The Increasing Disparity in Mortality Rates Between Socioeconomic Groups in the United States, 1960 and 1986," *New England Journal of Medicine* 329 (2) (July 8, 1993); and D. R. Williams and C. M. Wilson, "Race, Ethnicity, and Aging," in *Handbook of Aging and Social Sciences*, fifth edition, R. H. Binstock and L. K. George, eds. (New York: Academic Press, 2001), pp. 160–78.

2. Cross-sectional studies that compare individuals who are high and low in socioeconomic status suggest that there may be as much as a thirty-year lag between the onset of health problems. (James House et al., *Milbank Quarterly, Journal of Health and Social Behavior*), 1990–1992.

3. For a detailed review of the relationship between stress and coping behaviors, see Shelley Taylor et al., "Health Psychology," *Annual Review of Psychology* 48 (1997), pp. 371–410.

4. Arline T. Geronimus, "The Weathering Hypothesis and the Health of African American Women and Infants," *Ethnicity and Disease* 2 (3) (1992).

5. It is not at all clear that young black women are conscious of their comparatively short life expectancy. For the weathering hypothesis to work it would have to be shown that they do and that this knowledge consciously influences fertility behavior. For the moment, it remains a plausible account of the early childbearing behavior of this population, but one whose causal mechanisms are yet to be confirmed.

6. Geronimus and her colleagues found that in 1990 two-thirds of African-American fifteen-year-olds in Harlem could not expect to reach age sixty-five. For black youth nationwide the situation is better, though still not as promising as among white youth. In 1990, 60 percent of black youth could expect to live to age sixty-five compared to three-quarters of white youth. Arline T. Geronimus et al., "Excess Mortality Among Blacks and Whites in the United States," *New England Journal of Medicine* (November 21, 1996); Arline T. Geronimus, "Economic Inequality and Social Differentials in Mortality," *Economic Policy Review* (September 1999). See also Paul Sorlie et al., "Black-White Mortality By Family Income," *Lancet* (August 8, 1992).

7. Numerous studies document a correlation between race and mortality and morbidity independent of socioeconomic status for individuals under the age of sixty-five. See Daisy S Ng-Mak et al., "A Further Analysis of Race Differences in the National Longitudinal Mortality Study," *American Journal of Public Health*

8 (11) (November 1999); Sorlie et al., "Black-White Mortality By Family Income." Correlations between race and mortality and morbidity above and beyond socioeconomic status have also been shown to hold for child health outcomes and infant mortality rates. See Laura E. Montgomery et al., "The Effects of Poverty, Race and Family Structure on U.S. Children's Health: Data From The NHIS, 1978 through 1980 and 1989 through 1991," *American Journal of Public Health* 86 (10) (October 1996); and Kenneth C. Schoendorf et al., "Mortality Among Infants of Black as Compared With White College Educated Parents," *New England Journal of Medicine* 326 (23) (June 1992).

8. According to David Williams a growing body of scientific research suggests that racism can affect morbidity and mortality through a number of pathways. First, individual and institutional racism can decrease mobility and adversely impact socioeconomic status among blacks. Second, racism may have a more direct impact on health because negative health outcomes are associated with residence in segregated neighborhoods, stress associated with experiences of racism, racial bias in medical treatment, and the acceptance of the societal stigma of inferiority racism. See David Williams, "Race, Socioeconomic Status, and Health: The Added Effects of Racism and Discrimination," *Annals of the New York Academy of Sciences* (1999); David Williams et al., "Racial Differences in Physical and Mental Health: Socioeconomic Status, Stress and Discrimination," *Journal of Health Psychology* 2 (3) (1997); and Chiquita A. Collins and David Williams, "Segregation and Mortality: The Deadly Effects of Racism?" *Sociological Forum* 14 (3) (1999).

9. (57.8 percent)

10. David Williams et al., "Socioeconomic Status and Psychiatric Disorder Among Blacks and Whites," *Social Forces* 71 (1992): 179–94.

11. Daniels, Kennedy, and Kawachi, *Is Inequality Bad for Our Health?*; and Marmot, "Social Differentials in Health Within and Between Populations."

12. While this is true, it is also the case that access to care tells us a lot about how early on the development of serious disease it is likely to be caught, which is one of the reasons that health insurance coverage plays a role in explaining differential death rates by race and income.

13. There are undoubtedly other barriers to care besides income. Recent research suggests that if we equalized income and health insurance, one-half to three-quarters of the racial differences in access to care remain (*Medical Care Research and Review*, December 2000, first paper in the issue).

14. Physical and Mental Health in the New York Sample

	Puerto Ricans	Dominicans	African Americans
Physical health is:			
Poor/Fair	34.4%	35.3%	23.5%
Good	34.4	35.3	32.4
Very good/Excellent	31.3	29.4	44.1
Mental Health is:			
Poor/Fair	9.4%	26.5%	15.2%
Good	56.3	32.4	45.5
Very good/Excellent	34.4	41.2	39.4

15.   Physical and Mental Health Self-Report by Age Groups

Age	<30	30–40	41–65	66+
Physical health is:				
Poor/Fair	21.4%	21.1%	36.8%	60%
Good	28.6	39.5	34.2	20
Very good/Excellent	50	39.5	28.9	20
Mental health is:				
Poor/Fair	15.4%	13.2%	15.8%	40%
Good	30.8	44.7	50.0	40
Very good/Excellent	53.8	42.1	24.2	20

16.   Physical and Mental Health by Levels of Education

Physical Health is:	Poor/Fair	Good	Very Good/Excellent
<High School	41.9	45.2*	12.9*
HS/GED	31.4	31.4	37.1*
Some College	23.8	33.3	42.9
BA+	20	10*	70*

*The difference between less than HS and BA+ is significant at the 0.05 level for "Good" health. The difference between (a) less than HS and BA+ and (b) HS and BA+ are both significant at the 0.05 level for "Excellent" health.

Mental Health is:	Poor/Fair	Good	Very Good/Excellent
<High School	30*	56.7*	13.3*
HS/GED	17.1	37.1	45.7*
Some College	4.8*	52.4	42.9*
BA+	10	20*	70*

*The difference between less than HS and Some College is significant at the 0.05 level for "Poor" health. The difference between less than HS and BA+ is significant at the 0.05 level for "Good" health. The differences between (a) less than HS and BA+, (b) less than HS and HS, and (c) less than HS and Some College are significant at the 0.05 level for "Excellent" health.

17. I report these trends here, but it should be noted that neither is statistically significant at the .05 level.

18. The National Center for Health Statistics shows that nationwide blacks have higher death rates due to heart disease and cancer than whites, while Hispanics are less likely than whites to die of heart disease or cancer. The death rates for 1998 follow:

	Cancer	*Coronary Heart Disease*
Black	161.2	136.3
Hispanic	76.1	68.3
White	121.0	95.1

Note: Rates are deaths per 1,000 residents

19. In order to classify functional disabilities and handicaps, there are many methods of assessment. Two are the basic activities of daily living (BADL) and the instrumental activities of daily living (IADL). The BADL are "feeding, grooming, dressing, bathing, toileting, and mobility" (p. 3). The IADL are more complex. They include "shopping, using transportation, telephoning, preparing meals, handling finances, and maintaining a household" (p. 3). Margaret Kelley-Hayes, James T. Robertson, Joseph P. Broderick, Pamela W. Duncan, Linda A. Hershey, Elliot J. Roth, William H. Thies, and Catherine A. Trombly, *The American Heart Association Stroke Outcome Classification: Executive Summary*, cited July 27, 2001. URL: www.americanheart.org/Scientific/statements/1998/069803.html

20. Although this is a standard measure, it may also be biased by self-reports. A fuller discussion of this issue would require comparisons of these self-reports on depression to data on clinical depression.

21. The differences were not statistically significant, but they do show evidence of directionality nonetheless.

22.

Ratings of Life Overall (scale of 1 to 10)

	<$10,000	*$10–$24,999*	*$25,000+*
Today	6.77	7.31	7.73
10 years ago	7.23	7.94	7.91
10 years in the future	8.35	8.56	8.93

23. It is also possible that there is a bias in this data due to "selection by death." That is, elderly minorities who survive this long may look better than their majority counterparts because so many of their age mates have been "lost" along the way.

24. Through a process called allostasis our body is able to respond to and protect itself against chronic and acute stress. Bruce S. McEwen, "Protective and Damaging Effects of Stress Mediators," *New England Journal of Medicine* 338 (3) (January 15, 1998), however, argues that the long-term effect of constant coping, which he calls allostatic load, is increased susceptibility to disease. That is, we manage and adapt to chronic stress at the expense of our long-term physical health. Also see Bruce S. McEwen, "Stress, Adaptation, and Disease: Allostasis and Allostatic load," *Annals New York Academy of Sciences* 840 (1998).

25. The latter finding could reflect lack of comparable access to physicians, but it may also mean a lower incidence of disease.

26. According to the Federal Interagency Forum on Child and Family Statistics, poor children are more likely to suffer from lead poisoning, asthma, and activity limitation due to chronic health conditions such as asthma, diabetes, injuries, or

vision, hearing, and speech impairments. During 1988–94 poor children between the ages of one and five were six times more likely to suffer from lead
poisoning than children in high-income families (12 percent vs. 2 percent, respectively). During 1992–95 poor children were 1.9 times as likely to have some
activity limitation such as playing or going to school as children from higher-
income households. During 1988–91 asthma hospitalization rates for children
living in communities where the median family income was below $20,000 were
2.4 times that for children living in communities where the median family income was at least $40,000. See "America's Children: Key Indicators of Well-
Being," *Federal Interagency Forum on Child and Family Statistics* (2000). Moreover, a
study by the Center for Children's Health and the Environment at Mount Sinai
hospital found that hospitalization rates for children with asthma were up to
five times higher for children who lived in New York City's poorest neighborhoods. L. Claudio et al., "Socioeconomic Factors and Asthma Hospitalization
Rates in New York City," *Journal of Asthma* 36 (4) (June 1999).

27. Jody Heymann, *The Widening Gap: Why America's Working Families Are in Jeopardy
and What Can Be Done About It* (New York: Basic Books, 2000), documents the
burdens parents who are poor face when they have children with special needs,
including chronic health conditions, learning differences, ADD, and other disabilities. Most poor parents, Heymann found, lack flexible work schedules, the
ability to take time off from work (paid or even unpaid), and the additional
funds for the special care their children require when they are at work. In fact
parents with the greatest needs often face the worst work situations: 60 percent
of parents who worked and had two or more children with special needs experienced "double jeopardy"—that is, they had neither paid sick leave nor paid
vacation leave allowing them to attend to their children's needs. This is particularly problematic given that these parents often have trouble finding and retaining adequate child care, need to bring their children to visit the doctor almost
twice as often as children without special needs, and all too frequently are called
into their child's school to address behavioral issues or oversee medication
schedules. In the end, many parents must choose between their work and giving
their children the care and attention they require and all too often their own
needs, not to mention sleep, are the first to go.

28. Katherine S. Newman, *No Shame in My Game: The Working Poor in the Inner City*
(New York: Knopf/Russell Sage Foundation, 1999).

29. See Carol Stack's *All Our Kin: Strategies for Survival in a Black Community* (New
York: Harper & Row, 1974) and *Call to Home: African Americans Reclaim the Rural
South* (New York: Basic Books, 1996). See also Newman, *No Shame in My Game*.

30. Vicki Helgeson and H. L. Fritz describe "unmitigated communion" as a situation
in which someone, usually a woman, cares for others to her own disadvantage.
They immerse themselves in others' problems, ignoring their own. Vicki Helgeson and H. L. Fritz, "A Theory of Unmitigated Communion," *Personality and
Social Psychology Review* 2 (1998), pp. 173–83.

31. See Sheldon Cohen and S. Leonard Syme, *Social Support and Health* (New York:
Academic Press, 1985). See also Jennifer Unger et al., "Variation in the Impact
of Social Network Characteristics on Physical Functioning in Elderly Persons:

MacArthur Studies of Successful Aging," *Journal of Gerontology* 54B (5) (September 1999).

32. Peggy Levitt, *The Transnational Villagers* (Berkeley: University of California Press, 2001), explores in depth the interwoven lives of Dominican migrants to the United States and the communities they come from. Far from the one-way ticket of past generations of immigrants, Levitt shows the persistent involvement in politics, social networks, and community life at both ends of the migration route. Return migration is often sparked by the need to take care of an elderly relative on the island. Carol Stack, *Call to Home*, makes the same point about African Americans who return to the rural South, also in response to the needs of their elders.

33. Sally Wyke and Graeme Ford, "Competing Explanations for Associations Between Marital Status and Health," *Social Science and Medicine* (1992); Noreen Goldman, Sanders Korenman, and Rachel Weinstein, "Marital Status and Health Among the Elderly," *Social Science and Medicine* (1995); Ingrid Waldron, Christopher C. Weiss, and Mary Elizabeth Hughes, "Marital Status Effects on Health: Are There Differences Between Never Married Women and Divorced and Separated Women," *Social Science and Medicine* (1997). See also Sven E. Wilson, "Socioeconomic Status and the Prevalence of Health Problems Among Married Couples in Late Midlife," *American Journal of Public Health* (January 2001).

34. Cohen and Syme, *Social Support and Health*; Sheldon Cohen, Lynn Underwood, and Benjamin Gottlieb, eds, *Social Support Measurement and Intervention: A Guide for Health and Social Scientists* (New York: Oxford University Press, 2000); Sheldon Cohen et al., "Social Ties and Susceptibility to the Common Cold," *Journal of the American Medical Association* 277 (24) (June 25, 1997).

6: Does Race Matter?

1. Katherine S. Newman, *Declining Fortunes: The Withering of the American Dream* (New York: Basic Books, 1993), explores this proposition in detail for the two generations of baby boomers and their postwar parents trying to come to grips with intergenerational downward mobility.

2. Indeed, the PATCO (Professional Air Traffic Controller Operator) strike is, even now, referred to as a watershed for organized labor. It broke the back of the union movement that lay nearly dormant for the succeeding twenty years. See Katherine S. Newman, *Falling from Grace: The Experience of Downward Mobility in the American Middle Class* (New York: Free Press, 1988).

3. Peggy McIntosh, "White Privilege and Male Privilege: A Personal Account of Coming to See Correspondences Through the Work in Women's Studies," in Margaret Anderson and Patricia Hill Collins, eds., *Race, Class, and Gender: An Anthology* (London: Wadsworth, 1992); David Wellman, *Portraits of White Racism* (Cambridge, England: Cambridge University Press, 1993); and Joe Kincheloe, Shirley Steinberg, Nelson Rodriguez, Ronnald Chennault, eds., *White Reign: Deploying Whiteness in America* (New York: St. Martins Press, 1998).

4. While the poverty rate is higher for nonwhites (approximately 23 percent) in

the United States than for whites (approximately 8 percent), there are more poor whites than nonwhites because whites form a much larger group in absolute numbers. According to the 2000 Current Population Survey roughly 15 million (14,875,000) whites were poor. In the same year, more than 8 million (8,360,000) blacks and approximately 7.5 million (7,439,000) Hispanics were poor.

5. Jennifer Lee, "From Civil Relations to Racial Conflict: Merchant-Customer Relations in Urban America," *American Sociological Review* (forthcoming).

6. Perhaps the most notorious former lieutenant of the Nation of Islam was Khallid Muhammad, whose frequent anti-Semitic speeches earned him a unilateral condemnation by the United States Senate (97 to 0) in 1994. Kevin Merida, "Trent Lott," *Washington Post* (March 29, 1999). Khallid Muhammad's incendiary rhetoric has been denounced by most black and white leaders, including those in the Nation of Islam, which formally ousted Mr. Muhammad from its organization in 1994. Steven Gray, "Two Marches Reflect Split in Black America," *Washington Post* (August 14, 1998).

7. Indeed, half of all spells on welfare last less than two years and only 14 percent last ten years or more. See Mary Jo Bane and David T. Ellwood, *Welfare Realities: From Rhetoric to Reform* (Cambridge, MA: Harvard University Press, 1994), p. 29. In addition, the average family size for a family on TANF in 1999 was 2.8, which is smaller than the average family size for all families (3.18) in the United States in the same year. "Characteristics and Financial Circumstances of TANF Participants: Fiscal Year 1999," *U.S. Department of Health and Human Services* (www.acf.dhhs.gov/programs/opre/characteristics/fy99/analysis.htm); *Statistical Abstract of the United States,* U.S. Census Bureau (2000).

8. David Ellwood, *Poor Support: Poverty in the American Family* (New York: Basic Books, 1988), argues that nearly everyone disliked Aid to Families With Dependent Children (AFDC), including the conservatives who viewed welfare as a disincentive to hard work and even the liberals who believed the system mistreated the poor. Indeed a poll conducted in 1984 found that 41 percent of Americans thought the government spent too much money on welfare while only 25 percent felt the government spent too little.

9. Only 12 percent of the respondents as a whole thought American-born blacks preferred welfare. An equally small proportion thought this was true of Puerto Ricans. None of the others even came close. Only 7 percent thought immigrant blacks wanted to be on welfare rather than work, for example. In other words, 90 percent or more were unwilling to fully agree with the proposition.

10. According to the 1990 General Social Survey more than three-quarters (78 percent) of whites responded that blacks were more likely to prefer living off welfare than whites. This type of negative stereotyping that perceives blacks as culturally inferior to whites is distinct from Jim Crow racism or biological racism. Lawrence Bobo has called this type of negative stereotyping "laissez-faire" racism, which he argues is characterized by persistent negative stereotypes of blacks, a belief that African Americans themselves are responsible for their poor economic plight and resistance to policies that would remove the barriers blacks continue to face. See Lawrence Bobo, James R. Kluegel, and Ryan A. Smith, "Laissez Faire Racism: The Crystalization of a 'Kinder, Gentler' Anti-Black Ide-

ology," in Steven A. Tuch and Jack K. Martin, eds., *Racial Attitudes in the 1990s: Continuity and Change* (New York: Praeger, 1997), pp. 15–44. See also David O. Sears, Jim Sidanius, and Lawrence Bobo, eds., *Racialized Politics: The Debate About Racism in America* (Chicago: University of Chicago Press, 2000).

11. Rankings for each individual dimension analyzed by Smith are listed below. Positive scores indicate that the group was rated more positively than whites; a negative score suggests the group was rated more negatively than whites.

Wealth		Work Ethic		Violence	
Jews	+.58	Jews	+.38	Jews	+3.6
S. Whites	−.56	Asian Amer	−.19	Asian Amer	−.15
Asian Amer	−.77	S. Whites	−.52	S. Whites	−.23
Blacks	−1.6	Hisp Amer	−.99	Hisp Amer	−.75
Hisp Amer	−1.64	Blacks	−1.24	Blacks	−1.00

Intelligence		Dependency		Patriotism	
Jews	+.15	Jews	+.40	S. Whites	−.31
Asian Amer	−.36	S. Whites	−.71	Jews	−.57
S. Whites	−.54	Asian Amer	−.75	Blacks	−1.03
Blacks	−.93	Hisp Amer	−1.72	Asian Amer	−1.16
Hisp Amer	−.96	Blacks	−2.08	Hisp Amer	−1.34

12. See Jennifer Lee, "The Salience of Race in Everyday Life: Black Customers' Shopping Experiences in Black and White Neighborhoods," *Work and Occupations* (August 2000). Jennifer Lee, "Cultural Brokers: Race-based Hiring in Inner City Neighborhoods," *The American Behavioral Scientist* (April 1998). Jennifer Lee, *From Civil Relations to Exploding Cauldrons: Blacks, Jews, and Koreans in Urban America* (Cambridge, MA: Harvard University Press: forthcoming).

13. Some of the worst cases of misconduct involve minority police as well.

14. Between 1993 and 2000, the number of major felony crimes in New York City dropped 57 percent from 8,259 felonies per week in 1993 to 3,556 felonies per week in 2000. New York City Mayor Rudolph Giuliani, "State of the City Address," delivered at New York City Hall (January 8, 2001). These statistics are available online at the following Web address: www.ci.nyc.ny.us/html/nypd/pdf/chfdept/cshist.pdf

15. In Boston, for example, serious crime declined by 48 percent between 1990 and 1999. Boston Police Department, *Annual Report* (1999). In Chicago the total number of violent crimes decreased by 30 percent between 1991 and 1998. Chicago Police Department, *Annual Report* (1998). And in Los Angeles between 1990 and 1999 the number of aggravated assaults decreased by 35 percent; the number of burglaries decreased 58.5 percent; the number of robberies by 60 percent; the number of rapes by 42 percent; and the number of homicides by 57 percent. Los Angles Police Department, *Statistical Digest* (1999).

16. Boston, for example, was able to reduce its homicide rate by a greater margin than New York during the 1990s (77 percent vs. 72 percent, respectively), but

unlike New York, Boston achieved this drop without aggressive measures. Instead, the Boston Police Department teamed up with a coalition of black clergy members called the Ten Point Coalition. Working together they built trust between the African-American community and the police and achieved better results while rejecting the notion that there was a necessary conflict between policing and a respect for civil liberties. See Orlando Patterson and Christopher Winship, "Boston's Police Solution," opinion-editorial, *New York Times*, March 3, 1999, p. A17; and Christopher Winship and Jenny Berrien, "Boston Cops and Black Churches," *The Public Interest* (Summer 1999), pp. 52–68.

17. African American attitudes toward crime and punishment reflect the mixed experience they have as likely victims of both criminals and a legal system that is often stacked against them. Hence, blacks are far less likely than whites to support the death penalty and somewhat more likely than whites to report that the criminal justice system deals too harshly with criminals. See *Sourcebook of Criminal Justice Statistics* (1999), Tables 2.60 and 2.56. In 1998, 77 percent of whites believed in the death penalty while only 65 percent of Hispanics and 39 percent of blacks believed in it. Also, in 1998, in response to the question "In general, do you think the courts in this area deal too harshly or not harshly enough with criminals?" 4 percent of whites felt the courts were too harsh while 10 percent of blacks felt the same. However, skepticism about the criminal justice system does not translate into tolerance of deviance or an acceptance of high crime rates in their neighborhoods. Robert Sampson and Dawn Bartusch, "Legal Cynicism and (subcultural?) Tolerance of Deviance: The Neighborhood Context of Racial Differences," *Law and Society* 32 (4) (1998), found that "contrary to received wisdom, . . . African Americans and Latinos are less tolerant of deviance-including violence than whites." However, at the same time, they are also more skeptical of the law and criminal justice institutions.

18. Harry Holzer, *What Employers Want: Job Prospects for Less Educated Workers* (New York: Russell Sage Foundation, 1996), found that fewer than 10 percent of central city jobs require only a high school diploma, even when the diploma is accompanied by previous work experience. This trend was already evident in the 1980s. According to William Julius Wilson, *When Work Disappears: The World of the New Urban Poor* (New York: Vintage, 1997), p. 32, New York City lost "135,000 jobs in sectors in which workers averaged less than twelve years of education and gained almost 300,000 jobs in sectors in which workers had thirteen years or more of education." For additional material on the increasing importance of education, see John Bound and Harry Holzer, "Industrial Shifts, Skill Levels and the Labor Market for White and Black Males," *Review of Economics and Statistics* 75 (3) (August 1993); and Harry Holzer, "Can We Solve Black Youth Unemployment," *Challenge* 31 (6) (November/December 1988).

19. See Katherine S. Newman, *No Shame in My Game: The Working Poor in the Inner City* (New York: Knopf/Russell Sage Foundation, 1999), for a discussion of adults bumping down into the youth labor market.

20. Nationwide, poverty increased for full-time workers between 1996 and 1998 by 2.7 percent. Linda Barrington, "Does a Rising Tide Lift All Boats? America's Full-Time Working Poor Recap Limited Gains in the New Economy," *The Conference Board* (2000). In New York City, workers are increasingly filling the ranks

of the poor. Poverty rates for families with children with at least one adult worker (part-time or full-time) increased by 8.2 percentage points between the late 1980s and late 1990s and fell (6.9 points) for families with no worker present. Looked at in another way, the share of poor families that include at least one worker has increased over the last decade by 18.4 percentage points. Mark Levitan, "More Work, More School . . . More Poverty? The Changing Face of Poor Families in New York City," *Community Service Society* (April 2000).

21. Ana Zayas Ramos, *Performing the Nation: The Politics of Race, Class and Space in Puerto Rican Chicago* (Chicago: University of Chicago Press, forthcoming).

22. Jorge Duany, Luisa Hernandez Angueira, and Cesar A. Rey, *Los Dominicanos En Puerto Rico: Migracion en la Semi-Periferia* (Huracin, 1990). Jorge Duany, "Reconstructing Racial Identity: Ethnicity, Color, and Class Among Dominicans in the United States and Puerto Rico," *Latin American Perspectives* (May 1998).

23. In Latin America, race is not dichotomized into simple black and white (or white and nonwhite) categories as is done in the United States. Color distinctions in Latin American countries are more fluid and involve distinctions based on color, hair type, and facial structure. Jorge Duany, "Reconstructing Racial Identity," states that in the Spanish-speaking Caribbean in particular, "phenotype and social status rather than biological descent define a person's racial identity." Also see Michael Jones-Correa, *Between Two Nations: The Political Predicament of Latinos in New York City* (Ithaca: Cornell University Press, 1998), pp. 119–23; and Pierre-Michel Fontaine, ed., *Race, Class and Power in Brazil* (Berkeley: University of California, 1985).

24. Immigrant children, such as Dominicans, whose phenotype more closely resembles African Americans, are more likely to confront discrimination and barriers to upward mobility in the United States. Though many may not see themselves as blacks, they are likely to be treated that way. See Jorge Duany, "Reconstructing Racial Identity." See also Alejandro Portes and Min Zhou, "The New Second Generation: Segmented Assimilation and Its Variants," *Annals of the American Academy of Political Social Science* (November 1993), pp. 74–97. Min Zhou, "Segmented Assimilation: Issues, Controversies, and Recent Research on the New Second Generation," *International Migration Review* (Winter 1997), pp. 975–1008.

25. Mary Pattillo McCoy, *Black Picket Fences: Privilege and Peril Among the Black Middle Class* (Chicago: University of Chicago Press, 1999), notes that in many working- and middle-class neighborhoods similar to that where Barry James raised his daughter, it is not so easy to steer clear of the negative element. Poor people live in adjacent communities and as a result the influence of their less salutary patterns of behavior is felt by kids in middle-class families.

26. George J. Borjas, *Heaven's Door: Immigration Policy and the American Economy* (Princeton, NJ: Princeton University Press, 1999), argues that post-1965 immigration, particularly from poor countries with a surplus of low-wage workers (like Mexico), has indeed hurt the employment prospects and wage levels of native-born workers who are not well educated. In fact, Borjas argues that immigration is largely responsible for the increase in income inequality in the United States since the 1970s: he attributes to immigration nearly half (44 percent) of the decline in the relative wage of high school dropouts.

27. William Julius Wilson, *When Work Disappears*, provides a great deal of support

for Barry James's observations. He notes that African Americans are believed to be lazy, belligerent, hard to manage, and undependable by employers and hiring managers. J. Kirschenman and K. Neckerman, "We'd Love to Hire Them, But . . . : The Meaning of Race for Employers," in Christopher Jencks and Paul Peterson, eds., *The Urban Underclass* (Washington, D.C.: Brookings Institution, 1991), pp. 203–32, argue the same. Newman, *No Shame in My Game*, confirms the employer preference for immigrant labor, even when the person doing the hiring is black.

28. Mary Waters discusses this issue at length in her book *Black Identities* (Cambridge, MA: Harvard University Press, 2000). She notes that West Indian blacks go to great lengths to make it clear that they are not American-born because they know how stigmatized African Americans are, particularly by employers.

29. Lee, *From Civil Relations to Exploding Cauldrons.*

30. Newman, *No Shame in My Game.*

31. William Julius Wilson, *The Truly Disadvantaged: The Inner City, the Underclass and Public Policy* (Chicago: University of Chicago Press, 1987), argues that part of the reason for the larger number of out-of-wedlock births among blacks is that African-American men in the inner city have disproportionately high rates of joblessness, incarceration, and mortality, leaving few in a position to be able to support a family. To highlight the problem, Wilson creates a marriageable pool index, which is a ratio of employed civilian men to women by race and age group. By plotting this ratio over time, Wilson shows the decline in nonwhite ratios for all ages since the 1960s and contrasts this with the increase in the white ratios.

32. Research shows that children function better in a single-parent family than in a conflict-ridden two-parent home. See James L. Peterson and Nicholas Zill, "Marital Disruption, Parent Child Relationships, and Behavior Problems in Children," *Journal of Marriage and the Family* 48 (May 1986), pp. 295–307. Sara McLanahan and Gary Sandefur, *Growing up With a Single Parent: What Hurts, What Helps* (Cambridge, MA: Harvard University Press, 1994), find that growing up in a single-parent family is also associated with diminished chances for a successful adult life. For example, children in single-parent families are more likely then their counterparts in two-parent homes to drop out of high school, be teenage parents, or remain idle—neither in school nor employed. However, McLanahan and Sandefur (1994) also show that low income is by far the most important factor in these children's lower achievement, accounting for approximately half the disadvantage. See also Andrew J. Cherlin, *Marriage, Divorce, Remarriage* (Cambridge, MA: Harvard University Press, 1992); and Frank Furstenberg Jr. and Andrew J. Cherlin, *Divided Families: What Happens to Children When Parents Part* (Cambridge, MA: Harvard University Press, 1991). (Note: Andrew Cherlin has argued more recently that while McLanahan and Sandefur established that negative outcomes were associated with living in a single-parent household, they did not establish causality. In his work, he found that children whose parents would later divorce already showed more emotional problems before the divorce than children whose parents would not. Moreover, Cherlin argues that the prevalence of problems tends to be overestimated. See Andrew

J. Cherlin, "Going to Extremes: Family Structure, Children's Well-Being, and Social Science," *Demography* [November 1999].)

33. For a collection of essays about African-American attitudes toward Jews and vice versa, see Paul Berman, ed., *Blacks and Jews: Alliances and Arguments* (New York: Delacorte Press, 1994).

34. Jonathan Rieder, *Canarsie: The Jews and Italians of Brooklyn Against Liberalism* (Cambridge, MA: Harvard University Press, 1985), examines the tensions that erupted in Canarsie, Brooklyn, when a judge ordered that the Jewish and Italian neighborhood's school desegregate. See also Jennifer Lee, "Business as Usual," *Common Quest: The Magazine of Black-Jewish Relations* 1 (2) (Fall 1996): 35–38.

35. See Albert Bergesen and Max Herman, "Immigration, Race and Riot: The 1992 Los Angeles Uprising," *American Sociological Review* 63 (1) (February 1998), pp. 39–54; and Melvin L. Oliver, James H. Johnson Jr., and Walter C. Farrell, Jr., "Anatomy of a Rebellion: A Political-Economic Analysis," in Robert Gooding-Williams, ed., *Reading Rodney King/Reading Urban Uprising* (London: Routledge, 1993).

36. For a description of Marcus Garvey's black nationalist struggle see Tony Martin, *Race First: The Ideological and Organizational Struggles of Marcus Garvey and the Universal Negro Improvement Association* (Westport, CT: Greenwood Press, 1976). For a description of Malcolm X's views on economic and cultural autonomy in his own words see Alex Haley and Malcolm X, *The Autobiography of Malcolm X* (New York: Grove Press, 1965). See also William L. Van Deburg, ed., *Modern Black Nationalism: From Marcus Garvey to Louis Farrakhan* (New York: New York University Press, 1997).

37. See Arthur Hertzberg, *The Jews in America* (New York: Simon & Schuster, 1989).

38. Duany, "Reconstructing Racial Identity"; Roger Lancaster, "Subject Honor and Object Shame: The Construction of Male Homosexuality and Stigma in Nicaragua," *Ethnology* 27 (2) (April 1988), pp. 111–25; and Roger Lancaster, "The Negro of the Family," in *Life Is Hard: Machismo, Danger and the Intimacy of Power in Nicaragua* (Berkeley: University of California Press, 1992).

39. It is interesting to note that Latinos, not blacks, make up the largest single racial/ethnic group on welfare (Temporary Assistance to Needy Families, TANF) in New York City. According to the New York City Human Resources Administration, Hispanics make up 41 percent of the TANF caseload, blacks make up 37 percent, and whites, 7 percent. Data were not collected on the remaining 15 percent. Andrew S. Bush, Swati Desai, and Lawrence M. Mead, "Leaving Welfare: Findings from a Survey of Former New York City Welfare Recipients," *New York City Human Resources Administration* (September 1998). Jason DeParle of the *New York Times* cites slightly different figures toward the same ends. In 1998 he wrote that the welfare (TANF) population in New York City was 59 percent Hispanic, 33 percent black, and 5 percent white. Jason DeParle, "Shrinking Welfare Rolls Leave Record Share of Minorities," *New York Times* (July 27, 1998).

40. See Newman, *No Shame in My Game.*

41. In New York City, 32.8 percent of all Hispanics in 1999 were poor, a higher poverty rate than that of whites (10.6 percent) and even blacks (28.5 percent). Mark Levitan, "A Rising Tide Lifts Some Boats: Poverty Rates for New York

City, 1999," *Community Service Society* (September 1999). According to the 1999 New York City Housing and Vacancy Survey, 37.7 percent of Dominicans are poor while 32.8 percent of Puerto Ricans are poor. The picture nationwide is no less bleak: according to the 1999 Current Population Survey 30.9 percent of Puerto Ricans were poor compared to 27.1 percent of Mexicans, 13.6 percent of Cubans, 19.9 percent of Hispanics of Central and South American origin (includes Dominicans), and 23.6 percent of "other" Hispanics. Among Hispanic children, the poverty rates are even higher: 43.5 percent of Puerto Rican children were poor, followed by 35.4 percent of Mexican children, 16.4 percent of Cuban children, 26.6 percent of Hispanic children from Central and South American origin (includes Dominicans), and 31.6 percent of "other" Hispanic children.

42. The Personal Responsibility and Work Opportunity Reconciliation Act of 1996–better known as welfare reform–and the Illegal Immigration Reform and Immigration Responsibility Act barred most legal immigrants (and all undocumented immigrants) from welfare (TANF) and the Federal Food Stamp Program. Nine hundred thousand legal immigrants lost their Food Stamp eligibility nationwide due to PRWORA–147,000 of whom were New Yorkers. However, in 1998, Congress passed the Agricultural Research, Extension and Education Reform Act, reinstating many immigrants, including children, the elderly, and people with disabilities, who were in the United States prior to the signing of PRWORA. Center on Budget and Policy Priorities, "The Agricultural Act Restores Food Stamps to Some Vulnerable Immigrants" (June 29, 1998). What is more, New York, along with states like Texas, Illinois, and California, provided state-funded partial restoration of food stamps for children and the elderly during the two-year federal lapse. Despite the federal changes and New York's benevolence, many immigrants do not apply for benefits for which they are eligible for fear that public dependency will jeopardize their chances at becoming a citizen. Michael Fix and Jeffrey S. Passel, "Trends in Noncitizens' and Citizens' Use of Public Benefits Following Welfare Reform: 1994–1997," *The Urban Institute* (March 1999); and Shawn Fremstad, "The INS Public Charge Guidance: What Does it Mean for Immigrants who Need Public Assistance," Center on Budget and Policy Priorities (January 7, 2000). Moreover, undocumented immigrants with children who are U.S. citizens are also afraid to apply for the benefits for which their children are eligible, in fear that their status might be discovered and the information passed along to the Immigration and Naturalization Service. See Hector R. Cordero-Guzman and Jose G. Navarro, "What Do Immigrant Service Providers Say About the Impact of Recent Changes in Immigration and Welfare Laws?" *Migration World Magazine* 28 (4) (2000).

43. Portes and Zhou, "The New Second Generation," pp. 74–96.

7: Local Caring: Social Capital and Social Responsibility

1. Robert D. Putnam, *Bowling Alone: The Collapse and Revival of American Community* (New York: Touchstone, 2000). See also Robert Putnam, "Bowling Alone:

America's Declining Social Capital." *The Journal of Democracy* (January 1995), pp. 65–78.

2. See Robert D. Putman, "The Strange Disappearance of Civic America," *The American Prospect* 24 (Winter 1996).

3. W. J. Wilson, *The Truly Disadvantaged* (Chicago: University of Chicago Press, 1987), and W. J. Wilson, *When Work Disappears* (New York: Knopf, 1996).

4. Lacking longitudinal data on these questions, it is impossible to say whether these means are higher or lower than they were in the past.

5. Citizens with higher socioeconomic statuses, whether measured by income, level of education, or occupation, are more likely to vote. Sidney Verba and Norman H. Nie, *Participation in America: Political Democracy and Social Equality* (New York: Harper & Row, 1972), pp. 125–27. A greater percentage of whites vote than blacks or Hispanics. Although the percentage of voters in each racial category decreased in the thirty years shown in the following table, the percentage of white voters decreased most dramatically, narrowing the gap among the categories.

Reported Voted by Race and Hispanic Origin

	White	*Black*	*Hispanic*
1998	43.3%	39.6%	20.0%
1988	46.7%	39.2%	21.0%
1978	47.3%	37.2%	23.5%
1968	69.1%	57.6%	NA

U.S. Census Bureau, "Reported Voted and Registered by Race, Hispanic Origin, Sex, and Age: November 1964 to 1998," *Current Population Reports*, Series P20-504, Internet release date July 19, 2000. URL: <www.census.gov/population/socdemo/voting/history/htab01.txt>

6. Alice S. Rossi, ed., *Caring and Doing for Others: Social Responsibility in the Domains of Family, Work, and Community* (Chicago: University of Chicago Press, 2001).

7. Ibid., Chapter 3.

8. Elijah Anderson, *Streetwise* (Chicago: University of Chicago Press, 1990), argues that ghetto communities distinguish between respectable families and deviant ones. U. Hannerz, *Soulside* (New York: Columbia University Press, 1968), makes the same distinction.

9. The recent rash of mass shootings in rural and suburban high schools may force a change in this view. In most of these cases, a troubled child who was known to family members and acquaintances as having expressed threatening intentions acts on those sentiments to devastating result. Retrospective accounts suggest that most of these individuals were known for their aberrant attitudes but either were not taken seriously or were regarded as being a private, personal problem for their families to tend to. When the consequences of that privatized approach become so painful for the community as a whole, we may see a more intrusive or communal definition of child-rearing responsibilities. In these tragic episodes,

middle-class communities take on some of the more unfortunate characteristics of the inner-city neighborhoods from which my interviews emerge: enclaves where the private matters become public concern in a hurry. See Tamar Lewin, "The Disturbing Trend: More Victims and Much Less Sense in the String of Shootings at Schools," *New York Times*, May 22, 1998, p. A20.

10. Middle-class white families who experience downward mobility often confront the discord that attends this conception of generational autonomy. Parents who have fallen on hard times or adult children who have lost their jobs and find that they need to borrow money feel intensely uncomfortable about this dependency. It violates a cultural code that separates love from money, demanding a continuous expression of the former and only the most time-limited demonstration of the latter. Parents are responsible for supporting children—with funds flowing in this direction only—until they reach maturity. Economic dependency thereafter is a source of shame.

11. Arline T. Geronimus, John Bound, Timothy A. Waidmann, "Poverty, Time and Place: Variation in Excess Mortality Across Selected U.S. Populations, 1980–1990," *Journal of Epidemiology and Community Health* 53 (6), 1999, pp. 325–34, and Arline T. Geronimus, John Bound, Timothy A. Waidmann, Cynthia G. Colen, and Dianne Steffick, "Inequality in Life Expectancy, Functional Status, and Active Life Expectancy Across Selected Black and White Populations in the United States," *Demography* 38 (2) 2001, pp. 227–51.

12. People living in impoverished public housing projects have numerous but superficial exchanges with their neighbors. Parents may not allow their young children to interact with others in the neighborhood so that their children do not identify with others from the projects. People believe they will not live in the projects for long, that they are better than their neighbors, so they keep their distance. Frank F. Furstenberg Jr., "How Families Manage Risk and Opportunity in Dangerous Neighborhoods," in *Sociology and the Public Agenda*, W. J. Wilson, ed., (Newbury Park, CA: Sage Publications, 1993), pp. 231–58. See also Anderson, *Streetwise*.

13. Families living in unkempt housing projects avoid public spaces around their homes because of unsanitary conditions. Their absence diminishes the surveillance of everyday neighborhood events, leaving these public spaces to be overrun by gang activities. Sudhir Alladi Venkatesh, *American Project: The Rise and Fall of a Modern Ghetto* (Cambridge, MA: Harvard University Press, 2000), pp. 120–21.

14. "Study Links Violence Rate to Cohesion of Community," *New York Times*, August 17, 1997.

15. Alice Rossi, personal communication.

16. Indeed, as Sarah Mahler shows, exploitative practices often emerge within groups, even within families. She documents the ways in which Salvadorean migrants to Long Island obtain housing leases and then charge members of their families exhorbitant rents with ten people to a room, sleeping in shifts. One of the more shocking discoveries for her informants was the insertion of market norms into family relations. S. Mahler, *American Dreaming* (Princeton: Princeton University Press, 1994). See also P. Kasinitz, *Caribbean New York* (Ithaca: Cornell University Press, 1992).

17. Fifty-two percent of the qualitative sample were working. Only 8.2 percent were unemployed. Across all three ethnic groups, approximately 18 percent reported AFDC receipt in their households.

18. For more on this see Newman, *No Shame in My Game: The Working Poor in the Inner City* (New York: Knopf/Russell Sage, 1999).

19. Some immigrants form ethnic enclaves in American cities. These clusterings can adversely affect immigrants' economic growth. It has been proposed that if an immigrant group were randomly spread throughout the country, then its members' wages would increase by 16 percent over the first ten years. "There is a negative correlation between the rate of economic assimilation and the geographic clustering of the immigrant group." George J. Borjas, *Heaven's Door: Immigration Policy and the American Economy* (Princeton, NJ: Princeton University Press, 1999), p. 56. See also Alejandro Portes and Ruben G. Rumbaut, *Immigrant America: A Portrait* (Berkeley: University of California Press, 1996), and Alejandro Portes and Robert L. Bach, *Latin Journey: Cuban and Mexican Immigrants in the United States* (Berkeley: University of California Press, 1985).

8: A Different Shade of Gray

1. Henry Aaron and Robert Reischauer, *Countdown to Reform: The Great Social Security Debate* (Washington, D.C.: The Brookings Institution Press, 1999).

2. Martin Feldstein is perhaps the most forceful critic of the existing system of social security and a major voice for privatization. See Martin Feldstein, ed., *Privatizing Social Security* (Chicago: University of Chicago Press, 2000).

3. William Beach and Gareth Davis, "Social Security's Rate of Return for Hispanic Americans," Heritage Center for Data Analysis, Heritage Foundation, available at www.heritage.org/library/cda/pdf/cda_98-.02.pdf.

4. For more on this debate see Henry Aaron, John Shoven, Benjamin Friedman, and Alvin Hansen, eds., *Should the United States Privatize Social Security?* (Cambridge: MIT Press, 1999).

5. See EPI Policy Brief, "The Problems with Privatization," December 2000, available at www.epinet.org.

6. My discussion of these initiatives draws heavily on a March 2000 memo to the Gore campaign by Jeffrey Liebman, an economist at the Kennedy School of Government who helped the campaign develop its proposals.

7. Social Security benefits are based on a person's thirty-five years of highest earnings. Hence workers who drop out of the labor force have reduced income, which cuts into their savings, but also lose credits toward retirement.

8. Margaret Price, "Efforts to Privatize Social Security Leave Many Women Worried," *Newsday*, September 9, 2001, p. 1.

9. Gore eventually put forth a specific proposal for the amounts.

10. Ironically, the reduction is steepest in households with two earner couples where the woman earns the same amount as the man, which is likely to be the case among black women in particular, since their earnings are often as high or higher than their husbands'. "For a woman who receives a Social Security benefit based on her husband's earnings, the reduction is 33 percent (the household

benefit falls from 150 percent of his Primary Insurance Amount to 100 percent of his Primary Insurance Account). For a woman whose earnings were exactly the same as her husband's, the reduction is 50 percent (from both receiving the primary insurance amount to only the survivor receiving her primary insurance account). . . . More generally, the more equal are the lifetime earnings of the two spouses, the larger is the percentage benefit reduction when one spouse dies" (Liebman memo, March 2000).

11. Children are defined as those under the age of eighteen or students aged eighteen to nineteen.

12. Paula England and Nancy Folbre, "Who Should Pay for the Kids?" *Annals of the American Academy of Political and Social Sciences*, 563 (1999): 194–207. Lynne Casper, "What Does it Cost to Mind Our Preschoolers?" *Current Population Report* (Washington, D.C.: U.S. Bureau of the Census, 1995).

13. Kathleen McGarry, "Guaranteed Income: SSI and the Well-being of the Elderly Poor," in *Distributional Aspects of Social Security and Social Security Reform*, Martin Feldstein and Jeffrey Liebman, eds. (Chicago: University of Chicago Press, 2002).

14. The Federal Reserve Bank's 1998 Survey of Consumer Finances points to the connection between race and ethnicity and asset holding. In every category, from CDs and savings bonds to life insurance to stocks and mutual funds, nonwhites and Hispanics fall well behind whites and non-Hispanics. For example, 22 percent of whites have savings bonds, but only 9 percent of nonwhites do. Over 50 percent of whites have retirement accounts, but only 32 percent of nonwhites follow suit. Arthur Kennickell, Martha Starr-McCluer, and Brian Surette, "Recent Changes in U.S. Family Finances: Results from the 1998 Survey of Consumer Finances," Federal Reserve Bulletin, January 2000.

15. Jeffrey Liebman, "Redistribution in the Current U.S. Social Security System," in *Distributional Aspects of Social Security and Social Security Reform.*

16. Bequests foster income inequality because they provide resources for the next generation only for those who have property or savings to pass along, while social security stops at death's door. See Jagadeesh Gokhale, Laurence Kotlikoff, James Sefton, and Martin Weale, "Simulating the Transmission of Wealth Inequality Via Bequests," National Bureau of Economic Research Working Paper No. 7183, June 1999, available at www.nber.org/papers/w7183

17. Judith G. Waxman, "Testimony Before the Joint Hearing of the Select Committee on Aging and the Congressional Black Caucus, U.S. House of Representatives," 102nd Congress, First Session, September 13, 1991 (Washington, D.C.: U.S. Government Printing Office, Aging Commission Publication No. 102–846, 1992), p. 56.

18. Between 1980 and 1990, the "Part A" deductible for Medicare for each hospitalization increased almost 250 percent, from $180 to $628. The part B premium increased 244 percent during the same period. Out-of-pocket costs for Medicare beneficiaries with one hospitalization at more than $1,000, not including the co-payment required by Medicare or the cost of prescription drugs. Waxman, "Testimony Before the Joint Hearing of the Select Committee on Aging and the Congressional Black Caucus, U.S. House of Representatives," p. 2.

19. U.S. Department of Health and Human Services, Administration on Children Youth and Families (2000), "Report to the Congress on Kinship Foster Care," p. 6, available at aspe.hhs.gov/hsp/kinr2c00/index.htm.

20. Some children are voluntarily placed by their families into kin care without the involvement of Child Protective Services, while others are placed by CPS because of documented abuse and neglect.

21. Tina Traster, "When Grandparents are 'Parents' Again," *Boston Globe Magazine*, March 26, 2000, p. 5.

22. Child Welfare League of America, "Grandparents Raising Children included in the Reauthorization of the Older Americans Act," November 6, 2000, available at www.cwla.org/newsevents/news001106gu.htm.

23. Robert Sampson et al., "Neighborhoods and Violent Crime: A Multi-level Study of Collective Efficacy." *Science* 277 (1997): 918–24.

24. Katherine Newman, *No Shame in My Game: The Working Poor in the Inner City* (New York: Knopff/Russell Sage, 1999).

25. Arlie Hochschild pointed out long ago that recognition of these markets is clear enough for middle-class women who wouldn't stay middle class long if they got divorced. In her book *The Second Shift*, she shows how recognition of this fact holds women back from demanding more work from their husbands in the household. They understand that men can find new wives pretty easily, but women (especially those who have kids in tow) have a more difficult time finding a new mate if they get divorced.

26. Timothy Nelson, Kathryn Edin, and Susan Clampet-Lundquist, "Doin' The Best I Can': How Low-Income Non-Custodial Fathers in Philadelphia Talk About Their Families," unpublished manuscript (May 16, 2000), have argued that fatherhood is actually very meaningful to noncustodial fathers, who bitterly resent being shut out of their children's lives. Skeptics might argue that those who don't pay child support or fail to show up for appointments with their kids are just handling gullible researchers a line when they say they care. Others note that poor men are often unable to provide much more than affection.

Appendix

1. For a complete understanding of the methodology, sampling design, and response rates of the MIDUS survey, readers are referred to the appendix of Alice Rossi's edited volume, *Caring and Doing for Others: Social Responsibility in the Domains of Family, Work and Community* (Chicago: University of Chicago Press, 2001), pp. 519–25.

2. For a more thorough description of this survey see Diane Hughes, "Cultural and Contextual Correlates of Obligation to Family and Community Among Urban Black and Latino Adults," in *Caring and Doing for Others*, pp. 179–223.

3. About 3 percent of those who self-identify as African American now were born outside the United States, in places like Panama.

4. The mean age of Puerto Rican arrival was fifteen and the mean age of Dominican arrival was twenty-five years.

5. The breakdown on education by ethnicity is as follows:

	Puerto Ricans	Dominicans	African Americans
Less than high school	37.5%	42.4%	15.6%
High School/GED	37.5	30.3	40.6
Some college/two-year degree	25.0	15.2	25.0
Four-year degree	0.0	12.1	18.8

To some degrees, this distribution is driven by the ages of the sample. The breakdown of education by age is as follows:

	Under 30	30–40	41–65	66+
Less than high school	14.3%	32.4%	36.1%	40.0%
High School/GED	50.0	32.4	30.6	50.0
Some college/two-year degree	28.6	24.3	19.4	10.0
Four-year degree	7.1	10.8	13.9	0.0

6. Marital status across the sample:

Currently married	41%
Never married	33%
Divorced	19%
Widowed	4%
Separated	3%

7. Marital status varies a great deal by ethnic group, as the following data show:

	Puerto Ricans	Dominicans	African Americans
Married	50.0%	44.1%	29.4%
Never married	28.1	23.5	47.1
Divorced	18.8	23.5	14.7
Widowed	3.1	2.9	5.9
Separated	0.0	5.9	2.9

There are a few differences here between the small interview sample and the main survey respondents. This may suggest the interview sample is skewed due to the relatively small sample size (i.e., number of respondents). A higher proportion of Puerto Ricans and African Americans are widowed in the New York survey. A higher proportion of people in all three groups was legally separated than in the small interview sample, and a smaller proportion of Puerto Ricans and Dominicans were married in the large sample than in the small one.

Index